"In this excellent study of German and Italian work-family policies, Blome offers a persuasive account of welfare state change that has lessons for both scholars and policy-makers. Showing that reform is possible, but only under certain conditions, Blome breaks with a longstanding view of welfare states as stagnant and unlikely to change. Thoughtful, deeply researched and lucidly written, this book is a model of how comparative policy research should be done."
Kimberly Morgan, *George Washington University, USA*

"Why did Germany but not Italy embark upon a bold new approach to family policy in recent decades? Blome's mixed-method analyses shed powerful new light on how work-family reconciliation is facilitated by women's political representation, egalitarian change in mass opinion, and competition between political parties. *The Politics of Work-Family Policy Reforms* is essential reading for scholars of gender, public policy, and welfare state development in Europe."
Clem Brooks, *Indiana University, USA*

"This book provides a rich comparative analysis of the politics of family policies in Germany and Italy."
Martin Seeleib-Kaiser, *University of Oxford, UK*

"This engaging book uses a comparative case study framework and an innovative methodological approach to assess the determinants of work-family reconciliation policy developments. Blome shines a light on an understudied policy arena, integrating multiple explanatory frameworks to untangle the puzzle of differing trajectories in similar countries. The result is a fresh look at the complexities of the policy-making process."
Janet C. Gornick, *City University of New York, USA*

The Politics of Work-Family Policy Reforms in Germany and Italy

One of the fundamental challenges facing modern welfare states is the question of work-family reconciliation. An increasing share of mothers work, but many European welfare states do not adequately support the dual-earner model, especially in southern Europe.

After 2005, German policy makers transformed the nature of Germany's family-policy regime through a number of legislative measures, whilst Italy, a country with many similarities, witnessed little change. Using a multi-methods approach, this book addresses the puzzle of why Germany was able to implement far-reaching reforms in this policy area after a long impasse and Italy was not. As such, it delivers a broad, systematic account of these reforms and sheds light on why similar reforms were not also adopted in other similar welfare states at the same time. More generally, it contributes to understanding the determinants of welfare policy change in modern European welfare states.

This text will be of key interest to scholars, students and professionals working on topics linked to European politics, welfare and work-family policies, comparative politics, social policy and, more broadly, to political science and gender studies.

Agnes Blome is Research Fellow of the Research Unit Inequality and Social Policy at the WZB Berlin Social Science Center, Germany.

Routledge Studies in the Political Economy of Welfare
Series editors: Martin Rhodes and Maurizio Ferrera,
The European University Institute, Florence, Italy

For a full list of titles in this series, please visit www.routledge.com

This series presents leading edge research on the recasting of European welfare states. The series is interdisciplinary, featuring contributions from experts in economics, political science and social policy. The books provide a comparative analysis of topical issues, including:

- reforms of the major social programmes – pensions, health and social security
- the changing political cleavages in welfare politics
- policy convergence and social policy innovation
- the impact of globalisation.

14 **The Role of Business in the Development of the Welfare State and Labor Markets in Germany**
   Containing social reforms
   Thomas Paster

15 **Politics of Segmentation**
   Party competition and social protection in Europe
   Georg Picot

16 **Pension Reforms in Central, Eastern and Southeastern Europe**
   From post-socialist transition to the global financial crisis
   Igor Guardiancich

17 **The Politics of Welfare State Transformation in Germany**
   Still a semi-sovereign state?
   Christof Schiller

18 **The Politics of Work-Family Policy Reforms in Germany and Italy**
   Agnes Blome

The Politics of Work-Family Policy Reforms in Germany and Italy

Agnes Blome

LONDON AND NEW YORK

First published 2017
by Routledge

2 Park Square, Milton Park, Abingdon, Oxfordshire OX14 4RN
711 Third Avenue, New York, NY 10017

Routledge is an imprint of the Taylor & Francis Group, an informa business

First issued in paperback 2018

Copyright © 2017 Agnes Blome

The right of Agnes Blome to be identified as author of this work has been asserted by her in accordance with sections 77 and 78 of the Copyright, Designs and Patents Act 1988.

All rights reserved. No part of this book may be reprinted or reproduced or utilised in any form or by any electronic, mechanical, or other means, now known or hereafter invented, including photocopying and recording, or in any information storage or retrieval system, without permission in writing from the publishers.

Notice:
Product or corporate names may be trademarks or registered trademarks, and are used only for identification and explanation without intent to infringe.

British Library Cataloguing in Publication Data
A catalogue record for this book is available from the British Library

Library of Congress Cataloging-in-Publication Data
Names: Blome, Agnes, author.
Title: The politics of work-family policy reforms in Germany and Italy / Agnes Blome.
Description: Abingdon, Oxon ; New York, NY : Routledge, 2017. | Series: Routledge studies in the political economy of welfare ; 18 | Includes bibliographical references and index.
Identifiers: LCCN 2016025362 | ISBN 9781138841406 (hardback) | ISBN 9781315732237 (ebook)
Subjects: LCSH: Work and family—Germany. | Work and family—Italy. | Family policy—Germany. | Family policy—Italy. | Germany—Social policy. | Italy—Social policy.
Classification: LCC HD4904.25 .B59 2017 | DDC 306.3/6—dc23
LC record available at https://lccn.loc.gov/2016025362

ISBN: 978-1-138-84140-6 (hbk)
ISBN: 978-1-138-36192-8 (pbk)

Typeset in Times New Roman
by Apex CoVantage, LLC

To my parents

Contents

List of figures x
List of tables xii
Acknowledgements xiv
Abbreviations xvii

1 Introduction 1

2 Theories of welfare state and work-family policy reform 22

3 Design and evolution of work-family policies: a European comparative overview 46

4 Policy developments in Germany and Italy: from a shared focus on the male-breadwinner model to diverging paths after the 1990s 81

5 How normative beliefs and voting behavior shape party competition on work-family policies 114

6 Women's descriptive representation: the more, the better? 142

7 Work-family policy reform processes in Germany: continuous change towards dual-earner model support 149

8 Italy: no consensus for change 178

9 Conclusion 200

Appendices 219
Index 245

Figures

1.1	Total fertility rates, Germany and Italy, 1960–2009	7
1.2	Women's employment rates (% of population aged 15–64), Germany and Italy, 1983–2009	7
1.3	GDP per capita (in Euro), Germany and Italy, 1983–2009	10
1.4	Educational attainment of women as a share of total educational attainment, Germany and Italy, 1976–2008	11
2.1	The impact of normative beliefs on policy reform	30
2.2	How normative beliefs and the dynamics of party competition influence policy reforms	31
2.3	How normative beliefs, the dynamics of party competition and women's representation influence policy reforms	32
3.1	Maternity and parental leave provisions, 1994 and 2007	55
3.2	The difference in net transfers to government (tax and social security contributions) between male-breadwinner families and dual-earner families as a proportion (%) of net transfers to government for male-breadwinner families	70
5.1	Share of progressive beliefs in population, Germany and Italy, 1990, 1999 and 2008	124
5.2	Development of normative beliefs on mothers' employment and childcare (pooled logistic regression model)	125
5.3	Attitudes towards mothers' employment and childcare, Germany, 1990, 1999 and 2008	127
5.4	Attitudes towards mothers' employment and childcare, Italy, 1990, 1999 and 2008	128
5.5	Probability of voting for "SPD", Germany, 1994–2009 (AMEs from multinomial logistic regression)	130
5.6	Probability of voting for "CDU", Germany, 1994–2009 (AMEs from multinomial logistic regression)	131
5.7	Probability of voting for "center-left party bloc", Italy, 1994–2008 (AMEs from multinomial logistic regression)	132
5.8	Probability of voting for "center-right party bloc", Italy, 1994–2008 (AMEs from multinomial logistic regression)	133

5.9	Multinomial logistic regression, average marginal effects (AME) for probability of preferring the SPD/left-wing coalition and the CDU/right-wing coalition of people having progressive normative beliefs in Germany and Italy, 1990, 1999 and 2008	135
6.1	Share of women MPs (in %) by age group in the German Bundestag, 1990–2009	144
6.2	Share of women MPs (in %) by age group in the Italian Camera and Senato, 1996–2011	144
6.3	Women MPs (in %) in governing parties and in opposition parties in Germany and Italy (%)	145

Tables

3.1	Dimensions of work-family policies	53
3.2	Replacement rates for maternity leave (ML) and parental leave (PL), 1994 and 2007	56
3.3	The development of child care coverage rates for the age group zero to three (1994–2006)	61
3.4	Childcare flexibility: opening hours	62
3.5	Childcare costs and affordability, 2004	64
3.6	Child-to-staff ratio for children under the age of three, approximately 2000 and 2006	66
3.7	Type of taxation system, 1990–2007	68
4.1	Regional variation in the public provision of childcare in Germany, 1994–2010	97
4.2	Regional variation in the provision of childcare in Italy, 1992–2008	101
4.3	Policy developments in Germany and Italy after 1990	104
5.1	Parliamentary elections in Germany: official results in % (1994–2009)	115
5.2	Parliamentary elections in Italy: official results in % (1994–2008)	117
5.3	The development of the Italian executive, 1994–2008	118
5.4	Religious denomination and religious activity in Germany and Italy (in %), 1990–2008	133
6.1	Women in the German Federal Cabinet, in absolute number and share of total number, 12–16 legislatures	146
6.2	Women in the Italian Council of Ministers, in absolute number and share of total number, 11–16 legislatures	147
A.1	Variables in most-similar systems design in Germany and Italy, pre-reform period 1990–2000	219
A.2	List of interviewees	221
A.3	The development of parties in Italy after 1992	222
A.4	Definition of variables	226
A.5	Development of normative beliefs about mothers' employment and childcare	228

A.6	Logistic regression, dependent variable: individual attitudes towards mothers' employment and childcare, Germany, 1990, 1999, and 2008, average marginal effects (AME) for probability of supporting mothers' employment	229
A.7	Logistic regression, dependent variable: individual attitudes towards mothers' employment and childcare, Italy, 1990, 1999 and 2008, average marginal effects (AME) for probability of supporting mothers' employment	231
A.8	Logistic regression, dependent variable: individual beliefs towards mothers' employment and childcare, Germany, 1990, 1999 and 2008, average marginal effects (AME) for probability of supporting mothers' employment	233
A.9	Logistic regression, dependent variable: individual beliefs towards mothers' employment and childcare, Italy, 1990, 1999 and 2008, average marginal effects for probability of supporting mothers' employment	235
A.10	Logistic regression, dependent variable: individual attitudes towards mothers' employment and childcare, Germany, 1991, 1992, 1996, 2000, 2004, 2008, average marginal effects (AME) for probability of supporting mothers' employment	237
A.11	Multinomial logistic regression, dependent variable: voting behavior, Germany, 1994–2009, average marginal effects (AME) for probability of voting for 'FDP'	238
A.12	Multinomial logistic regression, dependent variable: voting behavior, Germany, 1994–2009, average marginal effects (AME) for probability of voting for "Greens"	240
A.13	Multinomial logistic regression, dependent variable: voting behavior, Germany, 1994–2009, average marginal effects (AME) for probability of voting for 'Die Linke'	242
A.14	Multinomial logistic regression, average marginal effects (AME) for probability of preferring the SPD/left-wing coalition and the CDU/right-wing coalition of people having progressive normative beliefs in Germany and Italy, 1990, 1999 and 2008	244

Acknowledgements

This book originated in a project on intergenerational relations in the welfare state. We compared institutional regulations for young and old people and their living situations in four different welfare states, as well as the work-family context. Two of the welfare states – Sweden and France – were very supportive of mothers' employment, while the other two – Germany and Italy – had a long tradition of reliance on the male-breadwinner model. While working on the book, however, Germany started to reform its work-family policies with the aim of a better support of working mothers. This struck me as a surprise given the conventional wisdom that social policies seldom undergo paradigm shifts, and I became interested in the causal mechanisms that led to these reforms. I thank Jens Alber and Wolfgang Keck for numerous critical and enlightening discussions throughout the work on this project.

This present study accompanied me through a very intense phase of my life, and I am indebted to many people. I had the privilege to write the book while working as a research fellow at the WZB Berlin Social Science Center. I cannot imagine a better place to work as a young researcher, and my special thanks go to Jutta Allmendinger for both intellectual input and numerous efforts to fund and support my work.

For all their support during the dissertation phase of this book, I am particularly indebted to Chiara Saraceno and Friedbert W. Rüb. They believed in this project from the very beginning, constantly encouraged me to proceed with this topic and generously provided sound advice and extremely valuable suggestions. My thanks also go to my second supervisor Ellen M. Immergut for many fruitful discussions and constructive suggestions at various stages of the dissertation. These supervisors have devoted a great deal of their time to me and this work. Thanks to them, I was able to develop my theoretical and empirical work further than I would have on my own.

During the second phase of this book, when turning the dissertation into a book manuscript, I was very lucky to work in the Inequality and Social Policy (ISP) unit of the WZB led by David Brady. The manuscript has benefited enormously from his enthusiasm for my work, his meticulous comments and sound guidance. I feel truly honored and thankful that he invested so much time and intellectual effort in this project. I am also indebted to Felix Elwert who continued with this spirit and who gave me all the necessary time and motivation to finish the book. I thank him for his valuable feedback on parts of the book.

I am deeply grateful to Irene Böckmann, Lena Hipp, Wolfgang Keck, Manuela Naldini, Georg Picot and the editors of the series Routledge/EUI studies in the political economy of welfare, Maurizio Ferrera and Martin Rhodes, for giving very constructive comments that helped me revise the manuscript for publication. I also greatly appreciated the opportunities to spend time as a guest at the Università degli studi di Torino. Manuela Naldini and Lorenzo Todesco welcomed me with great warmth and never grew tired of explaining to me the Italian peculiarities and politics, but also demonstrated what Italy and its people make such a wonderful country. These research stays were funded by EQUALSOC, a Network of Excellence funded by the European Union's Sixth Framework Programme. Furthermore, I thank all of my interviewees for revealing their precious insights about work-family policy reform processes in their countries as well as Hans Schadee and Bernhard Weßels for sharing their knowledge about some of the datasets I used.

My friends and colleagues at the WZB and outside have made my PhD years and beyond both inspiring and enjoyable. With them I discussed not only work but also shared work-life issues. I very much thank Thomas Biegert, Irene Böckmann, Petra Böhnke, Martina Dieckhoff, Cassandra Engemann, Anette Fasang, Sonja Grimm, Miriam Hartlapp, Jan Paul Heisig, Lena Hipp, Sabine Hübgen, Wolfgang Keck, Achim Kemmerling, Sabine Kropp, Susanne Marquardt, Luicy Pedroza, Reinhard Pollak, Anke Radenacker, Lena Ulbricht, Christiane and Philip Wotschack, the NAWIs and the Postdocs an the WZB, the participants of the Berlin Graduate School of Social Sciences 2008 and the participants of the Leibniz Mentoring Programme 2014/2015.

The Demographic Development, Social Change, and Social Capital (DSS) and ISP departments of the WZB Berlin provided an open, stimulating and cooperative research environment from which I benefited immensely. Among others, I thank the attendees at the ISP writing workshop, the president's group colloquium, and the APL colloquium at the WZB. Roisin Cronin from the Academic Writing Clinic has provided much-needed suggestions for language editing the manuscript. Christoph Albrecht, Elisabeth Gößwein, Susanne Grasow, Marion Obermaier, Stefanie Roth and Reinhild Wagner have very much facilitated my job and always had an open door if I needed advice. I also thank Susanne Marquardt, Annika Holz and Moritz Kaiser for excellent research assistance. Andrew Taylor and Sophie Iddamalgoda at Routledge provided professional and friendly editorial guidance. Some of the ideas and analyses in this book were previously published in *Comparative Politics*, and I am thankful for the publisher's permission to reprint them.

My family has been a great source of support during my writing of this book. I thank my parents, Frauke and Arnulf, for their unwavering encouragement and support of all kinds throughout my studies. They have always shown great interest in my work, including nagging questions about its progress. I thank my brothers Christian and Mathis and my sister Annette for sparking my interest in work-family issues early and for shaping my thoughts on gender equality during numerous discussions at the kitchen table.

My greatest thanks go to my husband, Kai-Uwe Müller, for his tolerance and support, for countless discussions of my arguments, for reading and commenting draft after draft, and for his patient guidance through the world of quantitative analyses with Stata. His love and companionship have made it all worth it.

While I was working on this book, my daughters Lenya and Jonna were born. They provided unlimited joy in my life and let me delve into the intricacies of combining work and family life. I very much hope that having children and pursuing a career will be a more natural thing for them than it was for their grandmothers and great-grandmothers.

Abbreviations

Germany

CDU	Christlich Demokratische Union Deutschlands
CSU	Christlich Soziale Union
FDP	Freie Demokratische Partei
FRG	Federal Republic of Germany
GDR	German Democratic Republic
PDS	Partei des Demokratischen Sozialismus
SPD	Sozialdemokratische Partei Deutschlands
DGB	Deutscher Gewerkschaftsbund
DM	Deutsche Mark

Italy

AD	Alleanza Democratica
AN	Alleanza Nazionale
CCD	Centro Cristiano Democratico
CDU	Cristiani Democratici Uniti
DL	Democrazia e libertà – La Margherita
DS	Democratici di Sinistra
FI	Forza Italia
LN	Lega Nord
MSI	Movimento Sociale Italiano – Fiamma Tricolore
PD	Partito Democratico
PdCI	Partito di Comunisti Italiani
PdL	Il Popolo della Libertà
PDS	Partito democratico della sinistra
PPI	Partito Popolare Italiano
PR	Radicali
PRC	Partito della Rifondazione Comunista
PS	Partito Socialista
PSI	Partito Socialista Italiano
UDC	Unione dei Democratici Cristiani e di Centro
UDEUR	Unione Democratici per l'Europea

Country Codes

AT	Austria
BE	Belgium
DE	Germany
DK	Denmark
ES	Spain
FI	Finland
FR	France
GR	Greece
IE	Ireland
IT	Italy
LU	Luxembourg
NL	Netherlands
PT	Portugal
SE	Sweden
UK	United Kingdom

1 Introduction

When and why do welfare states change? This question has been at the heart of comparative welfare state research for a long time. A central claim in this literature was that welfare states are fairly resistant to change and that they change only in path-dependent ways. Most of this research concentrated on the most resource-intensive pillars of welfare states such as the pension, health or unemployment schemes. By contrast, care services and policies addressing families more generally have received comparably little attention in the literature. This is surprising given that some of the key social changes that challenge contemporary welfare states are related to families: population ageing, fertility decline, women's increasing employment rates or the diversification of family forms. While these concerns affect the majority of wealthy countries, the welfare states of continental European countries are seen as especially unable to adapt. Family policies in these countries often provide support for the male-breadwinner model. Either explicitly or implicitly, social policies, the tax scheme and legal obligations facilitate a traditional gender division of labor which assigns women to the home and men to pursue paid labor. Policies to encourage maternal employment are virtually absent.

At the beginning of the 1990s, Germany and Italy stood paradigmatically for welfare states in which the lack of day care and other policies supporting mothers' employment led to a strong gender division of labor. Imagine for a moment the typical life course of a woman during the phase of childbearing and career advancement in the two countries.

Usually, a German[1] woman in her mid-twenties had an educational qualification and was in paid employment. She would also marry and have her first child around age 27 and then temporarily quit her job to take a three-year-long parental leave. Then she would have a second child and continue to be on leave. Women's long time away from employment in connection with childbirth was also shaped by the lack of publicly subsidized childcare places and cultural norms that saw maternal employment as detrimental to young children. When their last child turned three and started attending childcare for a few hours a day, most mothers would try to return to work on a part-time basis. If employers agreed to part-time employment, mothers frequently did so long term and with a significantly diminished career potential. At the same time, most male partners pursued careers without interruptions and many worked even more hours than before becoming fathers. For the majority of couples, it made economic sense to continue the male-breadwinner (part-time) female-homemaker model given the incentives from the tax and transfer system.

The situation was similar in Italy. Young women usually had an educational qualification before they married and on average had their first child at age 27. Having a child often meant women quit the labor force for considerable lengths of time. Those few who stayed in the labor market often relied on grandmothers to take care of their children. In contrast to Germany, part-time jobs were rare. If women were in the labor market, they worked full time. Similarly to Germany, men's employment situations did not change significantly when they became fathers. However, even though the male-breadwinner model was also widespread in Italy, it was neither explicitly supported by the welfare state nor by the tax system.

In both countries, traditional normative beliefs towards the role of the mother and the incidence of Christian-democratic governments supported this familialist work-family approach. The paradigm was not seriously disputed on a societal level, nor effectively contested by (leftist) political or societal actors. In the 1990s, changes seemed unlikely. Even in 2002, Esping-Andersen wrote: "One characteristic that is common to most, but not all, Continental European countries is their sustained adherence to traditional familial welfare responsibility – most powerfully in Southern Europe, and by far the least in Belgium and France" (Esping-Andersen 2002: 16).

At the beginning of the 2000s, however, this prognosis was challenged by unanticipated policy dynamism in some countries. During a relatively short period of time, substantial reforms were initiated which led to structural changes in work-family policies in a number of continental European countries (Morgan 2013). Most notably, German policy makers transformed the nature of Germany's family-policy regime through a number of legislative measures. In 2001 and in 2006, the parental leave scheme was reformed. The latter reform increased the maximum duration of paid parental leave for all parents (14 months including two "use-it-or-lose-it" fathers' months), raised the payment substantially (67 percent of previous wages) and abolished the means test. In 2004 and 2008, bills were adopted which aimed at increasing the number of public childcare places in particular in Western Germany. It also provided parents with a right to receive care for zero- to three-year-old children, with target coverage rates up to 33 percent beginning in 2013. In 2000, the legal right to part-time work in companies with more than 15 employees was established.

These reforms aimed not only at a better reconciliation of work and care for mothers but also for fathers. They incentivize mothers to return to work sooner and fathers to assume a greater share of childcare responsibilities. This unexpected appearance of these policy reforms on the political agenda and their speed of implementation has puzzled many observers, particularly because they happened under a coalition government led by the Christian Democratic Party (CDU) – a party that opposed policies supporting dual-earner families for a long time. Given the long-standing policy stagnation in Germany, these reforms raise several important questions: Why did this happen, why did it happen *in Germany*, and why did it happen *at this particular time*?

To tackle these questions, the book applies a comparative most-similar-systems-research design (Ebbinghaus 2005, Lijphart 1975, Mahoney 2003, Przeworski and Teune 1970). Comparing two countries that are similar to each other on several dimensions helps to isolate specific factors that differ across countries and can help explain why countries arrived at different policy outputs (King, Keohane, and Verba 1994). Germany and Italy represent classic cases of a "frozen" institutional landscape where reform capacity and in particular social policy reform activity was low (Esping-Andersen 1996, Palier and Martin 2007, Scharpf and Schmidt 2000). Italy and Germany are also similar on various other dimensions that matter for welfare state change (see the following section). Yet while Germany was experiencing this remarkable work-family policy change, Italy did not pursue comparable reforms. In spite of some attempts to reform both the parental leave scheme and the public provision of childcare places for children younger than three, a paradigmatic change from the male-breadwinner model to the dual-earner model has not happened. The country mainly concentrates on labor rights, e.g. leave and social rights when working part time. For instance, in 2000, extra months for the father were added to prolong the duration of parental leave (ten months in total). Yet Italy remains reluctant when it comes to state benefits. The parental leave payment is low (30 percent of previous wages), publicly provided childcare places for children younger than three are scarce (about 10 percent) and a right to part-time work does not exist.

This book addresses the puzzle of why Germany was able to implement far-reaching reforms in this policy area after a long impasse and Italy was not. More specifically, the book tackles the following questions: What conditions enable work-family policy changes? Why did Germany deviate from the traditional male-breadwinner model and adopt far-reaching work-family policy reforms oriented towards the dual-earner model, but Italy did not? Why did the German Christian Democrats become promoters of the dual-earner model which they opposed for a long time?

The analysis employs the rich theoretical literature on the politics of the welfare state to identify the conditions under which such significant welfare state reforms are possible, even in welfare states that are resistant to change such as Germany. Furthermore, the comparative approach enables the identification of factors which made similar reforms impossible in Italy, another strong male-breadwinner country that faced similar socio-demographic challenges. By examining far-reaching work-family policy reforms, this book adds to the literature on the occurrence and the causes of welfare state reform which has long been a neglected policy area. More generally, the book delivers a broad and systematic account of these reforms and provides a detailed analysis of the conditions under which work-family policy changes happen using a variety of different data sources. The findings of this book aim to enhance our understanding of the determinants of welfare policy change in contemporary European welfare states.

Explaining work-family policy changes

Over time, many theoretical approaches have been developed to explain social policy change. They can be broadly classified into three groups. Functionalist explanations emphasize social and economic challenges as driving forces of welfare state change (Bonoli 2007). Power resources theory and partisan theory stress class alliances and the impact of social-democratic parties on the generosity of welfare states (Brady 2009, Huber and Stephens 2001, Korpi 1983). Institutional theories highlight the role of policy legacies as well as institutional constraints such as veto points (Immergut 1992). All these explanations have proven useful for the analysis of policy reforms in various areas of social policy, but they have a difficult time accounting for the variation in work-family policy reforms across countries, in particular between Germany and Italy. For example, both countries are challenged by low fertility rates and low female labor-force participation rates combined with high predicted old-age dependency ratios, but reforms occurred only in Germany. Also, both institutional systems include a similar number of veto points (e.g. bicameralism, coalition governments) which remained stable over time. Thus they are unlikely to explain the different outcomes. Finally, partisan and power resources theories do not fully solve the puzzle of work-family policy change in Germany. The Social Democratic Party (SPD) had already been in office for seven years before the most far-reaching reforms were implemented. Also, in the grand coalition government, the CDU minister for family affairs took the lead in work-family policy reforms. In sum, prevailing explanations for policy change are neither able to fully explain the policy shift in Germany nor this particular contrast between German and Italian policy reforms.

In this book, I therefore propose an explanatory model of social policy change that integrates several more recent theoretical perspectives. First, a growing literature focuses on the influence of normative beliefs and discourses about the family, gender roles and care obligations for explaining work-family policy developments. According to that perspective, the design of work-family policies in a country is a function of the dominant "care ideal", i.e. the society's shared definition of what good care is and who should provide it (Kremer 2007, Lewis, Campbell, and Huerta 2008). Second, the role of voters and of electoral competition has increased in scholarly attention. These theories highlight changes in the electoral foundation of party support and the ways parties compete for (new) voters (Fleckenstein 2011, Häusermann, Picot, and Geering 2013, Morgan 2013, Picot 2012). For example, a party's core constituency may have changed policy preferences and put pressure on parties to adapt. Or, parties may mobilize different social groups more than before. This implies that the core constituencies keep to their beliefs, but they decline in importance to the party, while new social groups become electorally more relevant for the party. A third strand of the literature points to the impact of women's presence in parliament and in government on the development of the welfare state, which ultimately bears on the reconciliation of work and family. There is ample evidence on the impact of elected women on "women-friendly" policies (Caiazza 2004, Bonoli and Reber 2009, Lambert 2008, Mushaben 2005, Naumann 2005, Wängnerud 2000).

In line with the most-similar-systems research design, I focus on the systematic cross-country *variation* in the development of normative beliefs, political competition and women's representation to explain the different policy outcomes in Germany and Italy between 1990 and 2009. These factors vary sufficiently between Germany and Italy. The first two variables relate to the interplay between voters' normative beliefs, parties and the party system which followed different dynamics in Germany and Italy. Vote-seeking parties are responsive to voters' normative beliefs in situations where an increased party competition exists that is driven by changes in the electorate. The second set of variables refers to country differences in both women's descriptive and substantive representation in parliament and in government.

It will be argued that, first, the general change of normative beliefs is a crucial condition for any fundamental work-family policy change in a system of centripetal party competition. If it had not been for this average shift towards more progressive normative beliefs in Germany, the reforms likely would not have occurred. Second, the declining electoral importance of core constituencies and increasingly close election results intensified party competition for more progressive voters using the issue of work-family reconciliation policies. This fostered work-family policy reforms oriented towards the support of the dual-earner family model in Germany. Where normative beliefs on average remained traditional and parties were able to continue to rely on their core constituencies as in Italy, parties had a lesser incentive to compete with the issue of progressive work-family policies and reforms were less likely. Third, in order for work-family policy reforms to happen, a critical mass of women representatives has to be in parliament and female policy entrepreneurs have to put the topic onto the agenda. For far-reaching systemic reforms, the policy entrepreneurs' support of the government leader is indispensable.

This book challenges existing assumptions of welfare state change by analyzing work-family policy reforms in Germany and Italy between 1990 and 2009. It explains why Germany was able to adapt its family policies to the needs of dual-earner families and why Italy failed to do so. The book takes up recent debates about "values and norms", "political competition", "policy responsiveness" and "policy entrepreneurs"; combines them in a theoretical framework; and makes them fruitful for empirical analysis. While previous research often found that social policies develop slowly and in path-dependent ways, this book argues that cultural and structural changes may lead to a radical shift in work-family policies. Parties play an important role in this process, and this book demonstrates how, when and why party competition – and ultimately policymaking – is influenced by (changes in) citizens' normative beliefs and developments of voters' attachment to parties. By doing so, this book goes beyond traditional parties-do-matter and institutional theories. It takes seriously the dynamic and multifaceted interrelationship between citizens' beliefs, their voting behavior and the way parties react to them. The study also shows how women matter in the complexities of party politics – as voters, as political representatives and as female policy entrepreneurs who push the topic of work-family policies onto the agenda.

By comparing Germany with Italy, the book contributes to the literature of within-group comparisons of continental welfare states (Häusermann 2010, Palier and Martin 2007, Picot 2012). Within-regime studies are not widespread in comparative research, even though such similar-case comparisons make a lot of sense from a methodological point of view. They enable the identification of the crucial factors that account for reform differences. The following subsection will explain the similarities and differences between Germany and Italy in more detail and further justify the case selection.

Comparing Germany and Italy

While being a rather unusual case selection in comparative welfare state research, at a closer look, the unquestionable differences between Germany and Italy are limited compared to other advanced industrial countries. Hence there is much to learn from a comparison of these two countries. Both share several characteristics that matter for reforms of the welfare state, especially work-family policies: the welfare system, socio-economic and socio-demographic background and political and institutional structures (see also Table A.1 in the appendix for a concise summary of the most relevant context factors which the countries share and the dissimilarities in the dependent and the independent variables). The description focuses on the situation around the turn of the millennium – the time before the major changes happened in Germany. The graphs illustrate the development over a longer time span.

Socio-demographic structure and women's labor force participation

Germany and Italy have been confronted with similar problems in the socio-demographic structure of their populations and the labor-market integration of women. Fertility rates have remained at a level of approximately 1.3 since the beginning of the 1990s (see Figure 1.1) and old-age dependency ratios[2] in 2000 are rather high (24 percent for Germany and 27 percent for Italy).

Women's full-time equivalent employment rates were quite low compared to most rich democracies (46 percent in Germany and 37 percent in Italy 2000, see Figure 1.2). While participation is higher in Germany, Italian women work longer hours. In the middle of the 2000s, less than half of the mothers with children younger than six years old were in employment in both countries.

In both countries, women predominantly work in the service sector where they made up about 50 percent of the total workforce in 2000. By contrast, their share is about 24 percent in the industrial sector (ISTAT 2012, Statistisches Bundesamt 2012).

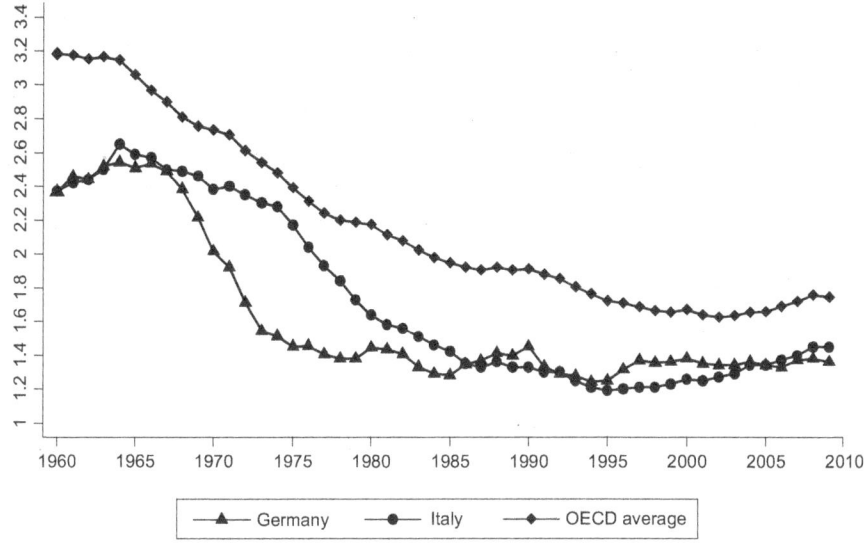

Figure 1.1 Total fertility rates, Germany and Italy, 1960–2009

Notes: Until 1991, figures for Germany refer to the territory of the former Federal Republic.
Sources: Eurostat, Statistisches Bundesamt, OECD Family Database

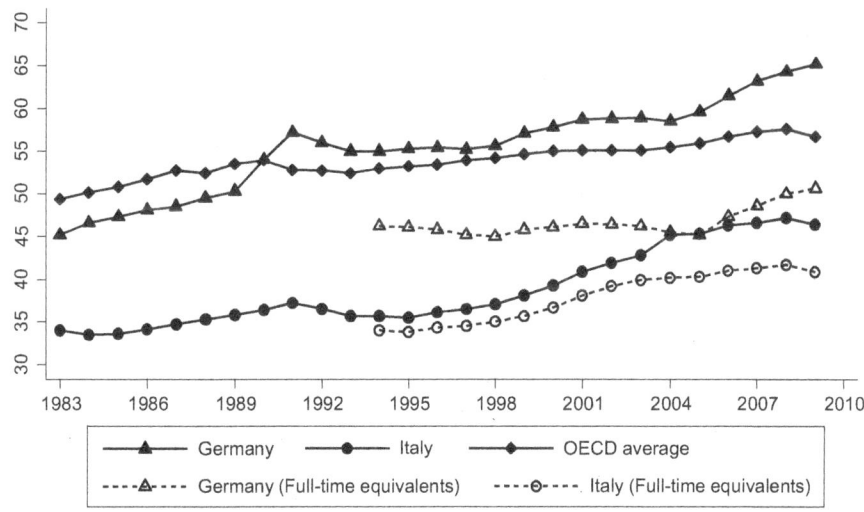

Figure 1.2 Women's employment rates (% of population aged 15–64), Germany and Italy, 1983–2009

Notes: Until 1991, figures for Germany refer to the territory of the former Federal Republic. FTE = full-time equivalent.
Source: Eurostat, OECD

Political structures and institutions

With regard to political structures and institutions, both Italy and Germany have been characterized as "frozen landscapes"(Esping-Andersen 1996) with political and institutional constraints that impede policy change (Bull and Rhodes 2007, Kitschelt and Obinger 2004, Schmidt 2003, Tsebelis 1995). Germany and Italy combine elements of majoritarian and proportional representation (Massicotte and Blais 1999: 347). This "mixed electoral system" tends to produce coalition governments which form less stable and effective executives compared to majoritarian systems. Executive power is in the hands of the government, but is strongly kept in check by parliament.

Both countries have a bicameral parliamentary system. Due to higher levels of party discipline, the lower house in Germany (*Bundestag*) usually does not impede government policy. The upper house (*Bundesrat*) consists of delegates from the 16 federal states (*Bundesländer*), who are elected at different points in time during the government term of office. The upper house may therefore have a different partisan majority than the lower house and may block legislation by the federal government. The veto right of the upper house is, however, restricted to legislation that concerns the interests of the states. In Italy, the upper house (*Senato della Repubblica*) and the lower house (*Camera dei Deputati*) are vested with the same rights regarding the legislative process (so-called *bicameralismo perfetto*). Party composition is generally consistent in both chambers (Kreile 1987). The upper chamber does not represent regional interests, but controls the lower chamber (and vice versa). Powerful parliamentary committees and the possibility of delaying proceedings put constraints on government policies.

The parliament exerts a control function over the government in both Germany and Italy. It is easier for the German government to push through bills compared to Italy, where each individual member of the parliament is allowed to propose or amend a parliamentary law. Moreover, in Italy, any law needs the consent of both the *Senato* and the *Camera*.

Division of competencies

Both countries are characterized by a division of competencies between the national state, the regions and the municipalities with respect to social-care services. In Germany, kindergartens and day-care centers are conceptualized as care (*Erziehung/Betreuung*).[3] Care is part of public welfare and as such subject to concurrent legislation. As stated in article 72 (2) of the Basic Law, this means that the federal states have the authority to legislate as long as the federal government does not make use of its legislative power. The federal government does in fact have a prior right to legislate where national interests (e.g. equal living conditions) are concerned (see Scheiwe 2009).[4] Before the reform of federalism in 2006, the federal government was entitled to framework legislation. This means that the federal government would frame the general outline of a law and leave regulatory details to the states. After 2006, this legislation was divided into exclusive and concurrent legislation.

In Italy, Law No. 1044, adopted in 1971, lays down that local authorities are responsible for the organization of childcare and receive financial support from the state level. Similar to Germany, the public provision of childcare is not part of the national education system. Instead, care is under the control of the Ministry of Health. Financial support is tied directly to the demand at the regional level, with annual increments from the Ministry of Health to be distributed to the regions (OECD 2001, Saraceno 2003). The national government is not responsible for monitoring the quality or defining minimum care standards. Children in the zero to two age group do not have a social right to a childcare place. A further decentralization took place with Law No. 382, adopted in 1975, which allowed regions to distribute national revenues (to a limited extent). The constitutional reform of 2001 further gave the regions more exclusive competencies (Madama 2010).

The national level, the federal states (in Germany) or regions (in Italy) and the municipalities are closely intertwined and are obligated to cooperate with respect to administration, legislation and funding of childcare. Hence different concerns have to be reconciled. In contrast to Italy, the German states have a dual role. First, they need to represent the policy interests of their region. On the other hand, they are part of party politics at the national level in their role as members of the Federal Council. Opposition parties might use the veto power if they control the Federal Council. This risk has proven to be a central obstacle for initiatives on childcare provision and efforts at the national level are often difficult endeavors (Erler 2005, Henninger and von Wahl 2010).

Welfare regime

In many typologies, Germany and Italy are classified as representatives of a common welfare state type termed Continental, Conservative or Bismarckian (Esping-Andersen 1990, Palier and Martin 2007). These systems have the following characteristics in common: access to benefits is in general linked to employment, most of the benefits are earnings related and paid in cash and much of their social expenditure is financed via earnings-related contributions. Sometimes a "northern" and a "southern" variant of the Bismarckian regime is differentiated (Bonoli 2006, Castles and Obinger 2008), or Southern Europe is even analyzed as a separate type (Ferrera 1996a, b, Leibfried 1993, Naldini 2003). For example, Ferrera (1996a; 1996b) emphasizes the high fragmentation of income maintenance and the high level of particularism with regard to cash benefits and financing in Italy that leads to clientelism.

Also, in contrast to Germany, Italy does not provide universal family benefits and more strongly relies on the family and kinship to provide care and financial support (Ferrera, Fargion, and Jessoula 2012, Naldini 2003, Saraceno 1994, 2003). With respect to the distribution of work and care, however, both countries are characterized by their reliance on the male-breadwinner model that traditionally assigns women the role of the primary caregiver (Ostner and Saraceno 1998). The parental leave schemes in both countries primarily encouraged mothers to withdraw from the labor market because of the low payment in both countries and the long duration in Germany. Until the beginning of the 2000s, only 10 percent of German children and 7.4 percent of Italian children younger than three received publicly subsidized childcare. The support of the male-breadwinner model was more comprehensive in Germany; for example, the joint taxation splitting system and the free co-insurance of non-employed spouses incentivizes mothers to opt out of the labor market or to reduce labor-market participation. While Germany made substantial changes in the work-family policies between 2000 and 2008, policy developments in Italy have been discontinuous and fragmentary.

Economy

Both Germany and Italy belong to the group of the largest economies in the European Union (EU). After World War II they experienced economic growth and industrialization (Flora, Kraus, and Pfenning 1987). The transition to a post-industrial economy in both countries has been marked by a steep increase in the share of people working in the service sector (64 percent in both countries in 2000). At the same time, the share of people working in the industrial sector had decreased to less than 30 percent by 2000.[5] Structural similarities notwithstanding, the two economies have performed differently in the period after 2000. The level of gross domestic product (GDP) per capita is higher in Germany compared to Italy (see figure 1.3).

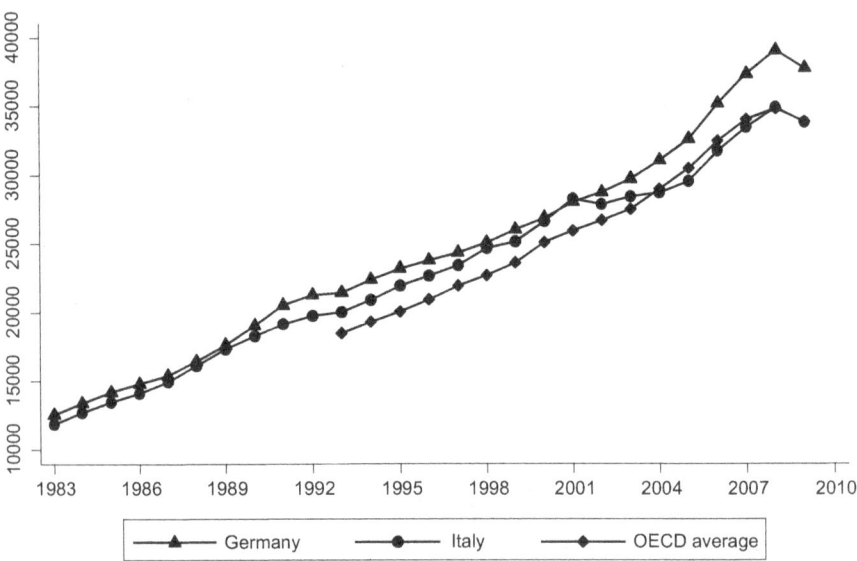

Figure 1.3 GDP per capita (in Euro), Germany and Italy, 1983–2009

Note: Levels of GDP per capita are presented in current prices (current PPPs).
Source: OECD stats

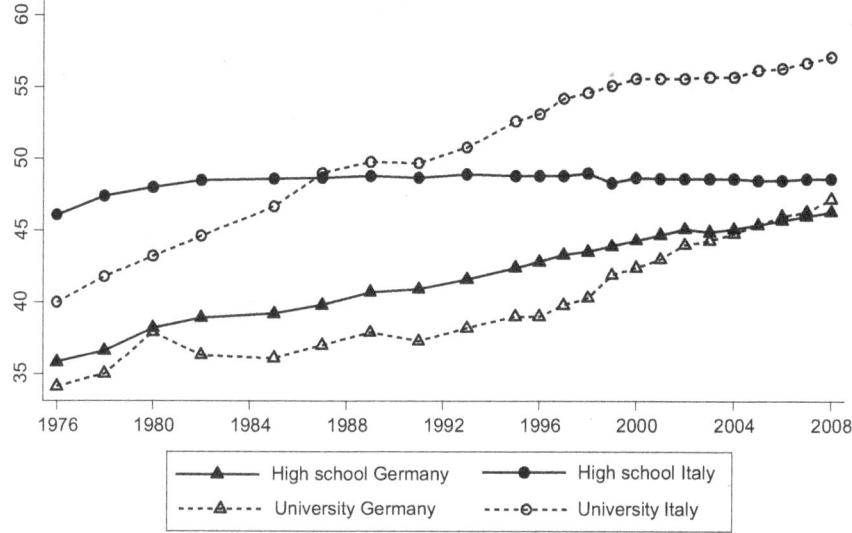

Figure 1.4 Educational attainment of women as a share of total educational attainment, Germany and Italy, 1976–2008

Note: Until 1991, figures for Germany refer to the territory of the former Federal Republic.
Sources: Statistisches Bundesamt based on Mikrozensus-Haushaltsstichprobe; ISTAT

In addition, during the period of observation, Italy has a debt ratio to total GDP of above 100 percent compared to Germany where the ratio fluctuates between 60 and 70 percent of GDP (Eurostat). The two countries both exhibit lasting regional differences in economic performance. The Southern Italian regions (*Mezzogiorno*) have much lower per capita income and higher unemployment rates than the northern regions. For Germany, a similar divide exists between the eastern and the western regions.[6]

Germany is characterized as a coordinated market economy, of which Italy shares several elements (Hall and Soskice 2001, Molina and Rhodes 2007, Trigilia and Burroni 2009). In both countries, women have a high skill level (in 2000, their share of tertiary education is 42.4% in Germany and 55.6% in Italy, see Figure 1.4).

The political landscape in the beginning of the 1990s

Both Germany and Italy experienced political shocks in the beginning of the 1990s, which also had consequences for the design of family policies. In Germany, two established work-family policy models had to be integrated following reunification in 1990. In contrast to the West, the East had one of the highest female-employment rates in Europe and had comparably progressive work-family policies. Thus working mothers were perceived quite differently in the East than in the West. Italy experienced a political crisis when a widespread system of clientelism and illegal party financing was uncovered in 1992, involving a large number of the political elite. In addition, the fall of the Berlin wall and the breakdown of the socialist regimes led to a collapse of the Italian party system. Together with the introduction of a mixed electoral system in 1993, this cleared the way for new parties and a change in party competition.

Thus in the beginning of the 1990s, windows of opportunity for family and work-family policies seemed to open: In Germany, a dual-earner-oriented system from the East was added to the male-breadwinner-oriented model of the West. In Italy, the parties that had been in government since the post-war years dissolved, and their many fragments entered into the emerging new parties. This process affected in particular the Christian Democratic Party, which had been the majority party for over 40 years and had also played a decisive role in family policies. Following the fall of the communist regimes, also the strongest opposition party, the Communists, re-oriented itself, changed its name and eventually merged with the former social left of the Christian Democrats.[7] This marked the beginning of an alliance, which was not always easy, between political cultures and individuals who until then had been on opposite sides.

The subsequent analyses will primarily focus on the period after the political and social changes in the two countries. Over the period 1990–2008, centripetal competition prevailed in both the German and Italian party systems, and the partisan composition of the government was also similar (Picot 2012). In the beginning of the 1990s, center-right coalitions ruled until the mid-nineties, which were succeeded by center-left governments that took over in Italy in 1996 and in Germany in 1998. In Italy, this government collapsed in 2001. Except for a two-year spell of another center-left administration, a center-right government ruled until 2011. The center-left coalition in Germany was replaced in 2005 by a grand coalition. Arguably, these similarities should have produced similar policy outputs.

This overview demonstrated the many similarities of Germany and Italy that make the two countries valuable for a comparison of their different work-family policy reform efforts. Despite sharing similar characteristics in welfare state and economic structures, socio-demographic challenges, work-family reconciliation approaches, political institutions and partisan composition of government, Germany and Italy, however, followed diverging paths in work-family policies after 1990 and in particular in the 2000s. The next section will briefly describe the methodological approaches and the data I use to explain these diverging paths. More details on the data and methods are provided in the substantive chapters.

Methods and data

The book offers a comprehensive study of the nation-specific policy context of working and caring parents. All proposals, initiatives and effective policy changes that have taken place between the beginning of the 1990s and 2008 are considered. For the explanation of the diverging developments, I use a multi-methods approach. The main advantage of this approach is that it allows me to both verify and generate theory (Tashakkori and Teddlie 2003). In addition, by combining different types of data, one type compensates for the weaknesses of the others (complementary design, see e.g. Small 2011). The study has a partially mixed concurrent equal status design (Leech and Onwuegbuzie 2007). This means that both the quantitative and qualitative elements have equal emphasis with respect to addressing the research question and are conducted simultaneously. Both elements are being mixed when it comes to the interpretation of the data (Leech and Onwuegbuzie 2007: 267 and 268).

The quantitative part of the study enables the statistical assessment of the relationship between normative beliefs, voting behavior and policy reforms. It also evaluates the impact of the share of women in parliament and in government. In a first step, logistic regressions are estimated with data from three waves (1990, 1999 and 2008) of the European Values Study (EVS) to analyze changes in normative beliefs towards mothers' employment. The findings are then related to a second set of regressions where group-specific voting behavior is analyzed. The database consists of national post-election surveys. Finally, I present descriptive statistics on the representation of women in the parliament based on data provided by the statistical departments of the parliaments.

The qualitative part of the book illuminates the mechanisms and processes linking these variables. Process tracing based on a variety of sources serves to validate the hypotheses tested in the quantitative part (method of triangulation, see e.g. Fielding and Schreier 2001). Theory-guided process tracing shows the conflicts and debates that accompanied the reform processes and illustrates in more detail the chronology of the reform processes. The method allows for the incorporation of a wide range of political actors and is sensitive towards temporal variations in meanings, problem definitions and interest representations. Moreover, the approach accounts for the relationship between political and social actors and political-institutional structures (George and Bennett 2005, Immergut and Anderson 2007, Mayntz and Scharpf 1995). This enables us to gain a better understanding of the causalities, processes and conditions allowing certain interests to enter into the decision-making process at a given point in time.

I use the method of process tracing, which provides "theoretically explicit narratives that carefully trace and compare the sequences of events constituting the process" (Aminzade 1993: 108). This method is particularly useful for small-N comparisons which study complex causal relationships that are characterized by multiple causality, path dependencies, policy feedback and interaction effects (Falleti 2006, George and Bennett 2005, Hall 2003). Process tracing not only helps to produce "thick" descriptions which reveal the intricacies of policymaking patterns (Fontana, Afonso, and Papadopoulos 2008: 534) but is also able to show whether causal mechanisms link the variables or whether a sequence is a spurious correlation (Mahoney 2003, 2000). By unfolding the process, causes and outcomes will be connected (George and Bennett 2005). A process-oriented approach allows me to analyze political decisions and the gradual transformation of preferences by treating politics in a dynamic way so that possible feedback mechanisms can be included (Trampusch 2006, Büthe 2002, George and Bennett

2005). It further sheds light on the role and the impact of policy entrepreneurs. This is particularly important for the analysis of women's substantive representation, because it reveals when, why and how women act for women; when they intervene or place the issue on the political agenda; and whether we can identify differences between women representatives of different parties.

The structured, focused comparisons of the reform processes in Germany and Italy rely on a number of sources: the minutes of parliamentary debates, documents and party manifestos from political parties[8] and relevant secondary sources such as national statistics, published books, papers and reports from experts. Fourteen in-depth expert interviews of relevant actors complement the analyses. I chose experts who either participated actively in the work-family policy reforms (such as ministers or members of Parliament) or who closely followed the political debates and reform developments (such as academic experts, representatives of ministries or members of interest groups). An anonymized list of the interviewees can be found in the appendix (see Table A.2). Due to the less comprehensive body of source material, I conducted more interviews in Italy (ten) than in Germany (four). The semi-structured interviews were highly useful because they provided background knowledge about the reform processes that is not accessible via the literature. Ultimately, they made the tracing of the processes and the dynamics of the reforms viable. In particular, they offer insights about the motivation of central actors and if, when and why they changed their views on family policies. The interviews also delivered information about how the dynamics of party competition were perceived and what role it played in work-family policy reforms. This information as well as data on the impact of timing and policy networks is not available in official (party) documents and media articles. All in all, the expert interviews enabled a more fine-grained analysis of reform processes.[9]

Structure of the book

Chapter 2 presents the theoretical framework that is situated in the extensive literature on welfare state reforms and family policies. Specific theoretical strands are selected to create a coherent perspective that can be adapted to the field of work-family policies. The framework is presented sequentially: It starts out by discussing the concept of normative beliefs drawing mainly on the literature on how norms and values concerning gender relations and child rearing shape the design and changes to policies. Policy responsiveness and competition between parties is added to the model in a second step. Finally, the role of women as an important group of actors is integrated into the framework.

Chapter 3 deals with work-family policy reforms. It discusses issues of measurement and then compares the nation-specific policy context of working and caring parents and the reforms that have taken place between the beginning of the 1990s and 2008 in 15 European advanced welfare states. Looking at the developments of Germany and Italy within the broader European context illustrates the relevant policy dimensions and differences and further justifies the case selection. Based on a custom-built database that includes a series of indicators suitable for policy comparison over time, it is shown that a large number of changes have taken place both in working-time policies and childcare services. These changes have led to policies that increasingly encourage both partners to be in paid employment. At the same time, there continue to be considerable cross-national differences. Germany and Denmark prove to be the most reform-active and Italy and Greece the least active countries in the sample during the observation period.

Chapter 4 focuses on Germany and Italy and describes the policy developments in the two countries in greater detail. The first part deals with the historical roots that influenced the similar starting situations in the beginning of the 1990s. Both countries lacked a coherent work-family policy framework that would encourage a dual-earner-family model. The fascist past, Christian Democratic Parties and the Catholic Church were important factors that contributed to the adherence to the male-breadwinner model in both Germany and Italy. The second part of the chapter gives a more detailed description of the policy developments after 1990 in terms of leave and working-time arrangements and childcare. I show that Germany initiated the renunciation of the male-breadwinner model through the introduction or expansion of work-family policies after the turn of the millennium. Italy, by contrast, mostly continues to implicitly encourage the male-breadwinner model through the lack of adequate policies that help parents to reconcile care and paid work.

Chapters 5 through 8 provide the empirical analyses of the reform activity and the differences between Germany and Italy. Quantitative evidence on normative beliefs, party competition and women's descriptive representation is complemented with a structure-focused, cross-case comparison. Taken together, they explain the shift in German work-family policies with the combined incidence of a change of normative beliefs towards the support of the dual-earner model, an increased salience of the issue of work-family policies for party competition, high women's representation in parliament and the commitment of female policy entrepreneurs who were supported by the chancellors. By contrast, the reasons for Italy's comparably low efforts to reform its work-family policy approach are shown to be the persistently traditional normative beliefs of the population, the disincentives for parties to compete with the issue of work-family reconciliation policies, the comparably low share of women representatives in government and the low support of female policy entrepreneurs by the political leadership.

Chapter 5 presents multivariate regression analyses and examines how electoral demand and party competition shape the development of work-family policies. Both the Italian and the German party systems foster centripetal competition, yet the continuous loss of votes for the two largest German parties and the erosion of their traditional constituencies also requires them to look beyond and try to attract new groups of voters. In Italy, the center-right and the center-left coalitions have more comfortable majorities. It is shown that Germans have on average become more supportive of the dual-earner-family model, while Italians have maintained traditional attitudes (i.e. more in favor of the male-breadwinner model). Thus a general change of beliefs in a society is a crucial condition for policy change. In both countries, women and highly educated persons are particularly likely to support the dual-earner model, while religious and less-educated people are more likely to approve of the male-breadwinner model. As their core constituencies declined, the large parties in Germany tried to compete for new groups of voters, i.e. women and other voters with more progressive work-family policy proposals.

Chapter 6 compares the political representation of women on different levels based on data from the statistical offices of the parliaments: in parliament, in governing coalitions and in cabinets. I compare levels for given legislative periods and also the trends over the period 1990–2008 between Germany and Italy. Looking both at the share of female MPs and of female ministers the chapter reveals that in Germany, the second red-Green government (2002–2005) and the subsequent grand coalition had the highest share of women representatives ever: one-third of the MPs were women. In Italy, even though the share of female MPs is on the rise, there was a lack of a critical mass of women in parliament.

Chapters 7 and 8 provide in-depth historical analyses of the reform processes in each country. Examining the intra-partisan conflicts and changing dynamics of party competition between 1990 and 2008 substantiates the analyses of Chapters 5 and 6. In Chapter 7, it is demonstrated when, why and how the parties in Germany have reacted to the changes in normative beliefs. Both large parties adapted their policy positions gradually starting in the late 1990s. At least since the 2002 election campaign, the Social Democrats had promoted policies that aimed at facilitating a better reconciliation of work and care for parents in the hope of electoral payoff. The CDU adapted its campaign accordingly. Yet it was not until the narrow election of 2005 that the CDU had fully realized the potential of work-family policies as a vote-seeking strategy. Chapter 7 further reveals the important role of women in decision-making processes. Two very strong ministers of family affairs acted as policy entrepreneurs and were able to persuade the critics within their own parties. Their support by the chancellors was a crucial condition for their success.

Chapter 8 traces the work-family policy reform processes in Italy and analyzes the causes of the failure to push through reforms. This chapter uses similar and parallel data to Chapter 7. Italian policymakers – irrespective of their party affiliation or membership in a coalition – did not have a strong incentive to reform work-family policies, because they were neither pushed by changes in the normative beliefs of the voters nor by structural changes in the electorate. Nonetheless, some reform efforts have been initiated by center-left coalitions after the 1996 and the 2006 elections. The laws that were adopted during the former period under a center-left government can be ascribed to the impact of female policy entrepreneurs who pushed them through as part of a joint effort and were supported by women from different parties. The reform initiatives of the second center-left coalition of 2006–2008, however, fell victim to the ideological debates about the family and the low priority ascribed to work-family policies.

Chapter 9 summarizes the findings from a comparative perspective. It offers a compact summary of the main results on how normative beliefs, the dynamics of party competition and women's representation interact to impact upon work-family reform processes. Then, after elaborating on the contributions of the study as well as its limits, avenues for further research are indicated. Finally, political implications of the study are discussed.

Notes

1 This description refers to women who grew up and lived in the western part of Germany. Eastern German women had a different life course trajectory. Yet, after unification in 1990, most of the Western German social policies, legal and tax regulations were transferred to common law so that Eastern Germans also had to cope with the dominance of the male-breadwinner model.
2 Old-age dependency ratio is defined as the number of elderly persons of an age when they are generally economically inactive (aged 65 and over) as a percentage of the number of persons of working age (from 15 to 64).
3 This is different from schools and formal education, which belong to the field of education (*Bildung*), where the regions have exclusive legislative power (Article 70 (1) of the Basic Law). This divergent conceptualization is, however, contested (see Scheiwe (2009).
4 Sozialgesetzbuch (SGB) – Achtes Buch (VIII) – Kinder- und Jugendhilfe – (Artikel 1 des Gesetzes vom 26. Juni 1990, BGBl. I S. 1163). Between 1953 and 1991, the Youth Welfare Act (*Jugendwohlfahrtsgesetz JWG*) regulated the child and youth services in Germany. Its predecessor was the Reich Youth Welfare Act (*Reichsjugendwohlfahrtsgesetz RJWG*) which was developed in 1922/24.
5 See Statistisches Bundesamt (https://www.destatis.de/DE/Startseite.html; access date: 17.02.2012) and ISTAT (http://timeseries.istat.it/; access date: 13.01.2012).
6 In 2011, the unemployment rate of Italians living in the north and the center was ca. 6.3 percent, while about 13 percent of Italians living in the south and on the islands were unemployed (ISTAT). After a period of increasingly high unemployment rates in the eastern part of Germany (a peak of almost 19 percent in 2005), the situation improved after the mid-2000s. In 2014, almost 10 percent of astern Germans were unemployed compared to about 6 percent of western Germans. Eastern Germans reach about 75 percent of western Germans' income (Statistisches Bundesamt 2015).
7 It should be noted that the leftist parties' views on mothers' employment did not greatly diverge from the Christian Democratic Party's attitude. Neither the Communist nor the Socialist parties, and especially their male leaders, supported a more equal gender division of labor. See Chapter 8 in this volume for more details.
8 I used the collection of party manifestos provided by the Manifesto Project (Volkens et al. 2011).
9 All quotes in this book have been translated to English by the author. Usually, the English version is found in the text and the originals are found in the notes.

References

Aminzade, Ronald. 1993. "Class Analysis, Politics, and French Labor History." In *Rethinking Labor History*, edited by Lenard Berlanstein, 90–113. Urbana: University of Illinois Press.
Bonoli, Giuliano. 2006. "New Social Risks and the Politics of Post-industrial Social Policies." In *The Politics of Post-industrial Welfare States. Adapting Post-war Social Policies to New Social Risks*, edited by Klaus Armingeon and Giuliano Bonoli, 3–26. London/New York: Routledge.
Bonoli, Giuliano. 2007. "Time Matters: Postindustrialization, New Social Risks, and Welfare State Adaptation in Advanced Industrial Democracies." *Comparative Political Studies* 40 (5):495–520. doi: 10.1177/0010414005285755.

Bonoli, Giuliano, and Frank Reber. 2009. "The Political Economy of Childcare in OECD Countries: Explaining Cross-national Variation in Spending and Coverage Rates." *European Journal of Political Research* 49 (1):97–118.

Brady, David. 2009. *Rich Democracies, Poor People: How Politics Explain Poverty*. New York: Oxford University Press.

Bull, Martin, and Martin Rhodes. 2007. "Introduction – Italy: A Contested Polity." *West European Politics* 30 (4):657–669. doi: 10.1080/01402380701500207.

Büthe, Tim. 2002. "Taking Temporality Seriously: Modeling History and the Use of Narratives as Evidence." *American Political Science Review* 96 (3):481–493.

Caiazza, Amy. 2004. "Does Women's Representation in Elected Office Lead to Women-Friendly Policy? Analysis of State-level Data." *Women and Politics* 26 (1):35–70.

Castles, Francis G., and Herbert Obinger. 2008. "Worlds, Families, Regimes: Country Clusters in European and OECD Area Public Policy." *West European Politics* 31 (1):321–344.

Ebbinghaus, Bernhard. 2005. "When Less Is More. Selection Problems in Large-N and Small-N Cross-National Comparisons." *International Sociology* 20 (3):133–152.

Erler, Daniel. 2005. "Public work-family reconciliation policies in Germany and Italy. Exploring the relevance of problem pressures, institutions, and actors." Department of Comparative and European Politics, Università degli studi di Siena.

Esping-Andersen, Gøsta. 1990. *The Three Worlds of Welfare Capitalism*. Princeton, NJ: Princeton University Press.

Esping-Andersen, Gøsta, ed. 1996. *Welfare States in Transition: National Adaptations in Global Economies*. London: SAGE.

Esping-Andersen, Gøsta. 2002. "Towards the Good Society, Once Again?" In *Why We Need a New Welfare State*, edited by Gøsta Esping-Andersen, Duncan Gallie, Anton Hemerijck and John Myles, 1–25. Oxford: Oxford University Press.

Falleti, Tulia. 2006. "Theory-Guided Process-Tracing: Something Old, Something New." *APSA-CP, Newsletter of the Organized Section in Comparative Politics of the American Political Science Association* 17 (1):9–14.

Ferrera, Maurizio. 1996a. "Il modello Sud-europeo di Welfare State." *Rivista Italiana Di Scienza Politica* 26 (1):67–101.

Ferrera, Maurizio. 1996b. "The 'Southern Model' of Welfare in Social Europe." *Journal of European Social Policy* 6 (1):17–37. doi: 10.1177/095892879600600102.

Ferrera, Maurizio, Valeria Fargion, and Matteo Jessoula. 2012. *Alle radici del welfare all'italiana. Origini e futuro di un modello sociale squilibrato*. Venezia: Marsilio Editori.

Fielding, Nigel, and Margrit Schreier. 2001. "Introduction: On the Compatibility between Qualitative and Quantitative Research Methods." Forum Qualitative Sozialforschung/ Forum: Qualitative Social Research 2 (1):Available at: http://www.qualitative-research.net/index.php/fqs/article/view/965/2106.

Fleckenstein, Timo. 2011. "The Politics of Ideas in Welfare State Transformation: Christian Democracy and the Reform of Family Policies in Germany." *Social Politics* 18 (4):543–571.

Flora, Peter, Franz Kraus, and Winfried Pfenning. 1987. *State, Economy, and Society in Western Europe 1815–1975*. II vols. Vol. II. Frankfurt a.M./New York: Campus.

Fontana, Marie-Christine, Alexandre Afonso, and Yannis Papadopoulos. 2008. "Putting the Special Case in Its Place: Switzerland and Small-N Comparison in Policy Research." *Swiss Political Science Review* 14 (3):521–550. doi: 10.1002/j.1662-6370.2008.tb00111.x.

George, Alexander L., and Andrew Bennett. 2005. *Case Studies and Theory Development in the Social Sciences*. Cambridge: MIT Press.
Hall, Peter A. 2003. "Aligning Ontology and Methodology in Comparative Research." In *Comparative Historical Analysis in the Social Sciences*, edited by James Mahoney and Dietrich Rueschemeyer, 373–404. Cambridge: Cambridge University Press.
Hall, Peter A., and David Soskice. 2001. *Varieties of Capitalism. The Institutional Foundations of Comparative Advantage*. New York: Oxford University Press.
Häusermann, Silja. 2010. *The Politics of Welfare Reform in Continental Europe. Modernization in Hard Times*. New York: Cambridge University Press.
Häusermann, Silja, Georg Picot, and Dominik Geering. 2013. "Review Article: Rethinking Party Politics and the Welfare State – Recent Advances in the Literature." *British Journal of Political Science* 43 (01):221–240. doi: 10.1017/S0007123412000336.
Henninger, Annette, and Angelika von Wahl. 2010. "Das Umspielen von Veto-Spielern. Wie eine konservative Familienministerin den Familialismus des deutschen Wohlfahrtsstaates unterminiert." In *Die zweite Große Koalition. Eine Bilanz der Regierung Merkel 2005–2009*, edited by Christoph Egle and Reimut Zohlnhöfer, 361–379. Wiesbaden: VS Verlag für Sozialwissenschaften.
Huber, Evelyne, and John D. Stephens. 2001. *Development and Crisis of the Welfare State: Parties and Policies in Global Markets*. Chicago/London: The University of Chicago Press.
Immergut, Ellen M. 1992. "The Rules of the Game: The Logic of Health Policy-Making in France, Switzerland and Sweden." In *Structuring Politics. Historical Institutionalism in Comparative Analysis*, edited by Sven Steinmo, Kathleen Thelen and Frank Longstreth, 57–89. Cambridge: Cambridge University Press.
Immergut, Ellen M., and Karen M. Anderson. 2007. "Editors Introduction: the Dynamics of Pension Politics." In *The Handbook of West European Pension Politics*, edited by Ellen M. Immergut, Karen M. Anderson and Isabelle Schulze, 1–45. Oxford: Oxford University Press.
ISTAT. 2012. Rilevazione trimestrale sulle forze di lavoro (fino al 2003); Rilevazione sulle forze di lavoro (dal 2004). In *SerieStoriche. L'archivio della statistica italiana*: http://dati.istat.it.
King, Gary, Robert O. Keohane, and Sidney Verba. 1994. *Designing Social Inquiry*. Princeton, NJ: Princeton University Press.
Kitschelt, Herbert, and Herbert Obinger. 2004. "From Stability to Stagnation: Germany at the Beginning of the Twenty-first Century." In *Germany. Beyond the Stable State*, edited by Herbert Kitschelt and Herbert Obinger, 1–36. London/Portland: Frank Cass.
Korpi, Walter. 1983. *The Democratic Class Struggle*. London: Routledge & Kegan Paul.
Kreile, Michael. 1987. "Die Reform der staatlichen Institutionen in Italien: symbolische Politik und parlamentarischer Prozeß." *Zeitschrift für Parlamentsfragen* (4):573–584.
Kremer, Monique. 2007. *How Welfare States Care. Culture, Gender and Parenting in Europe*. Amsterdam: Amsterdam University Press.
Lambert, Priscilla A. 2008. "The Comparative Political Economy of Parental Leave and Child Care: Evidence from Twenty OECD Countries." *Social Politics* 15 (3):315–344. doi: 10.1093/sp/jxn013.
Leech, Nancy L., and Anthony J. Onwuegbuzie. 2007. "A Typology of Mixed Methods Research Designs." *Quality and Quantity* 43 (2):265–275.
Leibfried, Stephan. 1993. "Towards a European Social Model?" In *New Perspectives on the Welfare State*, edited by Catherine Jones, 133–156. London: Routledge.

Lewis, Jane, Mary Campbell, and Carmen Huerta. 2008. "Patterns of Paid and Unpaid Work in Western Europe: Gender, Commodification, Preferences and the Implications for Policy." *Journal of European Social Policy* 18 (1):21–37.

Lijphart, Arend. 1975. "The Comparable Cases Strategy in Comparative Research." *Comparative Political Studies* 8 (3):158–177.

Madama, Ilaria. 2010. *Le politiche di assistenza sociale*. Bologna: il Mulino.

Mahoney, James. 2000. "Strategies of Causal Inference in Small-N Analysis." *Sociological Methods & Research* 28 (4):387–424. doi: 10.1177/0049124100028004001.

Mahoney, James. 2003. "Strategies of Causal Assessment in Comparative Historical Analysis." In *Comparative Historical Analysis in the Social Sciences*, edited by James Mahoney and Dietrich Rueschemeyer, 337–372. New York: Cambridge University Press.

Massicotte, Louis, and André Blais. 1999. "Mixed Electoral Systems: A Conceptual and Empirical Survey." *Electoral Studies* 18 (3):341–366.

Mayntz, Renate, and Fritz W. Scharpf. 1995. "Der Ansatz des akteurzentrierten Institutionalismus." In *Gesellschaftliche Selbstregelung und politische Steuerung*, edited by Renate Mayntz and Fritz W. Scharpf, 39–72. Frankfurt/Main: Campus.

Molina, Oskar, and Martin Rhodes. 2007. "Industrial Relations and the Welfare State in Italy: Assessing the Potential of Negotiated Change." *West European Politics. Special issue on "Italy: A Contested Polity"* (30):803–829.

Morgan, Kimberly J. 2013. "Path Shifting of the Welfare State: Electoral Competition and the Expansion of Work-Family Policies in Western Europe." *World Politics* 65 (01):73–115. doi: doi:10.1017/S0043887112000251.

Mushaben, Joyce. 2005. "Girl Power, Mainstreaming and Critical Mass: Women's Leadership and Policy Paradigm Shift in Germany's Red-Green Coalition, 1998–2002." *Journal of Women, Politics and Policy* 27 (1/2):135–161.

Naldini, Manuela. 2003. *The Family in the Mediterranean Welfare States*. London: Frank Cass Publishers.

Naumann, Ingela K. 2005. "Childcare and Feminism in West-Germany and Sweden in the 1960s and 1970s." *Journal of European Social Policy* 15 (1):47–63.

OECD. 2001. *OECD Country Note. Early Childhood Education and Care Policy in Italy*. Paris: Organisation for Economic Co-operation and Development.

Ostner, Ilona, and Chiara Saraceno. 1998. "Keine Arbeit, keine Kinder, keine Lösung? Italien und Deutschland in vergleichender Perspektive." In *Modell Deutschland – Modell Europa. Probleme, Perspektiven*, edited by Bruno Cattero, 183–206. Opladen: Leske + Budrich.

Palier, Bruno, and Claude Martin. 2007. "Editorial Introduction – From 'a Frozen Landscape' to Structural Reforms: The Sequential Transformation of Bismarckian Welfare Systems." *Reforming the Bismarckian Welfare Systems. Special Issue of Social Policy & Administration* 41 (7):535–554.

Picot, Georg. 2012. *Politics of Segmentation: Party Competition and Social Protection in Europe*. London: Routledge.

Przeworski, Adam, and Henry Teune. 1970. *The Logic of Comparative Social Inquiry*. New York: Wiley.

Saraceno, Chiara. 1994. "The Ambivalent Familism of the Italian Welfare State." *Social Politics* 1 (1):60–82. doi: 10.1093/sp/1.1.60.

Saraceno, Chiara. 2003. *Mutamenti della famiglia e politiche sociali in Italia*. Bologna: il Mulino.

Scharpf, Fritz W., and Vivien A. Schmidt, eds. 2000. *Welfare and Work in the Open Economy. From Vulnerability to Competitiveness. Volumes I + II* Oxford: Oxford University Press.

Scheiwe, Kirsten. 2009. "Slow Motion – Institutional Factors as Obstacles to the Expansion of Early Childhood Education in the FRG." In *Child care and Preschool Development in Europe. Institutional Perspectives*, edited by Kirsten Scheiwe and Harry Willekens, 180–195. Basingstoke: Palgrave Macmillan.

Schmidt, Manfred G. 2003. *Political Institutions in the Federal Republic of Germany.* Oxford: Oxford University Press.

Small, Mario Luis. 2011. "How to Conduct a Mixed Methods Study: Recent Trends in a Rapidly Growing Literature." *Annual Review of Sociology* 37 (1):57–86.

Statistisches Bundesamt. 2012. Erwerbstätige nach Wirtschaftsbereichen. Zeitreihe 1950–2010.

Statistisches Bundesamt. 2015. 25 Jahre Deutsche Einheit. edited by Statistische Ämter des Bundes und der Länder. Wiesbaden.

Tashakkori, Abbas, and Charles Teddlie, eds. 2003. *Handbook of Mixed Methods in Social and Behavioral Research.* Thousand Oaks, CA: Sage.

Trampusch, Christine. 2006. "Sequenzorientierte Policy-Analyse: Warum die Rentenreform von Walter Riester nicht an Reformblockaden scheiterte." *Berliner Journal für Soziologie* 16 (1):55–76.

Trigilia, Carlo, and Luigi Burroni. 2009. "Italy: Rise, Decline and Restructuring of a Regionalized Capitalism." *Economy and Society* 38 (4):630–653.

Tsebelis, George. 1995. "Decision Making in Political Systems: Veto Players in Presidentialism, Parliamentarism, Multicamerialism and Multipartyism." *British Journal of Political Science* 25 (3):289–325.

Volkens, Andrea, Onawa Lacewell, Pola Lehmann, Sven Regel, Henrike Schultze, and Annika Werner. 2011. *The Manifesto Data Collection. Manifesto Project (MRG/CMP/MARPOR).* Berlin: Wissenschaftszentrum Berlin für Sozialforschung (WZB).

Wängnerud, Lena. 2000. "Testing the Politics of Presence: Women's Representation in the Swedish Riksdag." *Scandinavian Political Studies* 23 (1):67–91.

2 Theories of welfare state and work-family policy reform

Many recent accounts of work-family policy reforms have their roots in comparative welfare state studies. Most of these theories have been developed to explain similarities and differences in states' approaches to provide for the economic security of their populations. State-provided social security schemes insure citizens against the risk of loss of employment and loss of income due to old age or sickness. They enable citizens to maintain a living without being forced to sell their working power on the market (decommodification). At the same time, their respective configuration stratifies society inasmuch as it determines who benefits from social policies and who does not. For example, in continental welfare states, wage earners are the main beneficiaries, while in universalist welfare states, all citizens receive benefits irrespective of their employment status. Hence functionalist, actor-centered and institutionalist theories have been applied to explain why countries differ in their approaches; when, why and how social policies are being reformed; and which groups prevailed in the distributive struggles.

Also, work-family policies are about the state provision of benefits and services. Parental leave, childcare, and other work-family policies insure against the risk of losing a job and an income because of becoming a mother. In that sense, they are comparable to the long-established social policies and the explanations that are used may be transferred to the area of work-family policies. However, work-family policies are not only about material redistribution in favor of certain groups of society. They also touch upon norms and beliefs about gender relations, proper childcare, emotional needs of children, and the family. To account for how these norms and beliefs impact upon work-family policy reforms and which actors play a role in this process is thus of central importance.

My approach builds on the influential theories of welfare state reform and integrates several more recent advancements. I start out by discussing the concept of normative beliefs. Here I mainly draw on the literature on how norms and values concerning gender relations and child rearing shape the design and changes to policies. Policy responsiveness and competition between parties is added to the model in a second step. These theories highlight changes in the electoral foundation of party support and the ways parties compete for (new) voters. Next, the role of women as an important group of actors is integrated into the framework. Women's presence in parliament and in government has played an important role in the development of the welfare state, which ultimately bears on the reconciliation of work and family. Lastly, I position my theoretical argument in the context of other influential theories of the welfare state.

Theoretical argument

Normative beliefs shape social policymaking

The fundamental starting point of my theoretical framework is that deeply embedded cultural values build a context for social policymaking (Jo 2011, van Oorschot 2006, van Oorschot, Opielka, and Pfau-Effinger 2008). The literature on care and family policies directs its attention to normative beliefs about the family, gender roles and appropriate state intervention for the design, the extent and changes to policies (Kremer 2007, Morgan 2006, Pfau-Effinger 2000, Strohmeier 2002). In a society, it is argued, there is a shared definition of what good care is and who provides it. This care ideal shapes both individual work and care practices and the agenda and decisions of policymakers. It is argued that the design of work-family policies is a function of the dominant care ideal or *care culture* (Kremer 2007) in a country.

It remains unclear how these normative beliefs enter the political arena and under which circumstances they are transformed into policies. One approach emphasizes the role of *ideas* and *discourses* that provide guidance for policymakers (Béland 2009, Padamsee 2009, Schmidt 2000). When new ideas enter the political discourse, the debate over definitions, the framing of problems and the possible solutions are altered. Subsequent policy decisions are then affected by the changed public discourse (Blum 2012, Bothfeld 2005, Nullmeier and Rüb 1993, Seeleib-Kaiser and Toivonen 2011: 335).

Several authors highlight the role of specific advocacy groups, such as women's organizations or the Catholic Church, in making policy demands to the state (Bertone 2003, Fix 2000, Kremer 2006, Morgan 2008, Naumann 2005). Important scientific studies may also be able to alter the public political discourse (Ahrens 2010, Rüling 2010). Ahrens, Blum, and Gerlach (2010) point to the importance of international actors in this process. International actors provide national policy makers with policy ideas for how to deal with the perceived challenges. Examples of this include the comparative education study Programme for International Student Assessment (PISA) by the Organisation for Economic Co-Operation and Development (OECD) or the Lisbon Strategy promoted by the European Union.

While the literature on ideational change and discourses puts particular weight on the role of elites and the importance of the framing of problems and solutions, *policy responsiveness theory* investigates the link between the citizens' preferences, normative beliefs and values and the formulation of a policy. This theory assumes that "[. . .] if the level of policy differs from the level the public prefers, the public favors a corresponding change in policy" (Soroka and Wlezien 2005: 667). The early literature on "dynamic representation" (Stimson, Mackuen, and Erikson 1995) postulates that policymakers calculate future implications of current public opinion. The elites are responsive to public preferences because in "democratic polities, elected officials have an incentive to incorporate the policy preferences of voters so as to reduce the risk of electoral losses for themselves (or for their party) [. . .]" (Brooks and Manza 2006: 479). Given the high levels of approval for the welfare state that are generally expressed (Bonoli 2000b, Svallfors 1997), there are compelling reasons to believe that politicians who wish to be re-elected will take the attitudes and value judgments of their electorate into account (see also Jo 2011, van Oorschot 2006).

This argument is also at the heart of Pierson's contribution (Pierson 1994). He claims that cutbacks in popular social policy programs are unlikely even for proretrenchment parties, such as the liberal or conservative parties, because politicians fear that they will be punished for these decisions at elections. This view places emphasis on the role of voters in the analysis of welfare state politics (Immergut and Anderson 2007, Immergut and Abou-Chadi 2014, Lupu and Pontusson 2011). Empirical studies have demonstrated, for example, that cross-national differences in the level of the population's policy preferences – measured as the preferred degree of government responsibility for providing employment opportunities and reducing income inequalities – are a factor behind comparative differences in welfare state spending (Brooks and Manza 2006). When applied to the study of work-family policies, this theory implies that a policy shift towards state support of the dual-earner model is presumed to be a reaction to a marked change in normative beliefs of the public towards more progressive attitudes toward mothers' employment and childcare.

The decisive role of political parties

Parties play a crucial mediating role in the process of transforming normative beliefs into policies. Political actors absorb the beliefs and help to put issues on the political agenda. A vote-seeking party tries to represent the interests of its constituencies and pursues policies that comply with its constituencies' preferences. This assumption originates in the influential power resources theory (Brady 2009, Brady, Blome, and Kleider 2016, Huber and Stephens 2001, Korpi 1983, 1989). It assumes that, in a capitalist democracy, businesses have far more political power than wage earners. To gain more power, the working class must bond with the middle class. By supporting leftist political parties, this bonding may then be mobilized in elections. When in office, these parties may enact their redistributive ideas and expand the welfare state. Conservative parties, by contrast, represent the interests of businesses and employers who are in favor of freedom of economy and small welfare states.

The theory thus postulates strong assumptions about the material interests of a party's constituencies and the relationship with social policymaking.[1] Indeed, how and to what extent parties matter in the development of social policies remains a major question in comparative welfare state research (see Häusermann, Picot, and Geering 2013 for a recent overview). Many studies that analyze the impact of leftist, and social-democratic parties in particular, on generous welfare states have confirmed the partisan effects on the welfare state (Allan and Scruggs 2004, Castles and Obinger 2007, Castles and Mitchell 1993, Huber and Stephens 2001, Korpi and Palme 2003).

On the other hand, the rather static left-right thinking has also provoked criticism from welfare state researchers. Some authors claimed that left-wing parties did not represent the entire working class, since parts of it were instead mobilized by religious parties. These authors found that the Christian-democratic movement is an alternative driving force of welfare state expansion, in particular when in competition with leftist parties for the working class (Alber 2000, Ferrera 1986, van Kersbergen 1995).[2]

The integration of the church-state cleavage[3] into the analysis of national variation and the extent of policy reforms has been shown to be particularly relevant for the development of social services and, hence, work-family policies (Alber 1995). This cleavage is nowadays described as a conflict between religious and secular values, where religious people are more likely to vote for a religious party (Pappi and Brandenburg 2010). As part of the process of secularization, this cleavage has over time been integrated into a more broadly defined values cleavage (Inglehart 1990) or cultural conflict between libertarian and authoritarian values (Kitschelt 1994, Kriesi et al. 2006, Niedermayer 2009). Libertarian values emphasize, among others, personal and political freedom, equality and concern over quality-of-life issues and environment, while authoritarian values concern security and order, as well as support for traditional religious and moral ideas (Flanagan 1987).

Parties and the values cleavage

Social-democratic parties are associated with libertarian values, and conservative and Christian-democratic parties are linked with authoritarian values. The social democrats strive for gender equality as a result of their commitment to social equality. In contrast to Christian-democratic parties, they aim to support individual family members, not the family as an institution. While Christian democrats deploy the principle of subsidiarity and see the family as the core provider of (care) services, social democrats promote equal opportunity through the public provision of social services (Seeleib-Kaiser, van Dyk, and Roggenkamp 2008). As a consequence, social democrats support emancipated family policies that promote women's employment. As they defend the rights of workers, they should favor labor-market regulations that enable parents to take parental leave or work part time. Christian-democratic parties, by contrast, are (1) assumed to hold traditional views about the role of women; (2) place more emphasis on women's role as carers, via incentives through cash transfers or derived social security rights; and (3) thus impede an expansion of work-family policies (Morgan 2003). Some scholars have used these findings to explain why social-democratic welfare states offer extensive childcare services and display high women's labor-force participation rates (Huber and Stephens 2000). While both social-democratic and Christian-democratic parties advocate state intervention into matters of the family (albeit favoring different directions of support), liberal-conservative parties, by contrast, reject the idea of state benefits to support a particular family model.

The empirical evidence of a positive relationship between leftist political power and dual-earner model-oriented work-family policies is not very strong. The social democracy thesis seems to be plausible for the Nordic countries but fails to explain policy patterns in Continental Europe. Morgan (2006) shows that the correlation between the extent of social-democratic power and the availability of public childcare is mainly driven by the Nordic countries. Despite the fact that countries such as Austria, Germany or the Netherlands all have had social-democratic governments at key points in recent history, childcare services and other work-family policies did not undergo improvement. The assumptions regarding Christian-democratic family policy are also not written in stone. Bleses and Seeleib-Kaiser (2004) attribute changes in family policies in Germany to a "modernized" Christian Democratic Party.

These findings raise the question of whether or not it is true that parties still represent their traditional constituencies and whether or not these constituencies still have the same preferences. In recent years, the assumed stable electoral patterns and stable beliefs of the parties' constituencies have been increasingly questioned. Some scholars argue that electorates and voter interests have likely undergone major changes during recent decades (Häusermann, Picot, and Geering 2013). In order to flesh out partisan theories more comprehensively, it is therefore necessary to analyze which groups a party is representing, whether there have been changes over time and whether or not the electorate has changed its preferences.

Party constituencies and their normative beliefs

In spite of some evidence that the Social Democrats incorporate libertarian values and promote the expansion of social services to support working women (Huber and Stephens 2000), it has also been suggested that their core constituency, the working class, holds traditional orientations toward mothers' employment (Lambert 2008). A party that mainly represents the working class might thus not be eager to adopt modern work-family policies – in particular if "[. . .] conservative parties have the potential to lure working- and middle-class voters, this could make it especially difficult for Social Democratic parties to adopt a more 'post-materialist' stance toward gender issues" (Morgan 2009: 63).

By contrast, libertarian voters attain a comparably high educational level, are relatively young and are often women. As they pursue a career and possibly have care responsibilities at the same time, they have a particular interest in work-family policies that help reconcile family and work life. It has been argued that the extent to which left-wing parties rely on these libertarian people's votes influences their policy agenda (Häusermann 2010, Kitschelt and Rehm 2005).

Conservative or Christian-democratic parties mobilize particularly religious people or people with traditional values. In the past, women, particularly those not in employment, have mainly voted for the political right (Inglehart 1977). As a consequence of secularization, the importance of the religious constituency might decline (Roßteutscher 2012). Given the effect of demographic change on labor supply, employers who are represented by conservative parties might become interested in the increase of female labor-force participation. Hence conservative parties could be faced with a conflict between their role as preserver of traditional gender roles and the claims of the employers to introduce work-family policies in order to make it possible for all women to work.

A closer look into parties' constituencies reveals that normative beliefs are ambiguous within political camps and might not be distributed distinctly along party lines. This might have either structural reasons (educational expansion, ageing) or be due to preference changes within the constituencies. Either way, heterogeneity and changes within the electorate should be taken into account when analyzing policy change.

To sum up, the traditional power resources theory and its operationalization through the relative strength of political parties have been refined in recent years. Scholars have argued to rethink conventional assumptions on parties' policy choices. For instance, the role of constituencies ought to be integrated more systematically into welfare state research. Social-democratic parties, for example, seem to face a dilemma: Should they engage in maintaining the status quo for their core constituency, the working class, or should they – in line with their attention for equality – promote work-family policies which would benefit mainly (young) women? Conservative parties might also be divided between promoting the male-breadwinner model and the demands of the employers for more support of working women.

Party competition and parties' policy choices

Although a party may have its own objectives and serve its constituency, policy choices in practice are further influenced by its relation to other parties (Ferrera 1993, Sartori 1976). Political parties perceive the competitive presence of other parties and move in the direction where they expect to gain the most votes. Many studies take the presence of the major opposition parties into account and assume that parties compete for the voters of the political center. Yet, depending on the configuration of the party system, different logics of competition may prevail (Sartori 1976). According to this line of argument, the structure of the party system determines which groups of voters parties compete for and, consequently, whose preferences are represented in the policy decisions (Picot 2012, Sartori 1976).

Kitschelt (2001) examines the role of party configurations in welfare state–retrenchment politics. He considers the relationship between parties as the most important explanatory factor for the likelihood of reform. Based on four variables,[4] he arrives at four distinct party configurations that "offer politicians opportunities to pursue unpopular social policy retrenchment with an office-seeking objective in mind" (Kitschelt 2001: 282). For instance, retrenchment is less likely in countries where party competition occurs primarily between a social-democratic and a Christian-democratic party, with liberal parties playing a limited role.

On a general level, the impact of the party system on policymaking has already been described by Sartori (1976). He argues to take into account the spatial constellation of the party system, because the positioning of the parties determines where the competition is concentrated and on what groups of the electorate the attention of the parties is focused. According to that logic, political parties perceive the competitive presence of other parties and move in the direction where they anticipate they will gain the most votes. Sartori developed the concept of centrifugal and centripetal competition which draws attention to the degree of ideological polarization. If polarization is low, parties try to capture votes from their main political competitor. In bipolar systems, competition focuses on voters in the center (centripetal competition). In party systems with a high degree of polarization between parties, centrifugal competition prevails – that is, competition focuses on the extreme ends. The party system itself is not assumed to be static. Significant changes, for instance, the appearance of a new party, may alter the mode of party competition and affect policy outcomes. Picot (2012) shows, for example, that the new spatial constellation of the party system in Germany, which came about because of the emergence of a new left-wing party, shaped reforms of the unemployment insurance scheme.

The idea that the nature of party competition affects work-family policymaking has more recently been taken up by family-policy researchers. Morgan (2009), for example, suggests that when left-wing parties compete with Christian-democratic parties they may espouse more traditional views on childcare and mothers' employment. She has shown that the lack of religiously based parties in the Nordic countries, and their weakness in France, helps to explain why the issue of mothers' employment has been less controversial in those societies than in some other parts of Europe. Others argue that in response to their electoral defeat in 1998 and increased competition with the Social Democrats, the Christian Democrats in Germany made an instrumental use of policy reforms in order to mobilize (young) women to vote for them (Fleckenstein 2011, Korthouwer 2008, Seeleib-Kaiser 2011). Also, from a comparative perspective, it is shown that the dynamics of electoral competition is an important factor in the explanation of work-family policy change (Morgan 2013).

To sum up, I propose that the analysis of political parties must take into account both the changing dynamics of representation and of party competition. Thus the commitment of political parties to reform work-family policies depends on the beliefs of their constituencies and how their beliefs and/or their composition might have changed. First, this requires analyzing the electoral foundations of party support to reveal which groups of voters parties are mobilizing. Second, the configuration of the party system influences which groups of voters are targeted in elections. Consequently, parties propose the kinds of policies that are favored by the voters they are competing for.

Women's agency and women's impact on work-family policies

Given that the gender division of labor is strongly unbalanced, women's electoral mobilization is a central variable for explaining work-family policy reforms. But women also play a major role as political actors. A host of studies have demonstrated the impact of women's agency on the construction of claims addressed to the state by demanding family policies and public support to care for children (Bertone 2003, Bussemaker 1998, Hobson and Lindholm 1997, Lewis 1994, Kremer 2006, Madama 2010, Misra 2003, Naumann 2005). But when and how do women make a difference? Feminist theories of representation draw on the concepts of descriptive and substantive representation (Pitkin 1967).[5] Descriptive representation occurs when representatives share similar characteristics of the represented such as age or sex (women stand for women). Sharing a group membership is supposed to mean to share "their experiences and policy goals, understanding their perspectives, and prioritize[e] their issues". (Cowell-Meyers and Langbein 2009: 492). Substantive representation is described as the representative's actual effort to advance a group's policy preferences (e.g. women act for women). There is not necessarily a relationship between descriptive and substantive representation. Some argue that party affiliation matters more than sex, particularly on highly contested issues. Feminist issues have been taken up more by women representatives of left-wing parties than right-wing parties (Lovenduski 1986). More recently, researchers have shown that independent of the left-right range, particular structures of party organization may also help to advance women's issues (Wiliarty 2010).

However, most studies contend that the presence of women in decision-making bodies such as political parties, the parliament, and the government is a necessary condition for the representation of women's interests (Campbell, Childs, and Lovenduski 2009, Phillips 1995). It is assumed that women will represent in a different way than male legislators by, for example, bringing issues such as equal opportunities or care work into the legislative arena. Female politicians tend to place a higher priority on social issues and gender equality as a substantial body of research demonstrates (Bolzendahl and Brooks 2007, Campbell, Childs, and Lovenduski 2009, Childs 2004, Lovenduski and Norris 2003, Reingold 1992, Wängnerud 2000). More broadly, it is argued that those issues are women's issues "where policy consequences are likely to have a more immediate and direct impact on significantly larger numbers of women than of men" (Carroll 1994: 15). The traditional gender division of labor issues of work-family reconciliation is a case in point for being more relevant for women than for men. Studies that look at the impact of women's representation on rights, such as maternity leave or reproductive rights, confirm this view (Brunsbach 2011, Lambert 2008). Also, since work-family policies affect young people in particular, work-family policy reforms are arguably more likely the younger the women in parliament are.

The argument that the presence of women leads to an increase of women-friendly policies was further qualified in the sense that a certain proportion of women is needed in decision-making bodies. Only if women have reached a certain numerical strength will they be likely to influence policymaking. Most studies refer to Dahlerup's suggestion of 30 percent (Dahlerup 1988).[6] Such a "critical mass" is essential, because the greater the number of women, the easier it is for them to form strategic alliances. Moreover, an increase in the number of women legislators may cause men to be more attentive to women's issues, and thus more prone to women-friendly policies. Even though these assumptions are contested (Childs and Krook 2008), many studies confirm the impact of a larger number of women legislators on policies. In her quantitative cross-country analysis of maternal employment policies, Lambert (2008) shows that the greater the number of women in parliament, the greater the likelihood that a country will have a generous paid leave policy (see also Bonoli and Reber 2009).

Others argue that it is not the number of women in parliament alone that makes the difference but rather who these women are, what positions they have and what they do. These "critical actors" are women who have a gender consciousness and aim at promoting policies that benefit women. Independent of their number, they initiate and promote policy proposals (Childs and Krook 2006, 2009). Such "policy entrepreneurs" are ideally close to powerful decision makers and are well equipped with financial means in order to be successful with their policy proposals (Mintrom 1997, Zahariadis 2003, see also Mackay 2008). The presence of women in decision-making bodies is thus advantageous for the representation of women's interests (Campbell, Childs, and Lovenduski 2009, Phillips 1995).

On the whole, an analysis of the development of work-family policies must take into account the role of women representatives. The most important opportunity to exert power and influence policymaking is to be represented in decision-making bodies. The analysis should differentiate between merely descriptive representation and substantive representation. A party might integrate women up to parity, but at the same time, neglect women's concerns in the party's policy or manifesto, and vice versa. Therefore, when and how women act for women is a central question for the study of political decision-making processes. The following section will briefly summarize the theoretical argument in its entirety. Figures will depict the evolvement of the analytical model.

The analytical model: how normative beliefs, party competition and women's representation matter for work-family policy changes

The analytic framework starts from the idea that work-family policy change is driven by a change of the population's normative beliefs. Policy responsiveness theory assumes that politicians who wish to be re-elected will take the attitudes and value judgments of their electorate into account. Hence a policy shift towards the dual-earner model is presumed to be a reaction to a marked change in

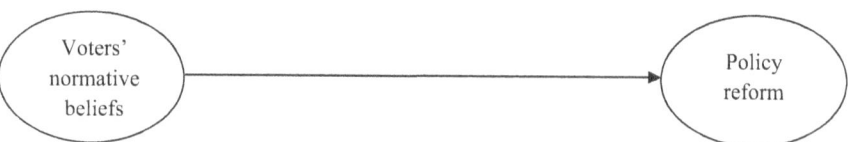

Figure 2.1 The impact of normative beliefs on policy reform

normative beliefs of the public that has led to more progressive attitudes toward mothers' employment and childcare.

According to power resources theory, parties play the crucial mediating role in this process. Political actors absorb the beliefs and help to put issues on the political agenda. A vote-seeking party aims at representing the interests of its constituencies and on pursuing policies that comply with its constituencies' preferences. Basically, leftist parties are more prone to expand work-family policies aimed at facilitating the compatibility of work and family, while such policy reforms are less likely if a Christian-democratic or liberal-conservative party takes over or remains in power.

On the other hand, the party system and the type and intensity of competition with other parties also affect a party's policy strategy. It is argued that the party system determines which groups of voters political parties compete for. In pluralist party systems, competition focuses on the margins of the political spectrum (centrifugal competition). Centripetal competition for voters in the center of the political space emerges in moderate pluralist and two-party systems. The party systems of Italy and Germany foster centripetal competition, which means that the major parties or party blocs compete for the center. A change in normative beliefs within the political center should thus induce a shift towards dual-earner oriented policies in centripetal party systems (figure 2.2).

The composition of the parties' constituencies may change over time. A different composition might also mean a change of the beliefs that play a role in a party's policy decision. The alternative possibility is that the composition of the constituencies remains intact but its members amend their preferences. A concrete example is the voting behavior of women who – because of rising education levels and increasing labor-market participation – are by no means a "natural" constituency of conservative parties anymore. Modifications of a party's policy responses can be the consequence of a) a change of its constituency's beliefs concerning mothers' employment and childcare, or b) a change of the electoral importance of the party's core constituency, or, related to that point, c) a turn towards new constituencies.

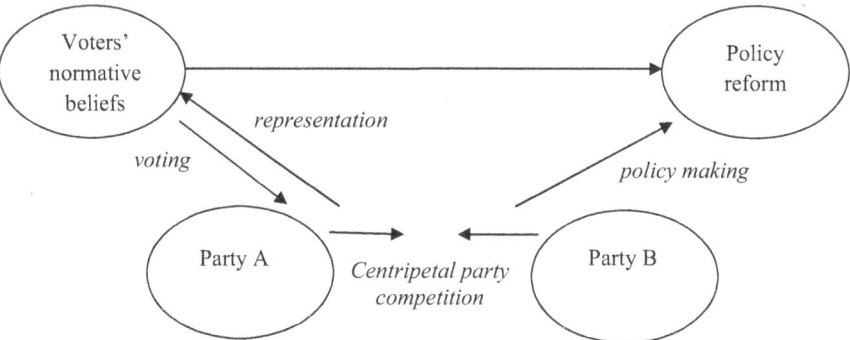

Figure 2.2 How normative beliefs and the dynamics of party competition influence policy reforms

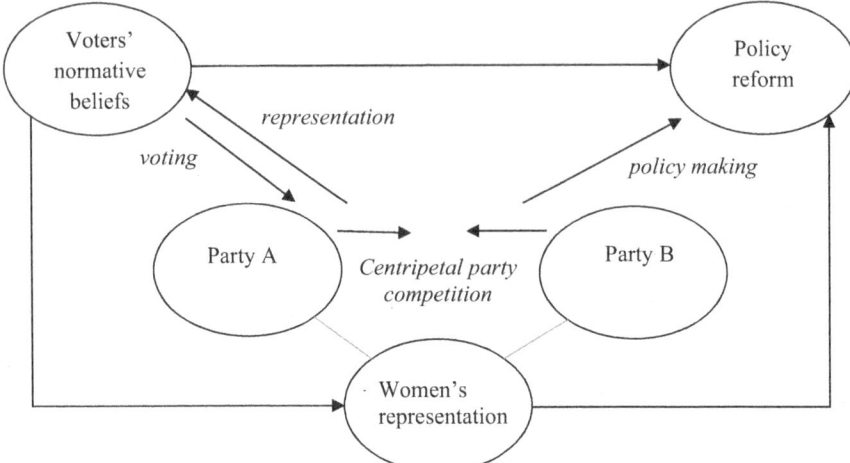

Figure 2.3 How normative beliefs, the dynamics of party competition and women's representation influence policy reforms

Also, internal dynamics matter for a party's policy positions. A change of values within the electorate may cause conflicts between factions of a governing party. Party members with a high interest in family policies should play a decisive role in putting the topic on the agenda. According to the concept of women's agency, women make a difference for the development of policies. The number of women in representative decision-making bodies has an influence on policymaking. Reforms of work-family policies are more likely when more women are represented in parliament and in government (figure 2.3). Their significance should also vary with their age composition, with younger women representatives being more dedicated on adopting work-family policies that support the dual-earner model. Arguably, the number and importance of women in parliament is influenced by a change of normative beliefs in the population. In a cultural climate of progressive gender norms, it becomes more "normal" for women to engage in politics.

Women in decision-making positions may also act on behalf of women's interests. The extent to which women in high-ranking positions in important committees or in government push for reforms will enhance the development of progressive work-family policies. On contested issues such as normative beliefs on mothers' employment and childcare, it is more likely that the Leftist party's women representatives engage in the enhancement of mothers' employment and supportive work-family policies in contrast to their Conservative counterparts.

Relating the theoretical framework to other established welfare state theories

The proposed theoretical framework for the explanation of work-family policy change builds on recent advancements of the extensive literature on welfare state development. In the following, I will explain how my theoretical argument is situated in the context of the well-known three most important schools of thought in comparative welfare state research: functionalist accounts, actor-centered theories and institutionalist explanations. I briefly discuss the theories with regard to their strengths and weaknesses for the explanation of work-family policy reforms.

Functionalist theories of welfare state growth saw the welfare state as developing to meet the demands of society at a certain period of industrialization or modernization. Industrialization, for example, created social needs, as the workers had no provision if they fell ill or became injured or too old to work (problem pressure). As a consequence, social policies were developed and the financial means administered to meet the demand (see Wilensky and Lebeaux 1958).[7] The functionalist thesis is also used to explain policy developments in post-industrial welfare states, albeit with a different focus. Here problem pressures emerge mainly from changing family patterns, rising part-time and temporary employment, mass unemployment and enhanced economic globalization, which create "new social risks" to which welfare states need to find a response (Bonoli 2006, Hantrais 2004, Häusermann 2006, Huber and Stephens 2001, Taylor-Gooby 2005).

The existing literature provides mixed empirical evidence for functionalist accounts. Studies that found a negative impact of globalization on social expenditure (e.g. Garrett and Mitchell 2001) are countered with studies that deny any direct influence on the welfare state (Brady, Beckfield, and Seeleib-Kaiser 2005, Castles 2004). Regarding work-family policies, the two most pressing issues that welfare states arguably have to react to are low fertility rates and low women's employment rates, which result in care and economic deficits (Bonoli and Reber 2009, Daly and Rake 2003). According to the theory, one would expect those countries with low scores on both indicators to adapt policies. However, this relationship does not hold for a number of countries. In particular, German-speaking and southern European countries face these challenges, but reforms have not always followed.[8] Nonetheless, the extent to which new social needs and problem pressures meet ineffective welfare contexts may trigger social policy reforms (Häusermann 2010).

In the late 1970s, functionalist theories were increasingly questioned. The main criticism concerned the "strong version" of the theory, which denied any role of politics in the development of social policies (Myles and Quadagno 2002). As a reaction, actor-centered theories were proposed which emphasized the mobilization of collective actors and the influence of left parties on welfare state development. As outlined earlier, the influential power resources theory argues that welfare state generosity depends on the role and the political strength of leftist actors and their ability to mobilize "power resources" in the state and the economy (Brady 2009, Huber and Stephens 2001, Korpi 1983). When it comes to work-family policies, however, the empirical evidence for a positive relationship between the strength of social-democratic parties and a generous support of working mothers holds mainly for the Scandinavian countries. The otherwise weak correlation can arguably be explained by the fact that leftist political actors represent the working class who may have a material interest in social policies that reduce income inequality and poverty, but who are not necessarily interested in achieving gender equality on the labor market. Rather, they often advocate the male-breadwinner model (Häusermann 2010, Morgan 2006).

Power resources theory and actor-centered theories more generally have also been criticized by scholars who point to the role of established and stable institutions, i.e. formal and informal rules, laws, and policies, for the analysis of social policy change. The literature on *welfare state institutions* postulates that existing welfare state arrangements, i.e. the structure of social provision, influence politics. The term welfare state institution refers to benefit generosity, entitlement regulations, the degree of universalism or targeting, the distribution between cash transfers and services and forms of governance and financing (Esping-Andersen 1990, Korpi and Palme 1998, Starke 2006). One mechanism of influence has been described by the *theory of path dependence*. It states that historical policy legacies largely determine both the extent and the types of change that may be possible, with a particular emphasis on the timing and sequencing of events (Brady et al. 2016, Pierson 2004). Previously established rules and arrangements become more important than politics as those rules and arrangements "lock in place" a certain level of welfare generosity (Brady and Bostic 2015, Ebbinghaus 2005, Pierson 1994).[9]

Many scholars have shown the ways existing or previous policy decisions and welfare state arrangements shape contemporary family policies. The welfare and gender-regime literature has demonstrated cross-regime differences in social policies, which also affect the policy approaches to mothers' employment (Esping-Andersen 1990, Lewis 1992, Orloff 1993, Saraceno 1997).[10] Other authors focus on the impact of early decisions or conflicts on the development of family policies. It has been shown that the nation-specific interplay between the church and the state in the early twentieth century (e.g. Morgan 2006, Naumann 2006, Pfenning and Bahle 2000), or some countries' efforts to distance themselves from a fascist past (Naldini 2003), had shaped the diverging development of social services in European countries.

Theories of *political institutions* focus on the influence of the structure of the political system on politics. On the whole, it is argued that features of the decision-making process' "rules of the game" (North 1990: 3) determine policy outputs by structuring the attempts to change legislation.[11] Political institutions thus shape the environment for political parties and other actors.[12] The concept of veto points as developed by Immergut (1992a, 1990, 1992b) and the related approach of veto players (Tsebelis 1995) share the idea that formal constitutional rules shape the likelihood that legislative proposals will be obstructed. Political actors may, however, use veto points strategically in order to bring their interests into the decision-making process and block, change, or accelerate legislative proposals. Generally, the veto perspective has frequently been applied to quantitative studies that try to understand social policy gridlock (Bonoli 2000a, Huber, Ragin, and Stephens 1993, Iversen and Soskice 2006, Kittel and Obinger 2003, Persson and Tabellini 2004, 2006, Siegel 2002).

So far, the approach has not been explored much in the literature explaining work-family policy change. Analyzing the determinants of policy change towards mothers' employment, Lambert (2008) finds that veto points impede the expansion of parental leave and childcare policies. She argues that a larger number of veto points make it easier for the opponents of employment policies directed at mothers to block the introduction or expansion of these policies.[13] Most criticism of the political-institutionalist approaches originates in the fact that we have witnessed a multitude of welfare state reforms despite a high number of veto players in some countries. The rather static character of the theory's assumptions is not able to account for behavior that deviates from the assumptions or for strategic or creative actions (Lamping and Rüb 2008).

Another institutionalist school focuses on the role of economic institutions such as labor markets or systems of skill formation. Since work-family policies affect labor markets, economic institutions could also impact the policies' development. It is argued that because of future labor shortages, employers are interested in retaining (or attracting) women workers and therefore encourage policies that make work and family life more compatible (Bonoli 2005, Estévez-Abe, Iversen, and Soskice 2001). However, the literature on the "varieties of capitalism" (Hall and Soskice 2001) has found country differences with respect to skill formation. It is argued that in Coordinated Market Economy (CME) countries where the training systems are oriented toward firm-based training that produce company- or industry-specific skills, employers defend social policies to protect their investments in such specific skills (Estévez-Abe, Iversen, and Soskice 2001).[14]

Based on this work, Fleckenstein, Saunders, and Seeleib-Kaiser (2011) argue that in countries that have witnessed an increase in jobs requiring high general skills, employers are more likely to be interested in policies that help women to stay in the labor force. In these countries, employers have invested much more in them than in low-skilled workers who can be replaced more easily. Morgan (2005) argues that Liberal Market Economies (LME), such as the USA, make low-wage, low-skilled childcare workers available who can be afforded by the middle and higher classes. In CME countries, childcare workers are required to have an apprenticeship or university degree, and, consequently, wages are higher and more strongly regulated. Parents, therefore, cannot afford the prices of private childcare. Hence pressure on the governments to increase public expenditure is higher. While these are convincing arguments for why CME countries should be interested in providing childcare, the empirical evidence is inconclusive. CME countries continue to vary to a great degree with respect to public childcare places.

To sum up, the large literature on the impact of institutions has convincingly shown that the context and the "rules of the game" are important to understand the strategies political actors embark on. Immergut and Anderson, however, claim that "institutional theories based on veto points and veto players must be revised to account for the impact of political competition" (Immergut and Anderson 2007: 37). They understand political competition as the "strategy and intensity with which politicians compete for votes" (Immergut and Anderson 2007: 3) and argue in favor of including more systematically the electoral system and the pattern of distribution of political preferences of voters. Hence different aspects of policy responsiveness should be taken into account. This entails a closer look at what voters want and how they think about issues of work-family reconciliation. Accounting for this and the role of critical political actors will improve our understanding of what drives social policy changes in advanced welfare states.

Notes

1 It should be acknowledged that this early materialist and self-interest-driven conception of power resources theory has been broadened over time to include other interests or ideological preferences (Brady 2009, Brooks and Manza 2007, Huber and Stephens 2001).
2 Others have argued that in times of budget austerity, leftist parties are more credible in their efforts to retrench or restructure the welfare state. Leftist parties may be able to sell the reforms as measures to stabilize the welfare state in the long run rather than to dismantle it (Kittel and Obinger 2003), as they are more credible as traditional defenders of the welfare state (Ross 2000).
3 In their seminal work, Lipset and Rokkan (1967) define four cleavages that divide supporters and opponents of an issue: center-periphery, state-church, owner-worker, and urban-rural. Three elements are central to the analysis: first the entrenchment of a cleavage within the social structure, i.e. the identification of groups (e.g. class positions); second their organizational counterpart at the intermediary level (e.g. associations); and third the equivalent in the party. Lipset and Rokkan have used their cleavage theory to explain the development of national party systems. It is often also used to explain electoral behavior.
4 The four variables are (1) the existence of liberal parties and of credible welfare state protectors; (2) the electoral trade-off faced by social policy retrenchers; (3) the strategic flexibility provided by existing party organizations to enable militants and party leaders to choose new policies; and (4) the alignment of party competition around economic or non-economic policy dimensions (Kitschelt 2001: 282).
5 Pitkin's concept is actually composed of four related dimensions: formal, descriptive, substantive, and symbolic representation. However, most research concentrates on descriptive and substantive representation. Formal representation refers to the rules of how representatives are selected, i.e. electoral institutions. Symbolic representation refers to the attitudes about representation among the population, i.e. when the public feels that the elected politicians are trustworthy and when underrepresented groups feel represented (see also Schwindt-Bayer 2010).
6 The exact number is controversial (see e.g. the debate in issue 2/2006 of the Journal *Politics & Gender*).
7 Modernization, a multidimensional concept that comprises various processes, such as an increasing differentiation and the growing size of societies, as well as the social and political mobilization, was seen as another driving factor of the welfare state (Flora and Alber 1981).
8 Bonoli (2006) argues that differences can be explained by the different pace at which these social transformations have progressed and overlapped. For example, he attributes the emergence of more gender equal and universal welfare states in Scandinavia to an earlier change of family patterns and an earlier deindustrialization compared to the continental countries where these developments occurred later and coincided with higher financial pressures due to population ageing. Still, this argument has difficulties explaining differences in work-family policy reforms between latecomer countries such as Germany and Italy, which face similar problems.
9 The "lock-in" effect refers to the emergence of vested interests when certain social rights are granted and the problems that occur when governments attempt to curtail or reverse these rights.

10 In conservative welfare states, for example, the aim to maintain the status quo through employment-related social insurance schemes that provide generous derived rights for dependent family members encourages a traditional family model. The focus is on cash transfers, not on services. Liberal welfare states are based on liberal work-ethic norms and the idea of not intervening into matters of the family. In this regime, the welfare state provides means-tested assistance and modest social insurance; opting out of employment is difficult, and the welfare state neither promotes nor hinders female or mothers' employment. The social-democratic welfare state, by contrast, is characterized by the ideals of equality and universalism. In this regime, a strong welfare state creates individual independence both from the market and the family and at the same time supports full employment of all adult members of society. The social-democratic welfare state facilitates mothers' or women's employment, as the state is the main provider of services and at the same time also the main employer for women.

11 According to Rüb (2011: 34), political institutions also determine whether and to what extent actors who break the rules are sanctioned by jurisdiction. Further, political institutions must be legitimate and effective in the sense that they are regarded as fair and feasible by the actors.

12 An influential early account, for example, argues that consensus democracies which provide for more inclusive representation of minorities and grants them more institutionalized power to impede actions of the majority produce better outcomes. This is because policies that are based on a broad consensus can be implemented more successfully and are more sustainable. In contrast to majoritarian systems that are characterized by abrupt shifts in government, the more predictable, steady and coherent politics of consensus democracies is necessary for achieving good policy outcomes (Lijphart 1984, 1999).

13 Meyer (2003) examines care-related rights and finds that the expansion of care rights in the pension scheme and the provision of childcare for all children older than three years in Germany was mainly driven by stipulations of the Federal Constitutional Court, which forced the government to adapt policies. Yet with respect to the more recent developments in Germany, Ahrens and Blum (2012) or Henninger and von Wahl (2010) show that work-family policy reforms have been enacted without reference to the Federal Constitutional Court and even though partisan and institutional veto players played an impeding role.

14 Liberal market economies (LME) such as the United Kingdom are, in contrast, based on general skills that are portable between industries and firms.

Reference

Ahrens, Regina. 2010. "Sustainability in German Family Policy and Politics." *German Policy Studies* 6 (3):195–229.

Ahrens, Regina, and Sonja Blum. 2012. "Zwischen Stau und Stimulus: Hemmende und fördernde Vetospieler in der Familienpolitik." In *Vetospieler in der Policy-Forschung*, edited by Florian Blank, 13–48. Wiesbaden: VS Verlag für Sozialwissenschaften.

Ahrens, Regina, Sonja Blum, and Irene Gerlach. 2010. "Introduction: Family Policies in the German-Speaking Countries. Reforms and Explanations." *German Policy Studies* 6 (3):1–11.

Alber, Jens. 1995. "A Framework of the Comparative Study of Social Services." *Journal of European Social Policy* 5 (2):131–149.

Alber, Jens. 2000. "Der deutsche Sozialstaat in der Ära Kohl: Diagnosen und Daten." In *Der deutsche Sozialstaat. Bilanzen-Reformen-Perspektiven*, edited by Stephan Leibfried and Uwe Wagschal, 235–275. Frankfurt a.M./New York: Campus.

Allan, James P., and Lyle Scruggs. 2004. "Political Partisanship and Welfare State Reform in Advanced Industrial Societies." *American Journal of Political Science* 48 (3):496–512.

Béland, Daniel. 2009. "Gender, Ideational Analysis, and Social Policy." *Social Politics: International Studies in Gender, State & Society* 16 (4):558–581. doi: 10.1093/sp/jxp017.

Bertone, Chiara. 2003. "Claims for Child Care as Struggles over Needs: Comparing Italian and Danish Women's Organizations." *Social Politics* 10 (2):229–255. doi: 10.1093/sp/jxg013.

Bleses, Peter, and Martin Seeleib-Kaiser. 2004. *The Dual Transformation of the German Welfare State*. New York: Palgrave Macmillan.

Blum, Sonja. 2012. *Familienpolitik als Reformprozess. Deutschland und Österreich im Vergleich*. Wiesbaden: Springer VS.

Bolzendahl, Catherine, and Clem Brooks. 2007. "Women's Political Representation and Welfare State Spending in 12 Capitalist Democracies." *Social Forces* 85 (4):1509–1534. doi: 10.2307/4494997.

Bonoli, Giuliano. 2000a. *The Politics of Pension Reform. Institutions and Policy Change in Western Europe*. Cambridge: University Press.

Bonoli, Giuliano. 2000b. "Public Attitudes to Social Protection and Political Economy Traditions in Western Europe." *European Societies* 2 (4):431.

Bonoli, Giuliano. 2005. "The Politics of the New Social Policies: Providing Coverage Against New Social Risks in Mature Welfare States." *Policy & Politics* 33 (3):431–449.

Bonoli, Giuliano. 2006. "New Social Risks and the Politics of Post-industrial Social Policies." In *The Politics of Post-industrial Welfare States. Adapting Post-war Social Policies to New Social Risks*, edited by Klaus Armingeon and Giuliano Bonoli, 3–26. London/New York: Routledge.

Bonoli, Giuliano, and Frank Reber. 2009. "The Political Economy of Childcare in OECD Countries: Explaining Cross-national Variation in Spending and Coverage Rates." *European Journal of Political Research* 49 (1):97–118.

Bothfeld, Silke. 2005. *Vom Erziehungsurlaub zur Elternzeit. Politisches Lernen im Reformprozess*. Frankfurt a.M./New York: Campus Verlag.

Brady, David. 2009. *Rich Democracies, Poor People: How Politics Explain Poverty*. New York: Oxford University Press.

Brady, David, Jason Beckfield, and Martin Seeleib-Kaiser. 2005. "Economic Globalization and the Welfare State in Affluent Democracies, 1975–2001." *American Sociological Review* 70 (6):921–948. doi: 10.1177/000312240507000603.

Brady, David, Agnes Blome, and Hanna Kleider. 2016. "How Politics and Institutions Shape Poverty and Inequality." In *Oxford Handbook of Poverty and Society*, edited by David Brady and Linda M. Burton, 117–140. New York: Oxford University Press.

Brady, David, and Amie Bostic. 2015. "Paradoxes of Social Policy: Welfare Transfers, Relative Poverty, and Redistribution Preferences." *American Sociological Review*. doi: 10.1177/0003122415573049.

Brady, David, Susanne Marquardt, Gordon Gauchat, and Megan M. Reynolds. 2016. "Path Dependency and the Politics of Socialized Health Care." *Journal of Health Politics, Policy and Law* 41 (3):355–392. doi: 10.1215/03616878-3523946.

Brooks, Clem, and Jeff Manza. 2006. "Social Policy Responsiveness in Developed Democracies." *American Sociological Review* 71 (3):474–494.

Brooks, Clem, and Jeff Manza. 2007. *Why Welfare States Persist. The Importance of Public Opinion in Democracies*. Chicago: The University of Chicago Press.

Brunsbach, Sandra. 2011. "Machen Frauen den Unterschied? Parlamentarierinnen als Repräsentantinnen frauenspezifischer Interessen im Deutschen Bundestag." *Zeitschrift für Parlamentsfragen* 1/2011:3–24.

Bussemaker, Jet. 1998. "Rationales of Care in Contemporary Welfare States: The Case of Childcare in the Netherlands." *Social Policy* 5 (1):70–96. doi: 10.1093/sp/5.1.70.
Campbell, Rosie, Sarah Childs, and Joni Lovenduski. 2009. "Do Women Need Women Representatives?" *British Journal of Political Science* 40 (1):171–194.
Carroll, Susan J. 1994. *Women as Candidates in American Politics*. Bloomington: Indiana University Press.
Castles, Francis G. 2004. *The Future of the Welfare State: Crisis Myths and Crisis Realities*. Oxford: Oxford University Press.
Castles, Francis G., and Deborah Mitchell. 1993. "Worlds of Welfare and Families of Nations." In *Families of Nations. Patterns of Public Policy in Western Democracies*, edited by Francis G. Castles, 93–128. Dartmouth: Aldershot.
Castles, Francis G., and Herbert Obinger. 2007. "Social Expenditure and the Politics of Redistribution." *Journal of European Social Policy* 17 (3):206–222. doi: 10.1177/0958928707078364.
Childs, Sarah. 2004. *New Labour's Women MP's: Women Representing Women*. New York: Routledge.
Childs, Sarah, and Mona Lena Krook. 2006. "Should Feminists Give Up on Critical Mass? A Contingent Yes." *Politics & Gender* 2 (4):522–530.
Childs, Sarah, and Mona Lena Krook. 2008. "Theorizing Women's Political Representation: Debates and Innovations in Empirical Research." *Femina Politica* 2/2008:20–30.
Childs, Sarah, and Mona Lena Krook. 2009. "Analysing Women's Substantive Representation: From Critical Mass to Critical Actors." *Government and Opposition* 44 (2):125–145.
Cowell-Meyers, Kimberly, and Laura Langbein. 2009. "Linking Women's Descriptive and Substantive Representation in the United States." *Politics & Gender* 5 (04):491–518. doi: doi:10.1017/S1743923X09990328.
Dahlerup, Drude. 1988. "From a Small to a Large Minority: Women in Scandinavian Politics." *Scandinavian Political Studies* 11 (4):275–297.
Daly, Mary, and Katherine Rake. 2003. *Gender and the Welfare State. Care, Work and Welfare in Europe and the USA*. Cambridge/Malden: Polity Press.
Ebbinghaus, Bernhard. 2005. "Can Path Dependence Explain Institutional Change? Two Approaches Applied to Welfare State Reform." In *MPIfG Discussion Paper 05/2*. Köln.
Esping-Andersen, Gøsta. 1990. *The Three Worlds of Welfare Capitalism*. Princeton, New Jersey: Princeton University Press.
Estévez-Abe, Margarita, Torben Iversen, and David Soskice. 2001. "Social Protection and the Formation of Skills. A Reinterpretation of the Welfare State." In *Varieties of Capitalism. The Institutional Foundations of Comparative Advantage*, edited by Peter A. Hall and David Soskice, 145–184. New York: Oxford University Press.
Ferrera, Maurizio. 1986. "Italy." In *Groth to Limits. The Western European Welfare States since World War II. Vol. 2: Germany, United Kingdom, Ireland, Italy*, edited by Peter Flora, 385–500. Berlin/New York: Walter de Gruyter.
Ferrera, Maurizio. 1993. *Modelli Di Solidarietà: Politica E Riforme Sociali Nelle Democrazie*. Bologna: Il Mulino.
Fix, Birgit. 2000. "Church-state relations and the development of child care in Austria, Belgium, Germany, and the Netherlands." In *Families and Family Policies in Europe. Comparative Perspectives*, edited by Thomas Bahle and Astrid Pfenning, 305–321. Frankfurt a.M.: Peter Lang.
Flanagan, Scott. 1987. "Value Change in Industrial Societies." *American Political Science Review* 81 (4):1289–1319.

Fleckenstein, Timo. 2011. "The Politics of Ideas in Welfare State Transformation: Christian Democracy and the Reform of Family Policies in Germany." *Social Politics* 18 (4):543–571.

Fleckenstein, Timo, Adam M. Saunders, and Martin Seeleib-Kaiser. 2011. "The Dual Transformation of Social Protection and Human Capital: Comparing Britain and Germany." *Comparative Political Studies* DOI: 10.1177/0010414011407473. doi: 10.1177/0010414011407473.

Flora, Peter, and Jens Alber. 1981. "Modernization, Democratization, and the Development of Welfare States in Western Europe." In *The Development of Welfare States in Western Europe and America*, edited by Peter Flora and Arnold J. Heidenheimer, 37–80. New Brunswick: Transaction Books.

Garrett, Geoffrey, and Deborah Mitchell. 2001. "Globalization, Government Spending and Taxation in the OECD." *European Journal of Political Research* 39 (2):145–177.

Hall, Peter A., and David Soskice. 2001. *Varieties of Capitalism. The Institutional Foundations of Comparative Advantage*. New York: Oxford University Press.

Hantrais, Linda. 2004. *Family Policy Matters. Responding to Family Change in Europe*. Bristol: The Policy Press.

Häusermann, Silja. 2006. "Changing Coalitions in Social Policy Reforms: The Politics of New Social Needs and Demands." *Journal of European Social Policy* 16 (1):5–21.

Häusermann, Silja. 2010. *The Politics of Welfare Reform in Continental Europe. Modernization in Hard Times*. New York: Cambridge University Press.

Häusermann, Silja, Georg Picot, and Dominik Geering. 2013. "Review Article: Rethinking Party Politics and the Welfare State – Recent Advances in the Literature." *British Journal of Political Science* 43 (01):221–240. doi: 10.1017/S0007123412000336.

Henninger, Annette, and Angelika von Wahl. 2010. "Das Umspielen von Veto-Spielern. Wie eine konservative Familienministerin den Familialismus des deutschen Wohlfahrtsstaates unterminiert." In *Die zweite Große Koalition. Eine Bilanz der Regierung Merkel 2005–2009*, edited by Christoph Egle and Reimut Zohlnhöfer, 361–379. Wiesbaden: VS Verlag für Sozialwissenschaften.

Hobson, Barbara, and Marika Lindholm. 1997. "Collective Identities, Women's Power Resources, and the Making of Welfare States." *Theory and Society* 26 (4):475–508.

Huber, Evelyne, Charles R. Ragin, and John D. Stephens. 1993. "Social Democracy, Christian Democracy, Constitutional Structure, and the Welfare State." *American Journal of Sociology* 99 (3):711–774.

Huber, Evelyne, and John D. Stephens. 2000. "Partisan Governance, Women's Employment, and the Social Democratic Welfare State." *American Sociological Review* 65 (3):323–342.

Huber, Evelyne, and John D. Stephens. 2001. *Development and Crisis of the Welfare State: Parties and Policies in Global Markets*. Chicago/London: The University of Chicago Press.

Immergut, Ellen M. 1990. "Institutions, Veto Points and Policy Results: A Comparative Analysis of Health Care." *Journal of Public Policy* 10:391–416.

Immergut, Ellen M. 1992a. *Health Politics: Interests and Institutions in Western Europe*. Cambridge, New York, Melbourne: Cambridge University Press.

Immergut, Ellen M. 1992b. "The Rules of the Game: The Logic of Health Policy-Making in France, Switzerland and Sweden." In *Structuring Politics. Historical Institutionalism in Comparative Analysis*, edited by Sven Steinmo, Kathleen Thelen and Frank Longstreth, 57–89. Cambridge: Cambridge University Press.

Immergut, Ellen M., and Tarik Abou-Chadi. 2014. "How Electoral Vulnerability Affects Pension Politics: Introducing a Concept, Measure and Empirical Application." *European Journal of Political Research* 53 (2):269–287. doi: 10.1111/1475–6765.12037.

Immergut, Ellen M., and Karen M. Anderson. 2007. "Editors Introduction: The Dynamics of Pension Politics." In *The Handbook of West European Pension Politics*, edited by Ellen M. Immergut, Karen M. Anderson and Isabelle Schulze, 1–45. Oxford: Oxford University Press.

Inglehart, Ronald. 1977. *The Silent Revolution. Changing Values and Political Styles Among Western Publics*. Princeton/New Jersey: Princeton University Press.

Inglehart, Ronald. 1990. *Culture Shift in Advanced Industrial Society*. Princeton, NJ: Princeton University Press.

Iversen, Torben, and David Soskice. 2006. "Electoral Institutions and the Politics of Coalitions: Why Some Democracies Redistribute More Than Others." *American Political Science Review* 100 (2):165–181.

Jo, Nam K. 2011. "Between the Cultural Foundations of Welfare and Welfare Attitudes: The Possibility of an in-between Level Conception of Culture for the Cultural Analysis of Welfare." *Journal of European Social Policy* 21 (1):5–19. doi: 10.1177/0958928710385736.

Kitschelt, Herbert. 1994. *The Transformation of European Social Democracy*. Cambridge: Cambridge University Press.

Kitschelt, Herbert. 2001. "Partisan Competition and Welfare State Retrenchment: When Do Politicians Choose Unpopular Policies?" In *The New Politics of the Welfare State*, edited by Paul Pierson, 265–302. Oxford: Oxford University Press.

Kitschelt, Herbert, and Philipp Rehm. 2005. "Work, Family, and Politics. Foundations of Electoral Partisan Alignments in Postindustrial Democracies." Annual Meeting of the American Political Science Association, Washington, September 1–4, 2005.

Kittel, Bernhard, and Herbert Obinger. 2003. "Political Parties, Institutions, and the Dynamics of Social Expenditure in Times of Austerity." *Journal of European Public Policy* 10 (1):20–45.

Korpi, Walter. 1983. *The Democratic Class Struggle*. London: Routledge & Kegan Paul.

Korpi, Walter. 1989. "Power, Politics, and State Autonomy in the Development of Social Citizenship: Social Rights during Sickness in Eighteen OECD Countries since 1930." *American Sociological Review* 54:309–328.

Korpi, Walter, and Joakim Palme. 1998. "The Paradox of Redistribution and Strategies of Equality: Welfare State Institutions, Inequality, and Poverty in the Western Countries." *American Sociological Review* 63 (5):661–687.

Korpi, Walter, and Joakim Palme. 2003. "New Politics and Class Politics in the Context of Austerity and Globalization: Welfare State Regress in 18 Countries, 1975–95." *The American Political Science Review* 97 (3):425–446.

Korthouwer, Gerben. 2008. "How German Christian Democrats have said Farewell to Familialism." In *ASSR Working Paper 08/01*. Amsterdam.

Kremer, Monique. 2006. "The Politics of Ideals of Care: Danish and Flemish Child Care Policy Compared." *Social Politics* 13 (2):261–285. doi: 10.1093/sp/jxj009.

Kremer, Monique. 2007. *How Welfare States Care. Culture, Gender and Parenting in Europe*. Amsterdam: Amsterdam University Press.

Kriesi, Hanspeter, Edgar Grande, Romain Lachat, Martin Dolezal, Simon Bornschier, and Timotheus Frey. 2006. "Globalization and the Transformation of the National Political Space: Six European Countries Compared." *European Journal of Political Research* 45:921–956. doi: 0.1111/j.1475–6765.2006.00644.x.

Lambert, Priscilla A. 2008. "The Comparative Political Economy of Parental Leave and Child Care: Evidence from Twenty OECD Countries." *Social Politics* 15 (3):315–344. doi: 10.1093/sp/jxn013.

Lamping, Wolfram, and Friedbert W. Rüb. 2008. "Introduction: Moving Bulky Goods. How New Ideas and Partisan Politics Are Transforming the German Welfare State." *German Policy Studies* 4 (2):1–18.

Lewis, Jane. 1992. "Gender and the Development of Welfare Regimes." *Journal of European Social Policies* 2 (3):159–173.

Lewis, Jane. 1994. "Gender, the Family, and Women's Agency in the Building of 'Welfare States': The British Case." *Social History* (19):37–55.

Lijphart, Arend. 1984. *Democracies: Patterns of Majoritarian and Consensus Government in Twenty-one Countries*. New Haven/London: Yale University Press.

Lijphart, Arend. 1999. *Patterns of Democracy. Government Performance in Thirty-six Countries*. New Haven: Yale University Press.

Lipset, Seymour M., and Stein Rokkan. 1967. "Cleavage Structures, Party Systems and Voter Alignments: An Introduction." In *Party Systems and Voter Alignments: Cross-National Perspective*, edited by Seymour M. Lipset and Stein Rokkan, 1–64. New York: Free Press.

Lovenduski, Joni. 1986. *Women and European Politics: Contemporary Feminism and Public Policy*. Amherst: University of Massachusetts Press.

Lovenduski, Joni, and Pippa Norris. 2003. "Westminster Women: The Politics of Presence." *Political Studies* 51:84–102.

Lupu, Noam, and Jonas Pontusson. 2011. "The Structure of Inequality and the Politics of Redistribution." *American Political Science Review* 105 (02):316–336. doi: doi:10.1017/S0003055411000128.

Mackay, Fiona. 2008. "'Thick' Conceptions of Substantive Representation: Women, Gender and Political Institutions." *Representation* 44 (2):125–139.

Madama, Ilaria. 2010. *Le politiche di assistenza sociale*. Bologna: il Mulino.

Meyer, Traute. 2003. "Reasonable Measures for a Sustainable Future? An Analysis of the Expansion of Family Policies in Strong Breadwinner Models. Britain and Germany compared." 1st ESPAnet Conference, Copenhagen, 2003.

Mintrom, Michael. 1997. "Policy Entrepreneurs and the Diffusion of Innovation." *American Journal of Political Science* 41 (3):738–770.

Misra, Joya. 2003. "Women as Agents in Welfare State Development: A Cross-national Analysis of Family Allowance Adoption." *Socio-Economic Review* 1:185–214.

Morgan, Kimberly J. 2003. "The Politics of Mothers' Employment: France in Comparative Perspective." *World Politics* 55 (2):259–289.

Morgan, Kimberly J. 2005. "The 'Production' of Child Care: How Labor Markets Shape Social Policy and Vice Versa." *Social Politics: International Studies in Gender, State & Society* 12 (2):243–263. doi: 10.1093/sp/jxi013.

Morgan, Kimberly J. 2006. *Working Mothers and the Welfare State. Religion and the Politics of Work-Family Policies in Western Europe and the United States*. Stanford: Stanford University Press.

Morgan, Kimberly J. 2008. "The Political Path to a Dual Earner/Dual Carer Society: Pitfalls and Possibilities." *Politics & Society* 36 (3):403–420.

Morgan, Kimberly J. 2009. "The Religious Foundations of Work-Family Policies in Western Europe." In *Religion, Class Coalitions, and Welfare State Regimes* edited by Kees Van Kersbergen and Philipp Manow, 56–88. New York: Cambridge University Press.

Morgan, Kimberly J. 2013. "Path Shifting of the Welfare State: Electoral Competition and the Expansion of Work-Family Policies in Western Europe." *World Politics* 65 (01):73–115. doi: doi:10.1017/S0043887112000251.
Myles, John, and Jill Quadagno. 2002. "Political Theories of the Welfare State." *Social Service Review* 76 (March): 34–57.
Naldini, Manuela. 2003. *The Family in the Mediterranean Welfare States*. London: Frank Cass Publishers.
Naumann, Ingela K. 2005. "Childcare and Feminism in West-Germany and Sweden in the 1960s and 1970s." *Journal of European Social Policy* 15 (1):47–63.
Naumann, Ingela K. 2006. "Childcare Politics in the West German and Swedish Welfare States from the 1950s to the 1970s." European University Institute. Department of Political and Social Sciences, Unpublished Dissertation.
Niedermayer, Oskar. 2009. "Gesellschaftliche und parteipolitische Konfliktlinien." In *Wähler in Deutschland. Sozialer und politischer Wandel, Gender und Wahlverhalten*, edited by Stefan Kühnel, Oskar Niedermayer and Bettina Westle, 30–67. Wiesbaden: VS Verlag für Sozialwissenschaften.
North, Douglass C. 1990. *Institutions, Institutional Change, and Economic Performance*. Cambridge: Cambridge University Press.
Nullmeier, Frank, and Friedbert W. Rüb. 1993. *Die Transformation der Sozialpolitik. Vom Sozialstaat zum Sicherungsstaat*. Frankfurt a.M./New York: Campus.
Orloff, Ann Shola. 1993. "Gender and the Social Rights of Citizenship: The Comparative Analysis of Gender Relations and Welfare State." *American Sociological Review* 58 (3):303–328.
Padamsee, Tasleem J. 2009. "Culture in Connection: Re-Contextualizing Ideational Processes in the Analysis of Policy Development." *Social Politics: International Studies in Gender, State & Society* 16 (4):413–445. doi: 10.1093/sp/jxp018.
Pappi, Franz Urban, and Jens Brandenburg. 2010. "Sozialstrukturelle Interessenlagen und Parteipräferenz in Deutschland. Stabilität und Wandel seit 1980." *Kölner Zeitschrift für Soziologie und Sozialpsychologie* 62 (3):459–483.
Persson, Torsten, and Guido Tabellini. 2004. "Constitutional Rules and Fiscal Policy Outcomes." *American Economic Review* 94 (1):25–46.
Persson, Torsten, and Guido Tabellini. 2006. "Electoral Systems and Economic Policy." In *Handbook of Political Economy*, edited by Barry Weingast and Donald Wittman, 723–738. Oxford: Oxford University Press.
Pfau-Effinger, Birgit. 2000. *Kultur und Frauenerwerbstätigkeit in Europa. Theorie und Empirie des internationalen Vergleichs*. Opladen: Leske und Budrich.
Pfenning, Astrid, and Thomas Bahle. 2000. "Introduction." In *Families and Family Policies in Europe. Comparative Perspectives*, edited by Astrid Pfenning and Thomas Bahle, 1–11. Frankfurt a.M.: Peter Lang.
Phillips, Anne. 1995. *The Politics of Presence*. Oxford: Oxford University Press.
Picot, Georg. 2012. *Politics of Segmentation: Party Competition and Social Protection in Europe*. London: Routledge.
Pierson, Paul. 1994. *Dismantling the Welfare State? Reagan, Thatcher and the Politics of Retrenchment*. Cambridge: Cambridge University Press.
Pierson, Paul. 2004. *Politics in Time: History, Institutions, and Social Analysis*. Princeton, NJ: Princeton University Press.
Pitkin, Hannah. 1967. *The Concept of Representation*. Berkeley: University of California Press.

Reingold, Beth. 1992. "Concepts of Representation among Female and Male State Legislators." *Legislative Studies Quarterly* 17 (4):509–537.
Ross, Fiona. 2000. " 'Beyond Left and Right': The New Partisan Politics of Welfare." *Governance* 13 (2):155–183.
Roßteutscher, Sigrid. 2012. "Die konfessionell-religiöse Konfliktlinie zwischen Säkularisierung und Mobilisierung." *Politische Vierteljahresschrift* Sonderheft 45:111–133.
Rüb, Friedbert W. 2011. "Politisches Entscheiden. Ein prozess-analytischer Versuch." In *Pluralismus – Strategien – Entscheidungen*, edited by Nils C. Bandelow and Simon Hegelich, 17–45. Wiesbaden VS Verlag für Sozialwissenschaften.
Rüling, Anneli. 2010. "Re-framing of Childcare in Germany and England: From a Private Responsibility to an Economic Necessity." *German Policy Studies* 6 (2):153–186.
Saraceno, Chiara. 1997. "Family Change, Family Policies and the Restructuring of Welfare." In *Family, Market and Community*, edited by OECD, 81–100. Paris: Organisation for Economic Co-operation and Development.
Sartori, Giovanni. 1976. *Parties and Party Systems: A Framework for Analysis*. Cambridge: Cambridge University Press.
Schmidt, Vivien A. 2000. "Values and Discourse in the Politics of Adjustment." In *Welfare and Work in the Open Economy. Volume I. From Vulnerability to Competitiveness*, edited by Fritz W. Scharpf and Vivien A. Schmidt, 229–309. Oxford: University Press.
Schwindt-Bayer, Leslie A. 2010. *Political Power and Women's Representation in Latin America*. New York: Oxford University Press.
Seeleib-Kaiser, Martin. 2011. "Socio-Economic Change, Party Competition and Intra-Party Conflict: The Family Policy of the Grand Coalition." *German Politics* 19 (3–4):416–428. doi: 10.1080/09644008.2010.515789.
Seeleib-Kaiser, Martin, and Tuukka Toivonen. 2011. "Between Reforms and Birth Rates: Germany, Japan, and Family Policy Discourse." *Social Politics* 18 (3):331–360. doi: 10.1093/sp/jxr016.
Seeleib-Kaiser, Martin, Silke van Dyk, and Martin Roggenkamp. 2008. *Party Politics and Social Welfare. Comparing Christian and Social Democracy in Austria, Germany and the Netherlands*. Cheltenham/Northampton: Edward Elgar.
Siegel, Nico A. 2002. *Baustelle Sozialpolitik. Konsolidierung und Rückbau im internationalen Vergleich*. Frankfurt/New York: Campus.
Soroka, Stuart N., and Christopher Wlezien. 2005. "Opinion–Policy Dynamics: Public Preferences and Public Expenditure in the United Kingdom." *British Journal of Political Science* 35 (4):665–689.
Starke, Peter. 2006. "The Politics of Welfare State Retrenchment: A Literature Review." *Social Policy & Administration* 40 (1):104–120.
Stimson, James A., Michael B. Mackuen, and Robert S. Erikson. 1995. "Dynamic Representation." *The American Political Science Review* 89 (3):543–565.
Strohmeier, Klaus Peter. 2002. "Family Policy – How Does It Work?" In *Family Life and Family Policies in Europe. Volume 2. Problems and Issues in Comparative Perspective*, edited by Franz-Xaver Kaufmann, Anton Kujsten, Hans-Joachim Schulze and Klaus Peter Strohmeier, 321–362. Oxford: Oxford University Press.
Svallfors, Stefan. 1997. "Worlds of Welfare and Attitudes to Redistribution: A Comparison of Eight Western Nations." *European Sociological Review* 13 (3):283–304.
Taylor-Gooby, Peter. 2005. "New Risks and Social Change." In *New Risks, New Welfare. The Transformation of the European Welfare State*, edited by Peter Taylor-Gooby. New York: Oxford University Press.

Tsebelis, George. 1995. "Decision Making in Political Systems: Veto Players in Presidentialism, Parliamentarism, Multicamerialism and Multipartyism." *British Journal of Political Science* 25 (3):289–325.
van Kersbergen, Kees. 1995. *Social Capitalism: A Study of Christian Democracy and the Welfare State*. London: Routledge.
van Oorschot, Wim. 2006. "Making the Difference in Social Europe: Deservingness Perceptions Among Citizens of European Welfare States." *Journal of European Social Policy* 16 (1):23–42. doi: 10.1177/0958928706059829.
van Oorschot, Wim, Michael Opielka, and Birgit Pfau-Effinger, eds. 2008. *Culture and Welfare State. Values and Social Policy in Comparative Perspective*. Cheltenham and Northampton: Edward Elgar.
Wängnerud, Lena. 2000. "Testing the Politics of Presence: Women's Representation in the Swedish Riksdag." *Scandinavian Political Studies* 23 (1):67–91.
Wilensky, Harold L., and Charles Lebeaux. 1958. *Industrial Society and Social Welfare*. New York: Free Press.
Wiliarty, Sarah Elise. 2010. *The CDU and the Politics of Gender in Germany. Bringing Women to the Party*. Cambridge: Cambridge University Press.
Zahariadis, Nikolaos. 2003. *Ambiguity and Choice in Public Policy: Political Decision Making in Modern Democracies*. Washington: Georgetown University Press.

3 Design and evolution of work-family policies

A European comparative overview

This chapter deals with the conceptualization and measurement of work-family policy reforms. It then gives an overview of the nation-specific policy context of working and caring parents and the reforms that have taken place between the beginning of the 1990s and 2008 for 15 European welfare states. Looking at the developments of Germany and Italy within the broader European context illustrates the relevant policy dimensions and differences and further justifies the case selection.

The policy instruments are measured and compared in light of empirical evidence of their impact on the division of work and care in the household and the gender-specific (dis)incentives they provide. To what degree does a country support families with children and to what extent does the design of a policy support a male-breadwinner or a dual-earner model? This approach enables assessment of the overall degree of policy support in a country and the distinction of reforms that aimed at maintaining the status quo from those that led to a shift in work-family policies. As no comprehensive and longitudinal data source was available, I have created a database that includes a series of indicators suitable for policy comparison over the time period based on a number of cross-sectional comparisons and national reports.[1]

By comparing policy changes cross-nationally, the chapter also shows which countries were the most reform-active and whether there has been a convergence towards a more coherent support of working mothers in European welfare states.

Work-family models and degree of state support

Work-family policies aim at supporting the reconciliation of parenthood,[2] care responsibilities and employment. The question is what kind of work-family arrangement is supported through public policies and whether and how this has changed in national welfare states. This implies looking both at work-family models, i.e. the arrangements couples[3] make to combine work and care, and the degree of state support, i.e. the extent to which the state sustains one (or more) models through policies.

Scholars started to engage in the analysis of work-family models as a response to the increase of female labor-market participation rates in the late 1960s and

1970s[4] and the resulting shifts in the division between the public and the private and patterns of organizing care (Hernes 1987, Leira 1993, Siim 1987). Feminist welfare state researchers have criticized the male bias of mainstream welfare state analysis and argued that the relationship between the family and the state as providers of welfare was neglected (Lewis 1992, 1997, Orloff 1993, Saraceno 1997). The critiques are linked to the "difference versus equality" discussion, which is based on critical engagement with the citizenship theory advanced by feminist scholars (Lister 1997, e.g. Pateman 1989). As a response to the insight that women do not fully participate as citizens in the public sphere because of their (socially constructed) responsibilities in the private realm, feminists outlined two perspectives. The "difference" line of argument holds that women differ from men because of their unique responsibilities or predisposition for care work. Citizenship should therefore be reconceptualized so that women's unpaid care work forms the basis for their social rights in the same way as men's paid work does. The "equality" perspective argues that women need to be on par with men in order to attain full citizenship. This would mainly be achieved through women's full participation in the labor market (Naldini 2011).

Even though both perspectives aim to improve women's status in society, they call for very distinct arrangements. One way is to strengthen women's economic and social position by recognizing care work, i.e. the birth and upbringing of children, as a basis for the eligibility for social rights. This approach is often called the *male-breadwinner* model (Crompton 1999b, Lewis 2001). Male-breadwinner families are characterized by a gender division of labor where men earn a salary outside the home, while women are responsible for unpaid home and care work. Ideally, the welfare state covers men with employment-related social protection schemes and their wives with derived rights. There are also countries that do not provide any rights or benefits to women, i.e. the state presupposes wives' unpaid work without supporting them by income transfers. The other approach is to promote employment for both sexes. This can be achieved through policies that aim to commodify or socialize caring responsibilities so that caregivers are able to work (Korpi 2000). In this egalitarian *dual-earner model*, both men and women are freed from caring obligations during the day in order to pursue continuous and full-time employment. Some critics have maintained that the dual-earner model represents an androcentric view, because it induces women to adopt men's life pattern. An egalitarian *dual-earner/dual-carer* model, by contrast, embraces both responsibilities (Gornick and Meyers 2008). Similar to the dual-earner model, this dual-earner/dual-carer model presupposes policies that support a flexible work-family balance and the provision of care services. In addition, in order to overcome the prevailing gender-specific division of work, in this latter model, incentives are provided for men to utilize such policies, e.g. well-paid parental leave.[5]

The attempt to systematically integrate gender into welfare-regime analysis has led to typologies that distinguish countries in terms of their commitment to the *male-breadwinner* model (e.g. Ostner and Lewis 1995, Sainsbury 1996) or the degree of *defamilization*, i.e. the degree to which social policies grant individuals resources and rights independent from their family membership (Leitner 2003, Lister 1997, McLaughlin and Glendinning 1994, Saraceno 1997, Saraceno and Keck 2010).[6] These typologies were helpful for demonstrating that the state may support different kinds of work-family arrangements either implicitly, by not providing alternatives, or explicitly, through specific measures. For example, social policies in Germany have long worked together with the tax system to provide incentives and thus actively encouraged the *male-breadwinner* model. In Italy, but also in countries such as the United Kingdom, however, such policies were absent or weak. In these countries, the *male-breadwinner* model existed because it was tacitly assumed that women would do house and care work. Furthermore, family law in Italy prescribes financial obligations for an extended period of time and range of family members. Thus in Italy the family is assigned responsibilities, but receives little support in the form of income transfers (Naldini 2003).

Work-family models need to be understood as ideal types; they do not exist in the pure form. Static classifications where countries can be mapped exactly are difficult; instead, a "flexible framework through which change may be conceptualized" (Crompton 1999a: 202–203) may be more appropriate. I will focus on the policies that aim at supporting women to both have children and to work for pay. The following sections will briefly describe how to measure change in this policy area. Subsequently, I will characterize each policy's contribution to the reconciliation of work and care and discuss each with respect to the broad nature of the incentives and disincentives for women and men to work and care.

Policies and how to measure policy change

Jane Lewis (2009: 83) conceptualizes policies which favor the reconciliation of work and care and which may be regulated, financed and/or provided by the state as encompassing the following:

- Time: the regulation of working time and the provision of time to undertake informal care (leave regulations).
- Services: childcare that is directly provided by the state, or provided by the independent sector or employers.
- Money: cash to buy formal care, cash for carers while they are on leave.

While the components "time" and "services" are rather straightforward, "money" requires additional clarification. First, not only do cash transfers reduce direct costs of childcare, but some cash benefits may also influence the work-family arrangement. Means-tested children's allowances, for example, might increase the indirect opportunity costs for parents, because payoffs from employment can be disadvantageous for some families (Saraceno 2003). If income from employment is just above the threshold that entitles parents to the means-tested family allowance, it is not beneficial for one of the parents to be additionally employed. These kinds of cash benefits should thus also be taken into account. The tax system also may, under the heading of family support, provide tax deductions for dependent family members and, consequently, incentivize one of the partners (usually wives) to refrain from employment. Second, carers on leave who receive cash benefits may use them for different purposes – not only as a compensation for care work that they themselves provide but possibly also to buy formal care. Hence it is not a question of either/or. Rather, cash for carers on leave does not necessarily mean a support of mothers to stay at home and care full time. In fact, in some countries, it is possible to work part-time for pay during parental leave. Third, I propose that, even though time to undertake informal care and cash benefits for carers while they are on leave are often distinct entitlements, they should analytically be treated together because it is the interaction of both of these that influences parents in their decisions about work *and* care, how to divide those tasks between themselves, and whether to buy formal care on the market.

The issue of how to measure policy change has been discussed intensely among scholars interested in comparative welfare state research (see Alber 1996, Clasen and Siegel 2007). There are three types of indicators that are most widely used in comparative research on social policy and welfare state change: social expenditures, social policy institutions and social rights. Social expenditure data figure the most prominently, particularly within quantitative comparative welfare state analyses. The use of social expenditure data is, however, problematic for two reasons. First, the distinction between the generosity of benefits and the social need for benefits is not clear-cut. For example, high outlays on children's allowances may be ascribed either to generous allowances or to a high number of children (or both). Also, there may be a shift from universal coverage to means-tested benefits but at the same time an increase of the amount. In both cases, social expenditures would stay the same. Second, expenditure data are associated with a "time-lag" problem. There is potentially a long way from the adoption of a policy to increase the number of childcare places and the actual implementation and impact. Consequently, many legislative changes are not immediately reflected in expenditure data (Green-Pedersen 2007).

The second approach focuses on institutional characteristics of social policy programs and, consequently, refers to the output perspective. This approach focuses on eligibility criteria, the duration of benefits, and the scope or coverage of a given scheme (Alber 1996, 1995, Ferrera 1996, Saraceno and Keck 2010). In this way, it is possible to avoid mixing up developments that are due to context changes and changes in the objectives and institutional frameworks of policies. An example of the context sensitivity is an unemployment insurance scheme that links benefits to earnings. Here the average benefit will decrease even with constant legislation if an increasing proportion of the unemployed come from lower earnings strata. Such a decrease could not be interpreted as an indication of curtailment (Alber 1996). Similarly, a decrease in expenditure in a given field owing to a change in private choices is not to be understood as retrenchment (Starke 2008). For example, a drop in the use of parental leave cannot be considered a cutback in entitlement unless it is the direct consequence of state action, such as the repeal of an obligation that employers guarantee the return to the prior job position.

A third approach includes the recipient and stresses measures of what is called "welfare state generosity" or the "social rights" approach (e.g. Clasen and Clegg 2007, Scruggs 2007). Only by looking at how rates of replacement, take-up or coverage have developed can we fully understand the role of the state in providing individual opportunities and resources. However, this approach is also associated with problems, because such indicators might also illustrate developments that cannot be influenced by the government. For instance, a relatively low childcare-coverage rate may indicate either low engagement of the state (supply) *or* different care preferences by parents (demand). Hence systematically tracing a policy field's developments cannot rely upon one approach alone, but requires the inclusion of both the institutional and the generosity indicators.

In summary, in order to have a comprehensive picture and to identify micro-level changes I will study the evolution of the program characteristics such as entitlement, duration and benefit levels, as well as measures of generosity such as replacement or coverage rates. As work-family policies comprise rights, transfers and services, the criteria have to be specified for each policy separately. All policy developments will be discussed in light of their (potential) impact on the gender division of work, i.e. to what extent they support the male-breadwinner or the dual-earner family. As argued earlier, it makes a difference whether a parental leave scheme was extended by six months for the mother or for the father only. Only counting the six months would not capture the direction of a reform (i.e. towards support of the dual-earner model or support of the male-breadwinner model). Before the policies will be compared cross-nationally and over time, I briefly discuss the policy instruments in light of empirical evidence of their impact on the division of work and care in the household and the gender-specific (dis)incentives they provide. To what degree does a country support families with children and to what extent does the design of a policy support a male-breadwinner or a dual-earner model? In doing so, I expect to be able to assess the overall degree of policy support in a country and to be able to distinguish reforms that aimed at maintaining the status quo from those that led to a shift in work-family policies.

The impact of work-family policies on the gender division of work – evidence from the literature

Time: leave regulations and working-time flexibility

Judging the impact of *leave schemes* is a complex task. Providing the option to take parental leave by definition implies the employee's right to return to her/his previous, or a similar, position within the company. The available evidence shows that, in general, leaves strengthen women's labor-force attachment (see Ruhm 1998). However, long leave periods may lead women to postpone their re-entry into the labor market, in particular if it does not make financial sense from a household perspective[7] to use expensive childcare rather than taking a longer leave (Boeckmann, Misra, and Budig 2015, Grunow, Aisenbrey, and Evertsson 2011, Rubery, Smith, and Fagan 1999). Leave that is too short, on the other hand, may have the consequence that women leave the labor market without the option to return because they might not want to put their very small infants into childcare (if at all available) or decide not to have children at all.[8] Thus the life course effects of both extended interruptions and short breaks are strongly negative for female labor-market participation – and, as some authors argue, consequently, also have a negative effect on birth rates (Evertsson and Duvander 2011, Lalive and Zweimüller 2009, Pylkkänen and Smith 2003, Schönberg and Ludsteck 2007, Ziefle 2004). In addition to duration effects, the amount of the payment leads to gender-specific take-up rates. Fathers' take-up of leave seems to be positively related to high wage-replacement rates (de Henau, Meulders, and D'Orchai 2006, Moss and Korintus 2008: 110). A low flat-rate sum does not provide an incentive to fathers who are the main breadwinners in the household to use parental leave. It may also disincentive higher-earning women to take long leave periods. In that case, therefore, it is mostly the lower-salaried women who interrupt their employment careers (Spiess and Wrohlich 2008).

Flexible working-time arrangements are another important condition for men and women to reconcile employment and care work. Part-time work and also individualized flexible working hours belong to that category. Seen from the perspective of promoting mothers' employment and gender equality, part-time work regulations are, however, a two-edged sword. They enable parents who do not want (or are not able) to put their children into full day-care institutions to combine employment and care work. On the other hand, they might contribute to a crystallization of gender-specific working arrangements, with all the likely consequences of career interruptions and working fewer hours (lower salaries, less chances of job promotion, lower pensions, etc.), in particular in combination with other policies, e.g. the availability of part-time only childcare services (Jaumotte 2003: 21f.).[9] Scholars have thus argued that flexible working hours should be universally available, not only for parents, in order to make nonstandard working hours more acceptable. In the case of a universal right, employers might not be as reluctant in hiring parents or young women or men (mothers or fathers-to-be), because each employee at any age could ask for a part-time job (Hegewisch and Gornick 2008). Another important element is the degree to which part-time work includes the rights and benefits associated with full-time employment. Moreover, it is obvious that the right to reduce working time should be accompanied with the right to go back to full-time employment. Otherwise, one could not call it flexible working-time arrangements.

Services: the provision of childcare

It is by now widely acknowledged that any successful work-family reconciliation strategy that intends to increase female labor-force participation, birth rates and gender equality is dependent upon available and affordable *publicly provided or financed childcare provision* (Anderson and Levine 2000, Büchel and Spieß 2002, Hofferth and Collins 2000, Jaumotte 2003). Childcare services represent the most direct way for governments to reduce the indirect parental opportunity costs associated with childrearing. Yet the decision of parents to rely on publicly provided childcare depends on the *availability*, the *affordability* and the *quality*. In an analysis of variation between countries, these three dimensions of childcare need to be assessed. The children's age also matters. Childcare institutions for children older than three years of age are quasi-universally available in most countries (Bahle 2008, OECD 2006).[10] What seems to make the difference are care options for infants and toddlers (children aged zero to three). If a parent discontinues employment until a child is three years old and able to attend childcare, this long break has negative consequences for the subsequent employment career (Lalive and Zweimüller 2009, Ziefle 2004). Hence the more full-time, low-cost and good-quality childcare places for children under three years of age that exists, the more this situation should lead to an increase in maternal employment.

Money: children's allowances and type of taxation

In contrast to leaves and services, which have no other function than to support and relieve the family in its care tasks, *monetary benefits* as I defined them earlier follow different aims. They are designed to reduce the direct costs of children and to alleviate poverty. Yet the design of children's and tax allowances or deductions might affect the mother's decision of whether to care for her children herself or to use childcare in order to return to the labor market. High marginal tax rates play a role when evaluating the tax system, particularly in the case of joint taxation. The average tax rate on the second-earner's earnings, defined as the proportion of these earnings that goes into paying increased household taxes, affects the decision to participate in the labor market or not. The higher this proportion is, the higher the probability that a married woman will withdraw from the labor market (Smith et al. 2003). Some authors have demonstrated that systems where the family rather than the individual citizen is the unit of taxation yield high marginal tax rates for the second earner, since the income obtained by the spouses is added up and then divided between the partners, as in Germany, or among all family members, as in France (Rubery et al. 1997). The marginal tax rate for the second earner is especially high if there is a large differential between the primary and the secondary income. This effect may occur also in the case of tax allowances for dependents and if children's allowances are granted on the basis of a means test (OECD 2007c, Saraceno 2003). According to Dingeldey (2000), joint taxation, rather than encouraging full withdrawal from the labor market by wives, supports their choice to work part-time. Individual or separate taxation schemes, by contrast, are more neutral with regard to wives' labor-force participation and de facto more friendly towards the dual-earner model. However, as critics often point out, the complexities of national tax schemes make such a clear distinction between joint and individual taxation and their effects almost impossible. The impact of a tax system depends on the individual income level and the progressivity of the system. In joint taxation schemes, the more progressive a system is and the higher the income of the primary earner, the more likely it is that additional labor supply will yield a relatively lower income.

In the following section, the development of the work-family policies in 15 European welfare states will be investigated empirically. Table 3.1 gives an

Table 3.1 Dimensions of work-family policies

Core program	Program characteristic	Definition
Maternity leave	Duration of leave	Weeks of benefit payable for fully insured mother (before + after childbirth)
	Single replacement rate	After-tax benefit for a mother divided by previous earnings
Parental leave	Duration of leave	Weeks of guaranteed saving of workplace/weeks of guaranteed job return for fully insured parent
	Duration of paid leave	Weeks of benefit payable for fully insured parent
	Single replacement rate	After-tax benefit for a parent divided by previous earnings
	Gender division	Weeks reserved for fathers
Flexible working time	Entitlement	The right to reduce working hours
	Full social rights	Part-time work includes the rights and benefits associated with full-time employment
Childcare services	Coverage rate	Percentage of children aged under three provided with a place (no. of places/no. of children aged <3)
	Membership category	Social right for a child or requirements concerning the employment situation of parents
	Flexibility of service	Number of opening hours per day
	Affordability	Fees in % of average wage
	Quality of services	Child-to-staff ratio for children <3
Transfers	Basis of taxation	The basis of taxation for a couple: separate or joint
	Entitlement to children's allowances	Entitlement based on a means test or universally available

Source: My compilation

overview of the included dimensions. The comparison will demonstrate the efforts of European welfare states to reform their policy support of working mothers.

Time: leave regulations and working-time flexibility

Regulations for parents to use leave for childcare

Leave facilities are an important element of work-family policies, particularly when children are very young. It is important to differentiate between *maternity* and *parental leave*.[11] Maternity leave is generally available to mothers only. The right to a time off work is intended to protect the health of the mother and newborn child, and it can be taken shortly before, during and immediately after childbirth. By contrast, parental leave is generally available equally to mothers and fathers and can only be taken after the end of maternity leave. Often it is conceptualized as a family right that parents can divide between themselves as they choose. In some cases, mothers and fathers have a non-transferable individual entitlement for a short period of time. Parental leave is intended to give parents the opportunity to spend time caring for a young child (Moss 2015).

While the introduction of the first maternity leave schemes dates back around the turn of the nineteenth century when, in the context of industrialization, some European governments[12] introduced unpaid leaves for mothers for reasons of health and children's well-being, parental leave has a more recent history. In all countries under examination, maternity leave is available to all officially working women for a comparatively short period (a few months) and is paid at a high rate (see Figure 3.1).

Due to the EU Directive 96/34/EC,[13] parental leave is now granted in all countries in the study and open both to mothers and fathers. Yet countries differ with respect to the payment that parents may receive during this leave. In some countries, parents are entitled to a – more or less generous – earnings-related benefit. In others, parental leave may be either unpaid or paid at a low flat rate.

Figure 3.1 gives an overview of the cross-country differences and the development over time of both maternity and parental leave durations. Table 3.2 provides information on the leave benefits and replacement rates.

Maternity leave provisions have changed little over the period of observation, but (also because of the EU directive) have been expanded to progressively include workers who before were not entitled to a leave, such as some kinds of part-timers and self-employed people. The length varies between 7 weeks in Sweden and 26 weeks in the United Kingdom. Countries differ with respect to the division of this time before and after childbirth, i.e. some countries oblige mothers to stop working two months before childbirth, and others leave it to the mother to decide when to use the leave. Mothers are granted an earnings-related payment which amounts to between 50 percent (in Greece) and 100 percent of previous wages.

Parental leave regulations vary substantially between the countries both in terms of duration and payment. Before the EU Directive 96/34/EC was approved, there were several countries without any parental leave regulation: the Benelux states, United Kingdom and Ireland. Except for Luxembourg, these countries together with Greece are also the ones with the least generous provisions after the implementation of the directive. Each parent may go on leave for 13 (or 14 in the case of Ireland) weeks, but will not be remunerated. Only in Belgium are parents entitled to a flat-rate sum that amounts to about one-third of the previous wage. Another cluster of countries combines long leave periods with low payment: Austria, Spain, Finland, France and Portugal belong to this category. Germany used to be part of this cluster, too. Since it changed its leave regulations in 2007, however, this country has moved in the direction of the third cluster, which is characterized by medium to long leave and comparably high replacement rates. Sweden is the prototype of this cluster, but Luxembourg also belongs to it. Denmark and Italy do not fit any of the clusters: both countries allow parents a leave of equal to or less than ten months.[14] Yet Denmark grants a generous payment of 100 percent of previous wages, while Italy remunerates only 30 percent of previous wages and only for six months in total for the couple.

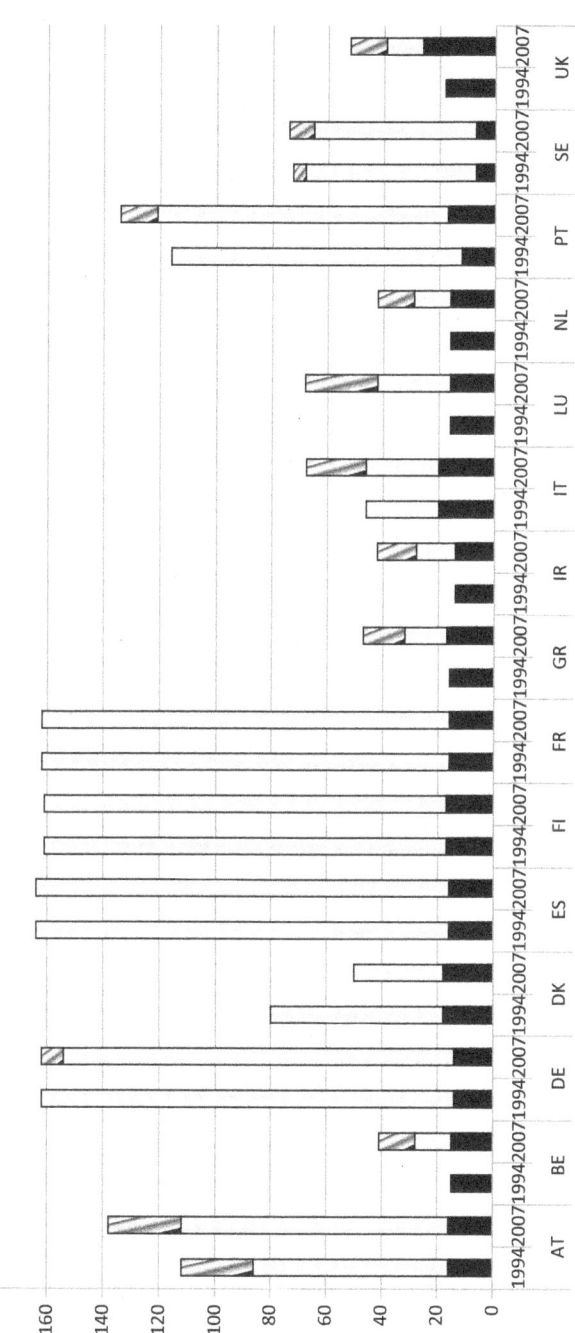

Figure 3.1 Maternity and parental leave provisions, 1994 and 2007

Notes:

1 The bars show the entitlement to leave in weeks. The black parts of the bars are weeks dedicated only to the mother (maternity leave), and the grey bars illustrate the maximum of parental leave in weeks. Shaded parts of the bars indicate the share of parental leave which is dedicated to the father only. Their positions do not indicate that fathers may only use parental leave after mothers have used up theirs. Rather, in most cases, fathers and mothers may use parental leave at the same time.

2 Note that in France, only parents of a second or subsequent child are entitled to parental leave.

Sources: European Commission (1995, 2007); European Data Service; Social Security Worldwide (https://www.issa.int/de/ssptw)

Table 3.2 Replacement rates for maternity leave (ML) and parental leave (PL), 1994 and 2007

Country		1994	2007
Austria	ML	100%	100%
	PL	23% (ca. 10 ECU/day) for up to 2 years (if father uses PL for at least 6 months, otherwise for 18 months)	21% (436 EUR/month) for up to 2 years
Belgium	ML	82% during the first month and 75% during the remaining 14 weeks	82% during the first month and 75% during the remaining 14 weeks
	PL	n.a.	36% (685 EUR/month) if full-time leave
Germany	ML	100 %	100%
	PL	16% (323 Ecu/month). A means test is applied as of month 7	67% for up to 12 months
Denmark	ML	90%	90%
	PL	96% (350 Ecu/week) for 10 weeks. 63% afterwards	86 % (460 EUR/week)
Spain	ML	100%	100%
	PL	0	0
Finland	ML	66% on average (entitlement varies between 42% and 82%)	66% on average (entitlement varies between 42% and 82%)
	PL	66% for 26 weeks, 19% (237 Ecu/month) for remaining 118 weeks	66% for 26 weeks, 20% (294 EUR/month) for remaining 118 weeks
France	ML	84%	100%
	PL	41% (455 Ecu/month)	27% (522 EUR/month) if full-time leave
United Kingdom	ML	90% for first 6 weeks, then 16% (196 Ecu/month)	90% for first 6 weeks, then 26% (771 EUR/month)
	PL	0	0
Greece	ML	50%	50%
	PL	0	0
Ireland	ML	70%	80%
	PL	0	0
Italy	ML	80%	80%
	PL	30% for 6 months	30% for 6 months
Luxembourg	ML	100%	100%
	PL	0	66% (EUR 1.778/month)

Country		1994	2007
Netherlands	ML	100%	100%
	PL	0	0
Portugal	ML	100%	100%
	PL	0	0
Sweden	ML	80%	80%
	PL	80% for 12 months, then 14% (183 Ecu/month) for remaining 3 months	80% for 13 months, then % (570 Ecu/month) for remaining 3 months

Notes: The maternity and parental leave benefit may either be a defined replacement rate or a flat-rate sum. In the latter case, I converted the amount into a replacement rate by dividing the sum by the average net income of a single person. The data on average net incomes is taken from the European Data Service (access date: 20.07.2009).

Sources: European Commission (1995, 2007); European Data Service; Social Security Worldwide (https://www.issa.int/de/ssptw)

Increasingly, parental leave schemes provide incentives for fathers to take up parental leave by giving them non-transferable rights in the form of either use-or-lose portions of shareable leave or individual entitlements. In most countries, regulations were modified following the EU Directive 96/34/EC (as discussed earlier). Parental leave is a family entitlement, i.e. to be divided between parents as they choose, in Austria, Denmark, France, Finland, Italy and Spain. An individual entitlement is granted in Belgium, Greece, Ireland, the Netherlands, Luxembourg and the United Kingdom. In Italy, parents may share the leave, and the total duration may not exceed ten months – except when a father uses at least three months. In this case, he is entitled to an additional month and the maximum time increases to 11 months. In Sweden and Germany (as of 2007), the total leave period can be shared between the parents, except for a reserved period of two months for each parent which is lost if not used. In order to increase the incentive to use at least the reserved period, the Swedish and German leave is comparatively highly paid (see Table 3.2).

Another condition for making leaves supportive of an early return to employment, thus reducing career penalties, is the possibility of combining the leave with part-time employment. Countries such as Belgium, Germany and France do not oblige parents to take up parental leave on a full-time basis. French parents are permitted to work up to 80 percent of full working hours and German and Belgian parents may take up leave on a half-time basis. Italian parents may take the leave in bits and pieces, even a day at a time, thus configuring a sort of vertical part time.

Flexible working-time arrangements

Flexible working-time arrangements, such as part-time work, but also individualized flexible working hours, are another important condition for men and women to reconcile employment and care work. The European Union once again played a role by stipulating the principle of non-discrimination against part-time work in terms of working conditions in the EU part-time Directive 97/81/EC (Leiber 2005). Often part-time arrangements are settled at the level of the firm, but some countries have national legislation. According to a report by the European Commission (2005), two forms of part-time[15] legislation can be distinguished with regard to the right of workers to ask for it. First, legislation that applies to all employees and second, legislation that focuses specifically on working parents. Only Germany and the Netherlands fall under the first category. Since the 2000 reform, German employees who worked for at least 6 months in a firm with no less than 15 employees have the right to request a part-time job. A similar right was enacted in the Netherlands in 2000. Here workers in firms with at least ten employees may ask for reduced working hours (Lewis 2009, see for more details Bosch, Deelen, and Euwal 2008). In Denmark, a law was enacted in 2002 making sections of collective agreements unlawful if they were obstacles to the creation of part-time jobs in any way (Lind and Rasmussen 2008). Interestingly, in Sweden, one of the countries with the highest part-time employment rates, employees do not have a statutory right to reduce working hours.

Five other countries introduced legislation that gives working parents the right to reduce their working hours: Austria, Greece, Finland, Portugal and the United Kingdom. They differ in regards to the target group and the period for which they might ask for part-time work. For example, in Austria, parents of children born after 1 July 2004 have a right to work part-time until the child reaches the age of seven and the right to return to full-time work thereafter. It is limited to companies with at least 20 employees, however, and the applicant must have been employed with the same employer for at least three years. The other countries differ regarding the age of the child for which a parent may request flexible work, with Portugal being the most generous (up to age 12) and Greece being the least generous country (four years of age) (European Commission 2005). Italian parents of newborn babies may take two hours of a day for "feeding the child" until the child turns one. In addition, workers in shift work may be exempted from the night shift if they have a child under three. Other countries are worth mentioning because they have introduced innovative working-time arrangements such as the career-break scheme in Belgium. The basic idea of the measure is that all employees – with the consent of their employers – can reduce working time (or stop) for a certain period of time. However, the right to reduce to part-time or the complete suspension is granted for only one year over the whole career.[16] An extension is possible only by a collective labor agreement.

Another important element is the degree to which part-time work includes the rights and benefits associated with full-time employment. This has been excluded explicitly from the scope of the EU directive, even though it recommended this practice.[17] Moreover, the right to reduce working time must be accompanied with the right to go back to full-time employment; otherwise, one could not call it a flexible working-time arrangement. However, there are countries where this is not the case.[18] Italy is another interesting case. Here a law concerning part-time work has already existed since 1984. Yet the law (*legge 863/1984*) was inspired by a negative evaluation of part-time work and aimed at protecting workers from this atypical form of employment. For example, it allowed collective agreements to determine caps for the share of part-time workers in a company, or prohibited overtime hours for part-time workers. In 2000, a decree-law (*decreto legislativo 61/2000*) abandoned these rules and introduced short-term financial incentives to recruit employees on a part-time basis. Moreover, the principle of non-discrimination was included in a broader sense than prescribed by the directive and included similar rights with respect to social security and access to vocational training (Leiber 2005).

To sum up, the crucial question is how to promote the expansion of part-time work in a way that is not detrimental to career prospects and offers adequate social protection. Our country sample does not include any country that fulfills all requirements. Germany and the Netherlands may, however, be singled out for providing a universal right to work reduced hours, even though in the case of Germany this entitlement is not accompanied by the right to return to a full-time job (except for parents who work part time while on parental leave).

Services: the provision of childcare

In international comparison, the public provision of care for the under threes may take different forms. Rostgaard (2000: 9–10) differentiates between (1) group care in centres with full-time services provided during normal work hours, such as the day nurseries;[19] (2) play groups,[20] which are often set up outside the educational system for children between two to compulsory school age, involve children attending part of the day, sometimes only a few days of the week, and may require that parents or other carers are obliged to stay there with the child; and (3) care not organised in centres but at the child's or carer's home, such as family day care.[21] Most family day carers take care of more than one child, normally three to five children, and operate on a full-day schedule. In recent years, a number of countries have conceptualized and integrated this third kind of care solution as part of the national day-care system (e.g. the French concept of *assistantes maternelles* and the German *Tagesmutter*).

However, because of differences in legal regulations and competencies, the availability, affordability and quality of publicly provided childcare institutions varies not only across countries but also, in some cases, even across regions within a country. I will address each of these factors in the following sections.

Availability

To capture the availability of publicly provided or financed childcare, coverage rates are calculated by dividing the number of available places by the number of children of the relevant age group. As previously noted, this kind of data is hard to obtain. Moreover, it is possible that the public care situation in a country is over- or underestimated because countries sometimes additionally report market-based forms of childcare, while, on the other hand, they do not always report all relevant public care forms, e.g. the use of family day care. The situation is further complicated by the fact that the definition of "public" provision of childcare is not always clear. Some countries directly finance childcare services and others fund programs for employers or tax measures for parents. Still others subsidize privately provided services and some provide all of these forms of subsidies (European Commission's Expert Group on Gender and Employment Issues (EGGE) 2009).

Countries also differ in whether they publish data on places available or enrolment rates. This makes a difference when a significant proportion of places are part time. Counting children attending day care will tend to overstate, by implication, the volume of available places. An additional difficulty is that enrolment rates might overestimate the time children spend in the facilities. As it is described by Eurostat (2004: 29),

> Whereas in Italy, data on childcare facilities relate to children enrolled, in Belgium, in both the French and Flemish Communities, data relate to all children who attend the childcare arrangement for at least one day during the year. This means that in Belgium more children who attended facilities only occasionally during the year are likely to be counted than in Italy.[22]

Table 3.3 illustrates the development of coverage rates for children aged zero to three in 15 European welfare states. Whenever possible, data on the number of publicly provided places based on national statistics are reported. The main difference between the periods before and after 2006 is the inclusion of family day care in the later data. In some cases, it is, therefore, not clear whether we really see an expansion or whether the increase is owed to differences in what is included.

Table 3.3 shows that, in 1994, there was a sharp divide between countries that provided many places for children under three (Nordic countries and France and Belgium) and German-speaking, southern European as well as English-speaking countries, where less than 10 percent of infants and toddlers were in a public childcare institution (except for Portugal). More than ten years later, the situation has changed. First, we have witnessed an overall increase in coverage rates. There is, however, still variation, which separates northwestern from Continental-southern European countries. Austria, Germany, Luxembourg, Greece and Italy still provide comparably few places. On the other hand, United Kingdom, the Netherlands, Portugal and Spain have considerably increased their provision.

As Kamerman and Kahn (1981: 120) pointed out, childcare facilities do not constitute a realistic choice unless they are quantitatively sufficient, well distributed geographically and accessible to all population groups. We take from Table 3.3 that the first condition is not met by all nations. Moreover, there are huge within-country differences. For instance, in Germany, coverage rates range from 2 percent in many western German states to up to 56 percent in the eastern German state Saxony-Anhalt. Childcare provision in Italy is comparatively low almost everywhere, but particularly so in the south, where it is similar to most southwestern German states (Blome, Keck, and Alber 2009: 220, Madama 2010; see also Chapter 4 in this book). In general, more urbanized areas provide more places than rural areas.

Table 3.3 The development of child care coverage rates for the age group zero to three[1] (1994–2006)

Country	1994	2000	2006	Change
Austria	3.0	7.7	10.8	7.8
Belgium	30.0	30.0	30.0	0.0
Germany	7.5	10.0	13.7[5]	5.2
Denmark	48.0	64.0	63.0	15.0
Spain	5.5	8.9	18.7	13.2
Finland	21.0	22.0	26.0	5.0
France	23.0	43.0	45.0	22.0
United Kingdom	2.0	26[3]	33.0	31.0
Greece	3.0	3.0	10.0	7.0
Ireland	2.0	15.0	18.0	16.0
Italy	6.0	7.4	11.4	3.9
Luxembourg	[2]	14.2	22.0	–
Netherlands	8.0	9.5[4]	16.5[4]	7.0
Portugal	12.0	12.0	33.0	11.0
Sweden	41.0	41.0	42.2	1.2

Notes:
1 Number of publicly provided/subsidized places as percent of children in the age group zero to three years.
2 Data not available.
3 England only.
4 For children under four years.
5 German childcare statistics changed in 2006. Coverage rates are no longer reported, but enrolment rates are. In addition, the figure now includes care provided by publicly subsidized child minders.

Sources: For 1994 data: Randall (2000). The figure for Italy refers to 1991, and the figures for Belgium, Ireland, Greece, France, Portugal and the United Kingdom refer to 1993. The source for Germany is Statistisches Bundesamt (2004), for Sweden Skolverket (2005) and for Spain it is the Instituto Nacional de Estadistica (2011).

For 2000 data: Germany and Greece (OECD 2001), France (Eurostat 2004), Austria (Statistik Austria 2011), Spain (Instituto Nacional de Estadistica 2011), the Netherlands (Centraal Bureau voor de Statistiek 2006), Italy (Fortunati 2002) and Luxembourg (Service central de la statistique et des études économique (STATEC) Luxembourg 2010). Figures for Belgium, Portugal, Finland (Eurostat 2004) and Ireland (OECD 2008a) refer to 2001, figures for Denmark and the United Kingdom refer to 1998 (OECD 2001).

For 2006 data: Denmark (Danmarks statistic 2007), France (Bailleau 2008), Greece, Finland, Ireland, Portugal and the United Kingdom (EU-Silc), theNetherlands (Centraal Bureau voor de Statistiek 2008), Belgium (Meulders and O'Dorchai 2008), Spain (Instituto Nacional de Estadistica 2011), Sweden (Skolverket 2010), Austria (Statistik Austria 2011) and Italy (Istituto degli Innocenti di Firenze 2009).

Countries differ in the commitment to childcare as a social right. Only in three countries do parents have a guaranteed place for each under three-year-old child: Finland,[23] Sweden[24] and Denmark.[25] The fact that enrolment is far from 100 percent suggests that not all parents decide to put their child(ren) into public facilities, but find other care solutions.[26] In 2008, Germany adopted a law that introduced a care right for children who are older than 12 months to be implemented from 2013 onwards.

Countries also vary in terms of opening hours. In some countries, childcare institutions are open for only half day, or close during lunch. In others, children attend childcare institutions just some days of the week. This situation merely encourages the parents to take up part-time employment. There is little data on the opening hours of care services for children between zero and three years of age. We therefore have to rely on information on pre-primary education, which is provided by Eurybase (European Commission 2009). Table 3.4 illustrates the

Table 3.4 Childcare flexibility: opening hours

Country	Usual hours of operation[1]	Remarks
Austria	n.a.	Great variation between regions and facilities. The maximum opening hours are 7 a.m. to 7 p.m. Only 42% of day nurseries are open until 5 p.m.
Belgium	Up to 12	At least 10 (French part) or 11 (Flemish part) consecutive hours between 6:30 am and 6:30 pm for a minimum of 220 working days a year.
Germany	n.a.	Great variation between regions and facilities: generally morning sessions (4 hours) without lunch. Only 8.3% of children between 0 and 3 years old received full-time care (more than 7 hours) in 2008.
Denmark	10	Some special day-care institutions are open all day and night.
Spain	7	This includes lunch breaks, rest or nap periods and recreation. This timetable can be extended for reasons related to employment. Children are not allowed to remain in school for more than 9 hours per day.
Finland	full time	
France	full time	Great variation between institutions, *crèches collectives* open for 11 hours, *école maternelle* for 5 hours plus flexible arrangements with *assistentes maternelles*.
United Kingdom	10	Minimum required by government funding: 2.5 hours/day. Day nurseries are typically open all day from 8:00 a.m. until 6:00 p.m. Parents (especially those in employment) may choose to pay additional fees so that their child can stay for longer than the 2.5 hours/day offered through government funding.
Greece	9	
Ireland	4	
Italy	8	Three weekly timetable models can be offered: minimum 25 hours service only in the morning, 40 hours service and maximum 48–49 hours service.
Luxembourg	6	Usually closed for two-hour lunch and closed on Tuesday and Thursday afternoons.
Netherlands	10	Regarding day nurseries, parents can only opt for blocks of 5 hours (morning and/or afternoon). Children attend play groups usually only twice a week for 2 or 3 hours each.
Portugal	10–12	Minimum 8 hours.
Sweden	12	

Sources: Country reports from Eurybase (European Commission 2009); Fuchs (2006), Statistisches Bundesamt (2009). Data for Luxembourg as cited in Gornick and Meyers (2003)

situation in 2007/2008. Estimating the change over time is unfortunately not possible. The numbers refer to the average hours of operation of a facility. This should not be mistaken for the actual daily caring time, but rather be understood as a measure of flexibility.

In the majority of European countries, public services generally provide extensive opening hours that take account of the needs of working parents. Full-day provision (including morning and afternoon sessions) is the norm in the Nordic countries, Belgium, Spain, France, Italy and Portugal.

Some countries offer only part-time subsidized provision or close during lunch. This is the case in Germany, Luxembourg, Ireland, the Netherlands and United Kingdom. In the latter cases, parents bear the costs for additional care services privately, or, as it often happens in Germany and Luxembourg, rely on the extended family.[27]

Affordability

Parents do not only have to pay for private forms of care. While free education for older children (usually from the age of three) is guaranteed in school settings in a majority of countries, parents of younger children usually have to contribute to the fees of publicly provided or subsidized care services. Research in particular on the United States and the United Kingdom has shown that costs matters for female labor supply and, thus, for the decision of parents to use childcare services (Blau and Ferber 1992, Ribar 1995, Viitanen 2005). The theoretical assumption is that since childcare costs increase the mother's reservation wage, high childcare costs may lead to a lower labor-force participation of women with children. For Germany and Italy, such effects have also been found. Wrohlich (2004) and del Boca, Daniela and Vuri (2007) show that, when subsidies to childcare facilities are cut and private childcare costs increase, the labor-force participation rate of mothers decreases. Changes in the opposite direction – namely, increasing state subsidy of childcare costs, produce increases in the labor-force participation of mothers and in average working hours. Parents, and particularly mothers, in fact, take into account the costs of childcare relative to the net gain from employment.

Most childcare services are (partly) subsidized, so parents do not pay full costs. There are basically two ways to subsidize childcare services, and countries can differ in the weight they put on either: support provided directly to families and allowing them to choose the types of childcare services they will purchase, or subsidies provided to various approved service providers. An example of demand-side subsidies are tax credits or vouchers; an example of supply-side subsidies are subsidies provided to private producers who meet certain specific requirements, e.g. aspects of quality (Cleveland and Krashinsky 2004).

The OECD computed childcare fees for a two-year-old child who attended accredited early years care and education services in 2004. According to their calculations, the average fee for two children[28] amounts to about 22.1 percent of the average wage, but fees range from 7.6 percent of the average wage in Sweden to almost 50 percent in countries such as the United Kingdom and Ireland (see Table 3.5). Since all countries except Sweden provide some sort of subsidies or

Table 3.5 Childcare costs and affordability, 2004

Country	Childcare fees[1]	Net childcare costs[2]	Childcare costs in % of the family net income[3]
Austria	19.1	19.1	14.9
Belgium	31.6	4.7	4.2
Germany	16.0	9.1	8.4
Denmark	11.4	8.4	7.8
Spain	n.a.	n.a.	n.a.
Finland	9.2	9.2	7.2
France	16.8	14.8	11.3
United Kingdom	47.8	43.1	32.7
Greece	8.9	6.6	4.7
Ireland	49.6	44.6	29.2
Italy	n.a.	n.a.	n.a.
Luxembourg	19.1	8.5	5.7
Netherlands	22.7	13.5	11.5
Portugal	27.8	5.9	4.2
Sweden	7.6	7.6	6.2

Notes:
1 For two children attending accredited care services in % of average wage.
2 Out-of-pocket childcare cost for two children attending accredited care services in % of net average wage. Childcare benefits, rebates and tax reductions are deducted.
3 Out-of-pocket childcare cost for a two-earner couple who earns 167% of the average income and use full-time care for two children aged two and three. The family net income is the sum of gross earnings plus cash benefits minus taxes and social contributions.

Source: OECD (2007)

tax reliefs for parents using childcare outside of the home, I also report *net* childcare costs for parents. This indicator is calculated by subtracting any childcare benefit, rebate and tax reduction from the fee. Table 3.5 reports net childcare costs in relation to the average wage (column 3) and for dual full-time earners with an overall wage income at 167 percent of the average wage (column 4).

Unfortunately, OECD data for Italy is not available. From a study by del Boca and Vuri (2007) we take that the costs of public childcare depend on family size, family income and family composition since in publicly provided or subsidized services it is defined on the basis of a sliding scale. Furthermore, fees vary enormously across municipalities, thus national averages are meaningless. In the northern Italian city of Monza, parents who earn €23,300 Euro per year[29] have to pay €172.30 per month for a public childcare institution (€504 for a private institution and €1120 for an individual child minder). This is about 9 percent of the parents' income (Sabatinelli 2008, Toto 2007). But the proportion increases almost three times in the case of attendance in a private service.

For dual-earner couples, average net childcare costs amount to about one-tenth of their average earnings. In most countries, parents receive some form of subsidy. In those cases, net childcare costs go down. The savings for parents can be estimated by looking at the difference between column 1 and column 2 in Table 3.5.

The level of difference depends on the country-specific policies with respect to tax reductions and childcare benefits or rebates. In countries where these direct or indirect transfers do not exist, or are very reduced (Austria, Denmark, Finland, France, Greece, Sweden), and fees are high, there is no incentive for a second earner to take up employment, and it is difficult also for a single parent (mother) to do so, although lone mothers in many countries receive additional subsidies either in the form of lower fees or that of higher transfers. As a result of a combination of high fees and low care-linked transfers, in Ireland and the United Kingdom, parents have to spend about one-third of their earnings to buy care services, followed at a distance by Austria with 14 percent.

In Germany, parents may deduct costs of childcare from their taxable income. As of 2006, dual-earner and working lone parents of children aged 0–14 can deduct two-thirds of the costs up to the limit of €4000 per year. This applies also to single breadwinner families, but only for three- to six-year-old children. In Italy, it is possible to deduct from taxable income only up to €360 for documented childcare costs (Sabatinelli 2008).

Quality

The extent to which parents engage in the labor market arguably depends on their trust in the quality of care that their children are receiving. Generally, the factors contributing to good-quality care include a favorable child-to-staff ratio, i.e. how many children are cared for by one caregiver, well-trained personnel in terms of education and empathy, and curriculum design (Gornick and Meyers 2003, OECD 2007a). However, these dimensions, and in particular changes in them over time, are particularly difficult to measure. It is, for example, tricky to determine what exactly constitutes empathy. Curriculum objectives, on the other hand, likely depend on the embeddedness of childcare institutions in the education system. Countries that focus on early childhood education, i.e. where institutions are part of the national schooling system and overseen by the national ministry of education, will have a different focus than countries with a predominantly pedagogical orientation of care services.[30]

For comparative purposes, the only meaningful indicator left is child-to-staff ratios that give a quantitative indication of the carer's time and attention available for each child. Table 3.6 provides the compilation of data collected by Gornick and Meyers (2003) for the year 2000 approximately and by the European Commission's Expert Group on Gender and Employment Issues for 2006.

The sources I use, unfortunately, do not provide detailed information on the calculation of the indicator. It is not always clear

- whether the figure reflects the number of persons who are engaged in caring for children aged under three years old or for children of all age groups;
- whether the number of persons employed in a public childcare institution reflects the number of persons who are in charge of care or includes facility managers, cooks, etc.; and

Table 3.6: Child-to-staff ratio for children under the age of three, approximately 2000 and 2006

Country	Approx. 2000	Approx. 2006
Austria	n.a.	5:1
Belgium	7:1	4:1[1]
Germany	n.a.	6.4:1
Denmark	Ranges from 3:1 (crèches) to 6:1 (age-integrated centres)	3:1
Spain	n.a.	10:1[2]
Finland	Ranges from 4:1 or 5:1	4:1
France	Ranges from 3:1 in family day care to 8:1 in day nurseries	n.a.
United Kingdom	3:1 for youngest, 4:1 for 2–3 year olds	3:1 for youngest, 4:1 for 2–3 year olds
Greece	n.a.	n.a.
Ireland	n.a.	3:1 for youngest, 5:1 for 1–2 year olds, 6:1 for 2–3 year olds
Italy	n.a.	5.5:1 for 0–1 year olds, from 7:1 to 10:1 for 1–3 year olds
Luxembourg	6:1	n.a.
Netherlands	4:1 for youngest, 6:1 for 2–3 year olds	4:1 for youngest, 5:1 for 1–2 year olds, 6:1 for 2–3 year olds
Portugal	n.a.	6:1
Sweden	varies locally, on avg. 6:1	5.1:1

Notes:
1 Ratio reported for regulated family day care.
2 Average ratio for children aged zero to six.

Source: European Commission's Expert Group on Gender and Employment Issues (EGGE) (2009), Gornick and Meyers (2003)

- which care scheme is taken into account, e.g. both day nurseries and family day care.

Keeping these problems in mind, the available data show that the child-to-staff ratio seems unchanged. One care worker per three children can be found in Denmark, the United Kingdom and Ireland (but only for the youngest) only. A rather high ratio of more than 6:1 is found in Germany, Portugal and Italy (note, however, that the figure for Portugal refers to a different age range).

In sum, we see a rather mixed picture of the childcare situation and development in the 15 European welfare states. First, the scope of publicly provided or subsidized childcare provision has increased over the last 12 years, yet there are still cross-country differences: while countries such as Portugal, Spain, Ireland and the United Kingdom provide more places than in 1994, Austria, Germany, Greece and Italy still come in last. Moreover, at least in Austria and Germany, the institutions often open only for a couple of hours during the day. One should, however, keep in mind the German government's decision to ensure a right to a childcare place for children aged zero to three from 2013 on. Here we should expect a considerable increase in coverage rates in the next couple of years.

Second, childcare is affordable in most of the countries. For dual-earner couples, average net childcare costs amount to about one-tenth of their average earnings. In high-cost countries such as Ireland and the United Kingdom, second earners might, however, be rather discouraged from taking up employment. This is also true for countries such as Austria, Germany, Denmark and Finland where the relief through taxes and benefits is not as high. Furthermore, where public or publicly subsidized childcare is scarce, the price of market services may be too high for low-income families/women, thus worsening the trade-off between working and caring full time. Third, childcare quality, measured as child-to-staff ratio, also varies between the countries. A rather high ratio of more than 6:1 is found in Germany, Portugal and Italy. A low ratio exists only in Denmark, but also for very young children in the United Kingdom and Ireland.

I argued earlier that full-time, low-cost and good-quality childcare places for children aged under three are the components in the broader support structure for working mothers. This constellation is found only in Denmark, Sweden and to some degree also in France, Belgium and Finland. Missing data for the situation in the beginning of the 1990s do not allow for the assessment of the intensity and direction of overall change. Taking into account only coverage rates, we see a change towards supporting mothers working in Spain, the United Kingdom and Portugal (and Germany because of the new law).

Money: children's allowances and type of taxation

Children's allowances

Children's allowances are a periodical payment to a household with dependent children to help with the cost of raising children. In contrast to parental leave benefits, children's allowances are in general paid for many years and until the child reaches a certain age, i.e. between 16 and 18 years in most countries (with higher age thresholds for children in education, military service, etc.). The benefit is not designed as a wage replacement or the like, but rather as a compensation for the additional costs that arise when raising a child. In most countries, children's allowances aim at balancing inequalities between families with and without children. There are cross-country differences in terms of level and degree of universality. As noted earlier, children's allowances based on a household means test may reinforce a high marginal tax rate for a second earner and thus present an adverse incentive for mothers to take up employment.

Three of the 15 countries follow a different approach than the rest regarding child support. In Italy, a household allowance (*assegno per il nucleo familiare*) was established in 1988, which is an entirely means-tested measure for low-income households. As part of the social security system, this allowance is limited to dependent employees and pensioners. In addition, it is targeted at households both with and without children. Due to the means test in Italy, children's allowances for a dual-earner family add up to only a very small amount and many dual-earner households do not get it at all. Portugal and Spain also employ a means test for children's allowances, reserving them for poor households. Germany and Greece,

68 *Design of work-family policies in Europe*

on the other hand, abolished the means test they had once applied to children's allowances in 1990. In 2005, a new scheme, in addition to the universal children's allowance and the substitutive tax deduction, and based on a household income test, was introduced in Germany (*Kinderzuschlag*). It aims at preventing low-income working parents from having to apply for unemployment benefit or social welfare benefits solely for the maintenance of their children. This scheme intends to uphold the benefit of staying in employment rather than applying for social assistance. In that sense, the *Kinderzuschlag* encourages mothers' employment.

Tax system and social security contributions

Earnings are an important part of the incentive for mothers to work, yet their influence is mediated by tax policies. Taxation of families can be separate or joint. In a joint taxation system, usually a quotient is applied, i.e. the taxable income is the sum of the incomes divided by a factor. This form of "income splitting" exists in Germany, Portugal and France. In Germany, the quotient is two, independent of how many people live in a household,[31] while in France, the number of household members is taken into account. In addition, it makes a difference whether employees have to pay social security contributions or whether social security is tax financed. In the first case, since social security contributions are generally based on individual, not the household, income, any additional income (up to a ceiling) will result in additional payments to the government. In the case of a tax-financed social security system, by contrast, tax exemptions for children may apply and reduce the overall burden.

Since the beginning of the 1990s, national taxation schemes have not changed fundamentally (except for Belgium, see Table 3.7). More essential changes took

Table 3.7 Type of taxation system, 1990–2007

Country	1990	1999	2006
Austria	Separate	Separate	Separate
Belgium	Joint	Separate	Separate
Germany	Joint	Joint	Joint
Denmark	Separate	Separate	Separate
Spain	Optional	Separate (Joint)	Optional (Joint)
Finland	Separate	Separate	Separate
France	Joint	Joint	Joint
United Kingdom	Separate	Separate	Separate
Greece	Separate	Separate	Separate
Ireland	Joint	Optional/Joint	Optional/Joint
Italy	Separate	Separate	Separate
Luxembourg	Joint	Joint	Joint
Netherlands	Separate	Separate	Separate
Portugal	Joint	Joint	Joint
Sweden	Separate	Separate	Separate

Sources: OECD (2001, 2008b)

place before the 1990s when the Nordic countries, Italy, Austria and the Netherlands switched from joint to separate taxation.

Joint taxation is associated with a reduced incentive for the partner with lower earnings to increase earnings because s/he will be faced with higher marginal tax rates under a progressive taxation scheme (OECD 2001). This effect can be reinforced in the case of income splitting, particularly when there is a substantial income unbalance between partners.

It has to be noted that while the systems in Italy, Austria and the Netherlands are classified as separate taxation systems, they provide a number of family-based tax measures. The Italian tax system, for instance, allows a tax credit for dependent spouses who earn an income below a certain limit. Together with the type of taxation (joint or separate), these additional benefits explain why in most EU countries a second income is effectively taxed more heavily than the income of primary or single earners, even in countries with separate taxation (Dingeldey 2000, Jaumotte 2003).

One way to illustrate the extent to which the state benefits families and encourages a certain family model is to compare the payments to the state (income tax plus social security contributions) as a percentage of gross earnings of a couple with two children with different earning compositions: one following the male-breadwinner model and the other following the dual-earner one. Figure 3.2 shows the difference in net transfers to government between male-breadwinner families and dual-earner families as a proportion (%) of net transfers to government for male-breadwinner families. Both families earn 200 percent of average worker earnings, yet in the male-breadwinner family, there is only one earner, while both partners earn 100 percent of average worker earnings in the dual-earner family. A higher value means that a dual-earner family pays more taxes and contributions than a male-breadwinner family. As the predominantly negative values in Figure 3.2 show, most countries favor dual-earner couples over male-breadwinner couples.

Two findings should be highlighted: First, dual-earner couples, where the partners equally contribute to the family's income, pay less taxes than couples in which only one of the partners earns this income in all countries, except for in Germany and France. This is due to the splitting systems in these two countries, which redistribute the taxable income among family members. In Germany, it can also be ascribed to the social security system which applies contribution ceilings for high incomes. This means that any additional income above the ceiling is not liable to social security contributions. Hence a couple in which only one partner has a considerable income benefits both from the tax and from the social security system.[32] This is different in the other countries, and the equal share of incomes pays off particularly in the Nordic countries Sweden and Finland, but also in Italy and Greece. Second, the situation did not change much between 2001 and 2008. In most countries, the difference in net transfers has become larger, which means that dual-earner couples increasingly pay less in taxes and social security contributions than male-breadwinner families. However, the figures are rather small, and we cannot speak of a trend towards a privilege of dual-earner couples.

70 *Design of work-family policies in Europe*

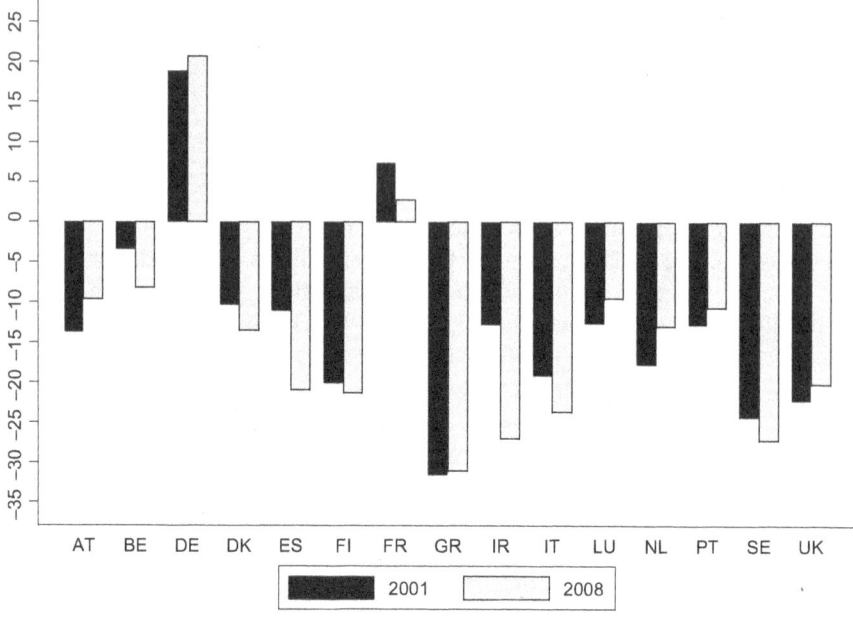

Figure 3.2 The difference in net transfers to government (tax and social security contributions) between male-breadwinner families and dual-earner families as a proportion (%) of net transfers to government for male-breadwinner families

Notes: The male-breadwinner family is defined as a couple with two children and with one income of 200 percent of the average wage (AW). The dual-earner family also has two children and two incomes of 100 percent of AW each.
Sources: OECD Social and Welfare Statistics (http://stats.oecd.org/Index.aspx; access date: 28.06.2011)

The calculations also demonstrate that the simple assumption that separate taxation is associated with higher incentives to earn a second income, and vice versa, does not hold. Belgium, which changed its taxation scheme in the 1990s and moved towards separate taxation, has one of the highest tax and social security contribution payments (similarly to Denmark). On the other hand, joint taxation does not automatically lead to a discouragement of a second earner, as the example of Portugal shows. Other factors such as the progressivity of the taxation scheme need to be taken into account.

To sum up, monetary benefits seem to be the policy that has the least impact on work-family arrangements and strategies. In particular, two factors need to be in place for monetary benefits to have a non-neutral impact with regard to the option between the male-breadwinner and the dual-earner arrangement: The first one is the presence of household means-tested children's allowances. The second one is a taxation system that substantially increases the tax rate for a second income. Both factors might be an adverse incentive for taking up a second, particularly full, income, thus supporting the male-breadwinner or also the one-and-a-half-earner model. On the contrary, the majority of the countries in the sample appear to have a combined system of universal child allowances and a tax system, that, at the same level of household income, is more favorable to couples where partners not only both work, but earn the same income.

Conclusion: more dual-earner support, but differences in reform tempo and intensity

Work-family policies in Europe are characterized by a wide variety of design and scope of the instruments. Not only do countries pursue quite different policies, but the most recent assessment of the situation in the years 2007 and 2008 shows also that there is not any absolute coherence between policies within a country. Except for Sweden, we find no systematically coherent dual-earner or male-breadwinner support model. Rather, the countries prioritize certain instruments over others, apparently irrespective of the specific goal they have with regard to work-family arrangements. This makes it very difficult to cluster them.

When we look at how the policies have developed over time, however, we do observe a trend towards supporting the dual-earner model. Changes have taken place both in time policies and childcare services that increasingly encourage both partners in a couple to be in paid employment – or rather encourage wives and mothers to be in work, at least part time, assuming that men are already there. Only the monetary benefits lag behind. These are, however, not the most relevant items for the reconciliation of work and care. Countries differ, however, with respect to both the extent to which they support the reconciliation of work and care for families and the pace of reform.

a   The most active countries in our time period are Germany and Denmark. In both countries, in part, substantial reforms towards the dual-earner model have been enacted. The two countries, however, differ greatly in the starting point. The dual-earner model prevailed in Denmark already before the 1990s, and public support for it was extended in the period observed. In Germany, by contrast, the system shift was more radical. Starting from a strong (West German) policy orientation favorable to the male-breadwinner model, the new parental leave scheme and support of early childcare shifted the focus towards supporting dual-earner households and working mothers. A full transformation to the dual-earner model is prevented by the maintenance of the taxation scheme.
b   Small to moderate changes have taken place in most of the remaining countries such as Belgium, Spain, the United Kingdom, Ireland, Luxembourg, the Netherlands and Portugal. In these countries, steps were taken towards the dual-earner model, or at least a trend towards it can be revealed. For these countries, the most reform-resistant policy area is the parental leave regulation, while in part substantial efforts were put into the expansion of childcare services.
c   Another category is composed of countries where hardly any change occurred at all. Yet one must differentiate between countries with a rather high base

level with regard to policies supporting the dual-earner model – i.e. where substantial reforms might not have been necessary (France and Sweden) – and countries where a change would be vital if the aim were to support dual-earner households and particularly working mothers: Italy and Greece. The latter countries leave room for action, in particular when it comes to the most important instruments: leave regulations and childcare services.

d   Finally, there are countries with an incomplete transformation. These are countries which have extended dual-earner-oriented policies but also pursued policies that lead in the opposite direction, i.e. which have enacted reforms that are more supportive of the male-breadwinner model. Austria and Finland belong to this category. Both countries have introduced measures in the parental leave scheme that encourage the gender-specific and long-term use of time out of employment. At the same time, Austria invested in childcare places, and both countries introduced flexible working hours for parents.

While there is a cross-country trend towards policies supporting mothers to participate in the labor market, there are much fewer efforts to encourage fathers to participate in care work. Wives and mothers are expected and encouraged to enter the labor market to a much larger degree than fathers are encouraged to enter the area of child care. Although there have been innovations in this field, with the degendering of parental leave and, in some countries, the introduction of specific incentives for fathers to take up some parental leave, this innovation, although symbolically important, is much more reduced in scope. Here, too, cross-country differences may be found, with some countries that strongly incentivize fathers, while others assume a neutral stance.

While this chapter has analyzed work-family policy changes from a broader European comparative perspective, the next chapter will look at the developments in Germany and Italy in more detail. It first explores the historical roots and the main shifts that brought about the similar starting situations of both countries in the beginning of the 1990s. It then describes the diverging developments of the parental leave schemes, the working-time regulations and childcare provision for children younger than three during the 1990s and the 2000s.

Notes

1   My database has information on leave regulations, childcare coverage rates and transfer benefits from the beginning of the 1990s until 2009. While data on maternity and parental leaves are available over time, it is often not differentiated between unpaid and paid periods and/or the periods are added. Yet to understand the impact of leave policies on maternal employment it is necessary to know whether a leave is paid and at what rate and whether the rates differ between periods. To my knowledge, there is no longitudinal database that covers the development of childcare coverage rates. These data are, however, essential to know a state's efforts in providing childcare. These data are especially scarce for the period before the mid-2000s. I therefore drew on national statistics and national reports. This enables a more coherent picture on the development of coverage rates within a country.

2 Policies that support the reconciliation of care responsibilities and employment also exist in the area of care for the elderly or other dependents, but are not part of the analysis.
3 Certainly, lone parents are also affected by policies which support one or another work-family model.
4 Even though, as Crouch (1999) has noted, arranging caring responsibilities and employment has been an issue for families, and mothers in particular, since the differentiation of production and reproduction spheres in the process of industrialization.
5 There are also mixed forms on the spectrum between the male-breadwinner and the dual-earner model, such as the one-and–a-half-earner model in which the family consists of a (male) main earner and a (female) part-time worker who is also responsible for care and housework (Crompton 1999a). The market version of the dual-earner model, i.e. when services are not provided publicly but privately, may lead to class inequalities, as only the better-off are in a position to pay for good-quality childcare.
6 Focusing exclusively on the degree to which policies shape and acknowledge care work, Leitner argues that familialistic policies are those policies that oblige (and enable) the family to meet the care needs of a family member and which reinforce the care recipient's dependency on his or her family. De-familialization means taking away caring obligations and reducing the dependency on family members.
7 I am aware of the fact that the couple usually makes decisions concerning care and employment, not the woman alone. However, the issue will be predominantly discussed from a mother's point of view owing to the fact that in reality it is the mother who takes up (the longest part of the) leave.
8 The effects of a leave scheme also seem to depend on women's education and position on the labor market. For example, it has been argued that a too short leave more likely impacts negatively on better-educated women's fertility. Also, low-educated women with low-paid jobs more likely leave the labor market than better-educated women (for a discussion of the empirical evidence, see Saraceno 2011b).
9 Another critical view focuses on employer-driven flexibility and needs. When part-time employment is used by employers for more flexible and efficient production patterns, it opens the way for cost reductions, where employers could save on wages, benefits and training costs (Lind and Rasmussen 2008).
10 Even though they may be places provided on a part-time or on a full-time basis. This makes a difference. Moreover, as Saraceno (2011a) notes, caring and supervision needs of children do not end when they reach school age. However, work-family arrangements are decided when a child is born, and the early years have long-term consequences.
11 Some countries also provide paternity leave. In these cases, fathers are allowed to take off some days around the time of birth in the name of gender equality in parenthood and of acknowledging some care responsibilities also to fathers. Where such a scheme exists, the period is usually two weeks at most (European Commission 2005, Moss and Korintus 2008: 79ff.).
12 The first (unpaid) scheme was introduced in Switzerland in 1877, Germany followed in 1878 and Austria in 1884 (Gauthier 1996: 51f.).
13 Directive 96/34/EC has set minimum standards regarding the duration (three months after the birth of a child for both female and male employees) and recommended to include rules regarding flexible use and the continuation of social security contributions. The entitlement might be dependent on previous work experience.
14 Italian parents are only entitled to six months each. If the mother uses six months and the father uses at least three months, he is entitled to one more month.
15 In the European context, it is important to keep in mind the cross-country differences in what constitutes part time. The official definition as put forward by the ILO or Eurostat is that "part-time employees are persons whose usual hours of work are less than the normal working hours" (http://stats.oecd.org/glossary/detail.asp?ID=1863; access

date: 10.07.2009). Yet part-time workers in Sweden might be employed for 30 hours a week, while in Germany or the Netherlands, a part-time worker might work less than 20 hours a week.
16 A one-fifth working-time reduction with a duration of five years over the whole career is also available.
17 Research has shown, however, that there are partly significant differences between full-time and part-time wages. Bardasi and Gornick (2008) investigated female part- and full-time workers in six OECD countries and found a part-time wage penalty of 11.5 percent in Canada, 20.8 percent in the United States and Italy, 10 percent in the United Kingdom and 9 percent in Germany, along with a 2.7 percent advantage in Sweden.
18 After parental leave, German parents are entitled to return to a full-time position (see http://www.bmfsfj.de/bmfsfj/generator/BMFSFJ/Service/rechner,did=16318.html; access date: 03.11.2009). In Sweden, even though a right to part-time employment does not exist, the government proposed a bill in 2006 regarding a right to full-time employment, not least in reaction to findings that pointed to the rather high share of involuntary part-time working women (see Hellmark 2006). The bill was not approved.
19 National terms for day nurseries are, e.g. Vuggestue (DK), Krippe (DE), Escuela Infantil 0–3 (ES), Créche collective (FR), Asilo nido (IT).
20 National terms for play groups are, e.g. Deltidsgruppe/Öppna förskolar (SE), Playgroup (UK), Peuterspeelzaal (NL).
21 National terms for family day care are, e.g. Child minder (UK), Dagpleje (DK), Familedaghem (SE), Tagesmutter/Pflegenester (DE), Créche Familiale (FR), Assistante maternelle (FR), Gastouder (NL), Ama (PT), Perhepäivähoito/Kolmiperhehoito (FI).
22 Since the 2000s, national statistics throughout Europe increasingly put an effort in providing reliable and comparable data on childcare. Still, however, the cross-country and time comparison should be handled with caution. The use of the available data requires a conversion to common standards in order to compare nation-specific constellations of childcare arrangements (see the variety of facilities noted earlier). In 2003, the European Survey on Income and Living Conditions (EU-Silc) survey was launched. This survey, which is now conducted in all EU member states, aims at providing comparable annual data on the use of formal childcare services "defined as preschool or equivalent, compulsory education, centre-based services outside school hours, a collective crèche or another day-care centre, including family day-care organised/controlled by a public or private structure" (European Commission's Expert Group on Gender and Employment Issues (EGGE) 2009: 29). Many studies on childcare rely on this source. Yet, as the definition shows, the figures include all forms of childcare; do not distinguish between public, publicly financed, and private care; and are based neither on enrolment nor on coverage, but on survey data collected for different purposes. Therefore, neither reliability nor comparability of the indicators is fully given (Keck and Saraceno 2011).
23 In Finland, all children, starting from the age of ten months, have had a right to a childcare place since 1990.
24 Since 2001, Swedish children who are older than one year and whose parents are in higher education, (un)employed or on parental leave have a right to be cared for in a day-care facility. Before 2001, only children of working or studying parents were entitled to a childcare place (Skolverket 2000).
25 Danish children aged nine months (six months before 2005) to six years are entitled to a place in a day care facility. As of 1998, the admission to a place is no longer based on a concrete assessment of (employment) needs, but it is rather stated that all children have equal access.
26 That 100% coverage is not reached in those countries could be due to other factors, too. In Denmark, for example, parents who decided to take a one-year leave in addition to parental leave did not enjoy the right to a childcare place before the child turned three years old (Ministry of Social Affairs 2000).

27 In eastern Germany full-day care is more common.
28 Fees are the gross amounts charged to parents of two children (aged two and three) for one month of full-time care, i.e. after any subsidies paid to the provider but before any childcare-related benefits for parents. Average wage refers to the gross earnings of an average worker (AW) as calculated by the OECD (OECD 2007b: 186ff.).
29 This is a rather low household income, though. The OECD calculation of the average wage of a single person is €22,662 in 2005 (OECD 2007b). When there are two earners, income is higher and therefore also the fee is substantially higher (and it is more difficult to get a place in a publicly financed institution).
30 Based on an analysis of the background reports and country notes from the OECD *Starting Strong* Project using Bennett's (2005) curriculum coding scheme, Jensen (2009) divides countries into two categories: following either a readiness-for-school-curriculum tradition or a social-pedagogical-curriculum tradition. Examples of the former tradition, which is characterized by an emphasis on focused cognitive goals in mathematical development, language and literacy skills, are Belgium, France, Ireland, Italy, the Netherlands, Portugal and the United Kingdom. Examples following the social-pedagogical-curriculum tradition characterized by an emphasis on overall development, including social competence and emotional well-being, are Austria, Denmark, Finland, Germany and Sweden.
31 Portugal only allows unrestricted income splitting if the second earner earns at least 5 percent of the total household income. Thus the pure male-breadwinner model is not supported.
32 Please note that the difference in net transfers to government between male-breadwinner families and dual-earner families is considerably smaller for families with lower incomes in Germany (see the information on the neutrality of tax/benefit systems provided by the OECD Family Database).

References

Alber, Jens. 1995. "A Framework of the Comparative Study of Social Services." *Journal of European Social Policy* 5 (2):131–149.
Alber, Jens. 1996. "Selectivity, Universalism, and the Politics of Welfare Retrenchment in Germany and the United States." 92nd Annual Meeting of the American Political Science Association, Panel 12.5: Inequality and Universalism, San Francisco, 31 August, 1996.
Anderson, Patricia M., and Philip B. Levine. 2000. "Child Care and Mothers' Employment Decisions." In *Finding Jobs: Work and Welfare Reform*, edited by David E. Card and Rebecca M. Blank, 420–462. New York: Russel Sage Foundation.
Bahle, Thomas. 2008. "Family Policy Patterns in the Enlarged EU." In *Handbook of Quality of Life in the Enlarged European Union*, edited by Jens Alber, Tony Fahey and Chiara Saraceno, 100–126. London/New York: Routledge.
Bailleau, Guillaume. 2008. L'accueil collectif et en crèches familiales des enfants de moins de 6 ans en 2006. Enquête annuelle auprès des services de PMI. In *Document de travail*: Direction de la recherche, des études, de l'évaluation et des statistiques DREES.
Bardasi, Elena, and Janet C. Gornick. 2008. "Working for Less? Women's Part-Time Wage Penalties across Countries." *Feminist Economics* 14 (1):37–72.
Bennett, John. 2005. "Curriculum Issues in National Policymaking." *European Early Childhood Education Research Journal* 13 (2):5–23.
Blau, Francine D., and Marianne A. Ferber. 1992. *The Economics of Women, Men, and Work*. Englewood Cliffs: Prentice-Hall.
Blome, Agnes, Wolfgang Keck, and Jens Alber. 2009. *Family and the Welfare State. Intergenerational Relations in Ageing Societies*. Cheltenham/Northampton: Edward Elgar.

Boeckmann, Irene, Joya Misra, and Michelle Budig. 2015. "Cultural and Institutional Factors Shaping Mothers' Employment and Working Hours in Postindustrial Countries." *Social Forces* 93 (4):1301–1333.
Bosch, Nicole, Anja Deelen, and Rob Euwal. 2008. "Is Part-time Employment Here To Stay? Evidence from the Dutch Labour Force Survey 1992–2005." In *IZA Discussion Paper No. 3367*. Bonn.
Büchel, Felix, and Katharina C. Spieß. 2002. "Kindertageseinrichtungen und Müttererwerbstätigkeit – Neue Ergebnisse zu einem bekannten Zusammenhang." *Vierteljahreshefte zur Wirtschaftsforschung* 71 (1):96–114.
Centraal Bureau voor de Statistiek. 2006. *Emancipatiemonitor 2006. Veranderingen in de leefsituatie en levensloop.* Den Haag. https://www.scp.nl/Publicaties/Alle_publicaties/Publicaties_2006/Emancipatiemonitor_2006.
Centraal Bureau voor de Statistiek. 2008. *Emancipatiemonitor 2008. Veranderingen in de leefsituatie en levensloop.* Den Haag: http://www.cbs.nl/NR/rdonlyres/DBA567B8-83E9-4BE2-9139-099DA9D25F44/0/Emancipatiemonitor2008.pdf.
Clasen, Jochen, and Daniel Clegg. 2007. "Levels and Levers of Conditionality: Measuring Change within Welfare States." In *Investigating Welfare State Change. The 'Dependent Variable Problem' in Comparative Analysis*, edited by Jochen Clasen and Nico A. Siegel, 166–197. Cheltenham/Northampton: Edward Elgar.
Clasen, Jochen, and Nico A. Siegel, eds. 2007. *Investigating Welfare State Change. The 'Dependent Variable Problem' in Comparative Analysis.* Cheltenham/Northampton: Edward Elgar.
Cleveland, Gordon, and Michael Krashinsky. 2004. *Financing ECEC Services in OECD Countries.* Paris: OECD.
Crompton, Rosemary. 1999a. "Discussions and Conclusions." In *Restructuring Gender Relations and Employment. The Decline of the Male Breadwinner*, edited by Rosemary Crompton. Oxford: Oxford University Press, 201–214.
Crompton, Rosemary, ed. 1999b. *Restructuring Gender Relations and Employment. The Decline of the Male Breadwinner.* Oxford: Oxford University Press.
Crouch, Colin. 1999. *Social Change in Western Europe.* Oxford: Oxford University Press.
Danmarks statistic. 2007. Stort set alle 3–5-årige passes ude. http://www.dst.dk/pukora/epub/Nyt/2007/NR077.pdf.
de Henau, Jérome, Danièle Meulders, and Síle D'Orchai. 2006. "The Childcare Triad? Indicators Assessing Three Fields of Child Policies for Working Mothers in the EU-15." *Journal of Comparative Policy Analysis* 8 (2):129–148.
del Boca, Daniela, and Daniela Vuri. 2007. "The Mismatch between Employment and Child Care in Italy: The Impact of Rationing." *Journal of Population Economics* 20 (4):805–832.
Dingeldey, Irene. 2000. "Einkommenssteuersysteme und familiale Erwerbsmuster im europäischen Vergleich." In *Erwerbstätigkeit und Familie in Steuer- und Sozialversicherungssystemen. Begünstigungen und Belastungen verschiedener familialer Erwerbsmuster im Ländervergleich*, edited by Irene Dingeldey, 11–47. Opladen: Leske + Budrich.
European Commission. 1995. *MISSOC. Social Protection in the Member States of the European Union.* Luxemburg: Directorate-General for Employment and Social Affairs.
European Commission. 2005. *Reconciliation of Work and Private Life: A Comparative Review of Thirty European Countries.* Luxembourg: Office for Official Publications of the European Communities.
European Commission. 2007. MISSOC. Social protection in the Member States of the European Union, of the European Economic Area and in Switzerland. Comparative Tables. Brussels: http://ec.europa.eu/employment_social/spsi/missoc_tables_de.htm.

European Commission. 2009. Eurybase. The Information Database on Education Systems in Europe. European Commission, Directorate-General for Education and Culture. http://eacea.ec.europa.eu/portal/page/portal/Eurydice/EuryCountry.
European Commission's Expert Group on Gender and Employment Issues (EGGE). 2009. *The Provision of Childcare Services. A Comparative Review of 30 European Countries.* Luxembourg: European Commission.
Eurostat. 2004. *Development of a Methodology for the Collection of Harmonised Statistics on Childcare.* Luxembourg: European Commission.
Evertsson, Marie, and Ann-Zofie Duvander. 2011. "Parental Leave-Possibility or Trap? Does Family Leave Length Effect Swedish Women's Labour Market Opportunities?" *European Sociological Review* 27 (4):435–450. doi: 10.1093/esr/jcq018.
Ferrera, Maurizio. 1996. "Il modello Sud-europeo di Welfare State." *Rivista Italiana Di Scienza Politica* 26 (1):67–101.
Fortunati, Aldo. 2002. I servizi educativi per la prima infanzia. In *Quaderni del centro nazionale di documentazione e analisi per l'infanzia e l'adolescenza.* Firenze: Istituto degli Innocenti.
Fuchs, Michael. 2006. Kinderbetreuungsplätze in Österreich. "Fehlen keine oder bis zu 650.000?" Bedarfsanalysen 2005–2015 im Auftrag der Industriellenvereinigung. Occasional Reports Series Vol. 3 Vienna: Europäisches Zentrum für Wohlfahrtspolitik und Sozialforschung.
Gauthier, Anne H. 1996. *The state and the family.* Oxford: Clarendon Press.
Gornick, Janet C., and Marcia K. Meyers. 2003. *Families That Work. Policies for Reconciling Parenthood and Employment.* New York: Russel Sage Foundation.
Gornick, Janet C., and Marcia K. Meyers. 2008. "Creating Gender Egalitarian Societies: An Agenda for Reform." *Politics & Society* 36 (3):313–349. doi: 10.1177/0032329208320562.
Green-Pedersen, Christoffer. 2007. "More than Data Questions and Methodological Issues: Theoretical Conceptualization and the Dependent Variable 'Problem' in the Study of Welfare Reform." In *Investigating Welfare State Change. The 'Dependent Variable Problem' in Comparative Analysis,* edited by Jochen Clasen and Nico A. Siegel, 13–23. Cheltenham/Northampton: Edward Elgar.
Grunow, Daniela, Silke Aisenbrey, and Marie Evertsson. 2011. "Familienpolitik, Bildung und Berufskarrieren von Müttern in Deutschland, USA und Schweden." *KZfSS Kölner Zeitschrift für Soziologie und Sozialpsychologie* 63 (3):395–430. doi: 10.1007/s11577-011-0139-0.
Hegewisch, Ariane, and Janet C. Gornick. 2008. *Statutory Routes to Workplace Flexibility in Cross-National Perspective.* Institute for Women's Policy Research. Washington, DC.
Hellmark, Ann-Britt. 2006. Part-time Employment an Issue for Policymakers. http://www.eurofound.europa.eu/eiro/2006/02/feature/se0602103f.htm: Access date: 11.7.2009.
Hernes, Helga Maria. 1987. *Welfare State and Woman Power. Essays in State Feminism.* Oslo: Norwegian University Press.
Hofferth, Sandra L., and Nancy Collins. 2000. "Child Care and Employment Turnover." *Population Research and Policy Review* 19 (4):357–395.
Instituto Nacional de Estadistica. 2011. Participación en la Educación. Cursos 1991–92 a 2008–09. http://www.ine.es/daco/daco42/sociales10/sociales.htm.
Istituto degli Innocenti di Firenze. 2009. Diritti in crescita. http://www.minori.it/down/pdf/3_4_rapporto_Governo_convenzione_Onu.pdf.
Jaumotte, Florence. 2003. Female Labour Force Participation: Past Trends and Main Determinants in OECD Countries. In *OECD Economics Department Working Papers No. 376*: OECD Publishing.

Jensen, Carsten. 2009. "ESPAnet/JESP Doctoral Researcher Prize Essay: Institutions and the politics of childcare services." *Journal of European Social Policy* 19 (1):7–18. doi: 10.1177/0958928708098520.

Kamerman, Sheila B., and Alfred J. Kahn. 1981. *Child Care, Family Benefits, and Working Parents. A Study in Comparative Policy*. New York: Columbia University Press.

Keck, Wolfgang, and Chiara Saraceno. 2011. Comparative Childcare Statistics in Europe. Conceptual and Methodological Fallacies. In *Multilinks Insights No. 1*. http://multilinksdatabase.wzb.eu/pdf/insight-no-1.pdf.

Korpi, Walter. 2000. "Faces of Inequality: Gender, Class and Patterns of Inequality in Different Types of Welfare States." *Social Politics* 7 (2):127–91.

Lalive, Rafael, and Josef Zweimüller. 2009. "How Does Parental Leave Affect Fertility and Return to Work? Evidence from Two Natural Experiments." *The Quarterly Journal of Economics* 124 (3):1363–1402. doi: 10.1162/qjec.2009.124.3.1363.

Leiber, Simone. 2005. *Europäische Sozialpolitik und nationale Sozialpartnerschaft*. Frankfurt/New York: Campus Verlag.

Leira, Arnlaug. 1993. "Mothers, Markets and the State: A Scandinavian Model?" *Journal of Social Policy* 22 (3):329–347.

Leitner, Sigrid. 2003. "Varieties of Familialism. The Caring Function of the Family in Comparative Perspective." *European Societies* 5 (4):353–375.

Lewis, Jane. 1992. "Gender and the Development of Welfare Regimes." *Journal of European Social Policies* 2 (3):159–173.

Lewis, Jane. 1997. "Gender and Welfare Regimes: Further Thoughts." *Social Politics* 4 (2):160–177. doi: 10.1093/sp/4.2.160.

Lewis, Jane. 2001. "The Decline of the Male Breadwinner Model: Implications for Work and Care." *Social Politics* 8 (2):152–169.

Lewis, Jane. 2009. *Work-Family Balance, Gender and Policy*. Cheltenham/Northampton: Edward Elgar.

Lind, Jens, and Erling Rasmussen. 2008. "Paradoxical Patterns of Part-Time Employment in Denmark?" *Economic and Industrial Democracy* 29 (4):521–540. doi: 10.1177/0143831x08096226.

Lister, Ruth. 1997. *Citizenship. Feminist Perspectives*. New York: New York University Press.

Madama, Ilaria. 2010. *Le politiche di assistenza sociale*. Bologna: il Mulino.

McLaughlin, Eithne, and Caroline Glendinning. 1994. "Paying for Care in Europe: Is There a Feminist Approach?" In *Family Policy and the Welfare of Women*, edited by Linda Hantrais and Steen Mangen, 52–69. Loughborough: University of Loughborough.

Meulders, Danièle, and Sîle O'Dorchai. 2008. Childcare in Belgium. In *DULBEA Working Paper N°08–08.RR*. Bruxelles.

Ministry of Social Affairs. 2000. *Early Childhood Education and Care Policy in Denmark – Background Report*. OECD: http://www.oecd.org/dataoecd/48/37/2475168.pdf.

Moss, Peter. 2015. International Review of Leave Policies and Research 2015. http://www.leavenetwork.org/lp_and_r_reports/.

Moss, Peter, and Marta Korintus. 2008. "International Review of Leave Policies and Related Research 2008." In *Employment Relations Research Series No. 100*. London.

Naldini, Manuela. 2003. *The Family in the Mediterranean Welfare States*. London: Frank Cass Publishers.

Naldini, Manuela. 2011. "Introduction. Feminist Views on Social Policy and Gender Equality. Symposium / Gender and Welfare State. A Feminist Debate." *Sociologica* 1/2011:1–10.

OECD. 2001. *Employment Outlook*. Paris: Organisation for Economic Co-operation and Development.
OECD. 2006. *Starting Strong II. Early Childhood Education and Care*. Paris: Organisation for Economic Co-operation and Development,.
OECD. 2007a. *Babies and Bosses. Reconciling Work and Family Life. A Synthesis of Findings for OECD Countries*. Paris: OECD Publishing.
OECD. 2007b. *Benefits and Wages 2007. OECD Indicators*. Paris: OECD Publishing.
OECD. 2007c. *Modernising Social Policy for the New Life Course*. Paris: OECD Publishing.
OECD. 2008a. *OECD Family Database*. http://www.oecd.org/document/4/0,3343, en_2649_34819_37836996_1_1_1_1,00.html.
OECD. 2008b. *Taxing Wages, 2006–2007*. Paris: OECD.
Orloff, Ann Shola. 1993. "Gender and the Social Rights of Citizenship: The Comparative Analysis of Gender Relations and Welfare State." *American Sociological Review* 58 (3):303–328.
Ostner, Ilona, and Jane Lewis. 1995. "Gender and the Evolution of European Social Policies." In *European Social Policy: Between Fragmentation and Integration*, edited by Stephan Leibfried and Paul Pierson, 159–193. Washington, DC: Brookings Institution Press.
Pateman, Carole. 1989. *The Disorder of Women. Democracy, Feminism and Political Theory*. Cambridge: The Policy Press.
Pylkkänen, Elina, and Nina Smith. 2003. "Career Interruptions due to Parental Leave: A Comparative Study of Denmark and Sweden." In *OCED Social, Employment and Migration Working Paper No. 1*. OECD Publishing.
Randall, Vicky. 2000. "Childcare Policy in the European States: Limits to Convergence." *Journal of European Public Policy* 7 (3):346–368.
Ribar, David C. 1995. "A Structural Model of Child Care and the Labor Supply of Married Women." *Journal of Labor Economics* 13 (3):558–597.
Rostgaard, Tine. 2000. "Developing Comparable Indicators in Early Childhood Education and Care." In *Working Paper OECD Thematic of Review Early Childhood Education and Care*.
Rubery, Jill, Mark Smith, and Colette Fagan. 1999. *Women's Employment in Europe: Trends and Prospects*. London: Routledge.
Rubery, Jill, Mark Smith, Colette Fagan, and Damian Grimshaw. 1997. *Women and European Employment*. London: Routledge.
Ruhm, Christopher J. 1998. "The Economic Consequences of Parental Leave Mandates: Lessons from Europe." *The Quarterly Journal of Economics* 113:285–317.
Sabatinelli, Stefania. 2008. "Local differences and social inequalities in access to childcare options. A comparison between and within Italy and France". *Working papers du Programme Villes & territoires*, 2008/1, Paris, Sciences Po: http://blogs.sciences-po.fr/recherche-villes/files/2010/05/Sabatinelli.pdf.
Sainsbury, Diane. 1996. *Gender, Equality and Welfare States*. Cambridge: Cambridge University Press.
Saraceno, Chiara. 1997. "Family Change, Family Policies and the Restructuring of Welfare." In *Family, Market and Community*, edited by OECD, 81–100. Paris: Organisation for Economic Co-operation and Development.
Saraceno, Chiara. 2003. "La conciliazione di responsibilità familiarie attività lavorative in Italia: Paradossi ed equilibri imperfetti." *Polis* 17 (2):199–228.
Saraceno, Chiara. 2011a. "Childcare Needs and Childcare Policies: A Multidimensional Issue." *Current Sociology* 59 (1):78–96. doi: 10.1177/0011392110385971.

Saraceno, Chiara. 2011b. Gender (in)equality: An Incomplete Revolution? Cross EU Similarities and Differences in the Gender Specific Impact of Parenthood. Discussion Paper 13, 03/2011. Harriet Taylor Mill – Institut für Ökonomie und Geschlechterforschung, Hochschule für Wirtschaft und Recht. Berlin.

Saraceno, Chiara, and Wolfgang Keck. 2010. "Can we Identify Intergenerational Policy Regimes in Europe?" *European Societies* 5:675–696.

Schönberg, Uta, and Johannes Ludsteck. 2007. "Maternity Leave Legislation, Female Labor Supply, and the Family Wage Gap." In *IZA Discussion Paper No. 2699*. Bonn.

Scruggs, Lyle. 2007. "Welfare State Generosity Across Space and Time." In *Investigating Welfare State Change. The 'Dependent Variable Problem' in Comparative Analsis*, edited by Jochen Clasen and Nico A. Siegel, 133–165. Cheltenham/Northampton: Edward Elgar.

Service central de la statistique et des études économiques (STATEC) Luxembourg. 2010. Élèves et enseignants dans l'éducation précoce 1998–2009 http://www.statistiques. public.lu/stat/ReportFolders/ReportFolder.aspx?IF_Language=fra&MainTheme=3&Fl drName=6&RFPath=58.

Siim, Birte. 1987. "The Scandinavian Welfare States – Towards Sexual Equality or a New Kind of Male Domination." *Acta Sociologica* 30 (3/4):250–277.

Skolverket. 2000. Childcare in Sweden. http://www.skolverket.se/content/1/c4/09/44/00-531.pdf: Access date: 2.7.2009.

Skolverket. 2005. "Childcare in Sweden." Last Modified 10 February 2005 http://www.skolverket.se/sb/d/190: Access date 11.12.2006.

Skolverket. 2010. Förskola – Barn och grupper – Riksnivå. www.Skolverket.se.

Smith, Nina, Shirley Dex, Jan Dirk Vlasblom, and Tim Callan. 2003. "The Effects of Taxation on Married Women's Labour Supply across Four Countries." *Oxford Economic Papers* 55 (3):417–439. doi: 10.1093/oep/55.3.417.

Spiess, C. Katharina, and Katharina Wrohlich. 2008. "Parental Leave Benefit Reform in Germany: Costs and Labour Market Outcomes of Moving towards the Nordic Model." *Population Research and Policy Review* 27 (5):575–591.

Starke, Peter. 2008. *Radical Welfare State Retrenchment. A Comparative Analysis*. Basingstoke: Palgrave MacMillan.

Statistik Austria. 2011. Kindertagesheimstatistik, Bevölkerungsregister. Erstellt am 31.05.2010. http://www.statistik.at/web_de/statistiken/bildung_und_kultur/formales_ bildungswesen/kindertagesheime_kinderbetreuung/021659.html.

Statistisches Bundesamt. 2004. Kindertagesbetreuung in Deutschland. Einrichtungen, Plätze, Personal und Kosten 1990 bis 2002. Wiesbaden.

Statistisches Bundesamt. 2009. Kindertagesbetreuung regional 2008. Ein Vergleich aller 429 Kreise in Deutschland. Wiesbaden: http://www.destatis.de/jetspeed/portal/cms/ Sites/destatis/Internet/DE/Navigation/Publikationen/Fachveroeffentlichungen/Soziallei stungen,templateId=renderPrint.psml__nnn=true.

Toto, Tiziana. 2007. *Gli asili nido comunali in Italia, tra caro retta e liste di attesa. Dossier a cura dell'Osservatorio prezzi & tariffe di Cittadinanzattiva*. Roma: http://www.cittadinanzattiva.it/il-punto-archivio-comunicazione/3855-asili-nido-comunali-in-italia-tra-caro-rette-e-liste-di-attesa.html (download 13.05.2010).

Viitanen, Tarja K. 2005. "Costs of Child Care and Female Employment in England." *Labour* 19 (special edition):149–170.

Wrohlich, Katharina. 2004. "Child Care Costs and Mothers' Labor Supply. An Empirical Analysis for Germany." DIW Discussion Paper No. 412. Berlin.

Ziefle, Andrea. 2004. "Die individuellen Kosten des Erziehungsurlaubs: Eine empirische Analyse der kurz- und längerfristigen Folgen für den Karriereverlauf von Frauen" *Kölner Zeitschrift für Soziologie und Sozialpsychologie* 56 (2):213–231.

4 Policy developments in Germany and Italy
From a shared focus on the male-breadwinner model to diverging paths after the 1990s

The previous chapter outlined the variety of work-family policies in Europe and the changes during the last two decades. This chapter will go further into detail and compare the legal regulations regarding work-family reconciliation across time in Germany and Italy. Describing the relevant historical developments in the first part of the chapter serves for a better understanding of the starting situation in 1990 and the subsequent (non)changes.

It will be shown that Germany and Italy pursued fairly similar work-family policy paths for a long time. Before and during World War II, both the German and the Italian fascist states established pronatalist policies which also aimed at discouraging mothers' employment. After the collapse of the systems, both states[1] abstained from such policies. However, as will be demonstrated, the experience with fascism continued to have an effect, as state support of working mothers did not play a role in welfare state development for a long time. After both Germany and Italy further strengthened the male-breadwinner model after World War II, they were then concerned with adapting their family laws to achieve gender equality in the married couple in the 1970s. Yet a comprehensive set of work-family policies that would support a dual-earner model did not follow suit. This led to similar starting situations of both countries in the beginning of the 1990s.

The second part deals with a more detailed description of the post-1990 reforms to parental leave, working-time arrangements and childcare. The chapter concludes with a comparison of the reforms in both countries between 1990 and 2008. It shows how both countries have diverged in their approaches to work-family reconciliation policies. The comparison of *what* has happened serves as the basis for the subsequent chapters, which deal with the question of *why* reforms took place or not.

Family law and policies during and after fascism

Establishing the male-breadwinner model in western Germany

After the fascist takeover in 1933, the Weimar Constitution (*Weimarer Reichsverfassung*) of 1919 remained in force. It was the first German (and European) constitution that codified the protection of marriage and the family (Gerlach 2010). It defined marriage as the basis of a family. Marriage was to be explicitly protected within society and supported through state measures. However, during the era of National Socialism, families were not able to make use of their right to protection because of a functional redefinition of the family in national-socialist terms. The new definition saw the family as the basis for the preservation and reproduction of the German nation. The family was delineated as the basic part of the state and could, therefore, by definition, no longer be protected against the state (Gerlach 2010). Moreover, the Nazis introduced population policies that had the explicit aim of quantitatively "improving" the German population by implementing selective racist policies. These policies included the prohibition of marriage between so-called Aryan and non-Aryan partners according to the Nuremberg racial laws (*Nürnberger Rassengesetze*) and enforced the sterilization of persons classified as inferior. On the other hand, policies were adopted that promoted the birth of many children to German parents, e.g. marriage loans that could be redeemed with the birth of the fourth child, children's allowances for the fifth (and later for the third) child as well as tax reductions for dependent spouses and children. Mothers who bore four and more children received the Mother's Cross (*Mutterkreuz*), which served as a distinction in a similar manner to the Knight's Cross. At the same time, the exclusion of women from the labor market was supported through transfer benefits (Gerlach 2010).

After 1945, the occupying powers in Germany aimed to repeal all regulations that were associated with the Nazi regime. Owing to the close linkage between policies for families and national-socialist ethics, both children's allowances and family-related tax deductions were abolished and no further measures were adopted that would support families (Gerlach 2004, Langer-El Sayed 1980).

In 1948, the three Western allies charged the Parliamentary Council (*Parlamentarischer Rat*) with the development of a Basic Law (*Grundgesetz*) for Germany on the basis of recommendations of the members of the Convention of Herrenchiemsee (*Herrenchiemsee-Konvent 10.-23.08.1948*). The final version established marriage and the family as being under special protection.[2] In contrast to the Weimar Constitution, an imperative to explicitly support the family was not mentioned. However, the obligation to protect the family has been understood both as a right of defense against the state intrusion into privacy and as an imperative to provide measures for the family (Moeller 1993). Moreover, marriage was not defined as the basis of a family, yet the Basic Law's wording linked the two institutions. The effect was a "primacy of marriage" in West German family policies, i.e. legal or political action for families has been linked to married couples rather than to parents with children.

The German Civil Code of 1900 that regulated the relationship between men and women in a marriage remained unchanged at first. It prescribed, among other issues, a gender division of work. By law, husbands were the single earners and wives were responsible for housekeeping. In their role as the *Familienoberhaupt*, husbands had the sole decision-making power in all matters of the family. In line with this rule, wives needed the permission of their husbands to take up paid employment and husbands had the right to terminate their wives' employment without notice. Yet when article 3, paragraph 2 was included into the Basic Law in 1949, the Civil Code had to be adjusted to bring it into line with the Basic Law.

Against strong opposition in parliament, but supported vigorously by women's organizations, female parliamentarian Elisabeth Selbert of the Social Democratic Party was able to push through this article. It maintains that all persons shall be equal before the law and that men and women shall have equal rights. The Federal Court ruled in 1953 that all regulations which contradicted the second paragraph of article 3 were void. However, it took the legislator four years to bring in the "law on equal opportunities for men and women" (*Gesetz über die Gleichberechtigung von Mann und Frau*). It abolished the paragraph on the sole decision-making power of men regarding matters of the family and the husband's right to terminate his wife's employment without notice. It also assigned parental custody to both the mother and the father. Several original regulations, such as the wives' duty to do housekeeping and the necessity of a husband's consent to take up paid employment, however, remained in place, and the living situations of women and men were far from equal.

The years after the foundation of the Federal Republic of Germany (FRG) in 1949 were characterized by a gradual increase and institutionalization of policies directed at families. In 1953, a Ministry for Family Affairs was set up.[3] Children's allowances were introduced in 1954 and made part of the dual family-support system (*dualer Familienlastenausgleich*).[4] The allowances were amended several times until the end of the Christian-Liberal coalition governments in 1969.[5] Another important law that affected the families' income situations introduced the income splitting for the taxation of spouses in 1958. As described in Chapter 3, splitting is associated with reduced incentives for the partner to take up employment or to increase his or her earnings because s/he will be faced with higher marginal tax rates under a progressive taxation scheme in contrast to individual taxation. A further field of family support was the promotion of housing, in particular owning homes. Housing subsidies, which have been both related to income and number of children since 1965, were additionally given. Moreover, maternity leave was expanded in both duration – two more weeks after delivery – and in remuneration, i.e. a benefit of 25 DM was granted for each calendar day (Gerlach 2010).[6] Furthermore, dependent spouses and children continued to be entitled to free co-insurance and derived rights within the accident, health and pension insurance schemes (Rust 1990). In order to profit from these benefits, two preconditions had to be fulfilled: first, a couple had to be married and second, the husband needed to be in dependent employment.

The predominant focus on cash benefits mirrors the ideal of the male-breadwinner who earns a "family wage" and makes it possible for the wife to stay at home. It was shared across parties and became widely accepted in the 1950s (von Oertzen and Rietzschel 1998). With respect to the provision of extra-familial childcare, not only men but also women members of parliament and the representatives of women's interests (e.g. the SPD and DGB departments of women's affairs) saw extra-familial childcare only as a supplementary social assistance measure. In their view, wages should be high enough to feed a family. Ongoing attention to children by mothers was seen as necessary for the healthy development of their children;[7] according to this perspective, they should not be forced by economic need to take up paid employment (Hagemann 2006).

Establishing the male-breadwinner model in Italy

In Italy, the period of fascist dictatorship lasted from 1922 to 1943. The Italian family law under fascism was grounded in *Pisanelli*'s civil code of 1865,[8] which established the primacy of the male head of the household (*capofamiglia*) while stipulating a large number of "obliged kin" in case of financial need. The fascist civil code of 1942 further strengthened the view of the function of the family as being primarily the "organic basis of the corporatist society, charged with superior purposes, and centralized on the head of the family" (Naldini 2003: 73). At the same time, the regime weakened the family's position towards the state as it declared the family a 'social and political institution' and, hence, family interests as subordinate to the state's interests.

The Mussolini regime was concerned about declining fertility rates and ideologically supported the patriarchal family. To impede the decline of the population, it introduced a rather comprehensive set of policies. In fact, the fascist regime is responsible for the first explicit policies towards families in Italy, and, as Naldini (2003) notes, "[. . .] fascist social policies would long remain (and still remain) the only systematic family policy that Italy has ever known." (Naldini 2003: 67). As in Germany, family allowances (*assegni familiari*, introduced in 1934) were the core of the pronatalist policies of the Mussolini regime. The policies rewarded only those in dependent employment, and benefits were paid to household heads[9] and inversely proportional to their wages. Women were expected to have children and to do house and care work. Higher education for women was discouraged. It was possible to dismiss women from work when they married and had children, and they were barred from many jobs as well as higher job positions. Disincentives to women's work, however, did not refer to work in agriculture or in the home (*lavoro a domicilio*) or work as servants for other families. This had been the kind of work were most female workers were concentrated and which was the least protected in terms of contracts and social security. Fascist hostility towards working women mainly concerned urban, educated women of the middle class – that is, women who were starting to have fewer children. Social benefits for married mothers in the form of derived rights were introduced or expanded in other policy areas such as pension or health insurance. In 1939, birth premiums (*premi di natalità*) for dependent workers replaced the hitherto existing maternity leave payment benefit[10] and signaled a shift from protecting pregnant women to encouraging large families. Fathers became the de facto recipients, because they outnumbered female dependent employed (Saraceno 1991).

The benefits of that time were seen as a "family wage" that was thought to encourage fatherhood through income support and promote the reproductive role of women with, as in western Germany, the aim of reproducing the "race". By giving support to fathers while weakening women's position in the labor market, the fascist regime ideologically supported the patriarchal family. The only "acceptable" working sphere for women (who were not yet supported through maternity protection) was seen in agriculture or work within the home, because that would not take them away from where they belongs: the home (Naldini 2003).

After World War II and the demise of Mussolini's regime, a democratic-republican regime was established. A new constitution (*La Costituzione della Repubblica Italiana*) came into effect on 1 January 1948. It states in article 29[11] that the family is the natural social unit based on marriage, which, in turn, is based on juridical and moral equality between the partners – as long as this does not violate the "unity of the family". Here the inherent antagonism between the rights of individual family members and the family as a unit becomes visible. Other articles support this potential contradiction: article 3[12] acknowledges the equality of all citizens irrespective of their sex and guarantees that all obstacles that prevent the full development of the person and the effective participation of all workers in the political, economic and social organization of the country will be removed; article 37[13] prescribes the same rights for female workers as for male workers. This same article 37, on the other hand, calls for the protection of working mothers in order to enable them to fulfill their essential family functions (see Bimbi 1999, Saraceno 2003).

While some legal legacies were taken into the republic, some social policies such as children's allowances were stripped off the pronatalist motives. As early as 1944, birth order and the number of children were no longer used to determine the amount (Naldini 2003). Yet the acknowledgement of the male worker's responsibility for his family remained, as eligibility was based on the head of household's (i.e. legally defined as the husband) wage work in the private sector, who had dependent family members. During the years and decades that followed, this entitlement was extended to the unemployed, pensioners and those working in the agricultural sector (Ferrera, Fargion, and Jessoula 2012). In contrast to most European countries, family allowances are financed by employers' contributions based on total wages; a ceiling was in place until 1974. The extension of coverage to other groups has resulted in an increase of spending; however, as family allowances are not subject to an inflationary adjustment, the value of the allowances declined steadily (Naldini 2003).[14]

After the Second World War, a bill was presented in parliament that intended to improve the health protection of pregnant women or new mothers. The finally approved law no. 860[15] extended the compulsory maternity leave period from a total of ten weeks to two months before and three months after childbirth and introduced a payment benefit of 80 percent of previous wage. The right to maternity leave and payment was not extended to all women workers, but remained restricted to dependent employees. Women working in the agricultural sector were included in 1951. In addition, mothers could not be dismissed from employment until after the baby was one-year-old, and they were entitled to a daily time out for breastfeeding. In firms that employed more than 30 women – who, however, had to prove they were married – employers had to provide the facilities for breastfeeding in the workplace. This measure supported the reconciliation of family and employment and facilitated mothers' re-entry into the labor force – at least for married women who were in dependent employment and in the agricultural sector.

Comparing western Germany and Italy during and after fascism

Both western Germany and Italy have a fascist past that was characterized by similar family policies and had a long-lasting impact on the approaches these countries adopted with respect to families. Both fascist regimes introduced active population policies and supported the patriarchal family. While active population policies became a political taboo after the demise of the regimes, the support of the male-breadwinner model existed forth. According to the western German Civil Code, the husband as the *Familienoberhaupt* had the sole decision-making power regarding the family life, such as on questions of children's upbringing or the wife's employment, until 1958. After this point, the wife could only take up employment if it was compatible with her duties for the family. Similarly, in Italy, the constitution retained the figure of the *capofamiglia* who had commanding authority over his wife and children and subordinated equality between spouses to the unity of the family. Although the rule of *autorizzazione maritale* had already been eliminated in 1911, a large part of the civil code still treated husbands and wives differently and punished women for breaches to their husbands' authority. In western Germany, these legal imperatives were translated into policies. This meant that in the 1950s, western Germany (re)introduced cash benefits, such as children's and housing allowances, as well as tax allowances and the optional spousal income-splitting system to protect the traditional family. Italy remained more reluctant with respect to family policies and instead implicitly attributed women the role of the carer and men the role of the family wage earner. Except for reforms of maternity leave, neither state introduced policies that would help mothers to reconcile work and care.

The late 1960s and 1970s: a period of radical changes?

The era of meaningful family law reforms but less significant policy changes in western Germany

The end of the 1960s and the beginning of the 1970s were marked by a spirit of optimism and a massive expansion of the welfare state (Schmidt 2005). It was also the time of the students' and women's movements. In 1969, a coalition of SPD and FDP took office. This shift to the left was accompanied by government promises to modernize family law and policies. The reform of the matrimonial law (1976) abolished the wife's obligation to do housekeeping; the reform of the divorce law (1977) replaced the "principle of fault" with the "principle of disruption"[16] and introduced a rule of accrual (*Zugewinnregelung*) which recognized and compensated the wife's housework in a marriage. In 1979, the law on parental custody was changed by redefining the goals and styles of parental upbringing. The "principle of parental responsibility" replaced the "principle of parental authority" with the aim of strengthening the rights of the child within the family.

The laws on the legal status of children born out of wedlock (1970) and on adoption (1976) furthermore stipulated an equal treatment of all children.

This change of policy orientation, which saw a shift towards the provision of equal opportunities for all children, caused a leap forward concerning the public provision of childcare, because the role of early childhood education for children (and society as a whole) became central. Yet the children concerned were preschool children aged between three and five years, and the childcare forms in question were half-day kindergartens. Furthermore, even the reform that aimed at establishing a right to a kindergarten place for every child aged three to five failed in the mid-1970s because of the veto players involved – such as the opposition-controlled second chamber (*Bundesrat*) – and a financial situation that was negatively affected by the oil price shock (Naumann 2005).[17] A pilot project that attempted to establish "day mothers" (*Tagesmütter*) in some municipalities to provide examples of "good practice" backfired. The idea that a mother would take care of a number of children in her own home besides her own child(ren) was met with heavy criticism and resistance. People spoke of "experiments with small children". Experts pointed to research findings according to which it is crucial for children in the first three years to have a very close relationship with the biological mother (Naumann 2006). In fact, the project had been scientifically evaluated; the main finding was that the care and education by day mothers was equivalent to that of biological mothers (Bundesministerium für Familie 1998). It was, however, not until the TAG reform in 2004 that these insights were implemented at large.

Another reform that was initiated by the opposition party CDU in 1974 also failed: the introduction of a parental leave scheme and care allowance. Here the main conflict revolved around the scope of the measure – all mothers or only working mothers – and the form of allowance, i.e. flat rate or earnings-related. Moreover, the question of whether the state should rather invest in childcare institutions than in a costly measure, whose effects were very much contested, divided opinions. In the end, a counter draft – namely, a law on maternity insurance, was adopted in 1979. It granted working mothers an extension of maternity leave to up to four months and a remuneration of up to 750 DM per month.[18] This law was in keeping with the tradition of maternity rights and aimed at protecting the working mother.

As regards transfer benefits, in 1975, the government reformed the law on child allowances and tax deductions with the aim of creating a more socially balanced benefit. It abolished the tax deductions and introduced a child allowance for the first child of 50 DM. The allowances for the second and the third (and each following) child were raised to 70 DM and 120 DM, respectively. Parents received the benefits regardless of their income. In the subsequent years, child allowances were raised a couple of times.[19]

The era of meaningful family law reforms and some substantial policy changes in Italy

In a climate of economic prosperity, welfare state expansion, a strengthening of trade unions and emerging social movements, particularly the women's movement, the family law and social policies towards the family underwent a modernization. The changes to family, gender and reproductive law, in particular the introduction of the right to (no-fault) divorce in 1970,[20] the repeal of legislation forbidding the sale of contraceptives in 1971, the establishment of family planning clinics and the change to the family law in 1975, the law on equality between men and women in the labor market in 1977 and the passing of the law on abortion in 1978, were of importance (Bernini 2008, Saraceno 2003). The 1975 reform of the family law (law no. 151/1975) abolished the figure of the (male) family head, putting an end to the hierarchical relationship between the male authority and the female obedience within the family by prescribing the formal equality of both spouses and the need for collaboration within the family (Bimbi 1999).[21] The reform, however, left in place a large number of "obliged kin". In 1977, law no. 903/1977 passed parliament. It prohibited any form of discrimination against workers on the grounds of their sex and strengthened the principle of equal pay that had been introduced in the 1950s. Despite the fact that Italy was a forerunner in this field, observers argued that this law only had a symbolic character because of a lack of administrative control mechanisms or any government effort to ensure non-discriminatory practices in the private market (see Erler 2005). Despite this, the pay gap was not eliminated and still continues to exist because of a persistent horizontal and vertical segregation in the labor market. Finally, law no. 194/1978 introduced the right to obtain an abortion during the first 90 days of a pregnancy in the case of a risk of physical or mental damage to the woman.

Moreover, at the end of the 1960s, some important laws concerning publicly funded childcare facilities and maternity leave were implemented. In 1968, law no. 444/1968 was adopted. This act integrated the existing municipality-funded kindergartens with a state-funded nationwide preschool system (*scuole materne* or *scuole per l'infanzia*) and placed them under the control of the central education system. The aim was to increase the number of kindergarten places in regions, mostly in the south, where both municipal and private kindergartens were scarce. The state paid the teachers and provided subsidies, while local authorities were responsible for running the day-to-day business. The law gave children older than three a right to childcare free of charge (except for food), although the attendance in preschools was (and still is) not compulsory (Saraceno 2003). Private kindergartens, often run by Catholic agencies, were and still are subsidized and are thus a part of the overall state-subsidized kindergarten system. The implementation of the law has resulted in almost universal coverage of three- to five-year-old children (97.4 percent)[22] today and has contributed to a fairly homogenous extrafamilial care situation across the regions.

The care situation for children aged under three in public crèches (*asili nido*) was tackled three years later when law no. 1044/1971 was passed. This law had been introduced as a people's initiative bill. This law established a new state-level financial support by local authorities for crèches, the responsibility for which was taken away from private companies. In contrast to the law on preschool care, the national state was not responsible for monitoring the quality or defining minimum care standards, and the law did not establish a right to a childcare place for children of the age group zero to three. Instead, care services were to be provided based on individual demand, and working mothers, lone parents, and children from multiproblem families were prioritized (Saraceno 2003: 159). According to the law, parents have to contribute to the costs on a sliding scale based on their household income. Both the level of coverage and the cost to parents with a similar income vary across municipalities depending on local decisions and priorities. The more local governments spend on childcare, the less parents have to pay. In effect, the very ambitious target for service expansion stated in the law – provision for 5 percent of all children under three within five years – has not yet been achieved in some regions to the present day, for example, in Calabria (see Istituto degli Innocenti di Firenze 2008). And the state has not maintained its funding levels, thus leaving the cost exclusively to local governments.

In addition to the law on childcare services for the youngest children, law no. 1204/1971 on working mothers was adopted. This law reformed the maternity leave scheme. It implemented demands that had already been made by women's organizations and trade unions in the late 1940s by extending the right to maternity leave and benefits to those who work in the home and domestic workers. Moreover, it introduced additional rights concerning the mother's health: if the expectant mother's work activity was particularly hazardous, she was allowed to leave three (instead of two) months before childbirth, and a mother could not be employed in dangerous or heavy activities for up to seven months after childbirth. Two additional features, which were innovative and advanced at that time compared to other European countries, were introduced: first, the extension of the leave period for an additional six months at 30 percent of the woman's previous wage and second, the right to take unpaid leave when the child(ren) aged under three are sick. Six years later, owing to a Constitutional Court ruling, the option to take maternity leave was extended to the father in cases where the mother could not care for the child, or where the father had the sole custody of his child (law no. 903/1977).

A last reform passed parliament in 1977: law no. 114/1977 replaced the system of joint taxation, under which the *capofamiglia* was the unit of taxation, with individual taxation, thus removing one disincentive to women's employment. This law also came as a response to a ruling of the Constitutional Court that – not least owing to the 1975 reform of the family law – had declared various aspects of joint taxation as unconstitutional. This was because, among other issues, it treated women and men unequally (owing to the commitment to the male head of household as the unit of taxation) and because it violated the principle of contributory capacity. This principle stipulates that the progressive taxation of the income must be attributed to each physical person according to his or her contributory capacity (Saraceno 2003). In order to compensate for the unequal treatment of dual- and single-earner households, a system of tax deductions for "family dependents" was set in place.

Comparing western Germany and Italy

The period until the late 1970s was in both cases characterized by far-reaching changes to family law. The reform of legislation on divorce, parental care, abortion, children born out of wedlock and antidiscrimination in the labor market (Italy) all had major implications for the gender and family models prevalent in these societies, as it changed the relationships both between the sexes and between parents and children. In contrast to the period before, this time Italy followed suit and reformed or introduced work-family policies to support this new normative model of division of labor, while western Germany continued to prioritize cash benefits over services or other work-family policies. In particular, Italy's law on the public provision of childcare and the law on maternity leave were rather progressive. Western Germany, in contrast, was not able to implement a right to a kindergarten place or support extra-familial childcare. Hence, compared to western Germany, Italy took the lead in policies supporting mothers' employment during this period.

The 1980s: enough of modernization? The rediscovery of the family

Consolidating the male-breadwinner model in western Germany: explicit support for mothers to provide care work

When the Christian Democrat-Liberal government took office in 1982, family policies were retrenched. For example, childcare cost deductions and training allowances for children older than 18 were abolished and an income test for children's allowances was introduced. The only expansionary measure was the reintroduction of the dual family-support system (*dualer Familienlastenausgleich*) in 1983, i.e. the reintroduction of tax deductions for children (Münch 1990).

From 1985 onwards, however, family policies experienced another wave of growth. With the "new family policy", the CDU aimed at upgrading family policies by introducing a "10 billion family package"[23] (Kolbe 2002: 366). The central component in this package was the introduction of paid parental leave in 1986, something the CDU had proposed more than ten years earlier. Regardless of their employment status, mothers and fathers were eligible for the flat-rate benefit of 600 DM for the first six months. As of the seventh month, an income test was applied. The payment was made for a total of ten months, which was extended to 12 months as of 1988. Part-time employment along the parental leave tenure was allowed if it did not exceed 18 hours per week. By presenting the parental leave regulation as an alternative to the provision of childcare outside the home, the CDU emphasized their view of the family as being the more economical way of raising children and the more human place to do so. In keeping with this, they also propagated the opinion that raising small children exclusively in families would prevent child deprivation and consequently reduce the number of children and young people placed in juvenile homes.[24] Even though expressed in unisex wording, "family" here, of course, stands for "mother" (Kolbe 2002). In the final ballot, the SPD abstained, because they in principle advocated the purpose of parental leave, but criticized the cutbacks to benefits for working mothers. Only the Green Party voted against the law (see Kolbe 2002).

In the same year, another law was adopted that underlined the government's efforts to recognize mothers' care work as being equivalent to employment: As of 1987, parents received pension credits for one year of care within the state pension system. This year counted towards parents' minimum insurance records and was valued at 0.75 earnings points.[25] At the same time, tax allowances for children and for training were increased and tax deductions for childcare costs were introduced.

In summary, this period of Christian Democrat-Liberal government can be described partly as a return to "established" forms of family support, i.e. the increase of direct and indirect family allowances, but partly also as a time when new measures were introduced that recognized care work in the family, e.g. the leave allowance or the acknowledgement of care work in the pension scheme (Schiller 2016). The government propagated the new "freedom of choice" for parents, which meant a family policy model that can be characterized as a support for a "three-phase model" of mothers' life courses and work-family reconciliation (Kolbe 2002: 341–344, Münch 1990: 173). The "three-phase model" is characterized as follows: In the first phase, i.e. before a woman marries and has children, she completes education and works for a couple of years. During the second phase, when the children are small, she stays at home or works only part time. The third phase starts when the children are old enough to look after themselves and mothers return to a job. While phase one (qualification) and two (family care) are supported through state benefits, phase three leaves women more or less to depend on their own resources. The "freedom of choice" rhetoric was obviously aimed at women. How men are able to combine parental responsibilities and employment was not part of the debates.

Consolidating the male-breadwinner model in Italy: the persistent implicit assumption that mothers do care work

After the struggles of the 1970s for gender equality in the workplace and in the private sphere, the willingness to reform policies on family issues and women's labor-force participation seemingly came to a halt. To be sure, some reforms were carried out, e.g. law no. 863/1984 eventually reformed part-time work in 1984, strengthening the rights of workers. Previously, the regulation of part-time work was left to the individual choices of employers and employees, and labor and social security law, originally designed for standard full-time employment, discouraged the reduction of working hours in some aspects. For example, severance pay was calculated on the basis of the wages received at the time when employment was terminated. A lower salary due to part-time work was therefore unfavorable. Overtime hours were prohibited. Another problem was related to contributions to the pension scheme. In the case of part-time employees, the employers were obliged to pay so-called minimum hourly social security contributions – which were, however, calculated on the basis of a full-time worker (Lo Faro 2004). Thus part-time work represented an obstacle both to the employer and to the employee. In effect, part-time employment was not widespread in Italy, and trade unions were hostile to this form of employment, as they feared labor-market deregulation and increasing atypical employment.

Law no. 863/1984 defined part-time work as "employment at reduced hours of work compared to the standard" and equalized working at reduced hours to full-time work in many aspects of social security (Donà 2009, Leiber 2005).[26] A social right to part-time work, however, was not established, and the part-time quotas for companies prevented all interested individuals from asking for a reduction of working hours. The persistently low part-time working rates in Italy illustrate the acceptance of this type of employment.

After a decade of near standstill, political parties gained a new impetus to address the issues at the end of the 1980s. A new "welfare mix" was promoted and the family was (re)discovered as a provider of social security and care. All major parties sooner or later mentioned the family in their electoral programs (Naldini 2003). The Christian Democratic Party DC, for example, wanted to confine state intervention to the support of family formation and stability and introduced a bill (no. 4832/1990) that would extend the period of maternity leave to five years in order to "recuperate a specific female identity related to the function of motherhood" (cited in Erler 2005: 169). The left parties PCI and PSI proposed laws that would further the equal rights of family members (including children born out of wedlock). Yet, except for the reform of family allowances in 1988, this new impetus was reflected mainly in policy *proposals*, not in concrete policy reforms.[27] And even in the case of the 1988 reform (law no. 153/1988), one cannot speak of a new instrument to support families. In fact, the reform reduced the number of recipients because it replaced the existing benefit with a means-tested measure for low-income households (*assegno per il nucleo familiare*). Due to the form of funding through social contributions, it is still limited to dependent workers. Income thresholds are defined for different family sizes. Hence the existence of family dependents and/or children in a household is no longer the basis for claiming entitlement, but "the amount of total family income with respect to the total number of household members is relevant" (Naldini 2003: 152). As such, it can no longer be defined a family benefit, but rather a means to support low-income households of dependent workers.[28]

Promoting female labor-force participation and "socialist education" in the German Democratic Republic GDR (1949–1990)

Apart from the fact that all family-oriented policies were abolished after World War II, the development of laws, policies and public discourse on the family in the GDR differed substantially from that in the FRG. The attitude of the socialist state towards the family was characterized by ambivalence. The family was seen as the basic unit of society on the one hand, and on the other it was a source of difficulty, as it was a private sphere in which children grew up and were socialized, which could not be controlled (Gerlach 1996). Family law in the GDR, therefore, was intended to steer family behavior with the intention of building family relations according to socialism. Within this system, the family was linked to and integrated into society. Hence, in contrast to the FRG, where the family was considered to be a place of privacy, in the GDR, family, society and the state were very closely linked to each other.

The other major difference concerned the fact that family law and support measures were in place in the GDR that aimed at gender equality. These policies did not promote gender equality at all levels, however, but focused exclusively on the labor market. In line with Marxism, it was expected that women's personality development would benefit from participating in the material production. In addition, an increase in female participation in the labor force would help to counteract the massive shortage of labor in the years after World War II (Gerlach 1996). Hence state support of families meant the elimination of obstacles to female employment. Therefore, a massive expansion of childcare facilities took place. Differently from the FRG where childcare facilities worked according to the Weimar tradition of emancipatory pedagogy (i.e. to strengthen children's potential for self-responsible democratic behavior), childcare in the East was taught according to the Soviet pedagogic philosophy, which aimed to train children in "socialist patriotism" and loyalty (Hagemann 2006). When, after 1965, the birth rates began to sink (from 2.5 in 1965 to almost 1.5 in 1975),[29] the government introduced reforms that would help reconcile family and employment – for women! That is, the model of the "two full-time workers/housewife family" (Hagemann 2006: 244) prevailed and was supported through an extension of maternity leave, the introduction of a "baby-care year" with full wage continuation (from 1986 onwards, even fathers were entitled), the reduction of mothers' working hours and the expansion of day-care facilities.

A crucial factor for the development of these two distinct German models was the deliberate demarcation from each other. Both sides repeatedly criticized each other for the way they dealt with the family and gender-role models (Langer 1985, Münch 1990: 161). It should be noted, however, that in spite of the mutual criticism, the two models over time converged to some degree: The GDR gradually acknowledged and placed increasing value on female reproductive work from the 1970s, while the FRG has increasingly accepted female labor-force participation in certain phases of life since the beginning of the 1980s. The role of men and the gender-specific division of labor (that is, the responsibility of women for housework) was not questioned in both states for a long time, however.

Germany and Italy: a comparative synopsis of the developments until 1990

This overview has shown similarities in the legal and policy developments in the two countries, but also the different emphases Germany and Italy put on the family and family policies in the post-war period and up to 1990. Western Germany explicitly supported the male-breadwinner model – support that persisted in spite of a gradual change toward a modernized version under the heading of "three-phases model" or "freedom of choice". This model implied that women would work before "choosing of their own free will" a period of taking care of children and, again at their choice, return thereafter on the labor market. Italy is also characterized by a reliance on the male-breadwinner model, yet in contrast to Germany, it provides limited financial support for families. After a period of changes both in family law and policies in the 1970s, the 1980s were in both countries characterized by a reorientation towards the family, even though the countries recognized the family in different ways. Western Germany once again concentrated on monetary support to explicitly acknowledge the care work provided by the family (i.e. women), while Italy confined itself to support for the unpaid care work done by women that was more rhetorical in nature. In summary, by the beginning of the 1990s, both countries lacked a coherent work-family policy framework that would encourage a dual-earner family model. In fact, the Italian situation was more ambivalent than the western German: while the maternity leave scheme was one of the most advanced in Europe and laws concerning equal pay existed, the public provision of care for infants and toddlers and a part-time regulation that would facilitate the reconciliation of paid work and care were almost absent. In western Germany, the support bias for transfers rather than services persisted and the newly introduced parental leave scheme did not encourage the equal sharing of care work.

The period after 1990: persistence of the implicit support of the male-breadwinner model in Italy and policy reforms in Germany towards the dual-earner model

The beginning of the 1990s was marked in both states by political upheaval. Even though they differed in scope, they both mattered for the subsequent ways of dealing with the family and family policies. Unification challenged Germany because of the dramatic differences in the two former states' family policy aims. As Erler (2005: 84) notes, German unification "[. . .] represented a critical juncture for German family policies, as policy makers had to make difficult choices in order to reconcile diametrically opposed family policy legacies." At the same time, the eastern German women's employment behavior differed considerably from that of women in the western states. In Italy, the political and institutional crisis of the early 1990s was responsible for the breakdown of the parties that had previously been the largest and most influential. This made way for new parties and, consequently, a new start for debates on the reconciliation of work and care. The following sections give a more detailed overview of the changes to policies regarding the reconciliation of work and care after 1990.

Germany

Leave and working-time flexibility

The parental leave period of 12 months introduced in 1986 was gradually extended until 1992: for children who were born after 1 January 1988, the length added up to 12 months, for those born after 1 January 1989 it extended to 15 months, for those born after 1 January 1990 to 18 months, and to 36 months for those born after 1 January 1992 (Bothfeld 2005: 28). The period for receiving the leave benefit was extended accordingly from 12 to 15 to 18 months. As of 1992, parents received the payment for two years. The benefit level remained the same over the years and amounted to €307 per month. From month seven on a means test was applied.[30] Parents who had more than €15,032 net income per year were not eligible to receive the full payment; those who earned less received a corresponding graduated payment. The right to receive the benefit was extended to nonmarried fathers in cases where they took primary care of the child(ren) and the mother agreed. The income limits remained fixed for 15 years (1986–2001). In 1996, almost 85 percent of parents with a newborn child received a payment for more than six months. The share of households who were entitled to the full benefit for more than six months decreased to about 60 percent (BT-Drs. 13/9794 of 05.02.1998, tables 6 and 7).

The next parental leave reform took place in 2000.[31] Notably, the government had to react to the EU Directive 96/34/EC,[32] which had set minimum standards regarding the duration and recommended rules regarding flexible use and the continuation of social security contributions. As Kolbe (2002: 395) points out, in spite of the replacement of the term "child-raising vacation" (*Erziehungsurlaub*) with "parental time" (*Elternzeit*),[33] the reform represented a continuation of existing legislation rather than a fundamental shift. The use of leave was rendered more flexible, as parents were allowed to take the leave at the same time, while before they had to take turns. The number of maximum working hours during parental leave was increased from 19 to 30 hours per week. Moreover, the income limits for receiving the payment after the sixth month were raised to €16,470/year (€13,498 for single parents) with the aim of making more parents eligible for the payment.[34] More innovative was the newly introduced so-called budget option (*Budget*): parents could choose whether they wanted a payment of €307/month for two years or €450/month for only one year (Bundesministerium für Familie 2004a). The second option was meant as an incentive for a faster re-entry of mothers into the labor market. However, the choice was restricted to those parents who would have been eligible for the full benefit after the seventh month, i.e. low-income parents. It was assumed that, because of a higher identification with their jobs, better-qualified and high-income women would opt for a shorter leave anyhow (Bothfeld 2005). In the same year, a law on part-time work and fixed-term contracts (*Gesetz über Teilzeitarbeit und befristete Arbeitsverträge (Teilzeit- und Befristungsgesetz – TzBfG)*) was adopted. It rules that any employed person in a firm with at least 15 employees may claim a reduction of the working time.[35] The law applies not only to parents (or other carers) but to all employed persons (Bothfeld 2005: 41).

In 2003, the financial improvements of the 2000 parental leave reform were withdrawn: the Budget Supplement Act[36] of 2004 (*Haushaltsbegleitgesetz 2004*) substantially lowered the income limits for the leave payment during the first six months from €51,130 to €30,000 for couples and from €38,350 to €23,000

Euro for single parents. In addition, the payment – if claimed for two years – was reduced from €307 to €300.[37]

On 1 January 2007, a new leave benefit came into effect. It constituted a radical change from the previously flat-rate sum to an income-related measure of 67 percent of previous net income with a cap of €1,800. It is paid for a total of 14 months after the birth of a child[38] with two use-it-or-lose-it months for each parent. In addition, working parents with low income are entitled to an upgrade: for those who earn less than 1000 Euro a month, the replacement rate is increased by 0.1 percent for each second earned Euro below 1000 Euro.[39] Parents who already have one or more children may be entitled to a "sibling's bonus"; that is, the replacement rate is raised by 10 percent and at least 75 Euro per month.[40] The new law aimed to increase mothers' employment, to add more gender equality and to offer a better reconciliation of work and life for both parents. However, persons not in employment, such as housewives, unemployed persons or students are also eligible for a minimum leave benefit of €300.[41]

Childcare

In contrast to the parental leave and working-time flexibility policies, within childcare policies, competencies are divided. The responsibility for childcare provision and funding rests at the level of the federal states and municipalities. According to Evers and Riedel (2002), the municipalities pay at least 60 percent of the running expenses, the federal states contribute around 20 percent, and parents and local providers share the rest. According to the regional kindergarten laws, the regions set the share of their subsidies and funding rules as well as criteria for the organization and quality of services. This decentralist organization has resulted in strong regional differences (see Table 4.1). First of all, although it is lessening in size, the continuing discrepancy between eastern and western Germany should be noted. In the middle of the 1990s, on average, 40 percent of eastern German children younger than three were offered a place, while in western Germany, only 3 percent of children of this age group attended childcare. In spite of increases in provision in western Germany, the discrepancy between western and eastern Germany still amounted to approximately 34 percentage points in 2010. In addition, most of the western German childcare institutions operate on a part-time basis, while full-time places are offered in eastern Germany.

As of 2004, the Day-Care Expansion Act (*Tagesbetreuungsausbaugesetz*, TAG)[42] requires the municipalities to provide enough places for children younger than three to meet the demand, or at least to make places available for those children whose parents are in paid employment or in training (§24). This goal was supposed to be reached at the latest by 2010 (§24a). The law foresees the provision of an annual €1.5 billion for the adequate supply of childcare, i.e. an expansion of places in western Germany and the maintenance of existing coverage rates in the eastern states. The additional 230,000 places were not to be solely provided by institutions; rather, the TAG explicitly aimed at establishing formal child minders

Table 4.1 Regional variation in the public provision of childcare in Germany, 1994–2010

	No. of childcare places for 100 children aged 0–2				
	1994	1998	2002	2006[1]	2010
Western German federal states					
Baden-Württemberg	1.2	1.3	2.3	8.8	18.4
Bayern	1.0	1.4	2.1	8.2	18.6
Berlin (West)	19.1	23.4	–	–	–
Berlin (total)	–	–	35.8	37.9	42.1
Bremen	6.4	6.8	10.0	9.1	16.2
Hamburg	11.9	11.7	13.1	21.0	28.7
Hessen	2.1	2.6	3.7	8.9	19.4
Niedersachsen	1.5	1.8	2.3	5.1	15.9
Nordrhein-Westfalen	1.5	2.5	2.0	6.5	14.0
Rheinland-Pfalz	0.9	1.4	2.7	9.4	20.3
Saarland	1.7	2.5	4.8	10.2	17.8
Schleswig-Holstein	1.4	2.3	2.6	7.5	18.2
Ø Western German federal states (without Berlin)	2.7	3.1	3.8	7.9	15.6
Eastern German federal states					
Berlin (East)	51.5	52.4	–	–	–
Brandenburg	54.1	51.9	44.8	40.4	51.0
Mecklenburg-Vorpommern	39.0	30.8	37.6	43.2	50.8
Sachsen	32.8	24.1	29.1	33.5	42.8
Sachsen-Anhalt	42.9	47.2	56.6	50.2	56.0
Thüringen	36.4	25.9	22.4	37.9	45.1
Ø Eastern German federal states (without Berlin)	41.0	36.0	38.1	41.0	49.1

Notes:
1 As of 2006, the statistics changed from coverage rates to enrolment rates. In addition, the figures now include child minders who receive public subsidies (Kolvenbach and Taubmann 2006). A comparison between the years is therefore limited.
Source: Statistisches Bundesamt (2004); Statistische Ämter des Bundes und der Länder (2007; 2011)

(*Tagesmütter/Tagesväter*) as a "qualitative alternative of equal rank" to childcare institutions (Bundesministerium für Familie 2004b: 4).

The government aimed at incentivizing employment in the formal childcare sector[43] and required regional youth welfare offices to pay for the child minders' social security expenditures. In principle, the federal states are responsible for defining quality standards in care, yet the national law articulates common quality criteria for institutions and child minders (§22).

The Child Support Law (*Kinderförderungsgesetz*, Kifög),[44] adopted in 2008, is based on the Day-Care Expansion Act of 2004. It introduces the legal right to a childcare place for children older than one year as of 2013. The government established a special fund (*Sondervermögen*) to pay for investment costs. The fund covered a total of €2.5 billion to be spent between 2008 and 2013. Moreover, the federal government increased its contribution to the running costs from year to year, starting from €100 million in 2009, and will continue the efforts after 2013 with €770 million per year (Bundesministerium für Familie 2007). The law also aims at providing a childcare place for children whose parents are in search of work. Previously, this group had not been explicitly considered. Thirty percent of the newly established places are also to be provided by formal child minders, who do not require a formal qualification as long as they do not care for more than five children. Until 2011, the coverage rate increased to 25.4 percent in Germany.[45]

Italy

Leave and working-time flexibility

The most important law in the field of work-family policies is law no. 53/2000 with the title "Provision for the Support of Mother- and Fatherhood, for the Right to Care and Education, and for the Coordination of City Times".[46] The final law, which two subsequent legislative decrees united with preexisting regulations (d.lgs. no 151/2001 and d.lgs. no. 115/2003), included several components that aimed to make the reconciliation of work and family possible. It introduced more flexibility in the use of the five months of maternity leave with the possibility to reduce the time before childbirth to one month in order to stay longer with the baby after childbirth. Also, an autonomous right for fathers to use parental leave was established, independent of the working status of the child's mother and her use of the leave. Either parent is eligible for six months of leave paid at 30 percent of previous wages; however, in total, parents may only use 10 months, increased to 11 if the father takes at least 3 months (Naldini and Jurado 2013). Unemployed persons, home helps and domestic workers are not entitled to the benefit. The self-employed as well as those who are enrolled with *Gestione separata*[47] are entitled to three months of paid leave if they meet certain criteria (see Corsetti et al. 2014). The law consisted of several other components which all aimed at providing more flexibility for leave takers (not only for care reasons) including financial incentives for companies that establish time policies or the organization of flexible work.

In recent years, the law underwent some changes: First, the budget law of 2007 (*legge finanziaria*, law no. 296/2006) extended the right to receive maternity pay as well as a daily sickness benefit to be paid by the National Social Security Institute (INPS) to women on a short-term contract. Second, the basis for financing the company projects with the aim to better reconcile family and employment was shifted from the Fund for Occupations (under the responsibility of the Ministry of Labor) to the newly established[48] Fund for Family Policies. Law no. 296/2006 increased the financial means available in the fund[49] and individualized the sum available for the company projects (before, the sum was fixed at 40 billion Lira, about €20 million). The Department of Family Policies, which is attached to the prime minister's office, now sets the sum via decree and decides about the allocation of the financial means. Third, a bill adopted by the Council of Ministers on 16 November 2007[50] established that parents with children who are less than a year old are entitled to work part-time for at least a year. In 2009, article 9 of law no. 53/2000 was changed due to a legislative decree (law no. 69/2009) that implemented the EU Directive 2006/54/EC[51] with the aim of meeting citizens' needs more effectively. In particular, the reform increased the number of parties eligible for funding and of reconciliation needs for which projects can be presented.

A 2010 survey shows that among working parents who have a child younger than eight, 45.3 percent of mothers and 6.9 percent of fathers have taken up parental leave at least once and at least for one month. Of those who have not used parental leave, more than 25 percent of women and almost 20 percent of the men stated that they were not eligible (ISTAT 2011). There is thus a comparably low take-up rate.

Part-time employment became an issue on the political agenda in 1997 when a major liberalization of the labor market was launched with the so-called Legge Treu (law no. 196/1997).[52] It introduced the option to use a variety of short-term work contracts and provided financial incentives for firms who hired part-time workers or allowed employees to reduce working hours. In the same year, a directive launched by the Council of the European Union[53] obliged the member states to bring regulations into force that ensure equal treatment of part-time workers and full-time workers with respect to working conditions. The directive also contained recommendations about the non-discrimination against part-time workers regarding their social security and proposed instruments to promote part-time work. In 2000, the Italian government approved a legislative decree (dl. no. 61/2000)[54] which aimed at eliminating the legal uncertainties and organizational difficulties that had characterized part-time work and introduced a set of incentives that were intended to create 100,000 new jobs. An important purpose of the new rules was to encourage the use of part-time work in order to foster job creation (Pedersini 2000). The main points of the legislative decree establishing the new rules on part-time work are the distinction between vertical part-time work (full working day, but only in certain fixed periods during the week, month or year), horizontal part-time work (reduced daily working hours) and mixed part-time work (combining elements of horizontal and vertical); the introduction of equal rights between full-time and part-time workers as regards matters such as trade-union rights, pay, annual holidays, parental leave, protection against workplace accidents and occupational illness; access to company training schemes; and the abolition of the fixed limit of part-time workers in a company. Extra hours are paid at the same rate as ordinary hours. However, if they exceed the limit established by the law or by collective bargaining, a 50 percent premium is paid.

However, these regulations were withdrawn by the legislative decree 276/2003,[55] which introduced a more flexible use of part-time contracts on the demand side and reduced the rights of both the employees and the trade unions (Lo Faro 2002): In particular, this law made it easier for employers to change the form of the agreed working-time reduction on short notice and to directly agree with the individual employee on extra working hours. Moreover, the right to return to full-time employment was abolished (Bano 2005). In 2006, law no. 247/2007 again withdrew these rights on the part of the employers. At the same time, by building obstacles that hindered the transition from full-time to part-time employment, full-time employment was established as the norm. If an employee wants to reduce working time, both the employee and the employer have to provide a written agreement and the provincial labor office needs to confirm this agreement after hearing the employee. Moreover, if a firm wants to hire full-time employees, the right of precedence must be given to those who are already employed but had shifted from full-time to part-time employment (Treu 2011).

Childcare

In Italy, law no. 1044 of 1971 lays down that local authorities are responsible for the organization of childcare and receive state-level financial support. This division of competencies resulted in the territorial differentiation of service standards and availability of places as regions in the north and in the center, particularly those governed by left-wing majorities, passed regional framework laws on the provision of social services and compensated in part for the lack of national transfer payments while southern regions maintained an insufficient system of public welfare provision (Fargion 2000, Madama 2010). Still, since the bulk of the financial burden was left with the local authorities, budget constraints brought about an overall scarce offer of childcare places.

Unlike the data for the German case, the Italian data on the provision of childcare does not allow for a differentiation between publicly and privately provided places.[56] However, for 2000 and 2008, I have data on the share of publicly provided places of the total number of places (see column 3 of Table 4.2), which indicates the extent of the private provision of childcare.

The table demonstrates that there are dramatic differences between the regions and that coverage rates increased between 2000 and 2008. In 2008, childcare places were provided on average for more than 20 percent of zero- to two-year-old children in north and central Italy, while only 10 percent of children in the south had access to a place. The share of places provided by publicly supported institutions also differs across the regions: in some regions, more than two-thirds receive public financing, in others, such as Piemonte or Lombardia, privately run institutions prevail. The share of publicly provided places decreased overall between 2000 and 2008, however. Consequently, the increase of coverage rates can be attributed to the growth of privately run childcare institutions, and overall state involvement remains low.

In 1996, law no. 285/1997, which aimed at stimulating the provision of innovative childcare services, was adopted. Its main objective was the promotion of children's well-being, and it devoted special attention to the improvement of the relationship between children and parents and to parental and childcare service. At the same time, the "National Fund for Social Policies" was established by law no. 449/1997. It aimed at directing the financial resources for social policies to the regions, municipalities and also the third sector in order to guarantee a more clear and coordinated system of social planning.[57] Within this National Fund, a "National Fund for Children and Adolescents" (*Fondo Nazionale per l'infanzia e l'adolescenza*), which intended to incentivize the establishment of innovative

Table 4.2 Regional variation in the provision of childcare in Italy, 1992–2008

	No. of childcare places[1] for 100 children aged 0–2			Publicly provided childcare, share of total (%)	
	1992	2000	2008	2000	2008
Northwest					
Piemonte	10.8	10.7	17.6	78.6	27.4
Valle d'Aosta	7.6	12.3	17.2	100.0	93.9
Lombardia	9.1	9.7	17.6	84.3	29.4
Northeast					
Veneto	5.5	7.2	14.5	47.8	33.6
Friuli Venezia Giulia	5.4	7.8	15.6	68.4	40.4
Liguria	8.0	9.7	16.7	87.8	44.8
Emilia-Romagna	18.8	18.3	24.8	91.3	66.3
Central					
Toscana	7.9	11.3	20.1	92.9	64.5
Umbria	8.7	11.6	25.8	87.9	43.9
Marche	8.5	11.5	18.5	77.5	68.8
Lazio	6.6	8.5	15.7	83.1	52.6
South					
Abruzzo	4.7	4.1	9.2	92.9	n.a.[2]
Molise	2.1	2.9	10.3	80.0	70.0
Campania	0.6	2.2	n.a.	47.1	n.a.
Puglia	4.0	2.7	6.6	69.9	n.a.
Basilicata	3.4	5.2	11.4	82.1	n.a.
Calabria	0.9	1.9	6.2	55.0	n.a.
Islands					
Sicilia	2.4	4.7	n.a.	100.0	n.a.
Sardegna	3.3	6.4	n.a.	86.2	n.a.

Notes:
1 Publicly and privately provided places in day nurseries without *servizi integrativi* (which include playgroups and children's libraries together with parents or child minders).

Source: Centro nazionale di documentazione e analisi per l'infanzia e l'adolescenza (2002; 2008); my calculations

services for children and adolescents, was established. These services included childcare services for the under threes, which differed from standard childcare services in size and organization (such as *micro-nidi*, family-like care, *ludoteche*) and parental meeting places, as well as meeting places for adolescents. These services were intended to complement existing arrangements so that municipalities would have a more integrated service network at their command. As such, the law did not establish any social *rights* concerning care for children. Children and parents depended on the engagement of the local authorities to have their demands fulfilled. The idea of cofunding of local initiatives foreshadowed law no. 328/2000, which re-organized the competencies in the field of social services and strengthened the role of local authorities. Thus state intervention was provided only in those cases where local authorities cooperate with private and non-profit organizations and commonly develop a service. The fund was to be refinanced each year and a total of 750 billion Liras (approximately €387 million) was earmarked for the period between 1997 and 1999. However, this refinancing did not happen.

The absence of a law that would prescribe national standards and provide stable financial resources impeded the expansion of publicly provided childcare places for children younger than three. In 2000, a national care service framework law (law no. 328/2000) was adopted. The law established an integrated approach with cooperation between the central government, the regions and the local authorities and clearly defined these actors' respective tasks. The national actors were responsible for providing basic funds and guidelines for care services in terms of minimum coverage and quality standards (so-called essential levels, *livelli essenziali*).[58] The regions were supposed to develop regional norms based on the basic requirements by the national state and to work out action plans. Finally, the municipalities were in charge of delivering the services (Erler 2005, Saraceno 2003). Law no. 328/2000 also outlined the (lengthy) process for the establishment of common basic standards and coverage levels across the country (Naldini and Saraceno 2008). As a framework law, in order to be fully implemented, it had to be transposed by a series of follow-up regulations that would operationalize the general principles. Most of them were, however, never approved.

This also had to do with the fact that the law was largely weakened by the almost immediately following constitutional reform in 2001. Article 5 assigned the regions the exclusive responsibility for the provision of social services. The national state was therefore no longer allowed to set standards autonomously. Instead, the state and the council of regions must agree on the *livelli essenziali*, which must be *funded from the national budget*. Since 2001, however, these essential levels and national minimum standards have not been defined (Naldini and Saraceno 2008; Interviews IT2, IT5 and IT9) Some of the regions (particularly in the richer north and in the center) have developed their own laws and locally based rights. Consequently, regional differences have further increased.

Further, the constitutional reform constrained the national state's freedom to distribute financial resources based on its own goals. In the past, the state had been able to allocate conditional funds to the regions – that is, to explicitly require the regions to use the funding for, e.g. the provision of childcare places. After the constitutional reform, the national state may only distribute funds to the regions, while they decide how to use them. Nevertheless, in 2001, the National Fund for Interventions and Social Services (*Piano nazionale degli interventi e dei servizi sociali 2001–2003*) was introduced, which was intended to support the regions and local authorities in their efforts to provide social services.

Since the size of the National Fund for Social Policies is determined each year by the budget law (*legge finanziaria*), instead of providing continuous financial support through state funding, the financial support of care provision is each year dependent upon the government's priorities. The center-right government, for example, did not continue this funding, but rather provided €10 billion for the promotion of company crèches. Interested companies received 50 percent of the total sum (maximum of €125,000 Euros), while they had to repay the other 50 percent within seven years (Erler 2005).[59] In 2006, the so-called Piano nidi 2007–2009 was proposed.[60] It envisaged the expansion of childcare places to meet the goal set by the European Union of providing childcare places for 33 percent of all children aged under three. An annual budget of €100 million was earmarked for the implementation of these proposals.[61] One of the most important provisions of the law in regard to this objective concerned the linkage between the implementation of the plan to the successive definition of the *livelli essenziali*.[62] However, despite fixing this plan in a law, the *livelli essenziali* have not yet been defined and further national state initiatives regarding the public provision of childcare for zero- to three-year-old children have not been implemented.

Comparing Germany and Italy after 1990: diverging work-family policy paths

This chapter has shown the diverging paths of Germany and Italy after 1990. In the beginning of the 1990s, neither Germany nor Italy provided sufficient support for working parents, but rather relied on the traditional male-breadwinner model. In particular, childcare services were largely neglected in both countries (except for in eastern Germany). The design of parental leave also made it difficult to reconcile both spheres. Even though in Italy the parental leave duration was generous, the payment was very low. Hence the scheme did not facilitate having children and being in paid work at the same time for either parent, especially mothers, particularly given the low provision of childcare services. The male-breadwinner orientation was more coherent in Germany where the parental leave scheme allowed for parental leave until the child was three years old, offered only little payment and provided no incentives for fathers to take advantage of it. Furthermore, children aged under three living in western Germany had virtually no access to childcare services.

A look at the development of policies between 1990 and 2008 (Table 4.3) reveals substantial changes in Germany: The parental leave scheme was replaced by a Scandinavian-style one that reduced the duration of paid leave and substantially increased the payment. The number of public childcare places was increased and complemented by a right to receive care for zero- to three-year-old children with target coverage rates to up to 33 percent in 2013.[63] In 2000, the legal right to part-time work in companies with more than 15 employees was established. With this law, the individual employee's position in the bargaining process over part-time and full-time work had been strengthened. These reforms move Germany quite close to the dual-earner model, yet it has to be noted that in the field of childcare services, large within-country differences continue to exist.

By contrast, hardly any change has occurred in Italy. State intervention into matters of the family remains low. Until now, this country concentrated on labor rights, e.g. leave and social rights when working reduced hours. For instance, extra months for the father have been added to prolong the duration of parental

Table 4.3 Policy developments in Germany and Italy after 1990

Core program	Program characteristic	Germany		Italy	
		Approx. 1994	Approx. 2008	Approx. 1994	Approx. 2008
Maternity leave	Duration of leave (weeks)	6 + 8	6 + 8	8 + 12	8 + 12
	Replacement rate	100	100	80	80
Parental leave	Duration of leave (total)	148	148	26	26 + 13
	Duration of paid leave (mother + father)	26	44+9	26	26 + 13
	Replacement rate	16	67	30	30
	Gender division	no	2 m/father	no	3m/father
Flexible working time	Entitlement to reduce working hours	no	yes	no	no
	Full social rights	no	yes	no	yes
Childcare services	Right to receive care for <3s	no	(yes)[1]	no	no
	Coverage rate	7.5	15.3	6	12.7[2]

Notes:
1 The legal right was enacted in August 2013.
2 The figure also includes privately provided childcare places.

Source: My compilation

leave. Yet when it comes to state efforts in the form of benefits, Italy was and remains reluctant. The parental leave payment is low and publicly provided childcare places for children under three are scarce (Naldini and Jurado 2013). A right to part-time work does not exist; the Italian legislation, however, allows the provision of financial incentives for firms in order to recruit people on a part-time basis. The relationship between the family and the state in Italy is characterized by regulation through law, not by explicit financial support.

In summary, while Germany began to move away from the male-breadwinner model in many respects, the more ambivalent picture of the previous decades has persisted in Italy, where the male-breadwinner model is not explicitly supported but implicitly encouraged through the lack of adequate policies that help women to reconcile care and paid work. How can we explain these divergences? Why can we observe a policy shift in Germany, but stagnation in Italy? The following chapters will explain the developments in both countries using the explanatory framework that was developed in Chapter 2.

Notes

1 It is important to note that I primarily describe the western German history. The eastern Germans took in many ways a rather different path, which I will also delineate in one subsection. After the unification, however, western German institutions were imposed

upon the Eastern part – not only in terms of policy instruments and goals but also of governance. Hence in this historical overview of the western German tradition will be given more room.

2 "Marriage and the family shall enjoy the special protection of the state" (*Ehe und Familie stehen unter besonderem Schutz der staatlichen Ordnung* (Art. 6 GG, Abs. 1)). Other articles concern the rights of parents regarding care and upbringing of children and the protection of mothers. The last article postulates that children born outside of marriage shall be provided by legislation with the same opportunities for their development as children born within marriage. This latter article was translated into law only in 1970 ("Law on the legal status of children born outside of marriage", *Gesetz über die rechtliche Stellung der nichtehelichen Kinder*).

3 The Ministry was set up against the will of the coalition partner FDP and the opposition party SPD. The opponents criticized both the supposedly pronatalist and family restorative motivation, which induced the establishment and the exceedingly modest financial equipment of the Ministry which would not be able to effectively support families (Langer-El Sayed 1980). In fact, the first minister Franz-Josef Wuerrmeling, who was a strict Catholic, made the moral, not the financial, support of families his aim. He saw the family as a buffer against the consequences of modern life, such as increasing divorce rates and neglected children, and circulated several publications in which he praised the nuclear family and the gender-specific division of work (Gerlach 2004, Münch 1990).

4 Dual family support system means the co-existent availability of child allowances and tax deductions for families.

5 The first law on child allowances (1954) granted 25 DM per month for each third and subsequent child. In 1959, this amount increased to 40 DM. In 1961, the government expanded the eligibility to include second-born children also. For them, 25 DM per month were paid. Note that child allowances for the third and subsequent children were paid out of an employers' fund, while the allowances for the second child were taken out of the federal budget. This employers' fund was deliberately implemented to demonstrate that the state stays out of family matters. Only in 1964, the employers' fund was resolved. Since then, allowances (25 DM for the second, 50 DM for the third, 60 DM for the fourth and 70 DM for the fifth and subsequent children) are paid out of the public budget (Gerlach 2004).

6 This benefit level (approx. €13) has not been changed until today.

7 This view was supported by studies of social scientists who continued to regard mothers' employment as a social problem and potentially harmful for children (Hagemann 2006).

8 This civil code, which was inspired by the Napoleonic civil code of 1804, unified for the first time the civil codes of all Italian territories – four years after the new united Italian Kingdom was established (1861). It introduced civil marriage. Religious marriage was possible, but as an addition to, not a substitution of, civil marriage. Other than in the Napoleonic civil code, divorce was not possible. The Pisanelli code, however, adopted the principle of inequality between children born within and those born outside wedlock and the principle of a husband's dominance over his wife from the Napoleonic civil code. A wife had to ask her husband's permission even with regard to the management of her own property (this rule was cancelled in 1911).

9 As established by the civil code, fathers were the heads of household. Married women were only eligible in case their husbands were unable to work.

10 The maternity leave system had been reformed in 1934, extending the previously granted four to ten weeks of leave and ruling that a woman could not be dismissed from employment during pregnancy. In firms with more than 50 female employees aged between 15 and 50 years, employers had to establish nursing rooms. Even though this law *de jure* improved the situation of working women, it de facto concerned only a minor share, because it excluded the numerically largest group of working women – home-workers,

106 *Policy developments in Germany and Italy*

      domestics and women working in agriculture – from the established rights (Saraceno 1991).
11 *Articolo 29: La Repubblica riconosce i diritti della famiglia come società naturale fondata sul matrimonio. Il matrimonio è ordinato sull'eguaglianza morale e giuridica dei coniugi, con i limiti stabiliti dalla legge a garanzia dell'unità familiare.*
12 *Articolo 3: Tutti i cittadini hanno pari dignità sociale e sono eguali davanti alla legge, senza distinzione di sesso, di razza, di lingua, di religione, di opinioni politiche, di condizioni personali e sociali. È compito della Repubblica rimuovere gli ostacoli di ordine economico e sociale, che, limitando di fatto la libertà e l'eguaglianza dei cittadini, impediscono il pieno sviluppo della persona umana e l'effettiva partecipazione di tutti i lavoratori all'organizzazione politica, economica e sociale del Paese.*
13 *Articolo 37: La donna lavoratrice ha gli stessi diritti e, a parità di lavoro, le stesse retribuzioni che spettano al lavoratore. Le condizioni di lavoro devono consentire l'adempimento della sua essenziale funzione familiare e assicurare alla madre e al bambino una speciale adeguata protezione.*
14 For example, the value deteriorated from about 10 percent of GDP per capita in 1960 to about 4 percent in 1988 (Naldini 2003).
15 Law on the physical and economic protection of working mothers (legge n. 860, *Tutela fisica ed economica delle lavoratrici madri*").
16 The family law in the GDR introduced the principle of disruption already in 1965 (Gerlach 1996).
17 The number of publicly provided childcare places rose nonetheless during the 1970s and by 1980 68 percent of all children between three and five years were in kindergarten (Neumann 1987).
18 The benefit was conceptualized as a wage replacement with the maximum of 750 DM per month. According to Kolbe (2002: 293), a woman in 1979 earned between 1664 DM (blue collar worker) and 2169 DM (white collar worker) gross per month. The individual tax burden amounted to 29.1 percent (Flora 1987: 336); hence the net earnings of women averaged to between 1180 DM and 1538 DM. The monthly maternity insurance benefit thus averaged to between 64 and 49 percent of the previous wage.
19 In 1978, it rose to 80 DM for the second and 150 DM for each additional child. In 1979, it increased to 100 DM for the second child and to 200 DM for each additional child, and in 1981, it increased to 120 DM for the second and 240 DM for each additional child. In 1982, a differentiation between the third and the fourth child took place. The third received 220 DM and the fourth 240 DM (Gerlach 2009).
20 Only three dissenting votes had impeded the anchoring of the indissolubility of matrimony as a principle in the Constitution. The reform of 1970 introduced the principle of remedy and allowed divorce under the following conditions: a) the marriage has not been performed, b) one of the partners was sent to jail and c) the partners have been legally separated for at least five years (three years as of 1987) (Saraceno 2003: 49ff.).
21 *Articolo 24: Con il matrimonio il marito e la moglie acquistano gli stessi diritti e assumono i medesimi doveri. Dal matrimonio deriva l'obbligo reciproco alla fedeltà, all'assistenza morale e materiale, alla collaborazione nell'interesse della famiglia e alla coabitazione. Entrambi i coniugi sono tenuti, ciascuno in relazione alle proprie sostanze e alla propria capacità di lavoro professionale o casalingo, a contribuire ai bisogni della famiglia.*
22 The figure refers to enrolment rates in 2008 (OECD Family Database, http://www. oecd.org/document/4/0,3746,en_2649_34819_37836996_1_1_1_1,00.html; access date: 29.02.2012).
23 Münch (1990) points out that, taking into account the earlier retrenchments, the introduction of new measures only put back the expenditure level to the level it had been before the retrenchment phase.
24 In 1984, the Ministry for Family Affairs wrote, "[i]t is not only more human, but also economically more reasonable that the father or mother brings up his/her children him/

Policy developments in Germany and Italy   107

herself than that s/he, without the care allowance, feels compelled to work due to economic reasons even though s/he would prefer to stay at home with the child. Not only because the public provision of care is associated with high costs. It seems to be more important that psychological or physical damages (deprivation) which might emerge owing to the lack of a close reference person (*feste Bezugsperson*) will have to be fixed in public institutions – such as children's homes, special needs schools or other expensive establishments – yet without the guarantee of any success" (Bundesministerium für Familie 1989, cited in Kolbe 2002: 367–368).

25 Since 1984, the minimum insurance record for receiving a pension is five years (previously this was fifteen years). Women who have five children, but were never employed, would thus be eligible for an old-age pension. Contributions paid to the pension insurance are converted into personal earnings points (*Persönliche Entgeltpunkte*). Per year, people who are insured and earn an income that corresponds to the average income of all insured persons within that year earn one point. Together with the pension type factor, the pension accrual factor and the current pension value, the total of earnings points determines the individual pension benefit (see Blome, Keck, and Alber 2009)

26 Moreover, the aim was to impede dismissals of full-time workers and to enable the unemployed to take up a position. For that so-called *contratti di solidarietà* could establish whose salary, based on a part-time working contract, would be topped up by state funds (Ferrera and Gualmini 2004, Gualmini 2000).

27 As Collozzi and Mattenei (1991) note, 69 proposals concerning the family were introduced in parliament between 1978 and 1990. Yet none of them made their way to a law.

28 However, owing to the fact that only those persons in paid employment are entitled to the benefit, the allowance is not granted to those families most in need: parents without a job, often lone parents.

29 See Statistisches Bundesamt http://www.destatis.de/jetspeed/portal/cms/Sites/destatis/Internet/DE/Content/Statistiken/Bevoelkerung/AktuellGeburtenentwicklung,template Id=renderPrint.psml; access date: 01.03.2012.

30 In 1994, another income threshold was introduced. Married parents with a yearly gross income of more than €71,580.86 were no longer entitled to the parental leave benefit, even during the first six months (BT-Drs. 13/9794 of 05.02.1998).

31 *Drittes Gesetz zur Änderung des Bundeserziehungsgeldgesetzes* (BErzGG, Bundesgesetzblatt Teil I 2000 Nr.46 26.10.2000 S. 1426)

32 Directive 96/34/EC has set minimum standards regarding the duration (three months after the birth of a child for both female and male employees) and recommended to include rules regarding flexible use and the continuation of social security contributions. The entitlement might be dependent on previous work experience.

33 A cross-party consensus emerged on the renaming of the parental leave as all acknowledged that bringing up children has nothing to do with a vacation (Kolbe 2002).

34 For each additional child, the income limit rose: for a family with one child the limit was increased by about 10 percent, for a family with four children by about 25 percent (Bundesministerium für Familie 2004a). In 2003, about 80 percent of all parents who received the leave benefit during the first six months were eligible to receiving the benefit after the sixth month. Since the benefit was gradually reduced according to the income, however, only 60 percent received the full benefit of 307 Euros (Fendrich, Fischer, and Schilling 2005).

35 The claimant needs to have been employed for at least six months and the firm may reject the request because of "company reasons" (*betriebliche Gründe*).

36 A budget accompanying law is a law that is brought in together with the yearly budget law and the budget plan and undertakes planned changes to other laws. It usually concerns measures to consolidate the state budget.

37 A study for the federal state North Rhine-Westphalia shows a clear decline in the number of recipients: the share of those who were eligible for the benefit during the first six months dropped by 50 percent. The data stems from a minor interpellation (*Kleine*

Anfrage) from a deputy of the North Rhine-Westphalian state parliament (Drucksache 14/4047, http://www.landtag.nrw.de/portal/WWW/dokumentenarchiv/Dokument/MMD14–4047.pdf; access date: 17.10.2009).

38 Compulsory maternity leave of 8 weeks is included in the 14 months. That means that the total paid leave time is reduced by these 8 weeks, and parents may share only 12 months.

39 For example, a mother earned €700 net per month before childbirth. The difference to €1000 is €300 Euro. That €300 when divided by 2 is 150. The percentage points 150 x 0.1 equals 15 percentage points. And 67 percent plus 15 percentage points equals 82 percent (Bundesministerium für Familie 2009).

40 In households with two children, this entitlement lasts until the older child turns three. In households with three or more children, the parent is entitled to this increase if at least two of the older children have not completed the sixth year of age (Bundesministerium für Familie 2009). In Sweden, this measure is called "speed premium" because it encourages parents to have children shortly one after the other.

41 This was recently changed: as of 1 January 2011, those unemployed persons who receive social assistance (so-called Hartz IV) are no longer entitled to the basic amount of the parental leave benefit.

42 Gesetz zum qualitätsorientierten und bedarfsgerechten Ausbau der Tagesbetreuung. Bundesgesetzblatt Jahrgang 2004 Teil I Nr. 76 (27.12.2004), p. 3853.

43 According to Erler (2005), the SPD had been skeptical with respect to private child minders because it had been equated with illegal employment, i.e. leaving child minders without social security and low quality standards.

44 Gesetz zur Förderung von Kindern unter drei Jahren in Tageseinrichtungen und in Kindertagespflege (Kinderförderungsgesetz – KiföG), Bundesgesetzblatt Jahrgang 2008 Teil I Nr. 57, 15. Dezember 2008, p. 2403.

45 See http://www.bmfsfj.de/BMFSFJ/kinder-und-jugend,did=118994.html; access date: 21.04.2012.

46 Disposizioni per il sostegno della maternità e paternità, per il diritto alla cura e alla formazione e per il coordinamento dei tempi di città, published in Gazzetta Ufficiale n. 60 on 13.03.2000.

47 The *Gestione separata* is a special insurance scheme among others for people with atypical work.

48 The *Fondo delle politiche per la famiglia* was established at the Council of Ministers and assigned three million Euros for the year 2006 and annually ten million Euros as of 2007 (decreto-legge no. 223 of 04.07.2006, published in *Gazzetta ufficiale* on 04.07.2006).

49 The 210 million Euros were earmarked for the year 2007 and 180 million Euros for each of 2008 and 2009 (see http://www.politichefamiglia.it/media/24999/testo%20 commi%20finanz%202007. pdf; access date: 13.02.2010).

50 With article 44 of law no. 247/2007, published in Gazzetta Ufficiale n. 301 of 29.12.2007, the legislative decree n. 61/2000 (published in Gazzetta Ufficiale n. 66 of 20.03.2000) was modified to establish the right to part-time work for parents with children under age 13.

51 The EU-Directive 2006/54/EC is the "Directive on the implementation of the principle of equal opportunities and equal treatment of men and women in matters of employment and occupation". Among others, the aim is to maintain, adopt or expand positive action with a view to ensuring full equality in practice between men and women in working life.

52 "Norme in materia di promozione dell'occupazione", *Gazzetta Ufficiale* n. 154 of 04.07.1997 — Supplemento Ordinario n. 136.

53 Council Directive 97/81/EC of 15 December 1997 concerning the Framework Agreement on part-time work concluded by UNICE, CEEP and the ETUC – Annex : Framework agreement on part-time work, Official Journal L 014, 20/01/1998 P. 0009–0014.

54 Decreto legislativo no. 61/2000, "Attuazione della direttiva 97/81/CE relativa all'accordo quadro sul lavoro a tempo parziale concluso dall'UNICE, dal CEEP e dalla CES", *Gazzetta ufficiale* no. 66 of 20.03.2000.
55 *Decreto Legislativo* 10.09. 2003, n. 276 "Attuazione delle deleghe in materia di occupazione e mercato del lavoro, di cui alla legge 14 febbraio 2003, n. 30" published in Gazzetta Ufficiale n. 235 of 9.10.2003 — Supplemento Ordinario n. 159.
56 As in the German case, the differentiation between publicly and privately provided places is not always clear. Also, private institutions may be totally or partly publicly funded. This problem of exact differentiation exists also in other countries. Here I follow the definition provided by the Centro Nazionale (see source below table).
57 In 1999, seven areas of spending were specified: disability, childhood and adolescence, drug addiction, social assistance and social protection, migrant care policies, voluntary sector and international solidarity (Bruno 2011).
58 The essential levels may be defined as a) subjective rights, b) the type of services offered, c) quantitative standards, d) quality levels or e) expenditure levels (Ranci Ortigosa, Da Roit, and Sabatinelli 2007).
59 According to interview IT9, the firms that did invest never received the money. The Constitutional Court had ruled this intervention unconstitutional, because – as noted earlier – the state may fund social services only within the framework of the essential level of services. Since this level was not yet defined, financing selected providers but not others was a constitutional breach. Consequently, the firms did not receive the funding. Also the local governments suffered a loss.
60 Extraordinary plan for the development of socio-educative services such as crèches, integrative and innovative services (*Piano straordinario per lo sviluppo dei servizi socio-educativi, al quale concorrono gli asili nido, i servizi integrativi e quelli innovativi*), article 193 of the Disegno di legge Finanziaria of 1.10.2006.
61 Note, however, that in order to reach the EU goal, three billion Euros per year would be necessary (Brunetti and Tardiola 2007).
62 See paragraph 1259 of law no. 296 of 27 December 2006, "Disposizioni per la formazione del bilancio annuale e pluriennale dello Stato (legge finanziaria 2007)", published in Gazzetta Ufficiale no. 299 of 27.12. 2006 — Supplemento ordinario no. 244.
63 According to surveys among parents, the average demand for a childcare place for children younger than three amounts to 39 percent. Due to low fertility rates and a limited demand for full-time places (11 percent), the government argues that it can fulfil the goal of 33 percent until 2013 and does not expect parents to take legal action (Bundesministerium für Familie 2012).

References

Bano, Fabrizio. 2005. "Variazioni sul tempo di lavoro. La contro-riforma del lavoro a tempo parziale." *Lavoro e Diritto* 19 (2):295–319.
Bernini, Stefania. 2008. "Family Politics: Political Rhetoric and the Transformation of Family Life in the Italian Second Republic." *Journal of Modern Italian Studies* 13 (3):305–324.
Bimbi, Franca. 1999. "The Family Paradigm in the Italian Welfare State (1947–1996)." In *Gender Inequalities in Southern Europe: Women, Work and Welfare in the 1990s*, edited by María González, Teresa Jurado and Manuela Naldini, 72–88. London: Frank Cass.
Blome, Agnes, Wolfgang Keck, and Jens Alber. 2009. *Family and the Welfare State. Intergenerational Relations in Ageing Societies*. Cheltenham/Northampton: Edward Elgar.
Bothfeld, Silke. 2005. *Vom Erziehungsurlaub zur Elternzeit. Politisches Lernen im Reformprozess*. Frankfurt a.M./New York: Campus Verlag.

Brunetti, Margherita, and Andrea Tardiola. 2007. "Il piano asili." In *Le politiche di sostegno alle famiglie con figli. Il contesto e le proposte*, edited by Luciano Guerzoni, 159–172. Bologna: il Mulino.

Bruno, Antonella. 2011. "Financing Italian Welfare State: The Analysis of National Fund for Social Policies." 9th Annual ESPAnet Conference. Sustainability and transformation in European Social Policy, Valencia, 8–10 September 2011.

Bundesministerium für Familie, Senioren, Frauen und Jugend. 1989. *Erziehungsgeld, Erziehungsurlaub und Anrechnung von Kindererziehungszeiten in der Rentenversicherung. Gutachten des Wissenschaftlichen Beirats für Familienfragen beim Bundesminister für Jugend, Familie, Frauen und Gesundheit, Schriftenreihe des BMJFFG*. Stuttgart: Kohlhammer.

Bundesministerium für Familie, Senioren, Frauen und Jugend. 1998. *Tagesmütter-Handbuch. Kinderbetreuung in Tagespflege*. Berlin/Köln: Out-of-print, see http://ww.dji.de/cgi-bin/projekte/output.php?projekt=692&Jump1=LINKS&Jump2=8.

Bundesministerium für Familie, Senioren, Frauen und Jugend. 2004a. Chronologie zentraler familienpolitischer Maßnahmen seit Beginn der 14. Legislaturperiode 1998 — Stand Mai 2004. http://www.bmfsfj.de/Politikbereiche/familie,did=4198,render=render Print.html.

Bundesministerium für Familie, Senioren, Frauen und Jugend. 2004b. *Das Tagesbetreuungsausbaugesetz (TAG). Gesetz zum qualitätsorientierten und bedarfsgerechten Ausbau der Tagesbetreuung und zur Weiterentwicklung der Kinder- und Jugendhilfe*. Berlin.

Bundesministerium für Familie, Senioren, Frauen und Jugend. 2007. *Einigung zur Finanzierung des Betreuungsausbaus erzielt*. Berlin: http://www.bmfsfj.de/BMFSFJ/aktuelles,did=100436.html.

Bundesministerium für Familie, Senioren, Frauen und Jugend. 2009. Elterngeld und Elternzeit. Das Bundeselterngeld- und zeitgesetz. http://www.bmfsfj.de/bmfsfj/generator/RedaktionBMFSFJ/Broschuerenstelle/Pdf-Anlagen/Elterngeld-und-Elternzeit,property =pdf,bereich=bmfsfj,sprache=de,rwb=true.pdf.

Bundesministerium für Familie, Senioren, Frauen und Jugend. 2012. *Familienreport 2012. Leistungen, Wirkungen, Trends*. Berlin.

Centro nazionale di documentazione e analisi per l'infanzia e l'adolescenza. 2002. I servizi educativi per la prima infanzia. In *Quaderni no. 21*. Firenze: Istituto degli Innocenti.

Centro nazionale di documentazione e analisi per l'infanzia e l'adolescenza. 2008. Monitoraggio del piano di sviluppo dei servizi socio-educativi per 1 prima infanzia. Firenze: Istituto degli Innocenti.

Collozzi, Ivo, and Monica Mattenei. 1991. "La promozione sociale della famiglia: proposte legislative ed esperienze di servizi innovativi." In *Secondo rapporto sulla famiglia in Italia*, edited by Pierpaolo Donati, 446–514. Milano: Edizioni San Paolo.

Corsetti, Federica, Gianmarco Pagano, Antonella Parravano, and Francesca Valente. 2014. Reconciling Work and Family Life in Europe: A Comparative Perspective. Italian Report. In *European Working Group on Labour Law*. https://www2.le.ac.uk/departments/law/research/ewl/files/european-working-group-on-labour-law-italy-report-2014-pdf.

Donà, Alessia. 2009. "Why Is It So Difficult to Gender-mainstream the Italian Welfare State? The Case of Work-family Reconciliation Policies." 1st European Conference on Politics and Gender, Belfast, Queen's University. 21–23 January 2009.

Erler, Daniel. 2005. "Public Work-Family Reconciliation Policies in Germany and Italy. Exploring the Relevance of Problem Pressures, Institutions, and Actors." Department of Comparative and European Politics, Università degli studi di Siena.

Evers, Adalbert, and Birgit Riedel. 2002. Changing Family Structures and Social Policy: Child Care Services in Europe and Social Cohesion. National Report Germany. TSFEPS Project: http://www.emes.net/fileadmin/emes/PDF_files/Child_care/National_Reports/Child_care_NR_D.pdf.

Fargion, Valeria. 2000. "Timing and the Development of Social Care Services in Europe." In *Recasting European Welfare States*, edited by Maurizio Ferrera and Martin Rhodes, 59–88. London/Portland: Frank Cass.

Fendrich, Sandra, Jörg Fischer, and Matthias Schilling. 2005. *Erziehungsgeld und Elternzeit. Bericht des Jahres 2003. Im Auftrag des Bundesministeriums für Familie, Senioren, Frauen und Jugend*. Dortmund: Dortmunder Arbeitsstelle Kinder- und Jugendhilfestatistik.

Ferrera, Maurizio, Valeria Fargion, and Matteo Jessoula. 2012. *Alle radici del welfare all'italiana. Origini e futuro di un modello sociale squilibrato*. Venezia: Marsilio Editori.

Ferrera, Maurizio, and Elisabetta Gualmini. 2004. *Rescued by Europe? Social and Labour Market Reforms in Italy from Maastricht to Berlusconi*. Amsterdam: Amsterdam University Press.

Flora, Peter, ed. 1987. *Growth to Limits. The Western European Welfare States Since World War II. Volume 4. Appendix*. Berlin/New York: Walter de Gruyter.

Gerlach, Irene. 1996. *Familie und staatliches Handeln. Ideologie und politische Praxis in Deutschland*. Opladen: Leske + Budrich.

Gerlach, Irene. 2004. *Familienpolitik*. Wiesbaden: VS Verlag für Sozialwissenschaften.

Gerlach, Irene. 2009. "Wichtige Stationen bundesdeutscher Familienpolitik." *Informationen zur politischen Bildung* Familie und Familienpolitik (Heft 301):http://www.bpb.de/publikationen/HXBG2A,0,Wichtige_Stationen_bundesdeutscher_Familienpolitik.html: Access date: 25.10.2009.

Gerlach, Irene. 2010. *Familienpolitik. 2., aktualisierte und überarbeitete Auflage*. Wiesbaden: VS Verlag für Sozialwissenschaften.

Gualmini, Elisabetta. 2000. "Labour Market Policies In Italy. The 1990s and the New Wave of Reforms." *Österreichische Zeitschrift für Politikwissenschaft* 29 (3):329–340.

Hagemann, Karen. 2006. "Between Ideology and Economy: The "Time Politics" of Child Care and Public Education in the Two Germanys." *Social Politics* 13 (2):217–260.

ISTAT. 2011. "La conciliazione trafamiglia e lavoro." In *Statistiche report, Istat, 28*. http://www.istat.it/it/archivio/48912.

Istituto degli Innocenti di Firenze. 2008. Monitoraggio del piano di sviluppo dei servizi socio-educativi per 1 prima infanzia. Firenze.

Kolbe, Wiebke. 2002. *Elternschaft im Wohlfahrtsstaat. Schweden und die Bundesrepublik im Vergleich 1945–2000*. Frankfurt a.M./New York: Campus Verlag.

Kolvenbach, Franz-Josef, and Doreen Taubmann. 2006. "Neue Statistiken zur Kindertagesbetreuung." *Statistisches Bundesamt. Wirtschaft und Statistik 2/2006*:166-171.

Langer-El Sayed, Ingrid. 1980. *Familienpolitik. Tendenzen, Chancen, Notwendigkeiten. Ein Beitrag zur Entdämonisierung*. Frankfurt am Main S. Fischer.

Langer, Ingrid. 1985. "Die Mohrinnen hatten ihre Schuldigkeit getan... Staatlich-moralische Aufrüstung der Familien." In *Die fünfziger Jahre. Beiträge zu Politik und Kultur*, edited by Dieter Bänsch, 108–130. Tübingen: Gunter Narr Verlag.

Leiber, Simone. 2005. *Europäische Sozialpolitik und nationale Sozialpartnerschaft*. Frankfurt/New York: Campus Verlag.

Lo Faro, Antonio. 2002. "Fairness at Work? The Italian White Paper on Labour Market Reform." *Industrial Law Journal* 31 (2):190–198.

Lo Faro, Antonio. 2004. "Italy: Adaptable Employment and Private Autonomy in the Italian Reform of Part-time Work." In *Employment Policy and the Regulation of Part-time Work in the European Union: A Comparative Analysis*, edited by Silvana Sciarra, Paul Davies and Mark Freedland, 156–189. Cambridge: Cambridge University Press.
Madama, Ilaria. 2010. *Le politiche di assistenza sociale*. Bologna: il Mulino.
Moeller, Robert G. 1993. *Protecting Motherhood. Women and the Family in the Politics of Postwar West Germany*. Berkely, Los Angeles: University of California Press.
Münch, Ursula. 1990. *Familienpolitik in der Bundesrepublik Deutschland. Maßnahmen, Defizite, Organisation familienpolitischer Staatstätigkeit*. Freiburg im Breisgau: Lambertus.
Naldini, Manuela. 2003. *The Family in the Mediterranean Welfare States*. London: Frank Cass Publishers.
Naldini, Manuela, and Teresa Jurado. 2013. "Family and Welfare State Reorientation in Spain and Inertia in Italy from a European Perspective." *Population Review* 52 (1):43–61.
Naldini, Manuela, and Chiara Saraceno. 2008. "Social and Family Policies in Italy: Not Totally Frozen but far From Structural Reforms." *Social Policy & Administration* 42 (7):733–748.
Naumann, Ingela K. 2005. "Childcare and Feminism in West-Germany and Sweden in the 1960s and 1970s." *Journal of European Social Policy* 15 (1):47–63.
Naumann, Ingela K. 2006. "Childcare Politics in the West German and Swedish Welfare States from the 1950s to the 1970s." European University Institute. Department of Political and Social Sciences, Unpublished Dissertation.
Neumann, Karl. 1987. "Geschichte der öffentlichen Kleinkinderziehung von 1945 bis in die Gegenwart." In *Geschichte des Kindergartens, Vol. 1: Entstehung und Entwicklung der öffentlichen Kleinkindererziehung in Deutschland von den Anfängen bis zur Gegenwart*, edited by Günter Erning, Karl Neumann and Jürgen Reyer, 83–116. Freiburg i. Brsg.: Lambertus.
Pedersini, Roberto. 2000. "Government Approves Legislative Decree Transposing EU Directive on Part-time Work." In *EIROnline, european industrial relations observatory on-line*. http://www.eurofound.europa.eu/eiro/2000/02/feature/it0002261f.htm.
Ranci Ortigosa, Emanuele, Barbara Da Roit, and Stefania Sabatinelli. 2007. "Per una politica pubblica dei servizi per le famiglie con figli." In *Le politiche di sostegno alle famiglie con figli. Il contesto e le proposte*, edited by Luciano Guerzoni, 73–108. Bologna: il Mulino.
Rust, Ursula. 1990. *Familienlastenausgleich in der gesetzlichen Kranken-, Unfall- und Rentenversicherung, Beiträge zur Sozialpolitik und zum Sozialrecht Band 9*. Berlin: Erich Schmidt Verlag.
Saraceno, Chiara. 1991. "Redefining Paternity and Maternity: Gender, Pronatalism and Social Policies in Fascist Italy." In *Maternity and Gender Policies: Women and the Rise of the European Welfare States 1880s-1950s*, edited by Gisela Bock and Pat Thane, 196–221. London/New York: Routledge.
Saraceno, Chiara. 2003. *Mutamenti della famiglia e politiche sociali in Italia*. Bologna: il Mulino.
Schiller, Christof. 2016. *The Politics of Welfare State Transformation in Germany. Still a Semi-Souvereign State?* London/New York: Routledge.
Schmidt, Manfred G. 2005. *Sozialpolitik in Deutschland. Historische Entwicklung und internationaler Vergleich. 3., vollständig überarbeitete und erweiterte Auflage*. Wiesbaden: VS Verlag für Sozialwissenschaften.

Statistische Ämter des Bundes und der Länder. 2007. Kindertagesbetreuung regional 2006. Ein Vergleich aller 439 Kreise in Deutschland. Wiesbaden: http://www.sozialpolitik-aktuell.de/tl_files/sozialpolitik-aktuell/_Politikfelder/Familienpolitik/Dokumente/Kindertagesbetreuung_regional_2006.pdf: Access date: 11.03.2011.

Statistische Ämter des Bundes und der Länder. 2011. Kindertagesbetreuung regional 2010. Ein Vergleich aller 412 Kreise in Deutschland. Wiesbaden: http://www.destatis.de/jetspeed/portal/cms/Sites/destatis/Internet/DE/Content/Publikationen/Fachveroeffentlichungen/Sozialleistungen/KinderJugendhilfe/KindertagesbetreuungRegional5225405107004,property=file.pdf. Access date: 11.03.2011.

Statistisches Bundesamt. 2004. Kindertagesbetreuung in Deutschland. Einrichtungen, Plätze, Personal und Kosten 1990 bis 2002. Wiesbaden.

Treu, Tiziano. 2011. *Labour Law in Italy. Third revised edition.* Alphen aan den Rijn: Kluwer Law International.

von Oertzen, Christine, and Almut Rietzschel. 1998. "Comparing the Post-war Germanies: Breadwinner Ideology and Women's Employment in the Divided Nation, 1948–1970." In *The Rise and Decline of the Male Breadwinner Family?*, edited by Angélique Janssens, 175–196. International Review of Social History Vol. 5. Cambridge: Cambridge University Press.

5 How normative beliefs and voting behavior shape party competition on work-family policies

The previous chapter demonstrated how German and Italian work-family policies developed differently after 1990. While Germany focused on the expansion of the public provision of childcare and implemented a generous parental leave scheme especially in the mid-2000s, Italian work-family policies underwent only minor reforms. This chapter provides the first step of the empirical analyses that will explain these diverging paths. It presents multivariate regressions to examine how the development of normative beliefs and voting behavior shape party competition on work-family policies.

As is explained in Chapter 2, normative beliefs about mothers' employment are strongly related to peoples' demand for work-family policies. The design of work-family policies is thus a function of the dominant care ideal in a country (see Kremer 2007) and a change in this care ideal will eventually lead to policy reform. As policy responsiveness theory indicates, in order for reform to take place, the electorate must substantially change its normative beliefs. Also, political actors are more responsive under certain conditions, e.g. when political competition is intense (Hobolt and Klemmensen 2008). Political competition is again influenced by the spatial constellation of the party system, because the positioning of the parties determines where the competition is concentrated (Sartori 1976).

The questions this chapter aims to answer are whether the German and Italian populations changed their opinion regarding mothers' employment and whether the demand for more progressive work-family policies is driven by certain groups of the electorate. If these groups of voters become important for winning elections, parties might adapt their work-family policy agenda. A change in normative beliefs and shifts in voting behavior is likely to increase competition between parties regarding work-family policy issues. Before turning to the analyses of normative beliefs and voting behavior, the context of party competition is described. This includes the structure and key features of the German and the Italian party systems, as well as the parties' positions on family policies.

Party systems in Germany and Italy

Low polarization and centripetal competition in Germany

The German party system is characterized by low polarization and centripetal competition. Niedermayer (2006: 130) labels it as a "fluid five-party system": All parties that clear the 5 percent hurdle (up to five so far)[1] compete against each other and are able to form a coalition with each other (Mair 1997, Stöss, Haas, and Niedermayer 2006). The Christian Democratic Party (CDU) is an interdenominational center-right Christian party which has embraced the party ideology of a socially regulated market economy. The Social Democratic Party (SPD) is a center-left party. With respect to family policies, the SPD's focus is on redistribution and gender equality, whereas the CDU takes a more paternalist and a less redistributive orientation. Both parties accept the need for state intervention into matters of the family. For a long time, the CDU held traditional views about the role of women and put a larger emphasis on women's role as carers, while the SPD pursues emancipative family policies that promote women's employment (Gerlach 2004, Seeleib-Kaiser, van Dyk, and Roggenkamp 2008).

To the right of the CDU is the Free Democratic Party (Freie Demokratische Partei, FDP) which has remained rather vague and reserved with respect to state intervention into matters of the family (Dienel 2002). The Greens (Bündnis '90/ Die Grünen) complement the SPD on the left wing. The party is considered a proponent of gender equality, but is internally divided with respect to work-family policies (Bothfeld 2005). Further to the left is the Party of Democratic Socialism (Partei des Demokratischen Sozialismus, PDS), which is the successor party to the Socialist Unity Party of the GDR. The PDS calls for a strong redistributive welfare state. In 2005, the party renamed itself into the Linkspartei.PDS, and in 2007, it merged with the WASG (Wahlalternative Soziale Gerechtigkeit) to form the Die Linke (the Left).

Five elections took place in Germany during the period that I analyze here. A coalition between the CDU and the FDP ruled until 1998 and was then replaced by a coalition government consisting of the SPD and the Greens. They governed for two legislative periods, but called for early elections in 2005. Between 2005 and 2009, the CDU led a grand coalition government with the SPD (see Table 5.1).

The electoral defeat in 1998 marked a turning point for the CDU. For the first time in its history, the party received less than 40 percent of the votes in a federal

Table 5.1 Parliamentary elections in Germany: official results in % (1994–2009)[1]

	1994	1998	2002	2005	2009
CDU/CSU	41.5	35.1	38.5	35.2	33.8
SPD	36.4	40.9	38.5	34.2	23.0
Bündnis '90/ Die Grünen	7.3	6.7	8.6	8.1	10.7
FDP	6.9	6.2	7.4	9.8	14.6
Die Linke	4.4	5.1	4.0	8.7	11.9
Governing coalition	CDU, FDP	SPD, Greens	SPD, Greens	CDU, SPD	CDU, FDP

Notes:
1 Party results are % of party list votes for the Lower House. Only those parties with seats in parliament are reported.

Source: Bundeswahlleiter (http://www.bundeswahlleiter.de/de/; access date: 13.01.2015)

116 *Normative beliefs and party competition*

election. They needed a fresh start after the era of Chancellor Kohl, who had held office for 16 years. In the subsequent elections, the gap between the two largest German parties gradually closed. At the same time, the importance of both of the large parties diminished as their total share of votes decreased continuously. Structural changes in society pose a challenge for both parties. The CDU has to cope with the declining relevance of its core Catholic constituency. The SPD is struggling with the declining share of low-qualified and blue-collar workers.[2] At the same time, the attachment of the younger generations of blue-collar workers to the SPD and of the younger generations of the lower-middle class to the CDU has loosened (Müller and Klein 2011). In addition, the emergence and the growth of the Left party (Die Linke) provided a credible alternative to the SPD, even for voters in former West German states, which was important both during and after the contested so-called Hartz IV/Agenda 2010 reforms that were adopted under the second red-Green coalition in 2003 (Zohlnhöfer and Egle 2007). Hence both the CDU and the SPD were compelled to compete more strongly for centrist voters and to realign their focus by targeting new groups of voters.

Bipolar party system and centripetal competition in Italy

The Italian party system that had been in place from 1946 collapsed in the beginning of the 1990s.[3] In 1993, the electoral system was reformed[4] with the main intention to create a more concentrated system by reducing the number of parties. Yet, the fragmentation of the party system continued and the number of parties represented in parliament even increased (Bull and Rhodes 1997, 2007). On the right wing side, the neo-fascist Movimento Sociale Italiano (MSI) became the more moderate National Alliance (Alleanza Nazionale, AN), while a radical wing party, the Fiamma Tricolore, separated. The Northern League (Lega Nord, LN), which was founded in 1989, is a totally new political force. With a strong regional identity, LN endorses federalism and even secession. The most successful right-wing party was founded by Silvio Berlusconi. His party, Forza Italia (FI), is a conservative liberal party in favor of free markets and tax reductions. All the right-wing newcomers share certain features, e.g. the ability to demarcate themselves from the failed traditional party system and the presence of a dominant leader.

On the left wing side, the Communist Party transformed itself, and while it went through different stages and names, it remained the strongest party on the left. In 1998, the party by then named PDS (Partito Democratico della Sinistra) split into three different parties: the Democratic Party of the Left (Democratici di Sinistra, DS), which included the bulk of their original party, the Communist Refoundation Party (Partito della Rifondazione Comunista, PRC), and the Party of Italian Communists (Partito di Comunisti Italiani, PdCI). The former socialist party PSI, which had been strongly affected by the corruption scandals in the beginning of the 1990s, virtually disappeared. Its members were divided between those who entered the PDS and those who entered FI. A third group created a new center-left party, La Margherita. The former most important Christian

Democrats (Democrazia Cristiana, DC) later became the Italians People's Party (Partito Popolare Italiano, PPI) and gradually lost votes during the 1990s. Many former members joined FI, while still others formed smaller center-right parties, e.g. the Christian Democratic Center (Centro Cristiano Democratico, CCD) and the Christian Democratic Party (Partito dei Cristiano Democratici, CDU), which later allied with FI. The left of the former Christian Democrats merged with La Margherita to the social Christian party, Democracy and Liberty – the Marguerite (Democrazia e libertà – La Margherita, DL) in 2002 (see Table A3 in the appendix for an overview of the parties' development).

The high number of parties is the result of the fact that it remains attractive for small parties under the new system to stay autonomous, as 25 percent of the seats are allocated according to proportional representation. At the same time, it makes sense for parties to form pre-electoral coalitions, because small parties could potentially threaten any gains that might be made by larger parties with whom they had common ground (Cotta and Verzichelli 2007, Zohlnhöfer 2006).

At the beginning of the 1990s, the Italian party system was characterized by three poles: a left pole dominated by the post-communist party PDS, a center

Table 5.2 Parliamentary elections in Italy: official results in % (1994–2008)[1]

	1994	1996	2001	2006	2008
PSI	2.2				
PDS/DS[2]	20.4	21.1	16.6	31.2	
PRC[3]	6.1	8.6	5.0	5.8	
PPI/DL-Margh.[4]	11.1	6.8	14.5		
PD[5]					33.2
Di Pietro It Valori					4.4
Verdi				2.1	
FI[6]	21.0	20.6	29.4	23.7	37.4
AN	13.5	15.7	12.0	12.3	
LN	8.4	10.1	3.9	4.6	8.3
Patto Segni	4.7				
CCD/UDC[7]		5.8	3.2	6.8	5.6
Governing coalition	FI, LN, AN, CCD	L'Ulivo	FI, LN, AN, CCD-CDU	L'Unione	PDL, LN

Notes:
1 Party results are % of party list votes for the Lower House. Only those parties with seats in parliament are reported.
2 PDS transformed into DS in 1998. In 2006, Ulivo instead of DS (in coalition with DL).
3 In 1998, the Pdci splintered and, in contrast to PRC, further supported the left-wing government coalition.
4 PPI was part of "Popolari per Prodi" in 1996.
5 PD is a merger of DS and DL.
6 In 2008, FI and AN merged to a party with the name "Il Popolo delle libertà" (PDL).
7 The CCD formed an alliance with the CDU for the elections in 1996 and 2001. As of 2002, the party is UDC.

Source: Ministero dell'Interno (http://elezionistorico.interno.it/index.php?tp=C; access date: 20.05.2010)

pole and a right pole with FI, AN and LN. Since the political crisis, competition has concentrated more on the left and the right poles. As a consequence, the party system acquired a structure that was more clearly bipolar, which stimulates centripetal competition (Cotta and Verzichelli 2007). At the same time, the involvement of a high number of parties in coalitions encourages centrifugal competition and polarized behavior similar to the pre-1992 era (Bardi 2007, Picot 2012). This situation has resulted in a number of problems and restructurings of governments throughout the 1990s. Between 1994 and 2008, five elections and several reshuffles took place. Starting with a right-wing government, the party composition of the executive alternated between left-wing and right-wing parties (see Table 5.3).

For the coalitions, it is often difficult to agree on common platforms, goals, agendas and a broadly accepted leader because parties differ with regard to their ideological traditions and constituencies. This fosters internal competition. This is also reflected in the fact that voters tend to move more between parties of one coalition than between the two coalitions (Corbetta and Segatti 2004). Internal competition is particularly problematic for the center left, where parties support state involvement in matters of the family in principle, but are also affected by struggles between Catholic-oriented (e.g. La Margherita) and Social Democratic (e.g. Democratici di Sinistra, DS) positions. The new parties on the political right see themselves as the defenders of the traditional family and oppose state intervention into the family (Bernini 2008). Although the parties display a less religious profile than the previously dominant DC, FI in particular continues to rely on the ethical and moral support of the Catholic Church (Naldini and Saraceno 2008).

Table 5.3 The development of the Italian executive, 1994–2008

Legislative period	Parties in government[1]	Presidents of the Council
XII		
10.05.1994–22.12.1994	FI, LN, AN, CCD	Berlusconi
17.01.1995–17.05.1996	Cabinet of "technocrats"	Dini
XIII		
18.05.1996–09.10.1998	L'Ulivo	Prodi
21.10.1998–18.12.1999	L'Ulivo, PdCI, Udr	D'Alema
22.12.1999–19.04.2000	L'Ulivo, PdCI, Udeur	D'Alema
25.04.2000–11.06.2001	L'Ulivo, PdCI, Udeur	Amato
XIV		
11.06.2001–23.04.2005	FI, LN, AN, CCD-CDU	Berlusconi
23.04.2005–17.05.2006	FI, LN, AN, CCD-CDU	Berlusconi
XV		
17. 05.2006–08.05.2008	L'Unione, PRC, PdCI, Verdi, Italia dei valori, Udeur, RnP, I Socialisti, PP	Prodi
XVI		
08.05.2008–17.11.2011	PDL, LN	Berlusconi

Note:
1 See Table A.3 in the appendix for a description of the development of the parties.

Source: My compilation

In sum, centripetal party competition prevails in both countries. Since the center is crucial for parties in a system of centripetal competition, a change in the population's normative beliefs influences the political struggle for majorities. Parties are incentivized to adapt their policies in order to serve the demand of the centrist voter. When there is no change in beliefs, on the other hand, parties have less incentive to reform policies. Thus the first step of the analysis is to examine and compare the development of the population's normative beliefs about childcare and mothers' employment between Germany and Italy. To find out whether or not changes in beliefs may be explained by compositional changes in the population, several characteristics will be controlled for within a regression framework.

In addition to the focus on the political center, the two largest German parties are compelled to look for new voters because of the diminishing role of their traditional constituencies. The Italian alliances struggle with tendencies of centrifugal competition. What does this mean for party competition? There are two crucial questions to ask: First, which groups of voters prefer which kind of work-family policy? To this end, the evolution of beliefs towards childcare and mothers' employment is examined across population subgroups in a dynamic perspective between 1990 and 2008. This serves to identify the groups of voters that parties might target and compete for by offering policies that appeal to them. The second question asks which parties those same social groups vote for in the identical time period. By analyzing both normative beliefs and voting behavior along identical socio-demographic characteristics, the beliefs of specific constituencies (or certain groups that could be targeted by political parties) can be identified. This provides a more detailed understanding of the consequences of shifts in beliefs for party competition.

Empirical analyses: data and methods

Normative beliefs about mothers' employment

The development of normative beliefs is analyzed using the European Value Survey waves of 1990, 1999 and 2008 (EVS, see Halman 2001, Halman and Vloet 1994). The EVS is a large-scale, cross-national, standardized and repeated survey research program. Among various questions on the consequences of women working, I will concentrate on whether a preschool child suffers if his or her mother is working. Empirical studies have shown the impact of these beliefs on maternal employment (Steiber and Haas 2009) and on the preference for either state support of the male-breadwinner model or of the dual-earner model (Bolzendahl and Olafsdottir 2008). The sensitivity of the indicator is checked by replicating all analyses for a similar question, i.e. whether a working mother can establish as warm and secure a relationship with her children compared to a mother who does not work (see Table A.8 and Table A.9 in the appendix). It could be argued that the two indicators are somewhat limited in their capacity to measure the degree to which people (dis)approve of the mothers of small children holding employment, as they do not distinguish between very young and older children or between

120 *Normative beliefs and party competition*

differing working-time schedules (Saraceno 2011). However, precisely because these two statements are rather generic, they should be useful for unraveling deeply held beliefs on the issue of proper childcare and mothers' employment, which matters for paradigmatic shifts in work-family policies.

The dependent variable is whether an individual supports the employment of mothers, i.e. s/he thinks that it does *not* harm the well-being of children. The original answers measured on a four-item scale (strongly agree, agree, disagree, strongly disagree) are dichotomized (agree vs. disagree). The variables are dichotomized because it is unlikely that "strongly" has a consistent meaning across various countries (Brady and Finnigan 2014). They are equal to one if people support the employment of mothers, i.e. they disagree with the question. Correspondingly, the variables are coded zero if individuals are against mothers' employment during the child's early years, i.e. they agree with the question. The coding is the other way around for the second indicator, i.e. agreeing with the question means support of mothers' employment and disagreeing with the question means being against mothers' employment.

Binary logistic regressions are estimated separately for Germany and Italy, and average marginal effects (AME) for the probability of having progressive beliefs are reported. All three EVS waves are pooled and the models are estimated separately for Germany and Italy on these data. Time dummies for 1999 and 2008 (with 1990 as the base category) measure the average change in beliefs for each country while holding a number of covariates constant. In addition, groups of individuals who are more in favor of the male-breadwinner model or of the dual-earner model are identified. Control variables are region of residence, sex, age, employment status, marital status, children in household, religiosity, confession, union membership, and level of education. For the definition and the coding of the variables, see Table A.4 in the appendix. The longitudinal dimension in the data demonstrates whether or not there have been changes in the normative beliefs of the electorate to which political parties might respond. All the findings for Germany and Italy are systematically compared.

Voting behavior

In the second step, the voting behavior of the groups that emerged as significant in the analysis of normative beliefs is examined. In that way, the findings of the beliefs' analyses can be related to regression analyses of voting behavior. This sheds light on the dynamics of party competition. The time dimension in this data helps to identify changes in voting patterns which might prompt parties to align their policies.

The analysis of voting decisions is based on national post-election surveys. It is not possible to directly predict voting with the normative beliefs because the EVS does not include questions on the actual voting behavior, and the survey timings do not correspond to elections. Data for the 1994 Bundestag election, therefore, come from the "Nachwahlstudie Bundestagswahl 1994" (ZUMA et al. 2012). For the Bundestag elections of 1998, 2002, 2005 and 2009, I use data from the Comparative Study of Electoral Systems (CSES) study (The Comparative Study of

Electoral Systems (CSES) 2003, 2007, 2012). Italy only participated in the CSES project in 2006. However, ITANES (Italian National Election Studies)[5] provides comparable data for the elections of 1994, 1996,[6] 2001, 2006 and 2008. Because of the various transformations of the Italian party and electoral system, political parties are merged into party blocs of right wing, left wing and all remaining parties (see Table A.4 in the appendix). This procedure is warranted because political competition mainly happened along those lines (Bellucci and Heath 2012). For Germany, the analysis is focused on the two largest parties, the CDU and SPD, as they usually compete for the leadership in any governing coalition. Estimates for the other parties are given in Tables A.11–A.13 in the appendix. Multinomial logit models of voters' choices in national elections between 1994 and 2009 are specified for both countries. The dependent variable is the voting decision for a specific party in Germany and a coalition bloc in Italy. All estimation tables report average marginal effects of the independent variables with respect to the probability of voting for the respective party.

Explanatory variables

The selection of the covariates is guided by the literature on attitudes towards gender roles in international comparisons (e.g. Banaszak and Plutzer 1993, Lück 2009, Mischke 2014, Sjöberg 2004) and the literature on voting behavior of social groups (e.g. Pappi and Brandenburg 2010, Weßels 2011). Consistently using the same variables across both analyses enables us to see which parties social groups with a preference for a certain work-family model vote for. However, it also necessitates compromise with respect to the choice and definition of variables. For example, while it would theoretically make sense to differentiate between men's and women's experiences of employment for the explanation of normative beliefs towards mothers' employment (see e.g. Banaszak and Plutzer 1993), this interaction effect does not help to explain voting decisions. Therefore, only own employment is controlled for in both analyses. The following paragraphs outline the theoretical expectations regarding the relationship between the explanatory factors and normative beliefs and voting behavior, respectively.

Region of residence

The region of residence is a proxy for the living circumstances that affect individual beliefs. In regions with a (history of) high female-employment rates such as in the eastern German *Bundesländer*, for example, normative beliefs should be more supportive of mothers' employment (Goerres and Tepe 2012, Hank, Tillmann, and Wagner 2001). Regional differences in voting behavior exist in Germany with the dominance of the Die Linke party in eastern Germany and the CSU in Bavaria being two striking examples (Weßels and Wagner 2011). Similar regional patterns can be found in Italy. The emergence and success of the Lega Nord in northern Italy and the persistent support for the parties of the center-left in central Italy are cases in point (Cotta and Verzichelli 2007).

Sex

Since care responsibilities are gendered and women face more difficulties in reconciling work and care, women should be more likely than men to be in favor of policies that help to combine both. Hence women are expected to express more progressive normative beliefs concerning mothers' employment. There are no clear-cut gender cleavages with respect to voting decisions. In the past, women mainly voted for conservative parties, while in recent times, women tend to vote for left-wing parties (Giger 2009). However, women occupied in care work have traditionally been oriented towards parties that preserve the conservative model of the family, whereas employed women tend to vote for libertarian or social-democratic parties (Inglehart 1977, Manza and Brooks 1999).

Employment

Individual's employment experience should be positively related to the support of the dual-earner model, if the alternative is to give up the job (and income) for family reasons. It could be argued that this effect is more relevant for women and less obvious for men because of the gender division of work (Banaszak and Plutzer 1993). On the other hand, the effect may also be blurred for women: they may not be in employment either because they want to care for their children – in which case they may then support the male-breadwinner model – or they want to work, but cannot accept a job because adequate extra-familial childcare is not available; in this case, they may support the dual-earner model. In general, unemployed people tend to vote for leftist parties and self-employed people prefer liberal parties (Biorcio 2006, Faas 2010, Weßels 2011).

Marital status and children in the household

Both marital status and the presence of children in the household will be included in the analysis. Persons who follow a traditional path and are married might have different lifestyles than those who are either not married or are divorced. These lifestyles have an impact on their views on gender roles (Banaszak and Plutzer 1993). The impact of children on normative beliefs is unclear. They may raise the issue of how to reconcile work and care and should thus lead to more demand for dual-earner-oriented policies. On the other hand, they could reinforce the traditional division of work and hence be positively related to more traditional beliefs. By the same token, those types of individuals or families might rather favor conservative parties. Housewives, for example, tend to vote for conservative parties (Ceccarini and Diamanti 2006).

Age

A higher age has been shown to be associated with more traditional views. This might be a generational effect. For example, the generation that grew up during the 1950s when the male-breadwinner model was prevalent should have different attitudes than the generation of the 1970s, when feminist movements gained ground and gender roles were challenged (Lück 2009). But age should also matter because of material self-interest: younger people who have to reconcile work and care are more in need of dual-earner-oriented policies than older people and should thus have more modern normative beliefs (Goerres and Tepe 2012). While younger people tend to favor libertarian parties, such as the Greens in Germany, older people are less likely to vote for these parties (Goerres 2008, Weßels 2011).

Religious denomination and religious activity

Both the variables religious denomination and religious activity will be analyzed. Religious doctrine often includes norms of a gender division of work and the provision of (early) childcare by mothers. In addition, some religions, e.g. the Catholic Church, promote a subordinate role of women in church hierarchy more than others, e.g. the Lutheran churches (Gerhards and Hölscher 2003, Leitner 1999). An individual commitment to a religion likely increases the endorsement of its norm. This should be strengthened when the individual is actively religious. Individuals who go to church regularly will be less likely to support the dual-earner model. Religious people, especially Catholics, are the core constituency of Christian conservative parties. This well-known value cleavage is persistent and has been one of the strongest determinants of voting decisions (Roßteutscher 2012, Segatti 2006). A crucial difference between Germany and Italy might be that the prevalence of attachment to a religious denomination is much stronger in Italy and is therefore less decisive for individual voting behavior.

Education

A high level of education is in general associated with a higher social status and more liberal attitudes (Lück 2009). Larger investments in human capital are related to higher levels of work commitment because of better access to psychologically rewarding jobs and higher wages (Sjöberg 2004). Thus higher educational attainment should increase the approval of dual-earner-oriented policies. Similarly, high-educated persons rather favor libertarian or center-left parties, whereas low-educated individuals predominantly support left-wing parties that support social equality.

Union membership

Union membership serves as a proxy for whether a person is a labor-market insider or outsider. In theory, insiders are a group of privileged employees, mostly male, with secure jobs. These individuals are arguably not interested in work-family policies aimed at facilitating mothers' employment because they are afraid of losing privileges and earning reduced wages (Bonoli and Reber 2009). Union members should thus have more traditional attitudes. There is also a strong link

124 *Normative beliefs and party competition*

between union membership and the decision to vote for social-democratic parties (Debus 2011). The exact definition and information about the coding of the explanatory variables is given in Table A.4 in the appendix.

Normative beliefs about mothers' employment: towards support of the dual-earner model?

This section systematically compares beliefs between Germany and Italy. Has there been a shift in beliefs over time? Can we trace certain patterns across population subgroups which are relevant to party competition? Figures 5.1 and 5.2 show how beliefs about mothers' employment have evolved in Germany and Italy. Figure 5.1 presents the share of people holding "progressive beliefs" as defined earlier. In 1990, only about 18 percent of the people in Germany disagreed with the statement that a preschool child suffers if the mother works. This share rises dramatically to about 45 percent in 1999 and further increases to about 50 percent in 2008. According to this indicator, more progressive beliefs have clearly become prevalent in Germany.[7]

In Italy, however, normative beliefs have not changed. The low levels of disagreement with the first statement have virtually remained constant over the last

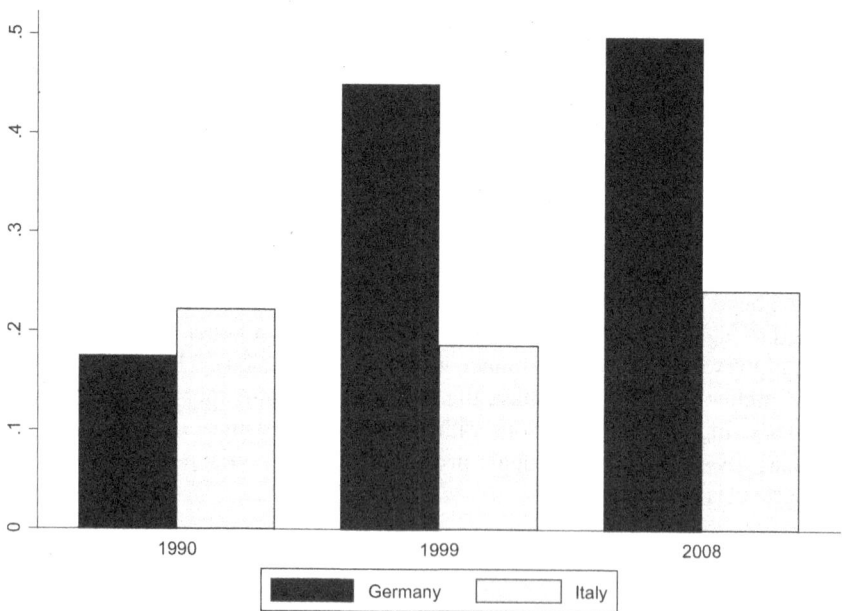

Figure 5.1 Share of progressive beliefs in population, Germany and Italy, 1990, 1999 and 2008

Notes: Progressive beliefs are measured as disagreement to the statement "A preschool child is likely to suffer if his or her mother works". See Table A.5 in the appendix for more details.
Source: European Values Study 1990, 1999, 2008; my calculations

20 years; they even slightly decreased until 1999 and have since returned to the level they were at in the beginning of the 1990s.[8]

What lies behind this average shift in normative beliefs among the German population? Individuals may simply have changed their opinion on the matter. An alternative explanation could be that the composition of the population has changed over the years. So even if people have kept their beliefs, the progressive types may have gained a higher weight in the overall population. To address this question, pooled cross-section models over all EVS waves are estimated separately for Germany and Italy. These models contain control variables for individual characteristics. In these models, the average change in normative beliefs is measured by using time dummies for the years 1999 and 2008 (with 1990 being the reference category) while holding the composition of the population constant.

Figure 5.2 shows that there is a strong and highly significant time trend towards more progressive beliefs in Germany between 1990 and 1999 (see for more

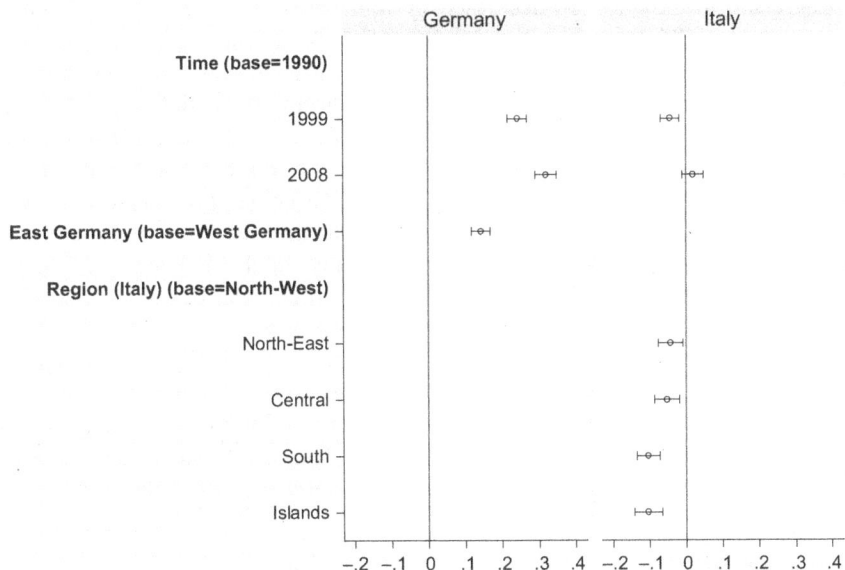

Figure 5.2 Development of normative beliefs on mothers' employment and childcare (pooled logistic regression model)

Notes: The point estimates show average marginal effects for probability of having progressive normative beliefs (measured as disagreement to the statement, "A preschool child is likely to suffer if his or her mother works"). Control variables in the regression include region, sex, age, employment status, marital status, children, religious denomination, religiosity, union membership, level of education. See Table A.5 in the appendix for more details.

Source: European Values Study 1990, 1999, 2008; my calculations

126 *Normative beliefs and party competition*

details Table A.6 in the appendix). The likelihood that someone will disagree with the first question had increased by about 24 percentage points in 1999. This trend continues between 1999 and 2008 as the difference to the base year in 2008 grows to 32 percentage points. These findings are confirmed by the findings for the second belief indicator. The probability of having progressive beliefs had decreased by 22 percent by 1999 and by 26 percentage points by 2008 (see Table A.8 in the appendix). It should be noted that the effect is smaller compared to the average shares of people discussed earlier, especially for the second indicator. The change in beliefs can thus partially be explained by shifts in the socio-demographic composition of the population. Figure 5.2 also shows that eastern Germans have a much higher probability of supporting mothers' employment than western Germans. This is not surprising given that mothers' employment was widespread in the former GDR. However, the climate for more progressive policies was not only favorable in the eastern part, but work-family policy reforms were also increasingly wished for in the western part of Germany.[9]

Again, Italy does not exhibit a trend towards more progressive normative beliefs. Between 1990 and 1999, the reverse is true for the first variable. Beliefs became slightly, but statistically significant, more traditional; the probability of disagreeing to the question decreased by four percentage points (see for more details Table A.7 in the appendix). By 2008, beliefs had once again become more progressive with results at a level similar to the baseline year 1990 and an insignificant coefficient. Measured by the second indicator, the beliefs of the Italians became slightly more progressive between 1999 and 2008 (see Table A.9 in the appendix). The magnitude of the change is only one-fourth the size compared to Germany. Figure 5.2 also demonstrates regional variation of beliefs in Italy. The traditional regional cleavage is between the industrialized north and the southern Mezzogiorno. The northwest, northeast, center, south and islands are distinguished. Persons living in all regions have more traditional beliefs compared to the northwest (see Table A.7 in the appendix).

To conclude, a marked change towards more progressive beliefs has taken place in Germany between 1990 and 2008, whereas the traditional attitudes remained at almost constant levels in Italy. This average change of attitudes is interpreted as a general shift of normative beliefs in a society. This should induce an increased demand of the electorate for progressive work-family policies in Germany.

Normative beliefs across subgroups of the population

In addition to the general trends in normative beliefs, the distribution of normative beliefs across subgroups of the population is also relevant for political competition, as parties may target specific constituencies. The investigation of the individual covariates shows that in both Germany and Italy, some groups are more likely to support mothers' employment than others (see Figures 5.3 and 5.4 and Tables A.6 and A.7 in the appendix).

Figures 5.3 and 5.4 show that, among the individual characteristics, sex is associated with a significant difference. Women are markedly more supportive of

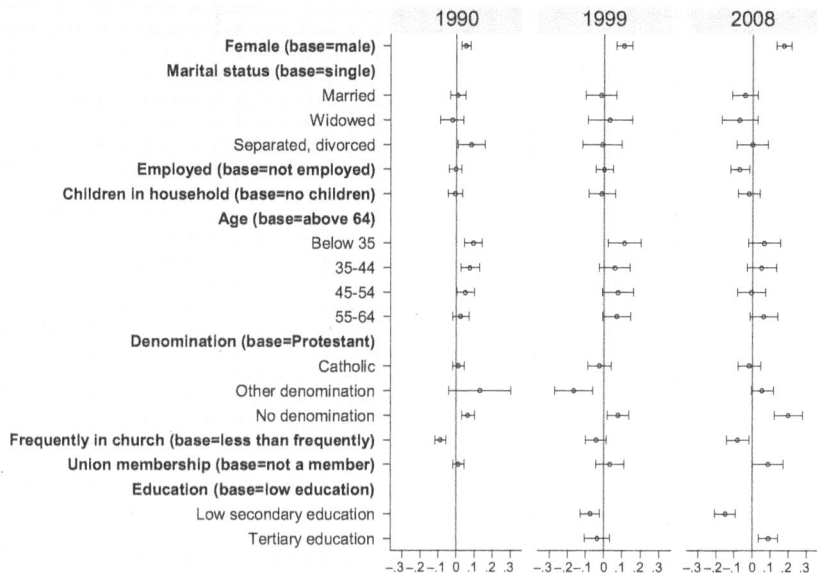

Figure 5.3 Attitudes towards mothers' employment and childcare, Germany, 1990, 1999 and 2008

Notes: The point estimates show average marginal effects for the probability of supporting mothers' employment. Control variables in the regression include region, sex, age, employment status, marital status, children, religious denomination, religiosity, union membership, level of education.
Source: European Values Study 1990, 1999, 2008; my calculations

mothers' employment than men. This effect is robust over both countries and all indicators. The magnitude of the effect ranges between 5 and 17 percentage points in Germany and is markedly higher in comparison to Italy. Women, as expected, strive much more for adequate work-family policies. Therefore, reforms in this policy field that strengthen the dual-earner model offer an opportunity to satisfy women's demands.

Marital and employment status in the household do not have a clear-cut relationship with attitudes. More surprisingly, the same holds for people who have children in the household; the effects of traditional male-breadwinner couples may offset those of families with working parents. As mentioned earlier, interaction effects between employment status and children in the household turned out to be insignificant. Trivariate interactions for women with small children in employment were impossible to identify or also insignificant.

In 1990, there was a significant difference between the beliefs of different age groups in Germany. Although the AMEs for younger individuals still point to more progressive attitudes in 2008, the effect seems to have vanished over time,

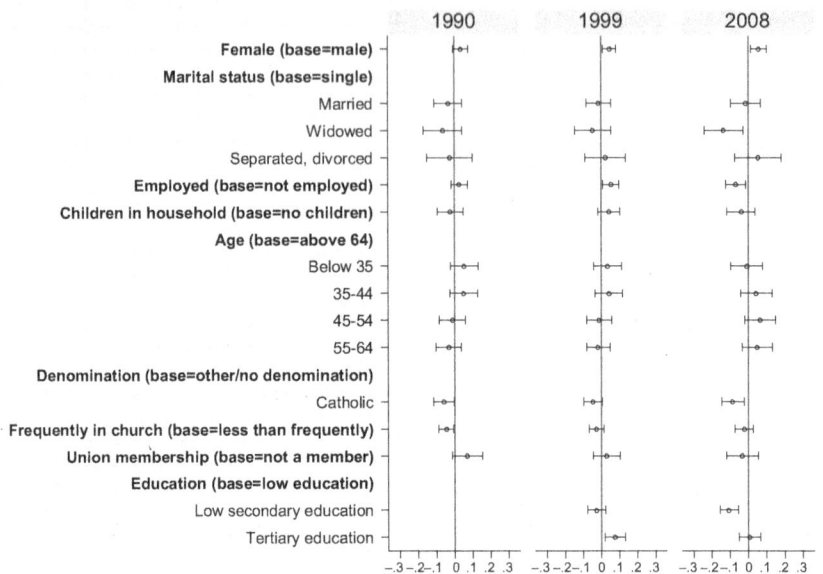

Figures 5.4 Attitudes towards mothers' employment and childcare, Italy, 1990, 1999 and 2008

Notes: The point estimates show average marginal effects for the probability of supporting mothers' employment. Control variables in the regression include region, sex, age, employment status, marital status, children, religious denomination, religiosity, union membership, level of education.
Source: European Values Study 1990, 1999, 2008; my calculations

as none of the AMEs is statistically significant. It could be that young women (and not the young people in general) exhibit particularly progressive beliefs. I estimated interaction effects of age and sex. Although there is some evidence that younger women are more progressive, not much is added to the main effects, as all interaction effects are insignificant. Unfortunately, it is difficult to identify the triple interaction effect of age, sex and children because of case-number restrictions. In Italy, beliefs never varied much with age.

Religious individuals express more traditional views. The difference between the religions is not relevant in Germany when religious activity is controlled for. But individuals who often go to church have clearly more traditional views on childcare. The effect was more pronounced in 1990, but it persists through 2008. In Italy, by contrast, being Roman Catholic matters more than religious activity. Both variables are associated with traditional attitudes. Although the number of religiously bound individuals is decreasing overall, the topic seemingly remains salient for religious voters. This fact certainly has to be taken into account among politicians and parties that target religious voters.

Finally, low-educated people are rather traditional and highly educated people display more progressive beliefs, which is not particularly surprising. The same is true for income: richer people have clearly more progressive beliefs. The income variable is not included in the main models and the results tables, as the response rate was low and too many observations would have been lost. The income effect estimated on a reduced sample was significant throughout for both countries and all indicators. Union membership – as a characteristic for labor-market insiders – is associated with modern attitudes. The effect is mostly insignificant, though, except for Germany in 2008.

To sum up the findings on the individual heterogeneity of normative beliefs on mothers' employment, it was shown that women, people in eastern Germany and Italy's northwest and highly educated people are more likely to favor policies supporting the dual-earner model, while actively religious and low-educated persons tend to prefer the male-breadwinner model.

The next section looks at which parties different social groups vote for. The aim is to understand why and when political parties have a particular interest in reforming work-family policies, where others have less interest. Political competition between parties or coalitions on work-family policy issues is likely to increase if key groups of voters demand more progressive work-family policies. Hence the analysis of voting behavior will be linked to the analysis of normative beliefs. If groups that were shown to be more progressive also become more important as voters for parties, then this could have an influence on the parties' work-family policy agenda.

Voting behavior of different social groups

The two largest parties in Germany have lost considerable ground since the beginning of the 1990s (see Table 5.1). For the first time ever, the CDU won less than 40 percent of the votes in 1998, while the SPD's share of the vote peaked in the same election. Afterwards, the share of votes for both parties consistently dropped, and in 2009, both parties' combined share of the vote was 57 percent of all votes, which marked a historical low point. As a consequence, party competition has stiffened. This has had two effects: First, the two large parties compete more strongly for the political center because their core clientele is shrinking. Second, both have to look beyond their traditional constituencies and attract new groups of voters to remain a decisive force in any coalition government. In Italy, political competition among blocs has not changed in a similar way. The coalitions had more comfortable majorities after each election and may rely on their core constituencies. However, the coalitions have to struggle with internal problems between the various parties.

Turning to those socio-demographic groups from the analysis of normative beliefs, it becomes obvious that regional variation is also important for voting behavior: western Germans, except for 2002, had a higher probability of voting for the Social Democrats than eastern Germans (see Figure 5.5). For the Christian Democrats, the reverse is true for 1994 and 2009: in 1994, they attracted a

130 *Normative beliefs and party competition*

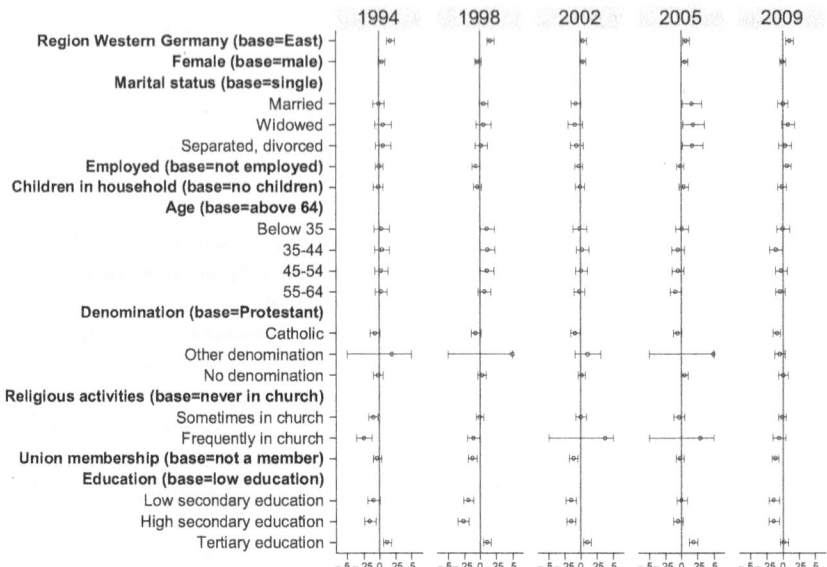

Figure 5.5 Probability of voting for "SPD", Germany, 1994–2009 (AMEs from multinomial logistic regression)

Notes: Confidence bands < -0.5 set to -0.5 and > 0.5 set to 0.5 in graph.
Sources: Nachwahlstudie Bundestagswahl 1994; CSES 1998, 2002, 2005, 2009; my calculations

disproportionate amount of eastern German voters; in the meantime, they became equally attractive for voters in both regions (see Figure 5.6). Regional heterogeneity also exists in Italy. The central region is a stronghold for the left alliance. Right-wing parties are more dominant in the northwest region (see Figure 5.7 and Figure 5.8). Hence, in both countries, people living in regions exhibiting more progressive normative beliefs do not vote for the leftist parties or coalitions.

For women, we do not find significantly different voting patterns compared to men holding other covariates constant. This result does not change when sex is interacted with age groups. It shows that women's significantly more progressive beliefs, as shown earlier, do not preclude them from voting for parties with rather traditional family policy agendas. The only exception is the German election of 2005, where women had a higher probability of voting for the SPD. Marital and employment status and the existence of children in the household do not exhibit consistent voting patterns over time in either Germany or Italy.

The German Christian Democrats clearly had a hard time attracting younger voters during the 1990s. In particular, the 1998 Bundestag election showed that younger individuals were turning away from the party in proportionately greater numbers compared to people older than 65. This pattern has lost some of its

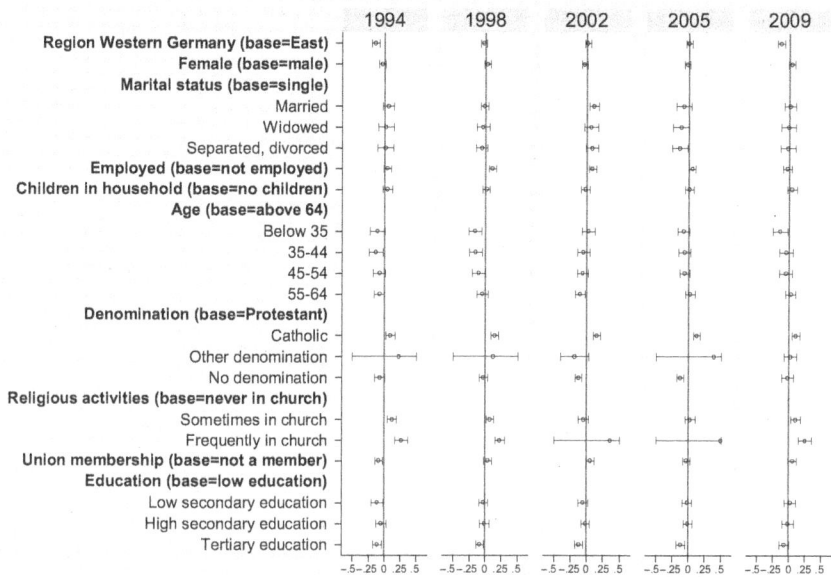

Figure 5.6 Probability of voting for "CDU", Germany, 1994–2009 (AMEs from multinomial logistic regression)

Notes: Confidence bands < -0.5 set to -0.5 and > 0.5 set to 0.5 in graph.

Sources: Nachwahlstudie Bundestagswahl 1994; CSES 1998, 2002, 2005, 2009; my calculations

significance. Although younger age groups are still less likely to vote for the CDU, most of the effects are no longer statistically significant. For Italy, the generation gap does not play a significant role for the voting decision.

Religious affiliation and religious activities are still a very strong predictor of the probability of voting for a Christian democrat or conservative party. Being Catholic, for example, increases the probability of voting for the CDU by more than ten percentage points compared to Protestants. An even stronger effect exists for religious activity. In 2009, e.g. the probability of voting for the CDU is 25 percentage points higher for people who frequently go to church. This relationship also holds for right-wing parties in Italy, although the significance of the "religious denomination" effect has vanished in the last two elections. Religiousness (particularly Catholicism) remains one of the strongest individual constituency characteristics for conservative parties. The salience of the beliefs of religious voters with respect to mothers' employment was shown earlier. This makes it clear why conservative Christian parties retained traditional views for a long time.

On the other hand, the quantitative importance of religious supporters has steadily decreased against a backdrop of secularization in Germany. Therefore,

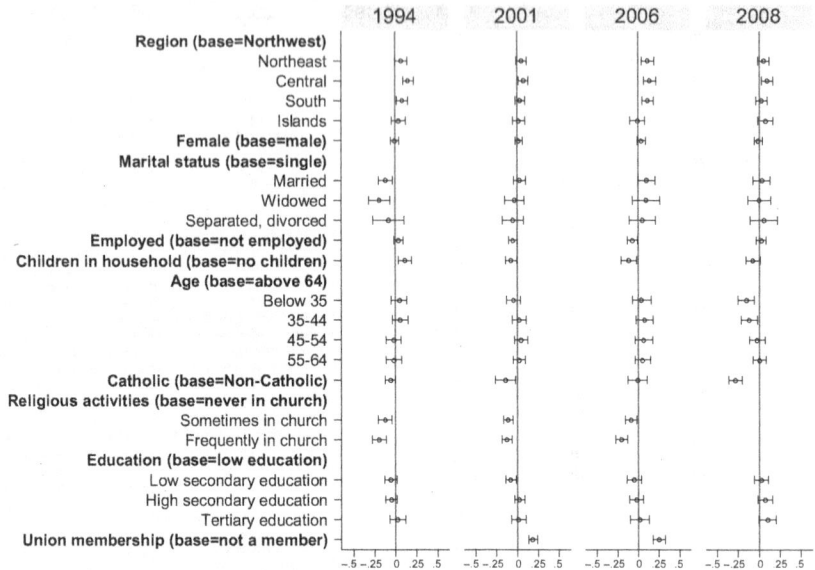

Figure 5.7 Probability of voting for "center-left party bloc", Italy, 1994–2008 (AMEs from multinomial logistic regression)

Notes: Confidence bands < -0.5 set to -0.5 and > 0.5 set to 0.5 in graph.
Sources: ITANES 1994, 2001, 2006, 2008; my calculations

the CDU has to cope with the declining relevance of its core Catholic constituency. The share of the German population that is Catholic has been declining for several years, as has the share of religiously active people (see Table 5.4). This trend has accelerated since unification, when the former GDR, an almost irreligious society,[10] joined the former FRG (Niedermayer 2006).

In contrast to the situation in Germany, religious activity and the Catholic Church have retained an important role in the life of Italians. According to the EVS data, about 80 percent of Italians are Catholic with half of them going to church regularly (see Table 5.4). Even though the numbers are in slight decline, the fact that Italy is the country with the most dioceses in Europe underlines the importance of the Catholic Church in the country (Jansen 2007). This could explain not only the stable attitudes in the majority of the population but also the reluctance of (any) political party to take up the issue and propose reforms, even if political leaders have different views.

Finally, education and union membership influence the probability of voting for the Social Democrats in Germany. Figure 5.5 shows that the AMEs for all

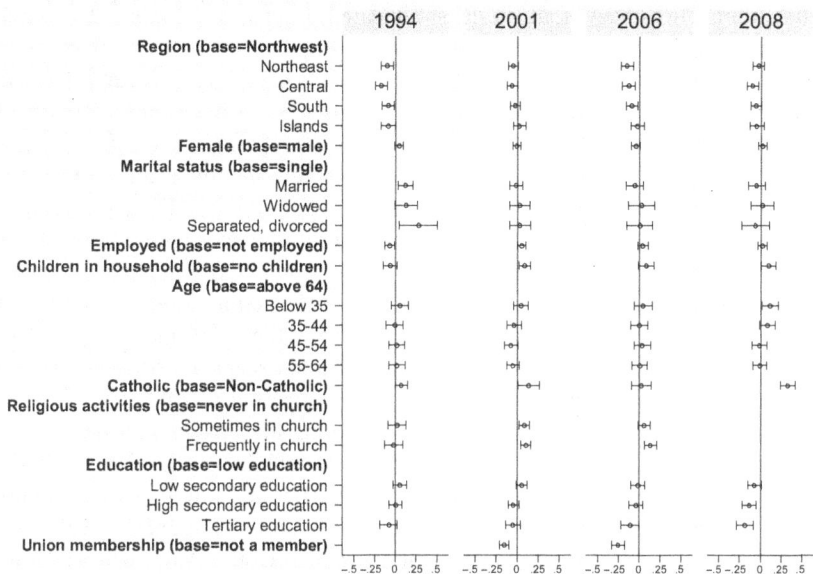

Figure 5.8 Probability of voting for "center-right party bloc", Italy, 1994–2008 (AMEs from multinomial logistic regression)

Notes: Confidence bands < -0.5 set to -0.5 and > 0.5 set to 0.5 in graph.
Sources: ITANES 1994, 2001, 2006, 2008; my calculations

Table 5.4 Religious denomination and religious activity in Germany and Italy (in %), 1990–2008

		1990	1999	2008
Germany				
Religious denomination	Protestant	38.8	34.2	27.4
	Catholic	29.6	21.2	22.9
	No denomination	30.7	40.0	46.2
	Other denomination	0.1	4.7	3.8
Religiously active population		28.0	24.3	15.9
Italy				
Religious denomination	Catholic	83.0	81.1	78.1
	Non-Catholic	17.0	18.9	21.9
Religiously active population		51.2	53.6	47.6

Source: European Values Study 1990, 1999, 2008; my calculations

levels of education compared to low education are negative and mostly statistically significant. The probability of voting for the SPD increases with the level of education. This means that the least-educated groups in the population have an above-average probability of voting for the SPD. Low-income, working-class people seem to form an important part of the party's constituency even today. As discussed earlier, those less qualified individuals tend to have more traditional values. Thus an important share of the electorate – comparable to religious voters for the CDU – tends to oppose work-family policy reforms for structural reasons. Until 2009, union members remained an important part of the SPD's constituency. The fact that their importance decreased should not, however, affect the SPD's positions on work-family policies, since we could not find evidence for either more traditional or more progressive normative beliefs. Italy does not exhibit a stable voting pattern differentiated by education for either coalition over the elections in the observed time span. The only noticeable exception is the opposition of highly educated individuals to vote for right-wing parties in 2008. Union membership, by contrast, is clearly associated with voting for left-wing parties.

To summarize the role that specific groups who exhibit predominantly traditional or progressive beliefs play for political parties, I show that in Germany both large parties continue to rely on their traditional constituencies. Religious persons vote much more likely for the Christian Democratic Party, whereas low-educated voters tend to favor the Social Democrats. Both groups are characterized by persistently traditional normative beliefs regarding mothers' employment. Those groups' persistently traditional normative beliefs may help to explain not only the long impasse in the field of work-family policies until beliefs changed overall but also the initially low reform efforts by the SPD (see Chapter 7 for more details).

The fact that the long-lasting core constituencies of the CDU and the SPD have continuously declined in the electorate may be part of the explanation for why the large German parties have modified their policy positions to attract new voters. Eastern German voters, who exhibit more progressive views on mothers' employment, have a lower probability of voting for SPD than western Germans; for the CDU, the opposite is true. There was, seemingly, potential for the SPD to attract more eastern Germans with a reformed work-family policy, which could have been a further motivation for the SPD to initiate reforms.

In the 1990s, younger individuals turned away from the CDU and voted for other parties. The age-related pattern has vanished in the last few elections and is no longer significant. This may provide the grounds to interpret it, albeit very cautiously, as another sign that the party has modernized itself over the last decade. Lastly, for the first time, women had a significantly higher probability of voting for the SPD in the elections in 2005. This was in all likelihood an alarm signal to the CDU that may have triggered the CDU's particular effort to surpass the SPD in the grand coalition in this policy area.

In Italy, the parties continue to be strongly supported by their long-established constituencies and shifts in support have not taken place. Hence Italian parties did not have an incentive to compete for other groups of voters by changing their policy positions. The strong ties to Catholics who are more male-breadwinner oriented can explain why the center-right coalitions staunchly oppose work-family policy reforms. Heterogeneity with respect to other characteristics seems to be of minor importance.

Normative beliefs and party preferences

These findings are supported by an analysis of the relationship between beliefs and party preferences in the EVS. Whereas the previous analyses link the groups' normative beliefs to evolving voting tendencies, the results shown in Figure 5.9 (see Table A.14 in the appendix for more details) provide direct evidence linking beliefs to party preferences. Keeping all other factors constant, the question is whether those people who have more progressive normative beliefs prefer certain parties. If there is a clear relationship or an observable pattern of change, this will provide us with further evidence on which groups of voters parties will focus on when trying to attract them with more progressive work-family policies.[11]

In Germany, people who have progressive beliefs are less likely to prefer the CDU/CSU than the SPD. People who support mothers' employment have a ten-percentage-point higher probability to prefer the SPD in contrast to people with

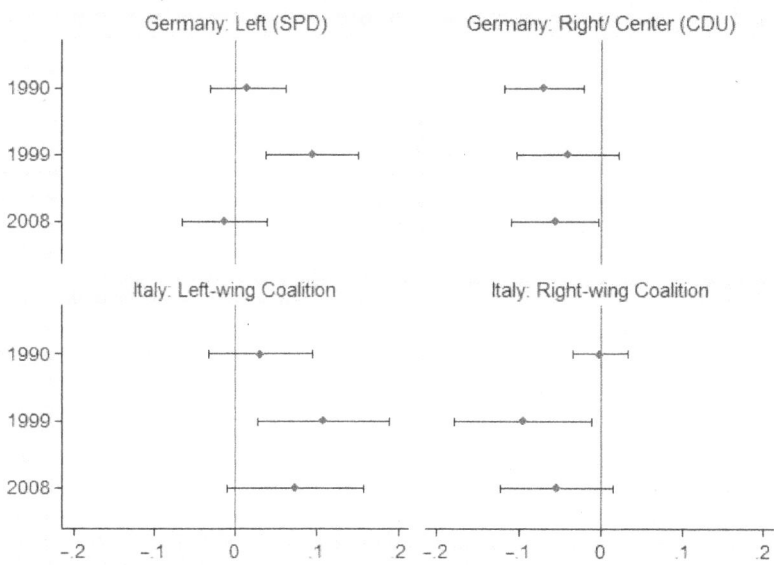

Figure 5.9 Multinomial logistic regression, average marginal effects (AME) for probability of preferring the SPD/left-wing coalition and the CDU/right-wing coalition of people having progressive normative beliefs in Germany and Italy, 1990, 1999 and 2008

Source: European Values Survey 1990, 1999, 2008; my calculations

more traditional beliefs in 1999 and a seven- and five-percentage-points lower probability to prefer the CDU in 1990 and 2008, respectively. There was thus a high potential for the SPD to attract voters who support the dual-earner model. In Italy, a difference in beliefs between proponents of right- and left-wing coalitions cannot be identified in 2008. Supporters of mothers' employment had a ten-percentage-point higher probability of preferring the left-wing coalition in 1999 and a ten-percentage-point lower probability of preferring the right-wing coalition; this discrepancy seems to have completely disappeared in recent years. Thus, at least in recent years, both coalitions did not seem to have an incentive to attract more progressive voters.

How changing normative beliefs and evolving voting behavior matter for party competition on work-family policies

This chapter showed that a broad shift in peoples' views on mothers' employment occurred in Germany between 1990 and 2008. The German population has on average become significantly more supportive of mothers' employment. As such a change did not happen in Italy, I conclude that this fundamental shift of beliefs in the population and the associated electoral demand for this type of policies was a key condition for work-family policy reforms in Germany.

Another important finding from the multivariate analysis is that normative beliefs are heterogeneous across the population. There are certain groups which exhibit traditional beliefs, e.g. religiously active individuals, Catholics or less-educated persons. By contrast, women and highly educated individuals have clearly more supportive views about mothers' employment. These belief patterns are very persistent over time and hold both for Germany and Italy. Not only the general trend but also this heterogeneity of beliefs is relevant for political competition.

A clear result of the empirical analysis of voting patterns for Germany is that the large parties rely on specific groups of the electorate: Catholics and religiously active people tend to vote for the CDU, while less-educated persons have a bond with the SPD. Both voter groups, although otherwise quite different, share sympathies for more traditional work-family policies. This explains why both parties for a long time hesitated to implement any fundamental reforms in the field.

The traditional constituencies, such as religious individuals or less-educated workers, have lost some of their relevance as their share in the overall electorate continues to decline. Consequently, the large parties have systematically sought new constituencies. This is why they are less loyal to their traditional core constituencies. At the same time, the parties had to be attentive to the voter of the center. The party system induces centripetal competition, which is further reinforced by the decline and narrowing of the large parties' votes share starting at the turn of the century. Thus, even if parties had wanted to attract new groups of voters, had it not been for this average shift towards more progressive normative beliefs, the reforms likely would not have occurred.

This conclusion is corroborated by the fact that in Italy, where beliefs remained traditional on average, a work-family policy change has not taken place to the same extent. In addition, even though certain groups of the Italian electorate such as women had increasingly more progressive views towards mothers' employment, the Italian parties did not have a similarly high incentive to compete for them with progressive work-family policies as it was in the German case. Rather, Italian parties appear to be able to still rely on their traditional constituencies.

In the following chapters, the quantitative analyses of normative beliefs, voting behavior and party competition will be complemented by examining the role of these factors in the concrete decision-making processes. Process tracing will provide a more deepened understanding of the (changing) positions the main political actors had, the conditions under which they proceeded and the constraints they faced. Given their central function in work-family policy reforms, a specific focus will be on the role of women's agency. Before I turn to these in-depth historical analyses of the reform processes in Germany and Italy, information on the descriptive representation of women in various political bodies is provided.

Notes

1 This description relates to the period of analysis, i.e. 1990 until 2009.
2 The declining share of low-educated people can be illustrated by a comparison of education levels between age cohorts: In 2004, only about 30 percent of the cohort of 30- to 35-year-old persons had a low education level (*Hauptschulabschluss*) compared to almost 70 percent of the 60- to 65-year-old persons in the same year. The share of persons who completed university education differed about ten percentage points, i.e. 10 percent of the cohort of 60- to 65-year-old persons versus 20 percent of the younger cohort have a higher education (cf. Figure B3–1 in Konsortium Bildungsberichterstattung 2006). The share of blue collar workers has declined from 50 percent in the middle of the twentieth century to one third of the total labor force at the turn of the millennium (Arzheimer and Schoen 2007).
3 A number of factors have led to this collapse: the fall of the Berlin wall, which challenged the role of the Communist Party, but also the role of the Christian Democratic party as a bulwark against the danger of Communism; the strengthening of territorial parties in the north, which seriously challenged the position of the DC; and, not least, the corruption impeachments against the top leadership of the parties (*mani pulite*) (Cotta and Verzichelli 2007).
4 The proportional representation electoral system that had been in place up to that point was reformed and a mixed system was established. Three-quarters of the seats are allocated following the majority principle; the remaining 25 percent are assigned following the PR system.
5 See http://www.itanes.org/
6 Unfortunately, the data for 1996 cannot be used. According to Hans Schadee, the coordinator responsible for the collection of the data set, the data is strongly biased towards the left since cases were selected on the basis of an already selective data set.
7 This is not an artifact of this specific variable. The second indicator reveals a change of similar magnitude for Germany between 1990 and 1999 (see Table A.8 in the appendix). The share of people agreeing with the assertion that a working mother can have a relationship with her child that is just as warm as a mother who does not work increased by almost 30 percentage points. This percentage had risen even further by 2008.
8 The picture is somewhat different for the second variable (see the appendix, Table A.9). Interestingly, in 1990, the share of people agreeing with the statement was about 65 percent, a much higher level than the level that existed in Germany at the time, which was 47 percent. According to this indicator, the Italian population has become

138 Normative beliefs and party competition

slightly more progressive over the years, the difference between 1990 and 2008, at five percentage points, is of a rather low magnitude. In contrast to the situation in Germany, there is overall little evidence for a noticeable change in normative beliefs towards mothers' employment in Italy.

9 Analyses with the ALLBUS show that between 1991 and 2008, the likelihood that a western German would disagree with the statement about mothers' employment and children's well-being had increased by about 21 percentage points (see Table A.10 in the appendix). The ALLBUS is a representative biennial survey that has been conducted since 1980 on the attitudes, behavior and social structure of persons who are residents of Germany (see http://www.gesis.org/allbus/allgemeine-informationen/). This dataset contains exactly the same attitudinal questions as the EVS and provides additional waves.

10 Only about a fourth of the eastern Germans belong to one of the Christian denominations.

11 The model is estimated with the full set of explanatory variables, resulting in an effect conditional on socio-economic characteristics. All indirect connections between party preferences and beliefs through observed covariates – e.g. older people are not interested in work-family issues and vote for conservative parties for completely unrelated reasons – are netted out in these multivariate models. In addition to the explanatory variables, the following indicator for party preference is included: "If there was a general election tomorrow, which party would you vote for?" The effect is a direct relationship between party preferences and beliefs.

References

Arzheimer, Kai, and Harald Schoen. 2007. "Mehr als eine Erinnerung an das 19. Jahrhundert? Das sozio-ökonomische und das religiös-konfessionelle Cleavage und Wahlverhalten 1994–2005." In *Der gesamtdeutsche Wähler. Stabilität und Wandel des Wählerverhaltens im wiedervereinigten Deutschland*, edited by Hans Rattinger, Oscar W. Gabriel and Jürgen W. Falter, 89–112. Baden-Baden: Nomos.

Banaszak, Lee Ann, and Eric Plutzer. 1993. "The Social Bases of Feminism in the European Community." *Public Opinion Quarterly* 57 (1):29–53. doi: 10.1086/269353.

Bardi, Luciano. 2007. "Electoral change and Its Impact on the Party System in Italy." *West European Politics* 30 (4):711–732.

Bellucci, Paolo, and Oliver Heath. 2012. "The Structure of Party-Organization Linkages and the Electoral Strength of Cleavages in Italy, 1963–2008." *British Journal of Political Science* 42 (01):107–135. doi: doi:10.1017/S0007123411000226.

Bernini, Stefania. 2008. "Family Politics: Political Rhetoric and the Transformation of Family Life in the Italian Second Republic." *Journal of Modern Italian Studies* 13 (3):305–324.

Biorcio, Roberto. 2006. "Professioni e scelte di voto: una polarizzazione tra lavoro autonomo e lavoro dipendente?" In *Dov'è la vittoria? Il voto del 2006 raccontato dagli italiani*, edited by Itanes, 93–108. Bologna: il Mulino.

Bolzendahl, Catherine, and Sigrun Olafsdottir. 2008. "Gender Group Interest or Gender Ideology? Understanding U.S. Support for Family Policy Within the Liberal Welfare Regime." *Sociological Perspectives* 51 (2):281–304.

Bonoli, Giuliano, and Frank Reber. 2009. "The Political Economy of Childcare in OECD Countries: Explaining Cross-national Variation in Spending and Coverage Rates." *European Journal of Political Research* 49 (1):97–118.

Bothfeld, Silke. 2005. *Vom Erziehungsurlaub zur Elternzeit. Politisches Lernen im Reformprozess*. Frankfurt a.M./New York: Campus Verlag.

Brady, David, and Ryan Finnigan. 2014. "Does Immigration Undermine Public Support for Social Policy?" *American Journal of Sociology* 79 (1):17–42.

Bull, Martin, and Martin Rhodes. 1997. "Between Crisis and Transition: Italian Politics in the 1990s." *West European Politics* 20 (1):1–13. doi: 10.1080/01402389708425172.

Bull, Martin, and Martin Rhodes. 2007. "Introduction – Italy: A Contested Polity." *West European Politics* 30 (4):657–669. doi: 10.1080/01402380701500207.

Ceccarini, Luigi, and Ilvo Diamanti. 2006. "'Semper fideles'? Genere e generazioni politiche al voto." In *Dov'è la vittoria? Il voto del 2006 raccontato dagli italiani*, edited by Itanes, 77–92. Bologna: il Mulino.

The Comparative Study of Electoral Systems (CSES). 2003. *CSES Module 1 Full Release [Dataset]*. Ann Arbor, MI: University of Michigan, Center for Political Studies [producer and distributor]: August 4, 2003.

The Comparative Study of Electoral Systems (CSES). 2007. *CSES Module 2 Full Release [Dataset]*: June 27, 2007.

The Comparative Study of Electoral Systems (CSES). 2012. *CSES Module 3 Third Advance Release [Dataset]*. May 31, 2012 version.

Corbetta, Piergiorgio, and Paolo Segatti. 2004. "Un bipolarismo senza radici?" In *Come chiudere la transizione: Cambiamento, apprendimento e adattamento nel sistema politica italiano*, edited by Stefano Ceccanti and Salvatore Vassallo, 125–150. Bologna: il Mulino.

Cotta, Maurizio, and Luca Verzichelli. 2007. *Political Institutions in Italy*. Oxford: Oxford University Press.

Debus, Marc. 2011. "Sozialstrukturelle und einstellungsbasierte Determinanten des Wahlverhaltens und ihr Einfluss bei Bundestagswahlen im Zeitverlauf: Westdeutschland 1976 bis 2009." *Politische Vierteljahresschrift* Sonderheft 45/2011:40–62.

Dienel, Christiane. 2002. *Familienpolitik. Eine praxisorientierte Gesamtdarstellung der Handlungsfelder und Probleme*. Weinheim/München: Juventa.

Faas, Torsten. 2010. *Arbeitslosigkeit und Wählerverhalten. Direkte und indirekte Wirkungen auf Wahlbeteiligung und Parteipräferenzen in Ost- und Westdeutschland*. Baden-Baden: Nomos.

Gerhards, Jürgen, and Michael Hölscher. 2003. "Kulturelle Unterschiede zwischen Mitglieds- und Beitrittsländern der EU. Das Beispiel Familien- und Gleichberechtigungsvorstellungen." *Zeitschrift für Soziologie* 32 (2):206–225.

Gerlach, Irene. 2004. *Familienpolitik*. Wiesbaden: VS Verlag für Sozialwissenschaften.

Giger, Nathalie. 2009. "Towards a Modern Gender Gap in Europe?: A Comparative Analysis of Voting Behavior in 12 Countries." *The Social Science Journal* 46 (3):474–492.

Goerres, Achim. 2008. "The Grey Vote: Determinants of Older Voters' Party Choice in Britain and West Germany." *Electoral Studies* 27 (2):285–304.

Goerres, Achim, and Markus Tepe. 2012. "Doing It for the Kids? The Determinants of Attitudes towards Public Childcare in Unified Germany." *Journal of Social Policy* 41 (02):349–372. doi: doi:10.1017/S0047279411000754.

Halman, Loek. 2001. *The European Values Study: A Third Wave*. Source book of the 1999/2000 European Values Study. Tilburg University.

Halman, Loek, and Astrid Vloet. 1994. "Measuring and Comparing Values in 16 Countries of the Western World. Documentation of the European Values Study 1981–1990 in Europe and North America." In *Worc Report 94.11.001*, edited by Work and Organization Research Centre-Tilburg University, Tilburg.

Hank, Karsten, Katja Tillmann, and Gert C. Wagner. 2001. "Außerhäusliche Kinderbetreuung in Ostdeutschland vor und nach der Wiedervereinigung. Ein Vergleich mit

Westdeutschland in den Jahren 1990–1999." *Zeitschrift für Bevölkerungswissenschaft* 26 (1):55–65.
Hobolt, Sara Binzer, and Robert Klemmensen. 2008. "Government Responsiveness and Political Competition in Comparative Perspective." *Comparative Political Studies* 41 (3):309–337.
Inglehart, Ronald. 1977. *The Silent Revolution. Changing Values and Political Styles Among Western Publics.* Princeton, NJ: Princeton University Press.
Jansen, Christian. 2007. *Italien seit 1945.* Göttingen: Vandenhoeck & Ruprecht.
Konsortium Bildungsberichterstattung. 2006. Bildung in Deutschland. Ein indikatorengestützter Bericht mit einer Analyse zu Bildung und Migration. Bielefeld.
Kremer, Monique. 2007. *How Welfare States Care. Culture, Gender and Parenting in Europe.* Amsterdam: Amsterdam University Press.
Leitner, Sigrid. 1999. *Frauen und Männer im Wohlfahrtsstaat. Zur strukturellen Umsetzung von Geschlechterkonstruktionen in sozialen Sicherungssystemen.* Frankfurt a.M.: Verlag Peter Lang.
Lück, Detlef. 2009. *Der zögernde Abschied vom Patriarchat. Der Wandel von Geschlechterrollen im internationalen Vergleich.* Berlin: edition sigma.
Mair, Peter. 1997. *Party System Change. Approaches and Interpretations.* Oxford: Oxford University Press.
Manza, Jeff, and Clem Brooks. 1999. *Social Cleavages and Political Change. Voter Alignments and U.S. Party Coalitions.* Oxford: Oxford University Press.
Mischke, Monika. 2014. *Public Attitudes towards Family Policies in Europe. Linking Institutional Context and Public Opinion.* Wiesbaden: Springer.
Müller, Walter, and Markus Klein. 2011. "Die Klassenbasis in der Parteipräferenz des deutschen Wählers. Erosion oder Wandel?" *Politische Vierteljahresschrift* Sonderheft 45/2011:85–110.
Naldini, Manuela, and Chiara Saraceno. 2008. "Social and Family Policies in Italy: Not Totally Frozen but far From Structural Reforms." *Social Policy & Administration* 42 (7):733–748.
Niedermayer, Oskar. 2006. "Das Parteiensystem Deutschlands." In *Die Parteiensysteme Westeuropas*, edited by Oskar Niedermayer, Richard Stöss and Barbara Haas, 109–134. Wiesbaden: VS Verlag für Sozialwissenschaften.
Pappi, Franz Urban, and Jens Brandenburg. 2010. "Sozialstrukturelle Interessenlagen und Parteipräferenz in Deutschland. Stabilität und Wandel seit 1980." *Kölner Zeitschrift für Soziologie und Sozialpsychologie* 62 (3):459–483.
Picot, Georg. 2012. *Politics of Segmentation: Party Competition and Social Protection in Europe.* London: Routledge.
Roßteutscher, Sigrid. 2012. "Die konfessionell-religiöse Konfliktlinie zwischen Säkularisierung und Mobilisierung." *Politische Vierteljahresschrift* Sonderheft 45:111–133.
Saraceno, Chiara. 2011. "Childcare Needs and Childcare Policies: A Multidimensional Issue." *Current Sociology* 59 (1):78–96. doi: 10.1177/0011392110385971.
Sartori, Giovanni. 1976. *Parties and Party Systems: A Framework for Analysis.* Cambridge: Cambridge University Press.
Seeleib-Kaiser, Martin, Silke van Dyk, and Martin Roggenkamp. 2008. *Party Politics and Social Welfare. Comparing Christian and Social Democracy in Austria, Germany and the Netherlands.* Cheltenham/Northampton: Edward Elgar.
Segatti, Paolo. 2006. "I cattolici al voto, tra valori e politiche dei valori." In *Dov'è la vittoria? Il voto del 2006 raccontato dagli italiani*, edited by Itanes, 109–126. Bologna: il Mulino.

Sjöberg, Ola. 2004. "The Role of Family Policy Institutions in Explaining Gender-Role Attitudes: A Comparative Multilevel Analysis of Thirteen Industrialized Countries." *Journal of European Social Policy* 14 (2):107–123.

Steiber, Nadia, and Barbara Haas. 2009. "Ideals or Compromises? The Attitude-behaviour Relationship in Mothers' Employment." *Socio-Economic Review* 7 (4):639–668. doi: 10.1093/ser/mwp015.

Stöss, Richard, Melanie Haas, and Oskar Niedermayer. 2006. "Parteiensysteme in Westeuropa: Stabilität und Wandel." In *Die Parteiensysteme Westeuropas*, edited by Oskar Niedermayer, Richard Stöss and Melanie Haas, 7–40. Wiesbaden: VS Verlag für Sozialwissenschaften.

Weßels, Bernhard. 2011. "Das Wahlverhalten sozialer Gruppen." In *Zwischen Langeweile und Extremen: Die Bundestagswahl 2009*, edited by Hans Rattinger, Sigrid Roßteutscher, Rüdiger Schmitt-Beck and Bernhard Weßels, 103–118. Baden-Baden: Nomos.

Weßels, Bernhard, and Aiko Wagner. 2011. "Regionale Differenzierung des Wahlverhaltens." In *Zwischen Langeweile und Extremen: Die Bundestagswahl 2009*, edited by Hans Rattinger, Sigrid Roßteutscher, Rüdiger Schmitt-Beck and Bernhard Weßels, 119–130. Baden-Baden: Nomos.

Zohlnhöfer, Reimut. 2006. "Das Parteiensystems Italiens." In *Die Parteiensysteme Westeuropas*, edited by Oskar Niedermayer, Richard Stöss and Melanie Haas, 275–298. Wiesbaden: VS Verlag für Sozialwissenschaften.

Zohlnhöfer, Reimut, and Christoph Egle. 2007. "Der Episode zweiter Teil – ein Überblick über die 15. Legislaturperiode." In *Ende des rot-grünen Projektes. Eine Bilanz der Regierung Schröder 2002–2005*, edited by Christoph Egle and Reimut Zohlnhöfer, 11–28. Wiesbaden: VS Verlag für Sozialwissenschaften.

Zuma, Mannheim, Manfred Berger, Matthias Jung, Dieter Roth, Wolfgang G. Gibowski, Max Kaase, Hans-Dieter Klingemann, Manfred Küchler, Franz U. Pappi, and Holli A. Semetko. 2012. *Nachwahlstudie zur Bundestagswahl 1994*. GESIS Datenarchiv, Köln: ZA2601 Datenfile Version 2.0.0, doi:10.4232/1.11460 http://dx.doi.org/10.4232/1.11460.

6 Women's descriptive representation
The more, the better?

The previous chapter presented quantitative evidence on the development of normative beliefs, patterns of voting behavior and the dynamics of party competition as one part of the explanation of work-family policy reforms in Germany and Italy. This chapter focuses on another crucial factor for the development of work-family policies: women's agency. Several studies have demonstrated that women's presence in parliament and in government has played an important role for the development of the welfare state, which ultimately bears on the reconciliation of work and family. While Chapters 7 and 8 will deal with the substantive representation of women, i.e. female representatives' efforts to advance women's policy preferences in Germany and Italy, respectively, this chapter focuses on the descriptive representation of women.

As laid out in greater detail in Chapter 2, a critical mass of women should affect the adoption of women-friendly policies. It is argued that the more women there are, the easier it is for them to form strategic alliances to pursue their policy goals. Also, an increase in the number of women legislators may cause men to be more attentive to women's issues and thus more prone to women-friendly policies. At the same time, this requires a number of "critical actors" as well, i.e. women who do have a gender consciousness and aim at promoting policies that benefit women (Childs and Krook 2006). The presence of women in decision-making bodies is a necessary condition for the representation of women's interests (Campbell, Childs, and Lovenduski 2009, Phillips 1995).

This concise chapter compares the political representation of women on different levels: in parliament, in governing coalitions, and in cabinets. Following and complementing the theoretical framework in Chapter 2, this empirical analysis is based on data from the statistical offices of the parliaments, differentiated by age and party affiliation. Levels for given legislative periods and also the trends over the period 1990–2008 between Germany and Italy are compared. It will be shown that the number of female parliamentarians and ministers increased in both Germany and Italy, but in contrast to Germany, there was a lack of a critical mass of women in the Italian parliament.

Women in parliament

To raise the number of women in parliament electoral gender quotas and party gender quotas have been implemented in several countries. However, a general electoral quota is applied neither in Germany nor in Italy. After the reform of the Italian electoral system in 1993, which introduced a majority element, women pushed for a quota system to counteract the probable negative effects for women candidates. As a consequence, in the 1994 election, a law was applied which foresaw a quota for the proportional element of the electoral system (allocating one-fourth of the seats). In 1995, however, it was declared unconstitutional. Afterwards, the parliament worked to amend the constitution in order to allow quotas, and a law was passed in 2003. However, a national-electoral gender quota has not been implemented to date (Guadagnini 2005).[1] There are specific party quotas among left-wing parties. The PDS, for example, adopted a quota of 40 percent for each sex, while the PD has a quota of 50 percent.[2]

In Germany, no electoral gender quota exists, but all parties except for the Free Democrats (FDP) had adopted specific gender quotas by the late 1990s at the latest, which range from 30 percent (CDU) to 40 percent (SPD) to 50 percent (Greens, the Left) (see www.quotaproject.org). The party quotas are not always enforceable by sanctions, thus making them a "soft" quota for some parties, e.g. the CDU (Meyer 2003).

In Germany, the total number of women increased between 1990 and 2009. During the thirteenth legislature under a CDU/FDP coalition government, only 136 women were members of the parliament (21 percent). This number rose to 207 under the first coalition government between the SPD and the Greens, and slightly fell when the SPD and the CDU formed a grand coalition in 2005. The share of women remained above 30 percent after 1998, which means that a critical mass, as defined by the theoretical considerations, has been reached. Figure 6.1 shows the development of the percentages of all MPs within specific age groups who were women in Germany between 1990 and 2009. In particular, in the younger age groups, women are increasingly more on par with men.

In Italy, the restructuring of the political and party system in the 1990s seemed to offer a window of opportunity for women to participate more in politics. Due to the *mani pulite* campaign, many men had to leave office, and the resulting gap might have offered chances for women in elections and to occupy decision-making positions (Gelli 2002).[3] The available data only allows us to describe the trends in women's participation in parliament and government after 1996. In that year, still only 10 percent of all MPs were women.

Even though more than ten years later we witness a doubling of this share, the level of female representation in Italy remains comparatively low and far below the 30 percent threshold. Looking at the age distribution of female representatives, an increase in the numbers of women MPs aged younger than 40 is noticeable, yet the total number of women parliamentarians of that age is still very low (29 of 193 women). The highest number of women is found in the age group of 50- to 59-year-old MPs.

Hence, even though the number and share of women in parliament is on the rise in both countries, only women MPs in Germany had reached critical mass by the end of the 1990s. The total number and also the proportion of women in the younger age category are also higher in Germany compared to Italy.

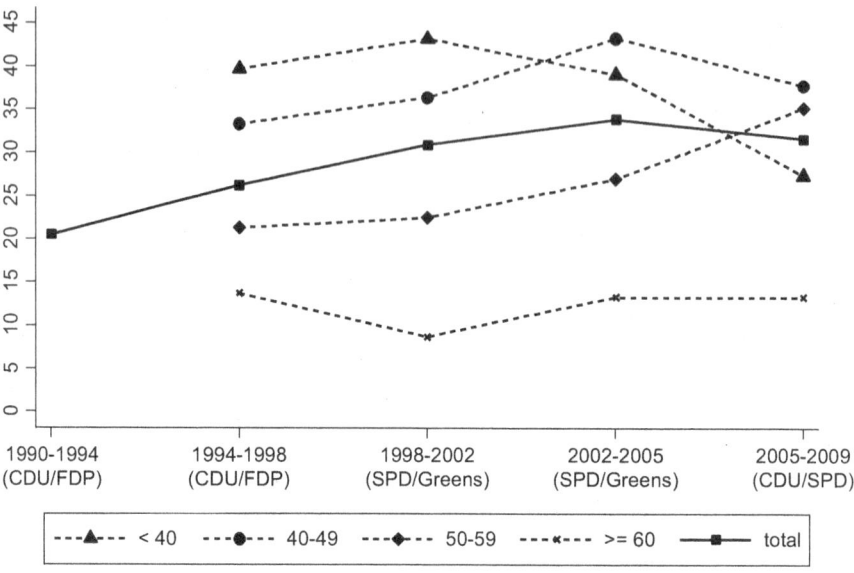

Figure 6.1 Share of women MPs (in %) by age group in the German Bundestag, 1990–2009

Source: Deutscher Bundestag, Abgeordnete (various issues), (http://webarchiv.bundestag.de/cgi/show.php?fileToLoad=215&id=1041; access date: 03.03.2011); Feldkamp and Sommer (2003); my calculations

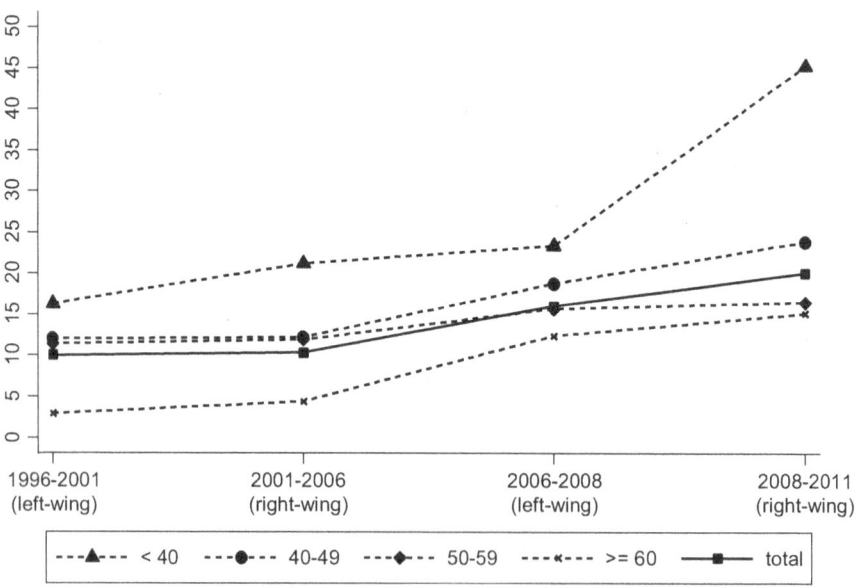

Figure 6.2 Share of women MPs (in %) by age group in the Italian Camera and Senato, 1996–2011

Source: Camera dei Deputati, Statistiche relative ai deputati (various issues), (www.camera.it, access date: 15.04.2010); my calculations

Women in government

When seeking to understand changes or gridlock in work-family policymaking, it is important to not only look at the share of women in parliament, but more specifically to consider those who are represented in government. As suggested by the theory of substantive representation, the presence of women in decision-making bodies is a necessary condition for the representation of women's interests (Campbell, Childs, and Lovenduski 2009, Phillips 1995). Arguably, an increase of the number of women in government has a positive effect on the adoption of work-family policies. Figure 6.3 shows that the share of women in governing parties in Germany almost doubled between the twelfth and the sixteenth legislatures.

The share of women is always higher in left-wing parties. Consequently, a critical mass of 30 percent has only been reached under left-wing governments (1998–2002 and 2002–2005). Interestingly, the average share of women in parliament often exceeds the share of women in governing parties. Keeping in mind that some decisive work-family policy reforms happened after 2005, it seems as if the

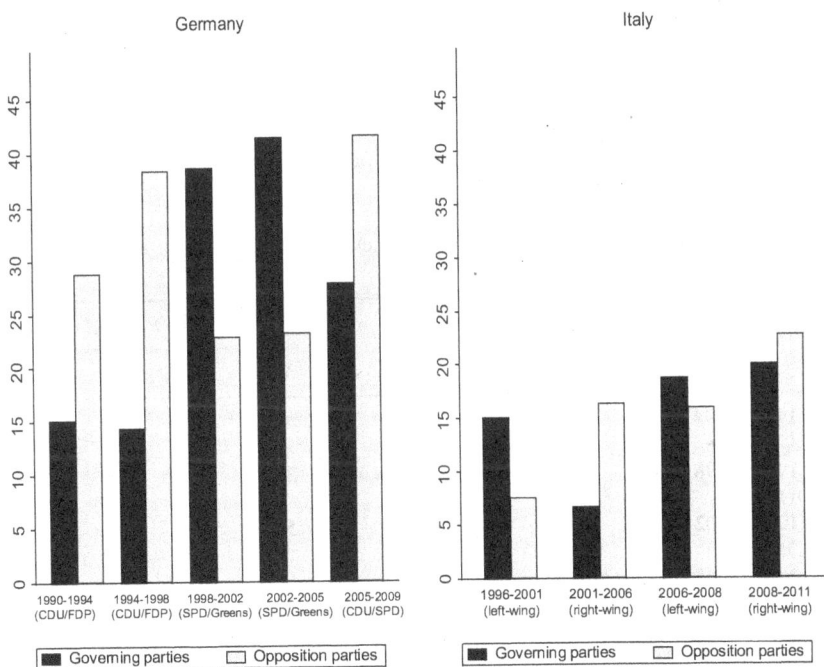

Figure 6.3 Women MPs (in %) in governing parties and in opposition parties in Germany and Italy (%)

Note: The information on the number of women MPs of each party represented in parliament is only given for members of the Camera, not the Senato.

Source: Deutscher Bundestag, Abgeordnete (various issues), (http://webarchiv.bundestag.de/cgi/show.php?fileToLoad=215&id=1041; access date: 03.03.2011); Feldkamp and Sommer (2003); own calculation; Camera dei Deputati, Statistiche relative ai deputati (various issues), (www.camera.it, access date: 15.04.2010); my calculations

146 *Women's descriptive representation*

quantitative representation of women in government was not a crucial factor for reforms in Germany.

In Italy, the share of women in governing parties also increased about four percentage points between the elections of 1996 and 2008 (Figure 6.3). Most notable is the leap between the first and the second right-wing coalition during this period, which saw the women' share go from only 6.7 percent to 20 percent. Similar to Germany, the share of women in left-wing parties (in government and in opposition) is always higher than in the right-wing parties.

How many women are represented in governing parties depends on the political configuration of the government: in left-wing governments, the share of women is markedly higher than in right-wing governments. This is true for both Germany and Italy (with significant differences in levels).

Women in cabinets

One of the most influential political positions is that of a minister. In Germany, the share of women ministers rose from about 20 percent at the beginning of the 1990s to more than 33 percent during the sixteenth legislature. The share mirrors the rise of women's representation in parliament. In 2005, a women chancellor took office for the first time in Germany in addition to five other women ministers (see Table 6.1).

Italian governments are in general far from an equal share of minister positions. Most women hold a ministry without a portfolio (ministri senza portafoglio).

Table 6.1 Women in the German Federal Cabinet, in absolute number and share of total number, 12–16 legislatures[1]

Legislative period	Federal Cabinet	Women in the Federal Cabinet	
	Total no.	No.	%
12 (1990–1994) (CDU/FDP)	18	4	22.2
13 (1994–1998) (CDU/FDP)	16	3	18.8
14 (1998–2002) (SPD/Greens)	14	5	35.7
15 (2002–2005) (SPD/Greens)	13	6	46.2
16 (2005–2009) (CDU/SPD)	15	6[2]	33.3

Notes:
1 Figures provided for the beginning of each legislature. In the course of a legislature, ministers may change positions or leave the cabinet.
2 In addition to the five women ministers, a female chancellor led the government of the sixteenth legislature.

Source: (http://www.bundestag.de/blob/196242/0c13976c9ca83bbd32f5396934908c85/kapitel_06_02_zusammensetzung_der_bundeskabinette_-_namensliste-data.pdf; access date: 09.08.2016)

These ministers are inferior to ministers with a portfolio with respect to decision-making possibilities and impact (Köppl 2007). If they exist at all, ministries for family affairs are usually ministries without a portfolio.

Throughout the time period under examination, there is a large difference between right-wing and left-wing governments (see Table 6.2). While the first Berlusconi government employed only one or two women ministers; in the first left-wing coalition government, there were between three and six women; and in the second Prodi government, a total of seven women were ministers. However, the latest Berlusconi government has also seen increases in the share of women ministers to almost 22 percent.

In summary, the number and share of women parliamentarians and ministers increased during the last 20 years in both Germany and Italy. In contrast to Italy, however, women make up a critical mass of more than 30 percent in Germany in all categories: parliament, government and cabinet. There is thus a pattern that is consistent with the proposed relationship between higher shares of women and work-family policy reforms. A closer look, however, reveals that some of the most essential work-family policy reforms in Germany took place at a time when the share of women in parliament and in the cabinet was comparably low. Consequently, the tracing of political decision-making processes in the next chapters

Table 6.2 Women in the Italian Council of Ministers, in absolute number and share of total number, 11–16 legislatures

Legislative period	Council of Ministers	Women in the Council of Ministers	
	total no.	no.	%
11 (1992–1994)			
Amato I	27	1	3.7
Ciampi	26	2	7.7
12 (1994–1996)			
Berlusconi I	24	1	4.2
Dini	26	1	3.8
13 (1996–2001)			
Prodi I	22	3	13.0
D'Alema I	25	6	24.0
D'Alema II	26	6	23.1
Amato II	25	4	15.4
14 (2001–2006)			
Berlusconi II	24	2	8.3
Berlusconi III	25	2	8.0
15 (2006–2008)			
Prodi II	26	7	26.9
16 (2008–2011)			
Berlusconi IV	23	5	21.7

Source: Governo Italiano (http://www.governo.it/i-governi-dal-1943-ad-oggi/i-governi-nelle-legislature/192; access date: 09.08.2016); my calculations

will more closely examine the substantive representation of women and in that way deepen the analysis of the influence of women's representation on work-family policy reforms.

Notes

1 There are, however, gender quotas on the regional level. Article 117 of the Constitution states: "Regional laws have to remove all obstacles which prevent the full equality of men and women in social, cultural, and economic life, and promote equal access for men and women to elective offices". Gender quotas have been adopted by 12 out of 20 regions (www.quotaproject.org; access date: 17.03.2012). The website provides an overview of the use of electoral quotas for women worldwide and is a joint project on the collection of global information on quotas between the Department of Political Science, Stockholm University and International IDEA.).
2 See www.quotaproject.org; access date: 17.03.2012.
3 In fact, after the elections of 1994, more than 70 percent of the previous composition in parliament was replaced (Cotta and Verzichelli 2007: 152).

References

Campbell, Rosie, Sarah Childs, and Joni Lovenduski. 2009. "Do Women Need Women Representatives?" *British Journal of Political Science* 40 (1):171–194.
Childs, Sarah, and Mona Lena Krook. 2006. "Should Feminists Give Up on Critical Mass? A Contingent Yes." *Politics & Gender* 2 (4):522–530.
Cotta, Maurizio, and Luca Verzichelli. 2007. *Political Institutions in Italy*. Oxford: Oxford University Press.
Feldkamp, Michael F., and Christa Sommer. 2003. *Parlaments- und Wahlstatistik des Deutschen Bundestages 1949–2002/03*. Berlin: Deutscher Bundestag Referat Öffentlichkeitsarbeit.
Gelli, Bianca R. 2002. "*Empowerment* femminile: un difficile discorso di intersezione tra passi e saperi femministi, politica e psicologia." In *Voci di Donne. Discorsi sul genere*, edited by Bianca R. Gelli, 9–40. Lecce: Manni.
Guadagnini, Marila. 2005. "Gendering the Debate on Political Representation in Italy: A Difficult Challenge." In *State Feminism and Political Representation*, edited by Joni Lovenduski, 130–152. Cambridge: Cambridge University Press.
Köppl, Stefan. 2007. *Das politische System Italiens. Eine Einführung*. Wiesbaden: VS Verlag für Sozialwissenschaften.
Meyer, Birgit 2003. "Much Ado about Nothing? Political Representation Policies and the Influence of Women Parliamentarians in Germany." *Review of Policy Research* 20 (3):401–21.
Phillips, Anne. 1995. *The Politics of Presence*. Oxford: Oxford University Press.

7 Work-family policy reform processes in Germany
Continuous change towards dual-earner model support

The chancellor was the only representative of the party's leadership who remained in the room for the whole of my speech and the ensuing discussion on work-family policies at the federal party convention in Nuremberg in 2001. Usually, when this topic is discussed, everyone leaves the room. [...] Family policy is nothing to write home about, but the modernized policy approach, that meets the wishes of young well-educated women (and men), paid dividends for the SPD. [...] The SPD was able to present itself as the more progressive and open-minded party in 2002 and 2005 which had developed substantial ideas. This changed completely with the arrival of Ursula von der Leyen[1] in 2009: the issue [of work-family policy] was then almost completely taken away from us. The SPD could no longer use this issue to distinguish itself from the CDU.[2]

This quote[3] from a former minister for family affairs puts the story of work-family policies in Germany in a nutshell. It underlines the importance of beliefs and demands of the population, the dynamics of party competition and the relevance of women's agency for significant work-family policy reforms to happen. While the previous chapters have used quantitative empirical evidence to depict how these variables shape work-family policy reforms, the following in-depth historical analysis of the reform processes in Germany will resume these explanatory variables by examining the role they play in the concrete decision-making process. For each legislative period, the positions the main actors had and how they have changed in response to changed normative beliefs, voting behavior and party competition are illustrated. In addition, the conditions under which actors proceed, the constraints they face and how they deal with them will be scrutinized in order to get a better understanding of why and when policy change occurred.

As with any democratic decision-making process, there was not a straightforward, linear path towards undisputed, previously defined political goals. In fact, the reform processes were shaped by debates, conflicts, contradictions, idiosyncrasies and, not least, compromises. It will be shown that the last two government terms of the CDU/FDP coalition between 1990 and 1998 were characterized by a continuity of the male-breadwinner model. In spite of claims for more gender equality and better childcare provision, the SPD in opposition was reluctant to clearly advocate the dual-earner model. Even after the government takeover in

1998 the SPD did not immediately turn out as a work-family policy reform activist. Only when the issue became salient for elections and female policy entrepreneurs pushed for changes, were reforms put on the agenda by the second center-left government. After the electoral defeat of 1998, a modernization course was also started within the CDU. Conservative female policy entrepreneurs – among them the later chancellor Merkel – were responsible for a change in the definition of the family and the role of mothers. When competition increased after 2002 and in particular in 2005, those who aimed at a modernization of the CDU were able to enforce the progressive policies.

Overall, this chapter shows that the work-family policy reforms enacted in the middle of the 2000s were the result of changes in normative beliefs and both large parties' deliberate strategy to attract new groups of voters against the backdrop of the decreasing electoral relevance of the parties' core constituencies for a longer period of time. Women played an important role in the decision-making processes. Two very strong ministers of family affairs acted as policy entrepreneurs and were able to persuade the critics within their own parties. Their support by the chancellors was a crucial condition for their success.

1990–1998: continuity of the male-breadwinner model

In the beginning of the 1990s, the large parties, the CDU and SPD, aimed at further work-family policy reforms. In their party manifestos for the 1990 election, both parties argued that children, in particular those aged younger than three, need high-quality care. To enable parents to provide this care, both parties proposed to prolong the leave entitlement to three years after the birth of a child. In quite vague terms, the SPD called for an anti-discriminatory benefit: "With respect to all benefits concerning mothers and childcare, priority should be given to those forms of financing that do not negatively affect the labor market chances of parents."[4] In contrast to the CDU, the SPD also called for an expansion of high-quality, extra-familial childcare in order to "enable parents in the long term to choose freely between paid parental leave up to three years and the entitlement to a childcare place" (Sozialdemokratische Partei Deutschlands 1990: 12).

In 1991, the parental leave reform was debated in parliament. The draft bill aimed at extending the leave period to three years and to increase the number of paid leave months by 6 months (24 months in total).[5] The CDU advocated for the extension of the leave period to up to three years – until, as Minister for Family Affairs Hannelore Rönsch (CDU) put it, children are old enough to attend kindergarten –[6] as an important factor in facilitating a better reconciliation of family and work. This statement mirrors the view of the conservative government that children under three are best cared for by the mother. It also underlines their intention to further support the three-phase model of mothers' life courses: an education/working period followed by a family care phase until children do not need to be cared for intensively followed by a re-integration into employment. However, the law proposal also aimed at providing improvements that would lead to more gender equality in the division of work. The minister appraised both the possibility to alternate leave periods between the mother and the father up to three times and the option to continue part-time employment while on parental leave.

The SPD agreed in principle. The party argued that providing parents with more time for their children would be extremely important for the relationship and the healthy development of children.[7] At the same time, the MPs demanded more childcare places for the under three-year-old children. The introduction of a replacement rate, which was once proposed by the SPD, was no longer part of the parental leave reform debates anymore.[8] Instead, the SPD demanded a higher flat-rate sum. Hence the faction of the SPD that had argued for a flat-rate sum in order to value all children equally prevailed over the faction that recommended an income-replacement rate that would serve the purpose of gender equality. In order to encourage fathers to do care work, the SPD proposed a bonus system similar to the Italian scheme, i.e. in the case that each parent claims at least four months, total parental leave would be extended by another three months.[9]

The SPD demands were denied by the government coalition, which pointed to their conviction that all parents (i.e. mothers) should freely choose how to raise their children and not be "forced" by incentives. This reasoning was based on the high take-up rates under the existing leave regulations. In their view, the broad use of the leave (96 percent of eligible parents) showed that the population accepted these regulations and demonstrated that parents would rather care for their children themselves. By making these arguments, the coalition also underlined their refusal of expanding extra-familial childcare institutions for children under three. As government member Norbert Eimer (FDP) put it,

> Men and women should have the freedom of choice whether they want to work or rather take care of their children. We do not prescribe any way of living, not the employment of women as a rule nor care at home. This is solely the decision of the parents. But I make no secret of the fact that I do not think that caring for children in daycare centers is optimal. I do not see the old GDR as a role model.[10]

An increasing awareness of family policies as work-family reconciliation policies

The debates reveal that the necessity for a better reconciliation of family and employment (for women) was increasingly acknowledged. Yet, within this, the parties referred to different forms of work-family reconciliation: While the SPD meant a simultaneous combination of both responsibilities, the CDU meant consecutive phases ("three-phase model").[11] Both parties used the "freedom of choice" rhetoric for justifying their approach to parental leave policies, which leaves the decision of how to combine care and employment to the parents (i.e. in reality, to the mothers). It allowed the conservatives to de facto continue to support the exit of women from the labor market for family reasons using different language. The low flat-rate sum, which replaced the previous income only inadequately and the lack of a comprehensive network of childcare places in extra-familial institutions discouraged fathers from giving up their employment and encouraged women, particularly with low incomes or those working part-time, to quit their jobs. Contrary to the CDU, the SPD used the concept in the hope of facilitating paid employment for women. At the same time, the party had never clearly supported the dual-earner model or any form of obligation or sanctioning of fathers who do not make use of parental leave (Bothfeld 2005, Erler 2005). The SPD instead hoped for a shift in the minds of parents and society.[12]

The new focus on family policies as reconciliation policies must be seen in the context of the heated debates concerning the reform of the abortion law, paragraph 218, in the beginning of the 1990s. Due to diverging legal situations in the former GDR and FRG, the Unification Treaty required the creation of a common legal basis (see Berghahn 1999, Gerlach 2010: 203ff.). The 1992 law,[13] which combined a three-month rule and the decision-making autonomy of pregnant women with an obligatory consultation, was, however, annulled by the Constitutional Court. It stipulated a law[14] that prescribed a consultation that normatively aimed to protect life. At the same time, the Constitutional Court lent support to an argument that had already been put forward during a parliamentary debate about abortion in 1975, according to which the living situation of families should be improved in order to ease the decision for having a child. Due to the high employment rates of women in the eastern German states and the increase in female labor-force participation in the western German states, many parliamentarians argued that work-family policies would be an effective method of improving the family's living situation. Hence they justified the extension of dismissal protection to three years within parental leave regulation in accordance with the Constitutional Court's ruling.[15]

Likewise, the introduction of a right to a childcare place for children older than three[16] was prompted by rulings of the Constitutional Court regarding the reform of the abortion law (Meyer 2003). Similar to the parental leave regulations, the right to a childcare place was seen as an element of support to women in order to avoid abortion. Women from the eastern states, among them CDU parliamentarian Angela Merkel, who was at that time minister for women and youth, played an important role in the adoption of the law (Interview DE1, see also Korthouwer 2008). These women would not accept regression in matters of childcare and continuously pushed for reforms. Together with the SPD, they also demanded an expansion of a public provision of childcare for children under three. For example, in her speech during the debate on the law proposals concerning the support of women in order to avoid abortion, Angela Merkel said that she regards "[. . .] the expansion of different childcare options for children aged under three for equally important as for children of pre-school age" and that she regrets the lack of an initiative for this issue.[17] Yet this went too far in the eyes of the CDU (Interviews DE1 and DE4).

To summarize the legislative periods between 1990 and 1998, the male-breadwinner model continued to dominate the work-family policy approach of the CDU. In spite of claims for more gender equality and better childcare provision, the SPD was reluctant to clearly advocate the dual-earner model. This strategic orientation is consistent with the findings on the average normative beliefs of the German population at the beginning of the 1990s. It is especially consistent with the findings of the particular traditional preferences of the core constituencies of both the SPD and the CDU. There was broad agreement on this issue by supporters of both large German parties. Since the section of the electorate with traditional beliefs continued to be of great importance during this period, incentives to start a reform process at that point remained limited. Interestingly, the foundations for an inter-party alliance between women who would later campaign on these issues were laid at that time. Moreover, critical actors, such as the future Chancellor Merkel, were already concerned with this issue at this point. Their claims were supported by the Constitutional Court's rulings that required adopting measures that improve the living situation of families.

1998–2002: a cautious shift in work-family policy orientation

In 1998, a coalition government of SPD and the Greens assumed responsibility. With the government takeover, a change in work-family policies was expected. In its party manifesto, the SPD had announced a "new start for women". The SPD had promised to support the reconciliation of work and care with an action program called "Woman and Work", and a parental leave reform which would create the preconditions for a more egalitarian division of work (Sozialdemokratische Partei Deutschlands 1998). This parental leave reform took place in 2000.[18] Except for the so-called budget option (*Budget*) where parents could choose between a lower payment for two years or a higher payment for one year, more flexibility in the use of leave and an increase in weekly working time during parental leave, the reform did not represent a shift towards firm support for the dual-earner family.

The draft law[19] was based on a bill the SPD had initiated in 1996.[20] At that time, the party had intended to introduce the budget option, but at a higher level than eventually adopted. A change towards an income-related benefit for working parents was neither mentioned in the 1996 bill nor in the draft law of 2000 – again because it was feared that cutting down a quasi-universal benefit[21] in favor of a payment benefitting mainly the employed and better-off parents would lead to opposition, and the SPD was eager to note that it refrained from privileging one way of living over the other (Bothfeld 2005: 185). Hence, at that time, the section of the SPD that considers redistribution between families as more important than dual-earner family support prevailed. Also, no measure to incentivize fathers to increase their use of parental leave, e.g. use-it-or-lose-it daddy months, could be enforced within the SPD. Rather, by referring to the "freedom of choice" motto, the SPD encouraged fathers and mothers to share the leave periods more equally.[22]

Also, the developments of the public provision of childcare fell short of the expectations. In its party manifesto, the SPD had promised to support the federal states financially in their efforts to expand the provision of childcare (Sozialdemokratische Partei Deutschlands 1998). Yet during this legislative period, the government did not provide additional financial means to the states for childcare. One reason was the tight budget (Erler 2005). The government had to struggle with the excessive level of debt the previous government had passed on (Zohlnhöfer 2003). In addition, a large part of the envisaged family policy budget had been reserved for an increase of children's allowances and tax benefits. In 1998, rulings of the Constitutional Court[23] had required the government to not only exempt the cost of living for a child within the tax system but to also consider the costs of childcare in a reasonable way. In an attempt to take account of the rulings, the government decided to combine an increase of children's allowances (in order to benefit low-income families) with an increase of the tax exemption for the child's subsistence level (to account for the Court's ruling to treat equal taxable persons with an equal income level) and a new tax exemption for care and education (Gerlach 2010).[24]

Thus, in spite of election promises, the highest share of women MPs in governing parties (38.7 percent) in the history of the German *Bundestag* and the highest number of women ministers (five) so far, a paradigm shift in work-family policies did not occur under the center-left government. In fact, the SPD achieved comparably minor improvements.

Another reason for this failure can be seen in the lack of initiatives by policy entrepreneurs and the lack of interest by the SPD leadership. Even though the then minister for family affairs Christine Bergmann emphasized issues of gender equality, a parental leave reform was not her top priority. As mentioned earlier, she was further restricted by budget constraints owing to the Constitutional Court rulings on the family tax allowance. In addition, family policies and the parental leave reform was not the party's leadership's main concern. Chancellor Schröder's disinterest in family policies is often illustrated with a statement he made during the 1998 election campaign where he described the proposed Ministry for Family Affairs, Senior Citizens, Women, and Youth as "responsible for women and all the other fuss" (Der Spiegel 21.02.2002). This mismatch between the gender equality-focused Bergmann and the chancellor is also illustrated by the failed attempt to introduce an equality act for the private sector in 2000 which aimed to strengthen women's representation in companies. The draft bill involved legally set minimum standards that would come into force if the social partners or employers and the works council on the company level could not come to an agreement. The employers' organizations strongly rejected this proposal, and Chancellor Schröder finally cancelled the initiative. In the end, the employers agreed on voluntary commitments of the companies and the draft bill was never discussed in parliament (Aust 2003, Fuhrmann 2002).

Changing approaches to families and family policies at the turn of the century

After 2001, the SPD changed its approach to family policies (Rüling 2010). The party adopted a definition of the family which identified the family as the most important source of comfort and context for education and socialization (Sozialdemokratische Partei Deutschlands 2002).[25] Previously, the SPD had rather emphasized the need to support the individual within the family. This new definition was close to the CDU's definition of the family, which saw the family as an institution that fulfils important tasks for society and should therefore be supported. The turnaround was brought forward by an internal working group on family issues presided over by Renate Schmidt and adopted at the National Party Congress in 2001 (Sozialdemokratische Partei Deutschlands 2001). This definition and its aims of supporting the family certainly paved the way for the party to be more attractive to centrist voters who might have disapproved of the party's focus on gender equality up to that point. Also, the employers, who traditionally have close links to the CDU and who had been put off by the SPD's proposal for an equality act for the private sector in 2000, could agree with the policy's aim of supporting the reconciliation of work and care.

The SPD's move can be seen as a response to the move by the CDU, which, in 1999, had adopted a new definition of the family, which was also published in the CDU's party manifesto of 2002. This shift had been the result of the proceedings in the context of the so-called *Projekt 21*. This project was initiated after the crushing electoral defeat in 1998, and it aimed to revise various policy fields. At that time, Angela Merkel, the former minister for women and youth and future CDU party chairperson, had been charged with the overhaul of family policies. The final resolution decided by the CDU Federal Committee acknowledged that families had changed significantly and faced different challenges than in the decades before. It also redefined families as "where parents carry responsibility for children and children carry responsibility for parents" – independently of marital status.[26] In addition, a priority was placed on policies that help parents to reconcile work and care, focusing especially on extra-familial childcare (even though the CDU emphasized that not only institutional forms of childcare should be supported but also company-provided childcare or child minders). All in all, this document represented a major innovation in the CDU's understanding of family policies (see also Fleckenstein 2010, Korthouwer 2008).

In summary, during this legislative period, taking steps towards the recognition of the dual-earner model and providing support for this model through policies became increasingly important for both large parties. The intra-party evolution of more progressive policies starts here. This must be seen against the background of a shift in public opinion about mothers' employment and childcare at the end of the 1990s. Also, the SPD arguably espoused the more conservative family definition in order to compete with the CDU for centrist voters. At the same time, parts of the CDU worked on a modernization of family policies to become more appealing to voters with progressive normative beliefs toward mothers' employment and childcare. The changes were more challenging for the CDU, which before had more clearly promoted the male-breadwinner model. Yet the electoral defeat in 1998 had triggered the desire to break away from the CDU's previous form and goals. Furthermore, this period saw the rise to prominence of some influential women who pushed the topic onto the agenda, for example the future minister for family affairs Schmidt (SPD) and the future chancellor Angela Merkel (CDU). They played a central role in subsequent reform processes.

2002–2005: family policies as an issue for party competition and the initial reforms

As mentioned earlier, one reason for the lack of substantial work-family policy progress under the first red-Green government was a lack of policy entrepreneurs and the disinterest of the SPD leadership. The support for and cooperation between the chancellor and the minister for family affairs, however, improved during the following legislature. The election of 2002 was very close, but sufficed for the continuation of the red-Green government. Renate Schmidt, who at that time was vice chairperson of the SPD with special responsibility for family policy and had been responsible for the change in the definition of the family, became minister for family affairs. She was also the one who had promoted an income-related parental leave benefit following the Swedish example as early as the 1980s (Interview DE1). Most importantly, Schmidt could rely on the support of Chancellor Schröder, who had recognized the importance of work-family policies. In the words of Schmidt,

> At the SPD's party convention in Nuremberg in 2001 Chancellor [Schröder, AB] was the only representative of the party's leadership who remained in the room for the whole of my speech and the ensuing discussion on work-family policies. Usually, after the major speeches and when it comes to this issue, all members of the party leadership leave the room. On top of that, by the time our turn came, it was an ungodly hour. Yes, and it was like this: He then understood. It might be because of his wife,[27] and maybe also because we like each other. In me he does not see a hysterical woman who runs around with a gender equality banner – although I actually do, just in a different way. So he thought, ok, she is capable and if she says so it will be right.[28]

Female policy entrepreneur Schmidt was arguably a persuasive person, and her words carried some weight. In addition, party competition on the issue of work-family policies increased. In this party convention at the very latest, family policies had become a decisive issue for the SPD. In April 2002 – five months before the elections – Chancellor Schröder made an official statement: "Family Is Where Children Are – Policies for a Family – and Children-Friendly Germany". In his speech, he made the case for better supporting parents who want to combine family and work responsibilities. He explicitly addressed young women by pointing to both the economic necessity to integrate the well-educated women into the labor force and young women's desires to be both in paid employment and have a family. In particular, he addressed the issue of childcare: "I think that there is nothing more important in family policies than to promote the expansion of childcare facilities. This will be the focus of our family policies within the next legislative period."[29] Thus the SPD tried to appeal to more libertarian voters with the focus on work-family reconciliation policies on the one hand and to please more conservative voters with the change in the family's definition at the same time.

How parties used work-family policy reform proposals in the 2002 election campaigns

Family and family policies continued to play an important role during the 2002 election campaigns (Rüling 2003). The CDU had noticed the SPD's change in direction and had begun to also put forth efforts in demonstrating a modernized image as regards family or women's issues However, individual CDU party members were still divided on what exactly constituted a modern family or a modern woman. While some party factions favored a change towards the dual-earner family support, some CDU members opposed this shift. For example, the CDU's fraction leader in parliament, Friedrich Merz, emphasized the importance of marriage for families with children and favored transfer benefits rather than services. He explicitly rejected the dual-earner model in his response to the government declaration in April 2002 and instead argued for a "real freedom of choice" for parents.[30] He received support from the sister party CSU. Consequently, even though both the CDU and the SPD mentioned the problems of reconciling work and care for parents in their 2002 party manifestos, the CDU promoted a family allowance to replace both the children's allowance and the parental leave benefit (Christlich Demokratische Union/Christlich Soziale Union 2002). As discussed earlier, a family allowance of this kind discourages rather than incentivizes mothers to return to work. The SPD, by contrast, emphasized an expansion of all-day public childcare by investing €1 billion in childcare infrastructure each year (Sozialdemokratische Partei Deutschlands 2002).

Hence, while it seems that the traditional wing of the conservatives, who wanted to preserve the status quo, had prevailed over those who wanted a change in work-family policies, the supporters of the dual-earner model were nevertheless able to push through some of their innovations. The party manifesto contained both the new definition of families and a proposal to take into account childcare costs within the tax system (Christlich Demokratische Union/Christlich Soziale Union 2002).

During the 2002 election campaign, the SPD drew on Chancellor Schröder's wife, who used to be a single mother with a career, in order to represent a modernized image of women. She figured prominently in the media on questions of childcare. In response, the CSU candidate, Edmund Stoiber, who had a reputation as a traditionalist, appointed a young woman parliamentarian who was pregnant with her second child to the election campaign team to epitomize the Christian Democratic emphasis on modern family policies (Lang and Sauer 2003). However, the heated discussions within the CDU about the fact that Katharina Reiche was not married to the father of her children (Der Tagesspiegel 13.08.2002) shows that the modern image did not represent all members of the party. The parties' attempts to project a modern family-friendly image were, however, accompanied with a rhetoric that focused almost solely on women, i.e. women as mothers who need to be supported in their efforts to reconcile work and care. Men did not play a role in this discourse. It was almost as if they were not also parents and affected by questions of reconciliation of work and care.

According to a survey, only 30 percent of the voters regarded the CDU and CSU as competent in family-policy matters at that time. By contrast, 43 percent of the voters believed that the SPD were better suited to solving family-policy problems. The difference becomes greater if we look only at women under the age of 35 for whom this policy field matters significantly; 48 percent of them trust the SPD more than the CDU to meet the challenges (Roth and Jung 2002: 11–12). This was ascribed to the fact that, in spite of the efforts during the election campaign to project a modern family- and woman-friendly image, the public's overall impression was that of a male-breadwinner-oriented CDU. The CDU party leader, Angela Merkel, named this as one of the reasons for their electoral defeat (Welt am Sonntag of 10.09.2003, cited in Lang and Sauer 2003).

In summary, the run-up to the 2002 election shows that progressive family policies had become a salient issue for political competition. This time the SPD more consistently used the issue of family policies to win votes and actively solicited women and libertarian voters. Women's agency, such as the female policy entrepreneur Schmidt and a large share of women MPs, played a considerable role in this strategy shift. The CDU observed the policy positions of the SPD and, as a consequence, also tried to demonstrate a modern approach to families. Yet in their party manifesto, the CDU preferred to compete with traditional policy proposals – in spite of more progressive positions regarding family policies within their own party. While the SPD started to respond to the shift in normative beliefs, the CDU was at odds with itself and did not present a coherent picture. This also had to do with the strong opposition of the CDU's parliamentary party leader to policies that support the dual-earner model and the traditional image of the male chancellor candidate. The 2002 elections have shown that Catholic housewives in particular voted for the CDU (Roßteutscher 2007), but this was not vital for winning the election. It led to yet another electoral defeat, which paved the way for more progressive CDU politicians. Shortly after the elections, Angela Merkel managed to strengthen her internal position by taking on the position of Friedrich Merz as leader of the parliamentary party.

Establishing "sustainable family policies" after the 2002 election

Right after having started in office, the new minister for family affairs, Renate Schmidt, started to develop and implement policies that would facilitate a better reconciliation of work and care as part of a "sustainable family policy".[31] She promoted an "Alliance for the Family" which, on different levels, aimed at bringing together all relevant actors in the field of childcare. On the municipality level, "Local Alliances for the Family" provide networks and exchange for local actors who wished to engage in family-oriented local initiatives. These local alliances are supported through a national service office, which, in particular, provides counseling. On the national level, employer organizations and trade unions cooperated and promoted work-family policies by referring to the effectiveness of such measures for companies and society in general. This has lead to various voluntary agreements. Most actors agreed that this appeasing approach had been very favorable for making previously suspicious actors (such as the employers' organizations) more sensitive to the issue and for putting the issue on the agenda (Erler 2005, Blum 2010).

At the same time, the government faced financial problems (Wagschal 2007). In spite of the promises made during the election campaigns regarding family support, the second red-Green government backtracked on the financial improvements of the 2000 parental leave reform in 2003 by substantially lowering the income limits for the leave payment during the first six months.

Another reform of the parental leave system was not intended until a closed meeting of the cabinet in July 2004. At that time, the government faced massive opposition to Chancellor Schröder's "Agenda 2010" and the so-called Hartz reforms.[32] Mass demonstrations – mainly in the Eastern states – took place, and a group of former SPD members splintered to set up the "Initiative Labor and Social Justice" party, which eventually merged with the PDS into the leftist party "Die Linke" in 2007 (Zohlnhöfer and Egle 2007). Against this background and in view of the upcoming elections in North Rhine-Westphalia in May 2005, the then minister of the chancellery, Frank-Walter Steinmeier, asked minister for family affairs Renate Schmidt to prepare a proposal that would break new ground and send a positive message (Interview DE1). So she presented her ideas on a Swedish-style, parental leave benefit reform that provided one parent with an income-related benefit for ten months and the other parent with two use-it-or-lose-it months. The proposed reform constituted a paradigm shift in two respects: First, the benefit is proportional to the previous income of the beneficiary. That is, in contrast to before, parents with a higher income would receive a higher benefit levels. Second, for the first time, the duration of paid leave would be reduced by two months if one of the parents did not take parental leave. There was thus a double incentive for fathers to take parental leave: the total length of paid parental leave is longer if both the father and the mother take it, and the use of the income-related benefit does not result in a sharp decline in disposable household income anymore.

After the cabinet meeting, Schmidt was charged with examining the implications of the parental leave reform for Germany with regard to the impact on the demographic developments and the compatibility of work and care. However, not all members of the cabinet had been persuaded. There were, in particular, reservations regarding the additional €1 billion per year financial burden (in total €4 billion/year). In addition, some SPD members disagreed with the principle of the income replacement. Above all, male members of the left wing argued that an income-related benefit would value children of high-income families more than children of low-income families and advocated a needs-based benefit. Schmidt managed to convince the critics by emphasizing the positive effects for birth and female-employment rates (Interview DE1). She also benefitted from the support of the (increased) number of women within the party. In her words,

> In the today's SPD no man would dare anymore to rail against such a reform. For sure, this has to do with the party gender quota. Due to the increase of women representatives these issues have become socially acceptable in the

SPD. In 1980 – even though the SPD faction in the Bundestag had the highest share of women of all parties, but it was only 9.2 percent – a discussion about childcare was impossible. If [the women, A.B.] had started such a debate they would have called them crazy and had asked whether they not had other things in mind. These issues have gained in importance with the increase of the share of elected party members who are women. Women have initiated these debates and men had been told by their wives and daughters at home that there is no way around.[33]

Most importantly, the minister could rely on the support of Chancellor Schröder. The fact that Schröder had asked the minister of family affairs via his minister of the chancellery, Steinmeier, to prepare a reform proposal indicates the relevance they attributed to family policies, i.e. their hope that it would be well received by the electorate. The plan worked out: most of the newspapers reported positively about the proposed reform. Two months after the cabinet meeting, the cabinet decided to incorporate the parental leave proposal into the government program (Der Tagesspiegel 05.09.2004). The government intended to implement the new regulation in 2006.

The contentious route towards the first law on the expansion of day care for children younger than three

As proposed during the election campaigns, the SPD aimed to expand publicly provided childcare places for children under three. The coalition treaty between the SPD and the Green Party included a commitment to introduce a legal quota of places for 20 percent of children under three which the states should fulfill (Sozialdemokratische Partei Deutschlands and Bündnis 90/Die Grünen 2002). Yet when the draft bill for the Day-Care Expansion Act (*Tagesbetreuungsausbaugesetz*, TAG) was presented in parliament in 2004, the government retreated from the commitment on the basis that the states and the municipalities rejected the plan because it would not be appropriate in light of regional variations and needs.[34] At that time, the government faced a strong majority of the opposition in the *Bundesrat*,[35] hence a potentially rather strong veto player. The proposed bill required the municipalities to provide enough places for children under three to meet the demands, but at least make places available for those children whose parents are in paid employment or in training. The TAG explicitly aimed to establish formal child minders (*Tagesmütter/Tagesväter*) as a "qualitative alternative of equal rank" to childcare institutions (Bundesministerium für Familie 2004: 4). The law was heavily debated. Yet, notwithstanding earlier reservations against early childhood care and education, this time the Christian-democratic parties were in favor of the reform. Quite interestingly, during the first round of the parliamentary debate, Maria Böhmer (CDU) assured the minister for family affairs her support in her fight for more and high-quality childcare places. She went even further by stating that she sees a subjective right for children aged zero to three to a childcare place as a possible goal. In fact, Böhmer criticized the law's limitation on parents who are in paid employment or in training and argued for an extension of the entitlement to all families.[36]

The commitment of conservative female MPs to the provision of childcare had already been demonstrated during the reform of the legal right to a childcare place for children older than three in 1992. Even then, some of the female CDU representatives from eastern Germany, among them Angela Merkel, had argued for an expansion of childcare provisions to children under three. But back then they could not persuade the male-breadwinner-oriented CDU. At the beginning of the new century, not only had the share of women within the CDU increased to about 20 percent (Christlich Demokratische Union 2010), but Angela Merkel had become party executive. In 2003, the women's organization of the CDU, the *Frauen Union* (Women's Union) had presented a proposal for the provision of childcare at party conferences and, even though it was met with criticism particularly on the part of male members,[37] it increasingly enjoyed popularity (Interview DE2). It was part of the modernizing strategy of the CDU that had initiated after the electoral defeat in 1998. Certainly, the CDU was also cautious not to further offend the traditional constituencies. Thus the party would not go so far as to promote childcare *institutions*. Rather, the party endorsed the provision of childcare by child minders (Tagesmütter) in their private homes. In a motion,[38] the CDU praised child minders as particularly suitable for small children, because this form of childcare is more "binding and straightforward", "flexible" and child minders are more "capable of dealing with the child as desired by the parents". The SPD's move toward the endorsement of private child minders as an alternative to institutions can be seen as a concession to voters of the political center.

The parliamentary debates were dominated by disputes over financing and the division of authority between the national, the regional and the local levels. The government intended to finance the expansion with savings from the merging of unemployment and social assistance (part of the so-called Hartz IV reforms). It had calculated that the municipalities would save €2.5 billion, of which €1.5 billion was to be allocated for childcare. Yet the opposition-controlled *Bundesrat* considered the calculation unrealistic. The upper chamber argued that it was unclear whether and when such savings would materialize and demanded the direct financing of the additional costs. Yet a direct financing out of the public budget had not been possible because of the government's financial situation (Interview DE1).[39] Due to the reservations of the SPD-led municipalities and states regarding the investment, Minister Schmidt also had to persuade a large part of the SPD. But she could rely on the chancellor, who, for example, organized a dinner with the SPD mayors. The minister and the chancellor in the end persuaded the mayors to agree with the proposal (Interview DE1).

The *Bundesrat* also pointed to the possibly unconstitutional interference with state competencies. For these reasons, the *Bundesrat* rejected the law and formally called the parliament-senate conference committee (*Vermittlungsausschuss*). This move resulted in a division of the law into a part that could be adopted without the consent of the *Bundesrat* (law on day-care expansion) and one that required *Bundesrat* approval (reform of the German Child and Youth Aid Act (KHJG) – a

162 *Germany: work-family policy reforms*

standard strategy in Germany to bring through laws. The CDU-led states then voted against the law on day-care expansion (which now excluded the contentious administrative issues), but was overruled by the *Bundestag* majority.

The 2005 elections: a strong pledge for mothers' employment supportive policies by the SPD and an incoherent approach by the CDU

The policy process tracing made clear that because of efforts by women, the idea of extra-familial childcare for small children had eventually had an impact on the CDU. Yet not all conservatives, in particular the conservative-led federal states, were sympathetic to the modernization strategy. This became even more apparent before and during the election campaign in the summer of 2005.[40] In her effort to modernize the CDU, party leader Angela Merkel had set up a commission on "Parents, Children and Employment" in April 2005. The title reveals what the key challenge was perceived to be and where family policies were supposed to be heading: the promotion and support of the dual-earner model. Merkel appointed the then Lower Saxon minister of social affairs, women, family and health, Ursula von der Leyen, as chairwoman. She seemed to be the embodiment of a conservative woman who successfully combined family and work: she is married and has seven children, but had worked as a physician for almost 20 years before she became minister of social affairs (see also Korthouwer 2008). Due to the surprising call for early elections, however, the commission was not able to finish its work. Merkel and von der Leyen were accordingly not capable of thoroughly spreading their view into the party and having it approved. For the elections, the party, therefore, proposed a mixture of policies that aimed at supporting both the traditional male-breadwinner model and dual-earner families. In its party manifesto, the CDU no longer intended to introduce a family allowance (as in 2002), but rather proposed to recognize the importance of parental care with a number of different cash benefits such as a basic tax allowance or reduced contributions to the pension scheme. They also stated that they would more strongly support parents who needed to reconcile work and care, but only referred to the responsibilities of the federated states for providing childcare and proposed to focus the entitlement to part time to caring family members only (Christlich Demokratische Union/Christlich Soziale Union 2005).

By contrast, the SPD proposed the expansion of childcare places through to the introduction of a legal entitlement for children starting from their second birthday and the parental leave reform in its manifesto (Sozialdemokratische Partei Deutschlands 2005). The introduction of the income-replacement rate was justified by referring to the importance of maintaining the living standard of families after the birth of a child, supporting gender equality to the benefit of women and for men to be involved with childcare (Sozialdemokratische Partei Deutschlands 2005: 46). Hence the SPD linked the necessity of providing material security for families with a gender egalitarian concept of childcare. Thus the SPD competed

Germany: work-family policy reforms 163

with progressive policy proposals while the CDU wavered between different models of family support.

In summary, the legislative period from 2002–2005 was characterized by efforts to tackle the issue of reconciling work-family issues. The topic also increased in importance. The SPD even used the parental leave reform as a counterpart to the unpopular unemployment benefit reforms, knowing that this benefit corresponded to the changes in normative beliefs towards childcare and mothers' employment. At the same time, the CDU continued to work on a change in the party's approach to families in order to compete with more progressive parties. Women's agency was again a major factor. Backed by Chancellor Schröder, Minister Schmidt was able to pursue the work-family policy reforms in spite of opponents within the SPD. At the same time, the CDU Women's Union, backed by party leader Merkel, strove for a modernization within the CDU. Yet, in spite of the shift in normative beliefs of the population, the CDU gave in to the traditionalists and went to the polls with rather traditional proposals. This insistence on policy support that favored the male-breadwinner rather than the dual-earner model by the CDU also explains why more far-reaching policy reforms did not take place during this legislative period. With respect to the reform of childcare provision, the government had to struggle with the conservative-led states, which had the majority of places in the *Bundesrat* and spoke against such reforms. The CDU, however, did not benefit from this strategy. In spite of the fact that surveys predicted a landslide victory for the CDU, the 2005 election was again close (SPD: 34.2 percent; CDU: 35.2 percent). As shown in the regression analyses of the voting behavior, the SPD competition for libertarian voters had paid off. Women were more likely to vote for the SPD than for any other party. Hence the SPD's more modern approach seemed to have appealed to this group of voters. In view of the declining support, the CDU was consequently even more under pressure to look beyond their traditional constituency and to adapt its policy approach accordingly.

After 2005: fundamental work-family policy reforms under the grand coalition

The 2005 election results for the two large parties were very close again, but the CDU received slightly more votes. In the end, the CDU and the SPD agreed on forming a coalition government ("grand coalition") headed by the first female chancellor Angela Merkel (CDU). For observers familiar with the differences regarding work-family policy proposals in the party manifestos, the coalition treaty of the grand coalition government contained a surprise. In order to "support an effective and sustainable economic security of families" (Christlich Demokratische Union/Christlich Soziale Union and Sozialdemokratische Partei Deutschlands 2005: 100), the grand coalition proposed to introduce a parental leave benefit that mirrored the SPD proposal of 2005. Hence, instead of pursuing the proposals made in the CDU party manifesto, the CDU agreed on the more radical shift in work-family policies as had been proposed by the SPD.

The leave benefit was to be income-related (67 percent of previous net income with a cap of 1,800 Euros) and paid for a total of 12 months. Moreover, the proposal included two use-it-or-lose-it months for each parent. In contrast to previous SPD deliberations, even non-employed persons such as housewives or students were eligible to receive a minimum leave benefit. Hence the merit for including the dual-earne-oriented parental leave benefit into the coalition treaty can be attributed to the SPD. Yet the negotiations within the grand coalition resulted in several amendments to satisfy the various party factions within the CDU and the SPD. As it stands, the leave benefit is not inherently consistent.

During the coordination processes for the coalition treaty in 2005, the former and current ministers for family affairs, Schmidt and von der Leyen, closely collaborated. Both women had quite similar ideas about the direction of work-family policy reforms. This consensus of representatives of different parties was explained by von der Leyen in an interview:

> Both of us have experienced how difficult it is to pursue a demanding profession while having several children at the same time. And we both aim at improving this situation to spare our daughters and sons this experience.[41]

Hence the conservative von der Leyen agreed with most of the proposals that had been brought forward by the former minister for family affairs, in part, within the former legislature. The SPD insisted on including the legal right to a childcare place for children older than one year (Interview DE1). The coalition treaty then put forward that, under the condition that the municipalities would not be able to meet the goal of providing 230,000 additional places by 2010, the legal right was to come into force in 2013 (Christlich Demokratische Union/Christlich Soziale Union and Sozialdemokratische Partei Deutschlands 2005: 97).

By then, most of the CDU had accepted the importance of adopting a progressive vision of women and the family (not least because the reform was justified due to its positive effect on birth rates). The policy entrepreneur von der Leyen played a central role in framing and enforcing this view (Henninger and von Wahl 2010). She was supported by the CDU's *Frauen Union*, but also benefited from the overall relatively high share of women representatives in parliament. In the sixteenth legislature (2005–2009) – the third time in a row – women representatives made up more than 30 percent of the MPs. She could moreover rely on the backing of Chancellor Merkel who had long advocated for the support of working women. Merkel also managed to persuade most within the CDU that these progressive policies are vital for winning elections. It should be noted that the CDU support of the leave benefit can also be attributed to the fact that its design reflects a key principle of conservative family policies: high-income earners profit more from an income-related benefit than low-income earners. As the chairman of the working group "Family, Senior Citizens, Women and Youth" of the CDU/CSU fraction in the Bundestag, Johannes Singhammer (CSU) said during the first consultation of the law proposal (BT-Drs. Drucksache 16/1889), "We are satisfied, because the *Elterngeld* contains a bourgeois and performance-oriented structure

Germany: work-family policy reforms 165

which was most important to us."[42] This fact was indeed more problematic for the SPD, which often struggles internally about which social group should benefit from family policies.

Some high-ranking male CDU and CSU members were, however, dissatisfied with the two use-it-or-lose-it months for each parent. The first deputy chairman of the CDU/CSU fraction in the Bundestag, Peter Ramsauer, ridiculed the two daddy months as a "diaper traineeship" for men. He and others criticized the "enforced daddy months" as an illegitimate intervention into private matters of the family (Sueddeutsche Zeitung 27.04.2006, see also Blum 2012). In the end, Chancellor Merkel intervened and defended the daddy months (Frankfurter Allgemeine Zeitung 19.04.2006). The final compromise did not change the principle of reducing the entitlement by two months. Rather, the total duration was prolonged by two months to 14 months,[43] and the daddy quota was positively re-framed "daddy bonus". The opposition criticized this horse trade as an expensive compromise. The then deputy chairwoman of the *Bundestag* committee on Family, Senior Citizens, Women and Youth, Ekin Deligöz (Greens) said, "The two additional months only serve to spare the CSU a humiliation. For that, the taxpayer has to pay 750 billion Euros."[44]

Another example of how the coalition "bought" the internal agreement refers to a SPD demand. Even though the coalition originally intended to credit other social transfer benefits against the *Elterngeld*, the left wing within the SPD (together with the leftist party then named *Die Linkspartei.PDS*) demanded an exemption for people who receive basic-security welfare payments (so-called *Arbeitslosengeld II* – unemployment money II) (Blum 2012, Sueddeutsche Zeitung 28.04.2006). The SPD had insisted on this benefit for those who receive basic security because the party was under pressure after the rise of the Left party. This party had become a strong competitor for the SPD's traditional constituency. In fact, for the first time, low-educated persons were more likely to vote for the Left party than for the SPD in the 2009 election.

The parental leave reform is one example of a paradigm shift in the field of work-family policies which can be explained by the dynamics of party competition and policy responsiveness and women's agency. The other example concerns the public provision of childcare.

Two steps forward...

In 2006, the coalition agreed on reassuming the reform of federalism.[45] The law that came into effect in September 2006 had consequences for the financing and competencies in the field of childcare. The federation was no longer permitted to assign duties to the municipalities (Art. 84 Section. 1(7) GG). In addition, except for those fields in which the federation has the sole competency, federal co-financing was abolished (Art. 104b). Consequently, intervention and financial aid were from then on impossible for the field of childcare.

Nonetheless, the two parties of the grand coalition proceeded with the expansion of childcare provision. In February 2007, the Christian Democratic minister for family affairs, Ursula von der Leyen, publicly announced an increase to the number of childcare places to 750,000 by 2013 so that one-third of children aged zero to three would be cared for outside the family. This venture immediately led to protests from various corners: from their coalition partner, the SPD, from social actors, e.g. some Catholic bishops, but also within the CDU and from her sister party CSU. In particular, a Catholic bishop Walter Mixa figured prominently in the media. He criticized von der Leyen's approach as a measure to "reduce mothers to baby producers" who put their children shortly after birth into "state-provided external care" (Sueddeutsche Zeitung 22.02.2007). Yet he was not able to mobilize allies with these statements. Representatives of the Bavarian CSU, however, accused the minister for family affairs of undermining the "freedom of choice" for parents, because her ideas would "force" both parents to take up employment. Also, some CDU representatives criticized this apparent shift toward a new family model. At the same time, von der Leyen was backed by some heads of the federal states, who argued in support of childcare expansion.[46] Most importantly, Chancellor Merkel supported von der Leyens plans and referred to the CDU program which postulates the necessity for work-family policies (Frankfurter Allgemeine Zeitung 24.02.2007). The proponents could point to the increased support for progressive policies for dual-earner families in the German population. Furthermore, they were able to refer to the success of the parental leave reform, which is popular among the population.

The SPD was in a difficult situation. They had successfully competed for women voters in the 2005 election with the more progressive proposals in the party manifesto. Yet they could not benefit from this achievement because the CDU minister for family affairs had taken over. In the words of former minister Schmidt,

> I was so angry when the SPD had passed this topic[47] over [to the CDU]. The SPD had abandoned all topics of the future – family, education, environment [. . .]. In exchange we obtained the more 'important' areas of responsibility such as finances. But these were also the more problematic ones and even though we did a good job we could not benefit from them.[48]

The SPD could not oppose the principal direction of the reforms in public, but was faced with the challenge of demonstrating the party's authorship of the reform and, at the same time, distancing itself from its political opponent.

In the end, the SPD welcomed von der Leyen's initiative, but criticized the lack of a financing concept. The party put forward its own proposal by the end of February 2007 (Sozialdemokratische Partei Deutschlands 2007). To demonstrate that the SPD was a party of substance as far as the issue of childcare was concerned (and to remind the electorate that it is the SPD and not the CDU that stands for progressive work-family policies), five leading Social Democrats presented the proposal (Sueddeutsche Zeitung 26.02.2007). It foresaw the introduction of a legal right to a childcare place for children older than one and proposed a financing mix of cutting and recalibrating other benefits. Among others, the party

Germany: work-family policy reforms   167

intended to reform the splitting system of taxation by introducing a cap on the amount that can be transferred to the partner. In addition, the savings of children's allowances that resulted from the decreasing number of children were to be allocated to finance the expansion and the improvement of the quality of childcare. The CDU, however, criticized these plans as unjust since the costs would have to be borne by families, in particular those who could not benefit from the provision of childcare anymore (Stern.de 25.02.2007).

The minister for family affairs convened a meeting of the municipalities, the states and the federal government in April 2007. Notwithstanding the fact that the federal government has no competencies to financially assist the municipalities, the minister promised to support them in their efforts to raise the number of childcare places. She first intended to have the federal government only take part in investment costs[49] and – similar to the SPD proposal – to use the child allowance savings that would result from the decreasing number of children and from the predicted increase of the employment of lone mothers who would no longer need social assistance. Yet, after protests by the states and their coalition partner, the SPD,[50] the coalition committee agreed on using additional tax money to assist the states with the running costs in May 2007. Minister von der Leyen was able to use a window of opportunity with regard to financing possibilities, because due to improvements on the labor market, the federal government had a (unexpected) budgetary surplus (Bundesministerium der Finanzen 2008). This additional money had to be spent, so the minister of finance came up with a special fund which could be used for childcare expenses (cf. Der Spiegel 25.05.2007).

... and one step back

The states and the CDU accepted the SPD demand that children older than one year as of 2013 have a legal entitlement to childcare. Against the background that the issue of childcare provision by now figured so prominently in the media and had become such a hot topic for the parties' leadership, the parties were arguably prone to force each other to adapt policy positions. Yet electoral demand and policy responsiveness also played a role. Both the SPD and the CDU had realized the potential for childcare policies to win elections. At the same time, the CDU was split: in an attempt to satisfy its traditional constituency, the CDU's sister party CSU was able to force through a transfer benefit for those parents who would not make use of a publicly provided childcare place, but care for their children at home (childcare allowance, *Betreuungsgeld*). This childcare allowance was proposed by the Bavarian prime minister and CSU leader Edmund Stoiber. According to a member of the CDU women's organization (*FrauenUnion*), he was able to enforce this idea at the highest level without having had it debated within the party (interview DE2). In the course of the debates, Stoiber even linked his demand for the childcare allowance to the CSU's approval of the introduction of the legal entitlement to a childcare place.[51] He was heavily criticized – in particular by women representatives also of his party (see Sueddeutsche Zeitung 07.08.2007), but he also found support. Once again, the debates centered on the question of whether or not children younger than three are best cared for at home by one parent, i.e. the mother. The proponents of the childcare allowance argued in favor of a "freedom of choice" of parents and against a seemingly exclusive focus of family policies on dual-earner families.

It seems plausible that CSU leader Stoiber had the CSU's core electoral constituency in mind when making the childcare allowance proposal. But also gender played a role. He was criticized in particular by women, but was supported by a group of young conservative men who published a document entitled "Modern Bourgeois Conservatism" which urges the CDU and CSU to "think more again of the parties' roots" (Mappus et al. 2007). The authors felt that the conservative profile threatened to get lost. In their view, supporting marriage and families is one of the essential parts of the conservative image. For that reason, the authors point out that *all* families should receive benefits regardless of their care arrangement ("freedom of choice") and advocate the introduction of the childcare allowance.

The example of the childcare allowance illustrates the Christian Democrats' conflicts. One faction of the party – mainly represented by women – has tried to respond to the changed normative beliefs in the population. Centripetal competition and the quest for libertarian voters back up this course. The other section aims at preserving the more traditional path to satisfy the core constituencies. Often, male representatives share this view. In the words of the then acting spokeswoman on family affairs,

> In politics, unfortunately, men rule who have built their life on this family model. They are here in the *Bundestag* while their wives are at home to free them from all family obligations. This is, for all intents and purposes, a defense of the own life philosophy. This is why policies do not change as quickly as normative beliefs in society.[52]

In late summer, the federal/state committee agreed on the division of the costs of the childcare expansion, and in autumn, the parliament approved the establishment of a special fund (*Sondervermögen*) to finance the costs. The federal government will pay for investment costs up to a total amount of €2.5 billion between 2008 and 2013. Moreover, the federal government will increase its contribution to the running costs from year to year, starting from €100 million in 2009, and will continue these efforts after 2013 with €770 million per year (Bundesministerium für Familie 2007). The childcare allowance and the question whether or not it should find its way into the draft bill remained controversial. The SPD refused to have it mentioned in the wording of the law. At the CDU party convention in December 2007, the *FrauenUnion* put forward a motion to reject the inclusion of the childcare allowance into the program. However, a lot of pressure to withdraw this motion was exerted on the *FrauenUnion*. The organization backed the motion, but Chancellor Merkel spoke in favor of the benefit saying that she had to stick to her word and asked the delegates to avoid a fight with the sister party CSU (Die Welt 03.12.2007). Thus, even though the chancellor agreed with the policy approach the minister of family affairs had pursued, this time she had to give in to the traditionalists, knowing that the CSU otherwise would block the law on childcare expansion. The *FrauenUnion's* motion was rejected.

In February 2008, the Coalition Committee found a compromise (Henninger and von Wahl 2010): the legal entitlement to a childcare place for children older than one will be incorporated in the law without making explicit reference to the childcare allowance. At the same time, a sentence is included which postulates that, as of 2013, a monthly benefit (for example a childcare allowance) may be introduced to support parents who care for their children younger than three at home. This passage thus postponed the decision of how to design the benefit. The law[53] was adopted on September 26 and came into effect on December 15.

Conclusion

The process tracing of the work-family policy reforms in Germany has shown a striking change of work-family policies over the period of almost 20 years, in particular after 2005. This development was not the result of a party change in government. Rather, in a continuous process starting in the late 1990s, both large parties gradually adapted their policy positions. Especially for the CDU, which traditionally supported the male-breadwinner model, the change represented a surprise twist. Take the example of public provision of childcare. The CDU has made a remarkable leap from opposition to extra-familial childcare for infants and toddlers to the introduction of a legal right to childcare for children older than one. Even though the intended introduction of the childcare allowance counteracts the law in a sense, the policy processes reflect the changes in normative beliefs of the population and how the large parties have started to compete for groups of voters who are in favor of dual-earner family support. The additional evidence provided by process tracing based on expert interviews and document analyses in this chapter underlined the importance of the explanatory factors outlined in the quantitative chapter for the reforms.

It also became clear that the policy changes would not have occurred without the increase in the numbers of women MPs and without the female policy entrepreneurs Schmidt and von der Leyen. While their motivation and involvement was independent of their party membership, their achievements did relate to their political background. Even though Schmidt, as a member of the SPD, had successfully persuaded her fellow party members and initiated the reform processes, she faced opposition from the CDU and in particular the CDU-led federal states. This situation was different for von der Leyen. Being herself a member of the CDU, she was in a better position to persuade the strong critics within her own party than her predecessor. In the words of Schmidt,

> This has most likely been the only way to force through the right to a childcare place for children older than one year as of 2013. Being a minister from the SPD I would have gotten a bloody nose even in spite of the grand coalition

and the coalition treaty. The same is true for the parental leave and the daddy months. The CDU would have grappled with me. Hence, it was good that it was a minister who herself was a CDU member. She was the only person who was in a position to overcome this logjam in the CDU.[54]

For both Schmidt and von der Leyen, the support of the chancellors – which was arguably motivated by vote-seeking strategies – was a central factor for their success. The example of the two SPD-governed legislative periods (1998–2002 and 2002–2005) is telling. Chancellor Schröder's support of the minister for family affairs and her reform ideas coincides with realizing that progressive work-family policies are an issue for political competition and winning votes. Years earlier, when the issue was not seen as important to win additional votes, a lack of support for the minister was discernible. Also the CDU minister for family affairs could rely on the chancellor's support after 2005. Work-family policies had been an issue for Merkel as early as the early 1990s and, recognizing progressive family policies as a means to make the party more attractive, she had argued for a change in the CDU's family policy approach in the late 1990s.

Notes

1 Minister for Family Affairs, 2005–2009 (CDU).
2 "Beim Bundesparteitag in Nürnberg 2001 war der Bundeskanzler der einzige der gesamten Führungsriege, der bei meiner Rede und der gesamten Diskussion über Familienpolitik auf seinem Platz sitzen geblieben ist. Normalerweise gehen nach den großen Reden und dazu noch bei diesem Thema immer alle raus. [. . .] Familienpolitik lockt zwar nicht jeden Hund hinterm Ofen hervor, aber die moderne Linie hatte für die SPD positive Effekte. [. . .] Die SPD konnte sich 2002 und 2005 noch als die modernere, aufgeschlossenere Partei mit Konzepten profilieren. Das war 2009 mit Frau von der Leyen vollkommen anders: Da war uns das Thema nahezu vollständig genommen. Eine Profilierung gegen die Union war nicht möglich." (Interview DE1).
3 Unless noted otherwise, all translations are my own.
4 "Bei allen sozialen Leistungen für Mutterschaft und Kindererziehung sind solche Finanzierungsformen zu nutzen, die die Arbeitsmarktchancen der Eltern nicht beeinträchtigen." (Sozialdemokratische Partei Deutschlands 1990: 12).
5 Drucksache 12/1125, Gesetz der Bundesregierung "Entwurf eines Zweiten Gesetzes zur Änderung des Bundeserziehungsgeldgesetzes und anderer Vorschriften", 09.09.1991.
6 Bundestag, Stenographisches Protokoll 12/50: 4099, 17.10.1991.
7 Ulrich Böhme (SPD), Bundestag, Stenographisches Protokoll 12/50: 4101, 17.10.1991.
8 Already in the 1980s, the SPD working group on gender equality had discussed the example of the Swedish parental leave scheme, which provides an income replacement rate and use-it-or-lose-it months for the father. In 1985, the parliamentary group of the SPD introduced a law proposal aimed at the introduction of this scheme in Germany. At that time, the SPD was in the opposition and the law proposal was not successful (Interview DE1).
9 Rose Götte, Ulrich Böhme (SPD), Bundestag, Stenographisches Protokoll 12/19: 1237ff., 22.03.1991.
10 Norbert Eimer (FDP), Bundestag, Stenographisches Protokoll 12/50: 4101, 17.10.1991.
11 Hildegard Wester (SPD), Bundestag, Stenographisches Protokoll 12/50: 4107, 17.10.1991.
12 Rose Götte (SPD), Bundestag, Stenographisches Protokoll 12/19: 1248, 22.03.1991.

13 Gesetz zum Schutz des vorgeburtlichen/werdenden Lebens, zur Förderung einer kinderfreundlicheren Gesellschaft, für Hilfen im Schwangerschaftskonflikt und zur Regelung des Schwangerschaftsabbruchs (Schwangeren- und Familienhilfegesetz – SchwFamHiG) (Bundesgesetzblatt, Jahrgang 1992, Teil 1, S. 1398 vom 27. Juli 1992).
14 On August 21, 1995, the SchwFamHiG was amended by the Schwangeren- und Familienhilfeänderungsgesetz (SFHÄndG, BGBl. I S. 1050). It added an article on the consultation in case of conflicts regarding a pregnancy, i.e. when a parent considers abortion. It states that the consultation aims at protection of the unborn life.
15 For example, Family Minister Hannelore Rönsch (CDU) stated in a parliamentary debate of 1991, "Parents who know about the parental leave benefit may be more convinced to say "Yes to life". Together with children's allowances and tax exemptions, housing allowances or benefits from the federal foundation "Mother and Child", parental leave and the leave allowance is an important support for the protection of unborn life." (Hannelore Rönsch (CDU), Bundestag, Stenographisches Protokoll 12/19: 1236, 22.03.1991).
16 The right to a childcare place was part of the Schwangeren- und Familienhilfegesetz of 1992.
17 Angela Merkel, Bundestag, Stenographischer Bericht 12/99: 8246, 26.05.1992.
18 Drittes Gesetz zur Änderung des Bundeserziehungsgeldgesetzes (BErzGG, Bundesgesetzblatt Teil I 2000 Nr.46 26.10.2000 S. 1426)
19 BT-Drs 14/3553 of 07.06.2000.
20 BT-Drs 13/6577 of 13.12.1996.
21 It was a quasi-universal benefit because all parents, regardless of their employment status, were principally eligible, yet the income-test certainly excluded those with a higher income.
22 Christine Bergmann (SPD), Bundestag, Stenographischer Bericht 14/115: 10943, 07.07.2000.
23 2 BvR 1057/91, 2 BvR 1226/91, 2 BvR 980/91; see Gerlach (2004).
24 "*Betreuungs-, Erziehungs- und Ausbildungsfreibetrag*".
25 "Familie ist, wo Kinder sind. Die Familien sind Leistungsträger unserer Gesellschaft. Sie leben Zusammenhalt, ermöglichen freie Entfaltung der Individuen und sind Lebensmittelpunkt. Die meisten Menschen wünschen und erleben Familie als Ort der Geborgenheit und der Sicherheit, viele auch des privaten Glücks. In Familien übernehmen Eltern, Großeltern und Kinder Verantwortung füreinander. Familien sind die erste und wichtigste Instanz für Erziehung, Persönlichkeits- und Charakterbildung. Hier finden junge Menschen den Raum, in dem Vertrauen, Selbstbewusstsein und Bindung entstehen können. Im Zusammenleben in den Familien werden zentrale Werte, Tugenden und Regeln unserer Gesellschaft vermittelt." (Sozialdemokratische Partei Deutschlands 2002: 45f.).
26 "Familie ist überall dort, wo Eltern für Kinder und Kinder für Eltern Verantwortung tragen. Familie: das sind Ehepaare mit ehelichen, nichtehelichen, adoptierten Kindern oder mit Pflegekindern, erwachsene Kinder, die sich um ihre Eltern kümmern, alleinerziehende Mütter oder Väter oder Alleinerziehende mit Lebenspartner sowie nicht-eheliche Lebensgemeinschaften mit gemeinsamen Kindern." (Christlich Demokratische Union 1999: 8).
27 The interviewee refers to the fact that Chancellor Schröder's wife used to be a single mother with a career and, supposedly, is concerned with the lack of support of mothers' employment.
28 "Beim Bundesparteitag in Nürnberg 2001 war der Bundeskanzler der einzige der gesamten Führungsriege, der bei meiner Rede und der gesamten Diskussion über Familienpolitik auf seinem Platz sitzen geblieben ist. Normalerweise gehen nach den großen Reden und dazu noch bei diesem Thema immer alle raus, außerdem war es eine unchristliche Zeit, als wir endlich dran kamen. Ja, und es ist wirklich so: Er hat's begriffen. Das liegt vielleicht auch an seiner Frau, und vielleicht auch daran, dass wir

uns schätzen. Er sieht also bei mir nicht nur irgend so ein überkandideltes Weibsbild, das immer nur mit einer Gleichstellungsfahne durch die Gegend rennt – was ich zwar auch tue, aber halt auf eine andere Art und Weise. Er hat also gedacht, so, die ist patent und wenn die jetzt so etwas sagt, dann kann man ihr das auch glauben." (Interview D1)

29 Gerhard Schröder (SPD), Bundestag, Stenographischer Bericht 14/230: 22774, 18.04.2002.

30 "Wir wollen nicht, dass das frühere Leitbild der Familie, in der in der Regel die Mutter auf eine Erwerbstätigkeit außer Haus verzichtet, nun ausschließlich durch das neue Leitbild einer Familie ersetzt wird, in der grundsätzlich beide Elternteile ganztägig außer Haus berufstätig sind und Kinder vom ersten Lebensjahr an in Krippen, Horten, Ganztagskindergärten und Ganztagsschulen groß werden (Friedrich Merz (CDU), Bundestag, Stenographischer Bericht 14/230: 22777, 18.04.2002. (We do not want an exclusive replacement of the former model where, as a rule, the mother renounces employment, with a new model of a family where principally both parents work full-time outside the home and children, as of their first year of life, grow up in day-care centers, after school care centers, all-day childcare institutions and schools.)

31 The concept of "sustainable family policy" was developed by the economist Rürup and colleagues (Rürup and Gruescu 2003). They argued that family policy would contribute to economic growth (and hence be sustainable) if it aimed at higher birth rates and higher female employment. To reach these goals, better childcare facilities, flexible working hours and a more equal share of care work should be introduced and/or facilitated. Later applications of the concept (e.g. the Seventh Family Report of 2006) abstained from the focus on fertility, but rather promoted a triad of time policy, financial transfers and infrastructural support to help all families (Ahrens 2010, Bundesministerium für Familie 2006).

32 The Agenda 2010 was a strategy paper aimed at the reform of the labor market and social security schemes. Chancellor Schröder proclaimed it during his government declaration on 14.03.2003 (see http://archiv.bundesregierung.de/artikel/81/557981/attachment/557980_0.pdf; access date: 12.12.2011). The Hartz reforms among others substantially reduced the level of unemployment assistance and the maximum duration of unemployment insurance.

33 "In der SPD würde sich heute kein Mann mehr trauen, gegen eine solche Reform zu sein. Das war nicht immer so und hat sicherlich mit der Quote zu tun. Dadurch dass mehr Frauen im Parlament waren, sind solche Themen in der SPD gesellschaftsfähig geworden. 1980 – da waren wir zwar die frauenstärkste Fraktion im Bundestag, aber wir hatten nur 9,2% Frauen – da war eine Diskussion über Kinderbetreuung unmöglich, da hätte man Sie für verrückt erklärt und gefragt, ob wir denn noch was anderes im Kopf haben. Mit dem höheren Frauenanteil haben solche Themen auch an Bedeutung gewonnen. Die Frauen haben die Themen eingebracht und die Männer haben von ihren Frauen und Töchtern zuhause erzählt bekommen, dass es so nicht mehr weitergeht." (Interview DE1).

34 See Drs. 586/04, Gesetzentwurf der Bundesregierung, "Entwurf eines Gesetzes zum qualitätsorientierten und bedarfsgerechten Ausbau der Tagesbetreuung und zur Weiterentwicklung der Kinder- und Jugendhilfe (Tagesbetreuungsausbaugesetz – TAG)".

35 In 2004, the opposition parties had reached a share of almost 60 percent of votes (41 in absolute terms) in the *Bundesrat*. The governing parties had only ten votes. State governments which were governed by a coalition in which at least one party was also represented in the national government, had 18 votes (cf. http://www.wahlen-in-deutschland.de/bBundesrat.htm; access date 17.9.2009).

36 Maria Böhmer (CDU), Bundestag, Stenographischer Bericht 15/123: 11197, 09.09.2004.

37 The main argument was that families themselves should decide what their children should do in the afternoons. An interviewee of the CDU has explained that men and

women parliamentarians differ in their perceptions of the issue of childcare because of a different kind of involvement. Male representatives have usually a different family background, i.e. they make a (political) career while their wives are responsible for children and the household. Therefore, they either have a more traditional approach or see themselves not as suited for childcare policymaking. This view was confirmed by other interviewees as well (e.g. DE1 and DE4).

38 BT-Drs. 15/3488, Antrag der CDU/CSU "Elternhaus, Bildung und Betreuung besser verzahnen", 29.06.2004, p. 3.
39 In 2004, Germany had failed to meet the Maastricht criteria for the third time in a row, and the federal budget of 2005 had almost been declared as unconstitutional because the government borrowing had exceeded the investments (cf. Wagschal 2007 for more details).
40 When the SPD lost the elections in North Rhine-Westphalia in May 2005, Chancellor Schröder called early federal elections for September 2005.
41 "Uns eint, dass jede versucht hat, mit mehreren Kindern einen anspruchsvollen Beruf auszuüben. Wir haben beide bittere Erfahrungen gemacht – und wir tun etwas dafür, dass unseren Töchtern und Söhnen solche Erfahrungen erspart bleiben." (Sueddeutsche Zeitung 08.02.2007).
42 "Wir als Union sind zufrieden, weil das Elterngeld bürgerliche und leistungsorientierte Strukturen enthält, an denen uns besonders gelegen war." (Johannes Singhammer (CSU), Bundestag, Stenographischer Bericht 16/40: 3720, 22.06.2006).
43 Parental leave is counted against maternity leave. That means that the first eight weeks after birth are subtracted from the parental leave entitlement. Hence mothers (or fathers if the mother does not make use of maternity leave) are only entitled to a maximum of ten months of parental leave benefit.
44 "Die zwei zusätzlichen Monate dienen einzig dazu, dass die CSU keinen Gesichtsverlust erleidet. Das kostet den Steuerzahler 750 Millionen Euro." (Ekin Deligöz (Bündnis 90/Die Grünen), Bundestag, Stenographischer Bericht 16/40: 3719, 22.06.2006).
45 Problems with the federal system, i.e. the veto potential of the states and long decision-making processes, have been bemoaned for a long time. In 2003, the two chambers agreed on appointing a commission which should put forward proposals for a reform. However, the commission foundered on the restructuring of the competencies in the field of education in 2004.
46 Interestingly, both the prime minister of North Rhine-Westphalia Jürgen Rüttgers and the prime minister of Lower Saxony Christian Wulff used the concept of a "freedom of choice" to argue *in favor* of an expansion of childcare places, saying that even though parents were in a need of "freedom of choice", they were just not able to choose due to the lack of childcare places (cf. Sueddeutsche Zeitung 24.02.2007).
47 The interviewee refers to the distribution of ministerial offices and the fact that the Ministry for Family Affairs was headed by a CDU representative after 2005.
48 "[. . .] darum hab ich mich ja auch so geärgert, dass dieses Thema 2005 abgegeben wurde. Alle Zukunftsthemen hat die SPD aufgegeben – Familie, Bildung, Umwelt, alles Themen, die in die Zukunft reichen. Dafür haben wir zwar die 'wichtigeren' bekommen – Finanzen, etc., die aber die viel problematischeren waren und wo wir gute Arbeit geleistet haben, die uns aber nicht zugutegekommen ist" (Interview DE1).
49 Art. 104b allows the federal government to share the investment costs such as reconstruction, new building or equipment. The costs of operating childcare institutions – that is, labor costs in particular, but also heating, cannot be paid by the federal government.
50 Representatives of the states argued that not the investment costs, but rather the running costs are the problem and complained that they had expected more engagement. Also, the SPD argued in support of the states and the municipalities who should not be overburdened by the additional costs (cf. Frankfurter Allgemeine Zeitung 04.05.2007).

51 After the minister for family affairs had publicly announced not to include the care allowance in the draft bill of the childcare expansion law, Stoiber and others committed to linking the CSU's agreement to the reform with the introduction of a care allowance (Der Spiegel 25.05.2007).

52 "In der Politik bestimmen bedauerlicherweise immer noch die Männer, die ihr Lebensmodell auf dieses Familienbild aufgebaut haben. Sie sitzen hier im Bundestag, während sie zuhause eine Frau haben, die ihnen den Rücken mit der Familie frei hält. Also das wird auch eine Verteidigung der eigenen Lebensphilosophie. Darum verändert es sich in der Politik nicht so schnell wie die gesellschaftlichen Einstellungen." (Interview DE4).

53 Gesetz zur Förderung von Kindern unter drei Jahren in Tageseinrichtungen und in Kindertagespflege (Kinderförderungsgesetz – KiföG), Bundesgesetzblatt Jahrgang 2008 Teil I Nr. 57, 15. December 2008, p. 2403.

54 "Das ist vermutlich auch der einzige Weg gewesen, wie man das hätte durchsetzen können. Ich hätte mir als SPD-Ministerin auch in einer Großen Koalition und trotz Koalitionsvertrag den Kopf blutig gestoßen mit einem Rechtsanspruch auf Krippenplätze ab dem 2. Lebensjahr ab 2013. Das Gleiche gilt für die Elternzeit mit den Vätermonaten. Die Union hätte sich an mir abgearbeitet. Insofern war es gut, dass es eine Ministerin war, die aus den eigenen Reihen kam. Nur die konnte diese Blockade und diese Betonstruktur in der Union aufbrechen [. . .]." (Interview DE1).

References

Ahrens, Regina. 2010. "Sustainability in German Family Policy and Politics." *German Policy Studies* 6 (3):195–229.

Aust, Andreas. 2003. "Policy Map Germany: Labour Market Policy, Social Assistance and Women's Employment, Long-term Care." WRAMSOC meeting, Madrid.

Berghahn, Sabine. 1999. "50 Jahre Gleichberechtigungsangebot: Rechtliche Fortschritte und Enttäuschungen." *Femina Politica* (1/1999):11–29.

Blum, Sonja. 2010. "Between Instrument Tinkering and Policy Renewal: Reforms of Parental Leave in Germany and Austria." *German Policy Studies* 6 (3):83–118.

Blum, Sonja. 2012. *Familienpolitik als Reformprozess. Deutschland und Österreich im Vergleich*. Wiesbaden: Springer VS.

Bothfeld, Silke. 2005. *Vom Erziehungsurlaub zur Elternzeit. Politisches Lernen im Reformprozess*. Frankfurt a.M./New York: Campus Verlag.

Bundesministerium der Finanzen. 2008. Die Steuereinnahmen des Bundes und der Länder im 4. Quartal 2007 und im Jahr 2007 insgesamt. Monatsbericht des BMF – Februar 2008. Berlin.

Bundesministerium für Familie, Senioren, Frauen und Jugend. 2004. Das Tagesbetreuungsausbaugesetz (TAG). Gesetz zum qualitätsorientierten und bedarfsgerechten Ausbau der Tagesbetreuung und zur Weiterentwicklung der Kinder- und Jugendhilfe. Berlin.

Bundesministerium für Familie, Senioren, Frauen und Jugend. 2006. *Siebter Familienbericht. Familie zwischen Flexibilität und Verlässlichkeit. Perspektiven für eine lebenslaufbezogene Familienpolitik*, http://www.bmfsfj.de/RedaktionBMFSFJ/Abteilung2/Pdf-Anlagen/siebter-familienbericht,property=pdf,bereich=,rwb=true.pdf. Baden-Baden: Koelblin-Fortuna-Druck.

Bundesministerium für Familie, Senioren, Frauen und Jugend. 2007. *Einigung zur Finanzierung des Betreuungsausbaus erzielt*. Berlin: http://www.bmfsfj.de/BMFSFJ/aktuelles,did=100436.html.

Christlich Demokratische Union. 1999. *Lust auf Familie. Lust auf Verantwortung.* *Beschluss des Bundesausschusses der CDU Deutschlands.* Berlin: http://www.cdu.de/doc/pdfc/beschluss_131299.pdf.
Christlich Demokratische Union. 2010. *Bericht zur politischen Gleichstellung von Frauen und Männern.* Karlsruhe.
Christlich Demokratische Union/Christlich Soziale Union. 2002. Leistung und Sicherheit. Zeit für Taten. Regierungsprogramm 2002/2006 von CDU und CSU. Berlin.
Christlich Demokratische Union/Christlich Soziale Union. 2005. Deutschlands Chancen nutzen. Wachstum. Arbeit. Sicherheit. Regierungsprogramm 2005–2009. Berlin.
Christlich Demokratische Union/Christlich Soziale Union, and Sozialdemokratische Partei Deutschlands. 2005. Gemeinsam für Deutschland – mit Mut und Menschlichkeit. Koalitionsvertrag zwischen CDU, CSU und SPD. Berlin.
Der Spiegel. 21.02.2002. "Serie Schröders Wahlversprechen (6). Frauenpolitik – Erfolgsbilanz mit Schönheitsfehlern." http://www.spiegel.de/politik/deutschland/0,1518,179268,00.html: Access date: 14.02.2011.
Der Spiegel. 25.05.2007. "Kindererziehung. Von der Leyen provoziert Krach mit der CSU." http://www.spiegel.de/politik/deutschland/0,1518,484909,00.html: Access date: 12.10.2011.
Der Tagesspiegel. 05.09.2004. "Neuer Mut aus Bonn." 05.09.2004, http://www.tagesspiegel.de/politik/neuer-mut-aus-bonn/544672.html: Access date: 18.02.2011.
Der Tagesspiegel. 13.08.2002. "Mutter's Courage." *Der Tagesspiegel*, http://www.tagesspiegel.de/zeitung/mutters-courage/336892.html: Access date: 28.02.2011.
Die Welt. 03.12.2007. "Parteichefin Merkel bringt Delegierte mit Machtwort auf Kurs." http://www.welt.de/politik/article1426842/Merkel_bringt_Delegierte_mit_Machtwort_auf_Kurs.html: Access date: 13.10.2011.
Erler, Daniel. 2005. "Public Work-Family Reconciliation Policies in Germany and Italy. Exploring the Relevance of Problem Pressures, Institutions, and Actors." Department of Comparative and European Politics, Università degli studi di Siena.
Fleckenstein, Timo. 2010. "Party Politics and Childcare: Comparing the Expansion of Service Provision in England and Germany." *Social Policy & Administration* 44 (7):789–807.
Frankfurter Allgemeine Zeitung. 04.05.2007. "Krippenplätze. Leyen stellt Finanzierungskonzept vor." http://www.faz.net/aktuell/politik/inland/krippenplaetze-leyen-stellt-finanzierungskonzept-vor-1438590.html: Access date: 11.10.2011.
Frankfurter Allgemeine Zeitung. 19.04.2006. "Kampf um "Vätermonate". Die Kanzlerin verteidigt das Elterngeld / Union weiter uneins."
Frankfurter Allgemeine Zeitung. 24.02.2007. ""Gebärmaschinen"-Streit. Merkel gibt Mixa Kontra." http://www.faz.net/aktuell/politik/gebaermaschinen-streit-merkel-gibt-mixa-kontra-1411461.html: Access date: 07.10.2011.
Fuhrmann, Nora. 2002. "Drei zu eins für Schröder. Zur Geschlechterpolitik von Rot-grün." In *"Deutschland auf den Weg gebracht." Rot-grüne Wirtschafts- und Sozialpolitik zwischen Anspruch und Wirklichkeit*, edited by Kai Eicker-Wolf, Holger Kindler, Ingo Schäfer, Melanie Wehrheim and Dorothee Wolf, 187–211. Marburg: Metropolis-Verlag.
Gerlach, Irene. 2004. *Familienpolitik*. Wiesbaden: VS Verlag für Sozialwissenschaften.
Gerlach, Irene. 2010. *Familienpolitik. 2., aktualisierte und überarbeitete Auflage*. Wiesbaden: VS Verlag für Sozialwissenschaften.
Henninger, Annette, and Angelika von Wahl. 2010. "Das Umspielen von Veto-Spielern. Wie eine konservative Familienministerin den Familialismus des deutschen Wohlfahrtsstaates unterminiert." In *Die zweite Große Koalition. Eine Bilanz der Regierung*

Merkel 2005–2009, edited by Christoph Egle and Reimut Zohlnhöfer, 361–379. Wiesbaden: VS Verlag für Sozialwissenschaften.
Korthouwer, Gerben. 2008. "How German Christian Democrats have said Farewell to Familialism." In *ASSR Working paper 08/01*. Amsterdam.
Lang, Sabine, and Birgit Sauer. 2003. ""Doris ihr'n Mann seine Partei". Die Reduktion von Frauen- auf Familienpolitik im bundesdeutschen Wahlkampf 2002." *Österreichische Zeitschrift für Politikwissenschaft* 32 (4):429–441.
Mappus, Stefan, Markus Söder, Philipp Mißfelder, and Hendrik Wüst. 2007. Moderner bürgerlicher Konservatismus. Warum die Union wieder mehr an ihre Wurzeln denken muss http://www.stefan-mappus.de/uploads/media/Moderner_buergerlicher_Konservatismus.pdf: Access date: 12.10.2011.
Meyer, Birgit 2003. "Much Ado about Nothing? Political Representation Policies and the Influence of Women Parliamentarians in Germany." *Review of Policy Research* 20 (3):401–21.
Roßteutscher, Sigrid. 2007. "CDU-Wahl 2005: Katholiken, Kirchgänger und eine protestantische Spitzenkandidatin aus dem Osten." In *Die Bundestagswahl 2005: Analysen des Wahlkampfes und der Wahlergebnisse*, edited by Frank Brettschneider, Oskar Niedermayer and Bernhard Weßels, 321–348. Wiesbaden: VS Verlag für Sozialwissenschaften.
Roth, Dieter, and Matthias Jung. 2002. "Ablösung der Regierung vertagt: Eine Analyse der Bundestagswahl 2002." *Aus Politik und Zeitgeschichte* 49–50:3–17.
Rüling, Anneli. 2003. "Einleitung. Familienpolitik=Frauenpolitik? Konturen einer Debatte." *Femina Politica* 12 (1):9–16.
Rüling, Anneli. 2010. "Re-framing of Childcare in Germany and England: From a Private Responsibility to an Economic Necessity." *German Policy Studies* 6 (2):153–186.
Rürup, Bert, and Sandra Gruescu. 2003. "Nachhaltige Familienpolitik im Interesse einer aktiven Bevölkerungsentwicklung." *Gutachten im Auftrag des Bundesministerium für Familie, Senioren, Frauen und Jugend*. Berlin.
Sozialdemokratische Partei Deutschlands. 1990. Der neue Weg: ökologisch, sozial, wirtschaftlich, stark. Regierungsprogramm 1990–1994. Beschlossen vom SPD-Parteitag in Berlin am 28. September 1990.
Sozialdemokratische Partei Deutschlands. 1998. "Arbeit, Innovation und Gerechtigkeit". SPD-Programm für die Bundestagswahl 1998. Leipzig.
Sozialdemokratische Partei Deutschlands. 2001. *Parteitag der SPD in Nürnberg. 19. bis 22. November 2001. Beschlüsse*. Berlin.
Sozialdemokratische Partei Deutschlands. 2002. Erneuerung und Zusammenhalt – Wir in Deutschland. Regierungsprogramm 2002–2006.
Sozialdemokratische Partei Deutschlands. 2005. Vertrauen in Deutschland. Das Wahlmanifest der SPD. Berlin.
Sozialdemokratische Partei Deutschlands. 2007. Gute Betreuung ab eins. Unser Konzept für einen Rechtsanspruch auf Kinderbetreuung. Berlin, 26.02.2007.
Sozialdemokratische Partei Deutschlands, and Bündnis 90/Die Grünen. 2002. *Koalitionsvertrag 2002–2006: Erneuerung – Gerechtigkeit – Nachhaltigkeit. Für ein wirtschaftlich starkes, soziales und ökologisches Deutschland. Für eine lebendige Demokratie*. Berlin.
Stern.de. 25.02.2007. "Kinderbetreuung Von der Leyen schießt gegen die SPD." http://www.stern.de/politik/deutschland/kinderbetreuung-von-der-leyen-schiesst-gegen-die-spd-583342.html: Access date: 07.10.2011.
Sueddeutsche Zeitung. 07.08.2007. "Betreuungsgeld: CSU-Frauen fallen Stoiber in den Rücken." http://www.sueddeutsche.de/bayern/betreuungsgeld-csu-frauen-fallen-stoiber-in-den-ruecken-1.422630: Access date: 11.10.2011.

Sueddeutsche Zeitung. 08.02.2007. "Familienpolitik". "Ich bin es leid, ständig die alten Gräben zu schaufeln". http://www.sueddeutsche.de/politik/familienpolitik-ich-bin-es-leid-staendig-die-alten-graeben-zu-schaufeln-1.429276: Access date: 11.10.2011.
Sueddeutsche Zeitung. 22.02.2007. "Bischof Mixa kritisiert Familienpolitik. "Von der Leyen degradiert Frauen zu Gebärmaschinen"." http://www.sueddeutsche.de/politik/bischof-mixa-kritisiert-familienpolitik-von-der-leyen-degradiert-frauen-zu-gebaermaschinen-1.894163: Access date: 11.10.2011.
Sueddeutsche Zeitung. 24.02.2007. "Streit um Krippen. Harsche Kritik an Bischof Mixa." http://www.sueddeutsche.de/politik/streit-um-krippen-harsche-kritik-an-bischof-mixa-1.895398: Access date: 07.10.2011.
Sueddeutsche Zeitung. 26.02.2007. "Stoiber attackiert SPD-Familienpolitik. "Familienpolitik von der rechten in die linke Tasche"." http://www.sueddeutsche.de/politik/stoiber-attackiert-spd-familienpolitik-familienpolitik-von-der-rechten-in-die-linke-tasche-1.786109: Access date: 07.10.2011.
Sueddeutsche Zeitung. 27.04.2006. "Streitpunkt Elterngeld. Gegen das "Wickelvolontariat"." http://www.sueddeutsche.de/politik/streitpunkt-elterngeld-gegen-das-wickelvolontariat-1.884278: Access date: 08.03.2011.
Sueddeutsche Zeitung. 28.04.2006. "Elterngeld. Beck fordert 300-Euro-Mindestbetrag." http://www.sueddeutsche.de/politik/elterngeld-beck-fordert-euro-mindestbetrag-1.887749: Access date: 08.03.2011.
Wagschal, Uwe. 2007. "Auf dem Weg zum Sanierungsfall? Die rot-grüne Finanzpolitik seit 2002." In *Ende des rot-grünen Projekts. Eien Bilanz der Regierung Schröder 2002–2005*, edited by Christoph Egle and Reimut Zohlnhöfer, 241–270. Wiesbaden: VS Verlag für Sozialwissenschaften.
Zohlnhöfer, Reimut. 2003. "Rot-grüne Finanzpolitik zwischen traditioneller Sozialdemokratie und neuer Mitte." In *Das rot-grüne Projekt. Eine Bilanz der Regierung Schröder 1998–2002*, edited by Christoph Egle, Tobias Ostheim and Reimut Zohlnhöfer, 193–214. Wiesbaden: Westdeutscher Verlag.
Zohlnhöfer, Reimut, and Christoph Egle. 2007. "Der Episode zweiter Teil – ein Überblick über die 15. Legislaturperiode." In *Ende des rot-grünen Projektes. Eine Bilanz der Regierung Schröder 2002–2005*, edited by Christoph Egle and Reimut Zohlnhöfer, 11–28. Wiesbaden: VS Verlag für Sozialwissenschaften.

8 Italy
No consensus for change

> Italian politics – also left-wing party politics, much to my regret – is very much attached to male welfare policies, the head of the household, and it does have a culture which is very familialistic, concerned with blue-collar workers, productive labour, the production. Hence, it is this culture of welfare and work that is an extremely tough nut.[1]

> In Italy, there is a growing demand for work-family reconciliation policies, [...] but it is not a demand which is perceived as being electorally decisive. More generally, I would say, the issue of equal opportunities is not perceived as being electorally decisive. So it's a much more general question.[2]

In contrast to Germany, Italy has not experienced significant changes in the areas of work and family in spite of a similar starting situation in the beginning of the 1990s. The two quotes[3] from a former minister for family affairs and a former advisor to the government put in a nutshell the problems and the challenges for work-family policy reforms to happen in Italy. They corroborate what has already been shown in Chapter 5 – that is, the important role of traditional normative beliefs which permeates the Italian society and the low incentives for Italian parties to compete on the issue of work-family policies.

By recounting the policy processes of each legislative period chronologically, this chapter will provide further evidence for the relevance of these explanatory factors. It makes three contributions: First, it shows clearly how normative beliefs and ideologies about the family shaped and, in part, paralyzed the political debates around work-family policies. Second, it demonstrates that the issue of work-family policies was never as salient as to impact upon electoral strategies of the parties. Third, the central role of female policy entrepreneurs for pushing the topic onto the political agenda becomes apparent. Yet it is also shown that their impact was marginal, in part, because of the mostly low support by the prime ministers.

Overall, this chapter demonstrates that even though reform initiatives were started, they often could not be sustained, as the overall agreement on the male-breadwinner model prevailed. There is a strong movement against changes to gender roles or to the function of the family in Italy. Parties thus have only marginal incentives to propose progressive family policies. The process tracing

Italy: no consensus for change 179

demonstrates that the legislative terms of the center-right coalitions were characterized by policy standstill or even retrenchment. During the coalition governments of the center-left parties, by contrast, steps towards more progressive policies were undertaken. However, many policy proposals were not adopted or led to reforms that do not radically question the responsibility of the family, usually the mother, for the provision of care work. It will be shown how ideological debates about the family are able to nullify leftist parties' efforts to better support mothers' employment. As in Germany, female policy entrepreneurs played a central role in putting reforms on the political agenda. Yet they were not as actively supported by the prime ministers as female politicians in the Bundestag. Their policy proposals, therefore, received lower attention.

1994–1996: neglecting the issue of work-family policy reforms

After the breakdown of the party system in the beginning of the 1990s and the introduction of a new electoral system, the Italian party system acquired a bipolar structure. The newly established parties positioned themselves on a left wing and right wing, while the center became insignificant compared to before (Picot 2012). Also with respect to family policies, partisan differences between left-wing and right-wing parties were extremely influential. The new parties on the center-right wing see themselves as the defenders of the traditional family and oppose state intervention into the family (Bernini 2008). The parties of the center left are more supportive of issues of gender equality and state involvement into matters of the family as a point of principle. At the same time, they are more heterogeneous with respect to issues of the family than the parties of the center right. They have continued to further the goals and values of their predecessors (Saraceno 2003). For example, similar to its Christian-democratic predecessor DC, the PPI upheld the belief that small children should be brought up within and by the family. The left-wing PDS, by contrast, continued to express the beliefs of its Communist predecessor PCI, which had paid attention to gender equality issues such as equal pay, antidiscrimination and gender equality in employment. At the same time, the PCI's focus on welfare and social policies had always been on the male worker, the head of household (*capofamiglia*) (Gelli 2002). Male party members even referred to the idea of including house and care work in welfare politics as an "abstract feminism" (*femminismo astratto*, interview IT10).

Interestingly, before the 1994 election, all parties called for a better support of the family. According to Saraceno (2003), this was the first time ever that the family played a role in election campaigns. At the same time, concrete policy proposals were not at hand. It became clear that the issue of care provision and reconciliation of work and care was neither on the agenda of the right-wing parties nor of the left-wing parties. Even though, for example the right-wing *Forza Italia* proposed increasing the number of childcare places, particularly in industrialized regions, the party at the same time praised the family as the most essential social institution, whose role can never be substituted by the state (Forza Italia 1994). The *Lega Nord* put it even more explicitly. According to their view, infants and toddlers need the

180 *Italy: no consensus for change*

"vicinity to the mother and growing up in a warm and affectionate familiar environment" (Lega Nord 1994). The left-wing PDS proposed a care and housework allowance. This proposal aimed at appealing to both leftist voters and the conservative female electorate. Yet it provoked protests, in particular from female left-wing party members, who argued that such an allowance would foster the gender division of labor and support the male-breadwinner model (Saraceno 2003). This example illustrates the cleavage within the left wing of the party system.

The fact that work-family policies were a low priority issue for the parties also had to do with the shift from centrifugal to centripetal party competition as described in Chapter 5. Winning the political center had become important for elections. As shown in Chapter 5, the average Italian adhered to more traditional beliefs and more likely supported the male-breadwinner model. Thus, even though the left-wing parties might have targeted women with their focus on gender equality, they at the same time had to consider the more traditional beliefs of the decisive groups of voters in the political center. All in all, the incentives for parties to compete with progressive policy proposals were limited anyhow because people with more progressive normative beliefs did not have a clear party preference at the beginning of the 1990s. As a consequence, the center-right government in office from 1994 to 1996 did not initiate any law to improve the work-family reconciliation.

1996–2001: small steps towards work-family reconciliation policies under the center-left coalition

Work-family policy reforms became increasingly important before the 1996 election. During the campaigns, the center-left coalition had already prioritized the reform of the welfare state and social services. The "Olive Tree" coalition's takeover in 1996 brought about a commitment to further reform the system (Erler 2005). Shortly after his appointment, the then leader of the government, Romano Prodi, convened an Expert Commission (known as Onofri Commission) which had the task of outlining a plan for a comprehensive reform of the national welfare system (Guerzoni 2008). Their propositions aimed above all at-cost containment and the recalibration of benefits.[4] In addition, the commission referred to the introduction of a social assistance scheme and nationally binding minimum service standards (Gori and Madama 2008). Even though policies targeted the family – in particular, those relating to the care of dependent persons were not mentioned in the commission's final report (Saraceno 2008) – the heated debates about the recommendations in the summer and autumn of 1997 created an environment which favored the development of a law on parental leave, a law that aimed at stimulating the provision of innovative childcare services and the development of a national care service framework law.

The long prologue of the parental leave reform in 2000

The responsible minister for family affairs, Livia Turco (PDS, then DS), initiated a number of work-family policy reforms. She was supported by an advisory board that included several feminist scholars (Interview IT10). Ten years earlier, she had been the spokesperson of the women's section within the Communist party PCI that had initiated the campaign "The women change the times" (*Le donne cambiano i tempi*) in 1987. This campaign originated in a conference of feminist scholars on "Production and Reproduction". According to an interviewee who participated in this conference, the debate on the interrelationship between productive and reproductive work and its effects on women's role in society was at that time new to the southern European country. Women's rights had been predominantly discussed in terms of women's – or rather mothers' – rights as employees. Their role as a family worker has never been at the center of any political debate let alone policy proposals before. In that conference, which women belonging to the women's section within the PCI also attended, the scholars proposed thinking about the gendered division of work, time use, life cycles and city times. Inspired by the speeches and the debates, the PCI women decided to invest in this new way of thinking about gender equality. In 1987, they initiated a popular law initiative with the aforementioned slogan of the campaign and brought a draft bill[5] into parliament in 1988. At the center of the bill was the resource "time" – i.e. how to better reconcile work and life, care, education, relationships and coordinate city times (Turco 2013). Even though the law proposal was not approved, it fueled the debate on the public regulation of the so-called city times.[6] The idea is to give the municipalities and cities the responsibility of coordinating and regulating the working times of their facilities and the resident companies. Caring time should be the pivotal element of the city times around which opening hours of various services and employment are to be organized (see Mairhuber 2001).

During subsequent legislatures, the law proposal was again and again presented. However, it never got past the parliamentary-debate state, which had to do with the fact that the proposers were in opposition. Furthermore, the PCI women lacked support both from their own party and other left-wing actors, such as the trade unions, who did not see the merit of the law (Interview IT10). At the same time, many cities reformed the city times and were in that way able to achieve evidently good results with respect to time organization. Even though the reconciliation of work and family was not mentioned as a specific objective, the problems of flexibility and the change of opening hours were seen as a matter full of implications for improving the work-family balance (Tempia 2005).[7]

This shows that, as in Germany, left-wing party membership was an important condition for the likelihood of developing work-family policy proposals that support dual-earner families. Left-wing parties seem to provide opportunities for women's collective action. On the other hand, even women representatives in left-wing parties face the challenges of prevailing traditional normative views. The idea of including care work in the social policy debate had not matured and been spread within the PCI. In particular, the PCI women lacked the support of the party leadership. Arguably, both facts also had to do with the low total number of women in parliament. In 1987, only 12.8 percent of the representatives of the lower house were women (Guadagnini 2005).

Bringing the parental leave reform proposal to parliament

After a period of parliamentary inactivity, the issue returned to the political agenda in 1996 under the aegis of the female minister of social solidarity, Livia Turco, the former spokesperson of the women's section within the PCI. In 1996, a parliamentary initiative was presented. The bill was supported by representatives not only of the governing coalition but also by women representatives of LN and FI (Interview IT10). Notwithstanding this seemingly broad parliamentary support, it took almost four years of debates – and the looming threat of legal action by the EU[8] – before the law was approved. On 8 March 2000, aptly the International Women's Day, Italy adopted law no. 53/2000 with the title "Provision for the Support of Mother- and Fatherhood, for the Right to Care and Education and for the Coordination of City Times".[9] Among others issues, the law introduced an autonomous right for fathers to use parental leave and more flexibility during the period in which parents may use the leave (see Chapter 4 for more details).

The long law-making process may seem surprising if one looks at the accompanying debates in parliament. All parties more or less agreed on the necessity of the law and the main goals involved – i.e. to support women's participation in the labor force and to improve the reconciliation of work and family life.[10] However, a total of 21 different law proposals from various MPs with different party backgrounds had to be integrated.[11] This high number indicates one reason for the time lag. None of the participants in the parliamentary discussion argued on supporting the traditional division of labor by proposing – e.g. a longer leave for mothers (as, for example, the DC did in 1990).[12] Yet the anticipated degree of state intervention was questioned by some of the representatives of the right wing.[13] In the eyes of Stefania Prestigiacomo (FI), for example, the future law was not able to respond to new labor-market challenges in a globalized economy that was characterized by flexible, nonstandard jobs.[14] She feared counterproductive results:

> If extending the guarantees for women means increasing the employers' expenses, then each guarantee in fact becomes a disincentive to hire potential mothers. Hence, if one wants to help working mothers, one will have to proceed promptly with a law that does not penalize the employers and renders the private sector more in favor of hiring women.[15]

The government, on the other hand, argued that state intervention was necessary in order to change long-standing cultural stereotypes both on the part of the companies and on the part of male family members. In the eyes of the governing center-left coalition, a dual-earner model could only be achieved by establishing rights (e.g. father's leave) and providing financial incentives for companies that established innovative time policies or the organization of flexible work with the aim to support the reconciliation of work and family life. Moreover, it was argued that companies would benefit from the greater productivity of individuals who are able to freely and autonomously govern their time.[16]

The law was brought into parliament and was adopted by a center-left coalition government. In contrast to the situation ten years earlier when the PCI leadership had not been interested in the law, the idea of acknowledging reproductive work had matured. At the same time, the adopted law left room for improvement. In particular, the benefit payment was too low to support a more equal division of labor between men and women. The willingness of the coalition's leadership to take on financial commitments was less marked. Arguably, political competition played a role. The political center, which is important for winning elections, did not claim a paradigmatic change.

Female policy entrepreneurs played a central role for the reform. By the end of the 1990s, the center-left government was already wounded – having had to reshuffle the government three times. This also became clear during the regional elections in April 2000 where the coalition performed poorly. The law was being debated in parliament when – compared to the previous (and following) legislative period – several ministries and other important decision-making positions were headed by women. It was the merit of women in decision-making positions that pushed it through by joint effort. Not only women representatives within or close to the government coalition supported the law but rather a cross-party coalition of women.

Debates on part-time work legislation: atypical employment versus mothers' employment support

While legislation on parental leave received some attention by policymakers, the idea of part-time work as a means to support the employment opportunities of mothers was not an issue for a long time. In fact, part-time work in Italy was considered to be atypical employment and not accepted by left-wing parties and the trade unions. The first law on part-time work,[17] adopted in 1984, aimed at protecting employees against this form of occupation (see Chapter 4). Given the bad reputation of part-time work, it came as a surprise that in 1997 a new effort was made by the first center-left government with the so-called Legge Tre" (Law No. 196/1997).[18] It allowed for the use of a variety of short-term work contracts and provided financial incentives for firms who hired part-time workers or allowed employees to reduce working hours. Due to its deregulatory purpose, Picot (2012) sees this reform as another attempt of the center-left coalition to appeal to centrist voters.

In contrast to Germany, the idea that part-time work could support the reconciliation of care and employment was not mentioned in any of the parliamentary sessions.[19] The MPs either spoke about the opportunities of flexible or part-time employment provided to reduce unemployment in general (in particular unemployment of youth and in the south), while others associated short-term work contracts with precarious employment. The increase of labor-force participation of mothers by means of legal regulations of part-time employment seemed not to be the goal. This is also reflected in the stance of the social partners which have strong opinions about part-time employment, but no voice in policymaking processes. While the employers' organizations support flexible work, the trade unions are traditionally hostile toward any type of atypical work. One of the three largest trade unions, CISL (*Confederazione Italiana Sindacati Lavoratori*), for example, advocates negotiations on the company level instead of on the national level. A female representative of CISL said,

> We did not want to impose the right to part-time work by law. We said: Let them regulate it in the company on the local level. The negotiation on the second level[20] and bilateral consultations are instruments where the company and the employee bring together funds to invest into education, flexible working-time arrangements, programs for the reintegration of women after maternity leave or for men who were absent for a long time due to sickness – all this on the local level in the company, not anymore with the government, not anymore with laws. [. . .] It's no use to go out shouting "Rights, rights!" – Stop, full stop, finish. By contrast, like this it is possible to pick up the problems and find solutions which are good for the company and good for the employee.[21]

The quote shows that a national law on part-time employment was not seen as appropriate, even though it could have sent a strong signal to employers and employees that work-family reconciliation is a legitimate social concern. Leaving it to the individual and committed employers and trade unionists to find solutions carries the risk of greater inequality in take-up and a marginalization of caring duties.

In 1998, the center-left government had to react to a directive launched by the Council of the European Union,[22] which was aimed at the equal treatment of part-timers and full-timers with respect to working conditions. In order to translate the European directive, the government decided to propose a legislative decree (dl. no. 61/2000).[23] The use of a legislative decree means that the parliament delegated the right to formulate a law to the government, but cannot change it afterwards.[24] This procedure is very common in the implementation of European directives (Lo Faro 2004). On 28 January 2000, the Italian Council of Ministers definitively approved the legislative decree, which intended to encourage the use of part-time work to foster employment creation (Pedersini 2000). The law included a number of regulations that made part-time work more attractive for employees (see Chapter 4 for more details).

This short overview of the treatment of part-time employment shows that Italian policymakers do not see a need to regulate part-time employment. The interesting difference to other policies that support work-family reconciliation is that even female policy entrepreneurs abstain from getting involved in this issue because of the overall agreement that part-time employment has negative effects on women's career chances. Policymakers only agreed to improve conditions for part-time employees after the move of the European Union.

Little steps towards an expansion of childcare services

The lack of a law that would involve a greater role for the state and provide stable financial resources impeded the expansion of publicly provided childcare places in

Italy. When voted into office, however, the center-left coalition had initiated a law that was entitled "Provisions of the Promotion of Rights of Childhood and Adolescence" (Law No. 285/1997).[25] It aimed at promoting children's well-being and devoted special attention to the improvement of the relationship between children and parents and to parental and childcare service. The law was adopted within a comparably short time.[26] The fact that the *Senato* sent the law proposal to a commission *in sede deliberante* – that is, the *Senato* abstained from deliberation and entitled instead the commission to vote on the proposal – contributed to its fast treatment and adoption. Law no. 285/1997 aimed at improving the well-being of children through a variety of so-called innovative child-related care supply, which explicitly includes parents, local welfare providers and the third sector. Hence the law did not include a right to childcare or enable the municipalities to increase the number of publicly provided childcare places. Rather, the aim was to complement existing provision with services featuring educational, playful or cultural elements involving a plurality of actors (Art. 6 of law no. 285/1997). As such, the law provided a first step towards a larger participation of the national state in the public provision of childcare.

The debate in parliament was not very controversial due to the fact that the law did not intend to crowd out the family as the core provider of childcare – and therefore did not touch upon the sensitive issue of proper childcare.[27] In principle, the law received the support of all political parties, because all could agree on its merit for the family. The representatives from right-wing parties, however, criticized the scarce resources and argued for a further decentralization of the competencies from the regions to the provinces (Resoconto stenografico della Seduta n. 199 of 26.05.1997: 16596; see also Erler 2005).

An imperfect reform: drafting a national framework for the provision of social services

At the same time, the government addressed the development of a national care service framework law. When law no. 328/2000 was finally adopted in 2000, a long parliamentary process had preceded its introduction. The proposal had been presented to the *Camera* in May 1996, was discussed in many sessions of several commissions, and it was finally approved in October 2000.

Similar to law no. 285/1997, this law made the family, its well-being and support through the welfare state, the point of reference (Saraceno 2003). The positive effects of the law for families and its members in need were highlighted by almost all parliamentarians.[28] As law no. 285/1997, it did not intend to usurp the family by providing services; instead, the family was to be supported in its role as the principal care provider. In a statement during the first general debate in parliament, the representative of the leftist *Partito Democratico* (PD), Giuseppe Fiorino, said the following:

> The family is recognized as essential for the provision of education and care of the person, for the support of well-being and the pursuit of social cohesion, for cooperation, and mutual assistance. The role of the family, therefore, is strengthened by policies that not only consider poor families, but families at large.[29]

This view was expressed in a similar vein by most other speakers.

The full implementation of law no. 328/2000 involved a series of follow-up laws that would operationalize the general principles. However, most of them wer never approved. One reason for this dilemma was the reform of article V of the Constitutional Act.[30] This reform, initiated by the center-left coalition in 1998, strengthened the principle of federalism and assigned the regions legislative authority in all issues that are not specifically attributed to the national state, including the provision of social services (Madama 2010). It thus contradicts the intentions of law no. 328/2000, which had explicitly assigned the state the responsibility for setting standards or targets. According to the reformed article, however, the state and the council of regions[31] have to come to an agreement about the essential levels – i.e. the guidelines for care services in terms of minimum coverage and quality standards (see Chapter 4 for more details). Even if essential levels were defined, the national state would have to commit itself to shouldering the financial responsibility (Naldini and Saraceno 2008). In times of budget austerity, this is not favored by the government, in particular not for an area such as childcare services, since care is not viewed as a spending priority (Interviews IT2, IT5, IT8, IT9). Moreover, the Constitution no longer allows the state to provide conditional funds – i.e. to provide funds directed at one specific target, for example, childcare services. The government may provide a general fund for social policies, but the regions themselves decide where to spend the money (Erler 2005).

Besides the fact that the national state has no means of controlling the regional use of the funds, the regions do not have a common interest. Up to now, taxes are redistributed across the regions with the result that the poorer regions in the south benefit from this redistribution, while the richer regions in the north pay the greatest part. Increasing expenditure on social services could, therefore, mean to increase the burden on the richer regions. This conflict in particular was taken up by the LN, which strongly advocated for fiscal federalism– that is, a complete financial autonomy of the regions. Since most other parties objected to this, they did not engage too strongly in fighting for more resources for social services in order avoid letting the conflict escalate (Interview IT5).

This contradictory situation regarding the competencies has persisted until the present day with the result that the regional gap in childcare facilities for children younger than three has widened ever more. While some regions adopted regulations regarding the operation and accreditation of early childhood care institutions early on (e.g. Lazio or Lombardia), others did so only very recently or still have not developed any plans (Basilicata, Calabria, Sicilia) (Istituto degli Innocenti di Firenze 2008, Naldini and Saraceno 2008).

A comparably high reform activity, yet no paradigmatic changes to the male-breadwinner model

In summary, the legislative period of the first center-left government was characterized by a comparably high reform activity in the field of work-family policies.

Yet the reforms involved only little financial resources and, most importantly, did not question the responsibility of the family for the provision of care. The view of the family being the core provider of care was shared across parties and facilitated the adoption of the laws. It also accommodated the views of the population who did not ask for paradigmatic changes, but maintained rather traditional normative beliefs (see Chapter 5). Thus, similar to Germany, the first left-wing government in Italy at the end of the 1990s did pursue some efforts to improve the work-family situation of parents, but – different to Germany – the maintenance of traditional beliefs in society and the low competition on family policies resulted in only incremental policy changes in Italy.

As in Germany, female policy entrepreneurs played a central role in putting the topic onto the agenda and pushing for reforms. Yet the overall low levels of women representatives in parliament arguably prevented a stronger support for work-family policy reforms. And since the left-wing coalition leader could not hope for an electoral payoff with an expansion of more progressive policies because of the lack of demand from the population, work-family reconciliation issues did not become a priority. Further, even the law adopted on the national state's support for childcare provision had its shortcomings, because the constitutional reform created an institutional barrier against state intervention in the form of divided competencies. Yet, if it wishes so, the government was still in a position to provide financial means to the regions. This was, however, not the case in the following legislative period.

2001–2006: curtailing the progress of work-family policy reforms under the center-right government

In 2001, a center-right coalition government took over. Before the election, the coalition had praised the family and promised to put huge efforts in supporting families in their party manifesto:

> All our policies, from the tax to the pension system, from the day nurseries to the working contracts, will be aimed at supporting and developing the family, as a cornerstone of a new social pact, as the basis for solidarity between the generations, as a source of positive values and dynamic protagonist of the modernization of our country.[32]

At the same time, it remained quite vague about concrete policies, in particular concerning work-family reconciliation policies and assigned local and regional governments the responsibility for social services. The coalition emphasized the importance of federalism and the principle of subsidiarity and decried the role of the central state as "obsolete, costly and inefficient" (La Casa delle Libertà 2001: 7). Hence implementing law no. 328/2000 in the form of concrete follow-up laws was not a priority for the new government and it stopped the process of fully implementing the national services framework law no. 328/2000 (Saraceno 2003).

Another (lukewarm) trial and failure to reform childcare services

It should be noted, though, that the government, on the initiative of FI deputy Maria Burani Procaccini, did introduce a bill for a national framework for the development of childcare services (p.l.n. 172/2001).[33] The proposal focused in particular on the support of company crèches, but also envisaged the definition of the *livelli essenziali*. The final proposal – after consultations in the commissions – also included a monitoring of the development and ongoing scientific evaluations of childcare services, yet it lacked a statement on how to finance the proposed measures. The debate in the *Camera* about this bill was quite controversial with mutual accusations that necessary reforms were being blocked.[34]

The leftist parties criticized in particular the lack of quality standards and of universal and social provision – e.g. access for children of (illegal) immigrants or housewives, or an upper limit of the costs for parents – and disapproved of the lack of any article concerning the financing of the law. The rightist parties, by contrast, emphasized the freedom of choice for parents and pointed to the fact that the yearly budget law (*legge finanziaria*)[35] of 2002 had already earmarked €300 million for childcare services at the workplace[36] and the *legge finanziaria* of 2003 assigned €10 million annually for the support of company crèches.[37] Facilitating the reconciliation of employment and care work was a theme that played an important role for most speakers, also in combination with its merit for increasing the birth rates. Yet we can also note a shift in issue framing. In contrast to previous debates, many references were made to the well-being of the child and its right to education. The left accused the government of establishing "parking lots" for children instead of investing in their education.[38] Thus the previous emphasis on working mothers was broadened by taking into account the children's needs.

However, the *Camera* representatives were not able to find common ground. In the end, the proposal was rejected by the leftist parties. With a nevertheless comfortable majority, the *Camera* passed the law to the *Senato*, where it got stuck. The failure of the law cannot be attributed to a veto from the opposition since the government coalition also had a majority in this house. Rather, the reason must be seen in the low priority which the center-right government has accorded to family policies (see Erler 2005). The provisions earmarked in the budget laws did not constitute a continuous and sustainable funding which would have been necessary for an expansion of services, but rather a sum that could be altered (or abrogated) each year according to the household situation.[39] In addition, the reform of the Constitutional Act V, which prevents the national government from earmarking funds for a specific policy that comes within competency of the regional level, in this case, the expansion of childcare facilities, posed a problem. The funds that were introduced with the *legge finanziaria* of 2002 and 2003 were eventually declared unconstitutional by the Constitutional Court, which specifically referred to the funding of childcare services (Constitutional Sentence n. 370/2003 and Constitutional Sentence n. 320/2004).

This low priority is also evident in the fact that during the 2001–2006 legislative period, the government neither initiated another law that would address the failures of the proposals before nor defined the *livelli essenziali*; they also did not resolve the contradictions with respect to the competencies. Despite the strong rhetorical emphasis on the family, the center-right government in the end did little more than pay lip service to the topic, which had no lasting effect.

Revisions to part-time legislation and the reluctance of women representatives to intervene

The center-right government also withdrew the regulations that made part-time work more attractive for employees that the previous government had introduced. Already during the election campaigns the center-right coalition announced a thorough revision of part-time legislation and the liberalization of the labor market. After the party was voted into office, a white paper titled "Proposals for an Active Society and for Quality in Work" was issued by the Italian Ministry of Labor in October 2001, which proposed profoundly modifying a number of regulations that related to the labor market, employment relations, collective relations, and labor litigations (Negrelli and Pulignano 2008). The corresponding law proposal aimed, among other issues (see Lo Faro 2002), at a major revision of the part-time provisions put in place by the precedent government. It was discussed during the summer of 2002 and, after one exchange round between the *Senato* and the *Camera*, was finally approved in February 2003 (so-called Biagi[40] reform). The reform process was accompanied by strong protests by the trade unions, who mobilized a large part of the workforce for various demonstrations and strikes in 2002. These protests notwithstanding, legislative decree 276/2003[41] introduced a more flexible use of part-time contracts on the demand side and cut rights of both the employees and the trade unions (Lo Faro 2002). Even though in the parliamentary debates the hope was expressed that the liberalization and flexibilization of work contracts would facilitate women's employment and eventually helps increase women's labor-market participation, the potential of part-time work for work-family reconciliation was not an issue in the parliamentary debates.[42] That is, questions of how to improve the rights of employees regarding flexible working hours were not raised. Rather, part-time work was seen as a means for employers to (re)act more flexibly to the dynamics of the economy.

The reluctance of women MPs to intervene in issues of flexible working time is telling. Part-time work as a means to reconcile work and care is very controversial since it is feared that an extension of part-time employment will lead women to have a more precarious position in the labor market. The prevailing belief states that employers appreciate full-time workers more because they see more commitment in them than in part-time employees (Piazza 2009; interview IT5 and IT8). It is thus feared that if women reduced their working-time, employers would exacerbate their career chances. In addition, the demand for part-time work is not very high, especially in times of economic crises. In couples where one partner is unemployed or in a precarious working situation, the other will not ask for a reduction of working hours. Due to an increase of atypical work contracts, this is one of the explanations for the low use of part-time employment (Interviews IT5 and IT7).

Low priority to work-family reconciliation issues, low reform activity

To summarize, in spite of proposing efforts to support the family during election campaigns, the government term of the center-right coalition was characterized by low reform activity in the field of work-family policies. Interestingly, even though a member of a governing party introduced a bill to improve the childcare situation, the bill vanished into thin air during the legislative process. Further, the government did not address the ambiguous situation that was brought about by the constitutional reform and the law on the national services framework. The government even torpedoed some of the changes that had been brought on track by the previous center-left government when it stopped the process of fully implementing the National Services Framework Law. This passivity resulted in the rejection of the funds earmarked for the expansion of childcare places by the Constitutional Court because they did not conform to the law.

This low priority regarding work-family policy reforms is in line with the overall low demand of the Italian population for work-family policies. In contrast to Germany, because of the relative stability of the voting behavior, the center-right coalition was not forced to compete for more modern-minded people. The center-right coalition parties could rely on their traditional constituencies who favor the male-breadwinner model.

It is also notable that the share of female representatives in parliament and of female ministers rose after 2000. Hence further reform efforts could have been expected. As the process tracing has shown, however, the decisive difference to Germany is the lack of female policy entrepreneurs. As a female former advisor to the government said,

> The main hurdle is there: I would first of all put women – not just women! But women who are aware of this issue – on decision-making positions. I believe this to be the method of change. If there were women who really were convinced that this is a political battle worth fighting for, then, consequently, we would see how reforms of the social services, part-time legislation, parental leave, of all these instruments of reconciliation, were feasible. But there are no women with significant understanding in such positions – neither in the trade unions, nor in the political parties nor in parliament.[43]

2006–2008: new reform initiatives under the center-left government

The 2006 election was very close. The center-left coalition *l'Unione*[44] won with a majority of only 24,775 votes in the lower chamber and two senators in the upper chamber (Cotta and Verzichelli 2007). The new electoral law[45] ensured a comfortable majority for the center-left coalition in the *Camera*, but only a tiny advance in the *Senato*. *L'Unione* consisted of a total of nine parties, including social-democratic parties, such as *Democratici di Sinistra*, Catholic parties, such as *La Margherita* or *UDEUR*, and more lay parties such as the *Radicali Italiani*. Thus *l'Unione* was an exceptionally broad and heterogeneous government coalition.

During the electoral campaign of 2006, *l'Unione* promised to work on the public services' offer for children with the explicit aims of a) promoting children's educational development and well-being and b) supporting the reconciliation of work and family life of parents.[46] It was the first time that both goals were connected with the availability of public services. The coalition also promised to define the *livelli essenziali* so that all families who wanted them would be entitled to services. At the same time, the coalition zealously emphasized the need to complement public services with offers from the third sector and contracted private suppliers. This double strategy can be interpreted as a first hint regarding the problems the coalition had with reconciling the differing views on family issues (and other ethical issues) between the parties involved. In fact, internal struggles caused difficulties for the electoral campaigning and the subsequent governing (Segatti 2006). An example of a contentious issue was the introduction of a new legal status for cohabiting couples (*coppie di fatto*). The drafting of this article in the electoral program proved a crucial test for the alliance since both the more liberal and the Catholic parties had to agree on a compromise (Bernini 2008).

The difficulties of reconciling the parties' differing views became evident when the government proposed the so-called Piano nidi 2007–2009 in their first *legge finanziaria* in the autumn of 2006. It envisaged the expansion of childcare places with the aim of providing places for 33 percent of all children younger than three.[47] The newly institutionalized ministry for family policies (without portfolio, led by a minister from the center-left DL) carried the responsibility for the *Piano nidi*. Besides this ministry, six other ministries had portfolios that pertained to social policy issues, three of them very close to the area of childcare: the ministries of Social Solidarity (PRC), of Education (DL), of Equal Opportunities (DS, without portfolio), of Health (DS), of Labour (DS) and of Youth (DS, without portfolio). Hence seven different ministries involving ministers from three different parties had to negotiate about resources regarding welfare, among other issues, the *Piano nidi*. This fragmentation hampered a more coordinated approach to childcare services in terms of budget – i.e. a more efficient usage of resources and quality standards (Gori 2008).

The budget law passed the *Camera* and was sent with modifications to the *Senato* in November 2006. One of the most important amendments concerned the linkage between the implementation of the plan to the definition of the *livelli essenziali* regarding socio-educative services that were to follow.[48] This was important since the constitution prohibited any budget dedicated to specific goals in areas that do not fall under the competency of the national state. In the general discussion of the budget law, the question of childcare was not a contentious issue. The opposition criticized the low expenditure, but did not question the policy as such.[49]

Since it was a budget law, the distribution of resources had to be renegotiated each year. While critics argued that the scheduled expansion of childcare places for children aged zero to three would need much more resources than earmarked in the law (Gori 2007a), the *legge finanziaria* 2008 only intended to increase the planned €100 million for 2008 by another €70 million. Instead of pushing the reforms forward, the government thus opted to phase out the reforms that had been initiated. This was due to internal debates on family issues, which overshadowed any effort to reform work-family policies and eventually proved to become the acid test of the coalition. In 2007, public debate was dominated by a bill on regulating the rights and duties of cohabiting couples (*Diritti e Doveri dei Conviventi, DiCo*). It had been written by the minister for the family, Rosy Bindi, and the minister of equal opportunities, Barbara Pollastrini, and presented a cautiously formulated compromise between the secular and the Catholic streams in the coalition. Similar to laws in other European countries (though much less comprehensive), the bill intended to give cohabiting partners, irrespective of their sexual orientation, inheritance and alimony rights, as well as the decision-making power on funeral arrangements and organ donation.[50] In spite of bringing together all actors to formulate the law proposal, it provoked harsh criticisms in particular from members of the Catholic Church. On March 28, the Italian Episcopal Conference (*Conferenza Episcopale Italiana, CEI*) appealed to all politicians, but in particular to Catholic parliamentarians, to vote against the law (Conferenze Episcopale Italiana 2007).[51] In May, various Catholic organizations and associations organized a demonstration under the heading "Family Day" with the aim to emphasize the importance of "the family" for society and the need for better social policies to support families. Half a million people took part. Even though it was not an official protest against the bill, the organizers made clear that cohabitating couples should not be treated the same as a nuclear family based on marriage. The debate about what constitutes "the family" dominated in that year and overshadowed any practical approach to improve the situation of families, let alone any efforts to expand childcare services. The bill, in fact, led to a split in the government when the minister for justice, Clemence Mastella of the *Udeur*, publicly announced his refusal to vote in favor of the law: "If they told me to be the minister or to vote against the law on civil unions in the *Senato* I will leave the government; I have no difficulties to do so".[52] The bill would not make it to a vote. It got stuck during consultations in various parliamentary commissions. In January 2008, the same Mastella resigned from his position. This led to a government crisis. Eventually, Prime Minister Prodi asked for the vote of confidence. While he won it in the *Camera*, six senators expressed their distrust and one abstained. Due to the tight majority for the center-left coalition in the *Senato*, this meant the end of the fifteenth legislative period after only two years (Köppl 2008). Prodi tendered his resignation, and new elections were appointed.

Conclusion

The process tracing of the work-family policy reforms in Italy has shown the low priority politics accords this issue despite strong rhetoric. In fact, all party blocs mentioned the family and the necessity to support the family in their election manifestos. Only the center-left coalition governments, however, tried to improve the situation of parents who work and care by initiating laws on parental leave, childcare and part-time work. The takeover of the center-right coalitions, by contrast, often meant only negligible efforts or the withdrawal of previously enacted reforms.

However, even those law proposals that entered the parliamentary arena were not introduced with the purpose of substantially changing the work-family model as had happened in Germany. The law on parental leave and the ones on childcare provision, for example, were not intensively debated, in part because they did not intend to crowd out the family, usually the mother, as the core provider of childcare. This indicates the pivotal role of the widespread and stable support of the male-breadwinner model in Italy. Given that the Italian party system induces centripetal competition, the centrist voter's traditional beliefs do not give parties on either sides of the spectrum a strong reason to compete on progressive work-family policies. Policies that support mothers' employment were apparently not seen as vital for winning elections.

The analyses of the parliamentary debates further underlined the central role of normative beliefs. Often, the debates on work-family policy reforms and debates about what constitutes "the family" and which kind of a "family" should be entitled to benefits mingled. Engaging in ideological debates about the family in the case of the law proposal concerning the DiCo even paralyzed law-making processes, such as the one on the *Piano Nidi*, and ultimately led to a breakdown of the government. Together with the parties' general disinterest in these issues, a "neutral" engagement with questions concerning real family life seems difficult in a climate of ideological debates.

Last, this chapter has shown that, as in Germany, female policy entrepreneurs were the main promoters of policy change. Yet they were only able to push through work-family policy reforms during the government term of the center-left coalition between 1996 and 2001. In contrast to Germany, conservative women in Italy did not actively fight for more progressive work-family policies. Altogether, the female policy entrepreneurs' effect was arguably not as strong because of the overall low numbers of women in parliament and in high-ranking positions. The endeavors of women in the second center-left government fell victim to the low priority the governing parties and their leader placed on the issue and the ideological discussions about the family, which overshadowed the efforts.

Notes

1 "La politica italiana – anche quella della sinistra, che io vedo con molto dispiacere – e molto allegata a una politica di welfare maschio, capofamiglia, e ha molto una cultura familialista, operaio, lavoro produttivo, la produzione. Quindi, c'é questa cultura di welfare e di lavoro che é un nocciero durissimo." (Interview IT10).
2 Interview IT9.
3 Unless noted otherwise, all translations are my own.
4 The Commission claimed in particular a better balance between labor-market insiders and outsiders and between the young and the old (Ferrera and Gualmini 2004).
5 "*Le donne cambiano i tempi. Una legge per rendere piu umani i tempi del lavoro, gli orari della città, il ritmo della vita*". (The women change the times. A law to render the working times, the hours of the city and the life rhythm more human).

6 The idea is to give the municipalities and cities the responsibility to coordinate and regulate the working times of their facilities and the resident companies. Caring time should be the pivotal element of the city times around which opening hours of various services and employment are be organized.
7 In fact, the term "conciliazione" (reconciliation) has been borrowed from official documents of the European Union in the mid-1990s (Tempia 2005).
8 In November 1999, an infringement case against Italy was referred to the European Court of Justice because of the failure to implement the EU directive 96/34/EC. This directive has set minimum standards regarding the duration of parental leave and recommended the inclusion of rules regarding flexible use and the continuation of social security contributions. The infringement case probably accelerated the lawmaking process (Erler 2005).
9 Disposizioni per il sostegno della maternità e paternità, per il diritto alla cura e alla formazione e per il coordinamento dei tempi di città, published in Gazzetta Ufficiale n. 60 on 13.03. 2000.
10 This impression was also conveyed by most of my interview partners.
11 See Camera dei Deputati, Resoconto stenografico della Seduta n. 453, 11.12.1998. The proposals and amendments did not question the law in principle. Among the different law proposals was, for instance, the claim by *Forza Italia* to enable more flexibility in maternity leave use and to reduce social security contributions for companies when hiring a temporary substitution, or the demand by *Rifondazione Comunista* to extend the rights to adoptive parents (see Camera dei deputati, Resosonto stenografico della Seduta n. 602, 13.10.1999 and Resoconto stenografico della Seduta n. 678, 22.02.2000).
12 However, one of the DC's successors, the CCD-CDU argued for obliging the family by law to provide care within the first five months of the child and prohibiting families from putting children under the age of five months into a public childcare institution (*asili nido*) (see Camera dei deputati, Resoconto stenografico della Seduta n. 678, 22.02.2000).
13 See the minutes of the parliamentary meetings on 11.12.1998, 03.06.1999 and 15.12.2000.
14 The law 53/2000 is in fact one of the last laws which was directed at the core workforce – i.e. employed persons with a permanent position – and, given the immensely increased number of persons with atypical work contracts (in particular among women), it was already then outdated (Interview IT9).
15 Statement of Stefania Prestigiacomo (FI), Camera dei Deputati, Resoconto Stenografico della Seduta n. 453 of 11.12.1998, pages 16f: "*Se ampliare le garanzie per le donne significa aumentare gli oneri per i datori di lavoro, di fatto ogni garanzia in più è un disincentivo all'assunzione di potenziali madri. Se si vuole, quindi, aiutare in concreto le lavoratrici madri, si deve porre mano con sollecitudine ad una normativa che non sia penalizzante per i datori di lavoro e renda il settore privato più favorevole all'assunzione delle donne.*" Similar statements were made by FI MPs in the parliamentary debates on 03.06.1999 or 15.02.2000.
16 Elena Emma Cordoni (Democratici di sinistra – l'Ulivo), Camera dei Deputati, Resoconto Stenografico della Seduta n. 548: 24f., 03.06.1999).
17 Legge n. 863/1984, „Misure urgenti a sostegno e ad incremento dei livelli occupazionali", *Gazzetta Ufficiale* n. 351, 22.12.1984.
18 „Norme in materia di promozione dell'occupazione", *Gazzetta Ufficiale* n. 154 of 04.07.1997 — Supplemento Ordinario n. 136.
19 See Camera dei Deputati, Resoconto stenografico della seduta n. 191 del 12.5.1997 and Senato della Repubblica, Resoconto stenografico della seduta n. 148 del 12.3.1997.

20 *La contrattazione di secondo livello* is a term used for describing negotiations between employers, trade unions and employees on the company level instead of the regional or national level (Namuth 2012, Ocmin 2010).
21 "Non abbiamo voluto imporre con una legge il diritto al tempo parziale. Abbiamo detto: facciamole regolarsi nell'azienda nel territorio. La contrattazione di secondo livello e la bilateralità che è un altro istrumento dove mettono insieme azienda e lavoratori fondi insieme per fare formazione, banca delle ore, flessibilità dell'orario, programmi per reinserimento della donna che è andato in gravidanza, programmi per reinserimento di un uomo che per malattie è stato lontano – tutto questo nell'azienda nel territorio, non più al governo centrale, non più con le legge [. . .] Non serve uscire alle piazze gridando "Diritti, diritti" – punto. Finisce. [. . .] Invece cosi, si riesce a intercettare i problemi, trovare soluzioni che vanno bene all'azienda, che vanno bene al lavoratore." (Interview IT6).
22 Council Directive 97/81/EC of 15 December 1997 concerning the Framework Agreement on part-time work concluded by UNICE, CEEP and the ETUC – Annex : Framework agreement on part-time work, Official Journal L 014, 20/01/1998 P. 0009–0014.
23 Decreto legislativo no. 61/2000, "Attuazione della direttiva 97/81/CE relativa all'accordo quadro sul lavoro a tempo parziale concluso dall'UNICE, dal CEEP e dalla CES", *Gazzetta ufficiale* no. 66 of 20.03.2000.
24 The parliament specifies in a delegation law (*legge delega*) the limits of the cabinet's legislative power and stipulates guidelines for the drafting of the subsequent legislative decrees (*decreti legislativi*) (Ferrera and Jessoula 2007, Weber 2008). The legislative decrees do not require parliamentary approval nor can they be amended by the parliament. This is often done when an issue is very complex and requires detailed knowledge.
25 Legge 28.08.1997, n. 285. Disposizioni per la promozione di diritti e di opportunità per l'infanzia e l'adolescenza, pubblicata nella Gazzetta Ufficiale n. 207 del 5 settembre 1997.
26 The law proposal was presented on 19.02.1997 and finally approved on 30.07.1997.
27 See Camera dei Deputati, Resoconto Stenografico della Seduta n. 199 of 26.05.1997.
28 See Resoconto Stenografico della Seduta n. 561 of 07.05.1999.
29 Camera dei Deputati, Resoconto Stenografico della Seduta n. 561 of 07.05.1999, pages 12f.: "*La famiglia viene riconosciuta come soggetto essenziale nella formazione e cura della persona, nella promozione del benessere e nel perseguimento della coesione sociale, nella cooperazione e mutuo aiuto. Il ruolo della famiglia, quindi, viene potenziato con una politica che riguardi non più solo la famiglia povera, ma la generalità delle famiglie.*"
30 Legge costituzionale 18.10.2001, n. 3, Modifiche al titolo V della parte seconda della Costituzione.
31 A regular exchange between the state and the regions is provided through the sessions of the Conference of the state and the regions (*Conferenza permanente per i rapporti tra lo Stato, le Regioni e le Province autonome di Trento e Bolzano*).
32 *Tutta la nostra politica, dalla fiscalità ai fondi pensione, dagli asili nido ai contratti di lavoro, sarà mirata a sostenere e sviluppare la famiglia, come fondamento di un nuovo patto sociale, come fattore di solidarietà fra le generazioni, come sorgente di valori positivi e protagonista dinamica della modernizzazione del Paese.* (La Casa delle Libertà 2001: 4).
33 Proposta di legge no. 172 of 20.05.2001, "Norme sugli asili nido e sui servizi integrativi".
34 See Camera dei Deputati, Resoconto stenografico della seduta no. 389 of 13.11.2003.
35 The *legge finanziaria* is adopted once a year and enables the financing of all measures in the year. Since it is restricted to only one year in question, the financing of a measure is not guaranteed for the next year.

36 The budget law of 2002 established the National Fund for the Construction and Operation of Crèches and Child Minders within the Working Place (*Fondo nazionale per la costruzione e gestione degli asili nido nonché di micro-nidi nei luoghi di lavoro*) which amounted to 50 million Euros in 2002, 100 million Euros in 2003, and 150 million Euros in 2004 (Gori 2007b).

37 The budget law of 2003 established the Fund of Rotation for Company Crèches (*Fondo di rotazione per i nidi in azienda*) with an annual budget of 10 million Euros (Gori 2007b).

38 "The day nurseries and the so-called innovative services (what this expression covers is unclear) are not educational or social instruments, but rather parking lots for the children! (*Gli asili nido e quelli che qui vengono chiamati servizi innovativi (espressione che non si sa cosa voglia coprire) non sono strumenti educativi e sociali per i bambini, ma sono aree di parcheggio per i bambini!*)" (Statement of Rosy Bindi of La Margherita, Resoconto stenografico della seduta n. 389 of 13.11.2003, p. 28).

39 A similar case was the introduction of the "baby bonus" (*bonus bebè*) in the budget laws: a flat rate sum of 1000 Euros for each second born child in the year 2004 and for each child in 2006.

40 The reform was named after Marco Biagi, a professor of labor law and advisor for the government who had contributed to the bill.

41 *Decreto Legislativo* 10.09. 2003, n. 276 "Attuazione delle deleghe in materia di occupazione e mercato del lavoro, di cui alla legge 14 febbraio 2003, n. 30" published in Gazzetta Ufficiale n. 235 of 9.10.2003 — Supplemento Ordinario n. 159.

42 Resoconto stenografico della seduta n. 234 of 17.09.2002.

43 "*La barriera principale è lì: Io, prima di tutto, metterai donne sensibile al tema – non donne! Donne sensibile al tema – nei luoghi dove si decide. Io credo che quello sarebbe il metodo di cambiamento. Se ci fossero donne che sono davvero molto convinte che questa è una battaglia politica da fare, allora, conseguentemente, si va vedere come si riesce anche intervenire sul servizio, sul part-time, sui congedi, su tutti gli strumenti di conciliazione. Ma la barriera fondamentale è che non ci sono donne consapevoli, attente al tema, nei luoghi di decisione – né nei sindacati, né nei partiti politici, né nel assemblea parlamentare.*" (Interview IT3).

44 *L'Unione* was a left wing coalition founded February 2005 and composed of the following parties: Democratici di Sinistra (DS), La Margherita (DL), Partito della Rifondazione Comunista (PRC), Partito dei Comunisti Italiani (PdCI), Italia dei Valori (IdV), Socialisti Democratici Italiani (SDI), Verdi, Popolari-UDEUR (UDEUR), Movimento Repubblicani Europei (MRE), later joined up by Radicali Italiani (November 2005), I Socialisti (January 2006).

45 In 2005, the center-right government had changed the electoral rules to improve the coalition's chances in 2005. The new electoral law had introduced a majority premium which automatically allocates the winning coalition 340 seats in the *Camera* (which equals 53.9 percent of all seats) independent of the margin. For the *Senato*, the winning coalition of each region is allocated 55 percent of all seats designated to a region. In 2006, the center-right coalition received in total 141,116 more votes than the center-left for the *Senato*, yet the votes of Italians living abroad (who were also responsible for the good performance of the coalition in the *Camera*) turned the balance in favor of the Prodi government (Köppl 2008).

46 In line with the competency on the national level, the coalition emphasized their role in supporting the regions by providing resources for the costs of operation and investments of crèches.

47 Extraordinary plan for the development of socio-educative services such as crèches, integrative and innovative services (*Piano straordinario per lo sviluppo dei servizi socio-educativi, al quale concorrono gli asili nido, i servizi integrativi e quelli innovativi*), article 193 of the Disegno di legge Finanziaria of 1.10.2006.

48 See Paragraph 1259 of law no. 296 of 27.12.2006, "Disposizioni per la formazione del bilancio annuale e pluriennale dello Stato (legge finanziaria 2007)", published in Gazzetta Ufficiale no. 299 of 27.12. 2006 — Supplemento ordinario no. 244.
49 See Resoconto stenografico della Seduta n. 89 on 20.12.2006, p. 17.
50 When presenting the proposal, the proponents emphasized that the rights would not constitute an alternative to marriage and should not be seen as a form of homosexual marriage but rather a long overdue acknowledgement for bureaucracy (see Bernini 2008).
51 In the note, the bishops made reference to a promulgation issued by the Congregation of the Doctrine of Faith (*Congregazione della Dottrina della Fede*) which had declared in 2003 that "in the case of a law that favors the legal recognition of homosexual partnerships, Catholic parliamentarians have a moral obligation to clearly and publicly express his/her disagreement and vote against the law proposal "([. . .] *un progetto di legge favorevole al riconoscimento legale delle unioni omosessuali, il parlamentare cattolico ha il dovere morale di esprimere chiaramente e pubblicamente il suo disaccordo e votare contro il progetto di legge*").
52 "*Se mi dicessero fai il ministro oppure voti no al Senato sul ddl sulle unioni civili io esco dal governo, non ho nessuna difficoltà*" (La Repubblica, 09.02.2007, Dico, Mastella: "Niente aut aut sono pronto a dimettermi", http://www.repubblica.it/2007/01/sezioni/politica/coppie-di-fatto2/polo-dico/polo-dico.html#up; access date: 20.04.2010).

References

Bernini, Stefania. 2008. "Family Politics: Political Rhetoric and the Transformation of Family Life in the Italian Second Republic." *Journal of Modern Italian Studies* 13 (3):305–324.
Conferenze Episcopale Italiana. 2007. Nota a riguardo della famiglia fondata sul matrimonio e di iniziative legislative in materia di unioni di fatto. Roma: http://www.chiesacattolica.it/pls/cci_new_v3/cciv4_doc.edit_documento?id_pagina=7790&p_id=12553: Access date: 16.04.2010.
Cotta, Maurizio, and Luca Verzichelli. 2007. *Political Institutions in Italy*. Oxford: Oxford University Press.
Erler, Daniel. 2005. "Public Work-Family Reconciliation Policies in Germany and Italy. Exploring the Relevance of Problem Pressures, Institutions, and Actors." Department of Comparative and European Politics, Università degli studi di Siena.
Ferrera, Maurizio, and Elisabetta Gualmini. 2004. *Rescued by Europe? Social and Labour Market Reforms in Italy from Maastricht to Berlusconi*. Amsterdam: Amsterdam University Press.
Ferrera, Maurizio, and Matteo Jessoula. 2007. "Italy: A Narrow Gate for Path-Shift." In *The Handbook of West European Pension Politics*, edited by Ellen M. Immergut, Karen M. Anderson and Isabelle Schulze, 396–453. Oxford: Oxford University Press.
Forza Italia. 1994. Programma Forza Italia. Cinque obbiettivi per quarantacinque proposte. Roma.
Gelli, Bianca R. 2002. "*Empowerment* femminile: un difficile discorso di intersezione tra passi e saperi femministi, politica e psicologia." In *Voci di Donne. Discorsi sul genere*, edited by Bianca R. Gelli, 9–40. Lecce: Manni.
Gori, Cristiano. 2007a. "Asili nido: lobby debole, la riforma si arena." *Il Sole – 24 ore*, 18.11.2007.
Gori, Cristiano. 2007b. "I 'livelli essenziali', un'opportunità per la prima infanzia." In *Le politiche di sostegno alle famiglie con figli. Il contesto e le proposte*, edited by Luciano Guerzoni, 135–158. Bologna: il Mulino.

Gori, Cristiano. 2008. "'Un emendamento per 100.000 bambini'. Storia di una poverty lobby all'italiana." *Rivista Italiana di Politiche Pubbliche* 2/2008:115–142.
Gori, Cristiano, and Ilaria Madama. 2008. "Le politiche socioassistenziali." In *La riforma del welfare. Dieci anni dopo la "Commissione Onofri"*, edited by Luciano Guerzoni, 425–440. Bologna: il Mulino.
Guadagnini, Marila. 2005. "Gendering the Debate on Political Representation in Italy: A Difficult Challenge." In *State Feminism and Political Representation*, edited by Joni Lovenduski, 130–152. Cambridge: Cambridge University Press.
Guerzoni, Luciano, ed. 2008. *La riforma del welfare. Dieci anni dopo la "Commissione Onofri"*. Bologna: il Mulino.
Istituto degli Innocenti di Firenze. 2008. *Monitoraggio del piano di sviluppo dei servizi socio-educativi per l prima infanzia*. Firenze.
Köppl, Stefan. 2008. "Prodis Sturz." *Politische Studien* 59 (419):75–83.
La Casa delle Libertà. 2001. Piano di governo per una intera legislatura.
Lega Nord. 1994. Programma Lega Nord.
Lo Faro, Antonio. 2002. "Fairness at Work? The Italian White Paper on Labour Market Reform." *Industrial Law Journal* 31 (2):190–198.
Lo Faro, Antonio. 2004. "Italy: Adaptable Employment and Private Autonomy in the Italian Reform of Part-time Work." In *Employment Policy and the Regulation of Part-time Work in the European Union: A Comparative Analysis*, edited by Silvana Sciarra, Paul Davies and Mark Freedland, 156–189. Cambridge: Cambridge University Press.
Madama, Ilaria. 2010. *Le politiche di assistenza sociale*. Bologna: il Mulino.
Mairhuber, Ingrid. 2001. Tempi della città: von Italien lernen. In *FORBA-Schriftenreihe 3/2001*. Wien.
Naldini, Manuela, and Chiara Saraceno. 2008. "Social and Family Policies in Italy: Not Totally Frozen but far From Structural Reforms." *Social Policy & Administration* 42 (7):733–748.
Namuth, Michaela. 2012. Gewerkschaften in Italien, edited by Friedrich-Ebert-Stiftung. Berlin: http://library.fes.de/pdf-files/id-moe/09340.pdf.
Negrelli, Serafino, and Valeria Pulignano. 2008. "Change in Contemporary Italy's Social Concertation." *Industrial Relations Journal* 39 (1):63–77.
Ocmin, Liliana. 2010. Relazione per la Giornata seminariale Cisl Roma, 18 Gennaio 2010, "Le Donne e il Lavoro: la risposta alla crisi". Roma.
Pedersini, Roberto. 2000. Government Approves Legislative Decree Transposing EU Directive on Part-Time Work. In *EIROnline, European Industrial Relations Observatory On-line*. http://www.eurofound.europa.eu/eiro/2000/02/feature/it0002261f.htm.
Piazza, Marina, ed. 2009. *Attacco alla maternità. Donne, aziende, istituzioni*. Portogruaro: Nuova Dimensione.
Picot, Georg. 2012. *Politics of Segmentation: Party Competition and Social Protection in Europe*. London: Routledge.
Saraceno, Chiara. 2003. *Mutamenti della famiglia e politiche sociali in Italia*. Bologna: il Mulino.
Saraceno, Chiara. 2008. "Le politiche della famiglia." In *La riforma del welfare. Dieci anni dopo la "Commissione Onofri"*, edited by Luciano Guerzoni, 399–418. Bologna: il Mulino.
Segatti, Paolo. 2006. "I cattolici al voto, tra valori e politiche dei valori." In *Dov'è la vittoria? Il voto del 2006 raccontato dagli italiani*, edited by Itanes, 109–126. Bologna: il Mulino.

Tempia, Anna. 2005. "Italia. Fasi e tipologie delle politiche di conciliazione." In *La Rivista delle Politiche Sociali* 3:221–260.
Turco, Livia. 2013. "Legge 8 marzo 2000 n. 53: Disposizioni per il sostegno della maternità e della paternità, per il diritto alla cura ed alla formazione e per il coordinamento dei tempi della città." In *le leggi delle donne che hanno cambiato l'Italia*, edited by Fondazione Nilde Iotti. Rome: ediesse.
Weber, Peter. 2008. "Gesetzgebung im politischen System Italiens." In *Gesetzgebung in Westeuropa. EU-Staaten und Europäische Union*, edited by Wolfgang Ismayr, 463–511. Wiesbaden: VS Verlag für Sozialwissenschaften.

9 Conclusion

Almost ten years after the debate on the DiCo in Italy led to the demise of the then left-wing government, another "Family Day" took place in Rome in January 2016. As in 2007, hundreds of thousands came and protested against a bill scheduled to be debated in parliament. The bill would give gay couples with civil unions – and unmarried heterosexual couples – the same rights as they would have under marriage, including the adoption of their partners' children. However, it is mainly the latter part that is much contested in the Italian society, while the issue of giving gay couples the same rights as heterosexual married couples is seen as less of a problem today than it was ten years ago. The bill – initiated by a member of the ruling Democratic Party PD – is expected to be approved in the Senato, despite being opposed by large numbers of center-right opposition lawmakers and divisions within the PD. Nonetheless, the events show how the Italians still struggle with the question of what constitutes a family. As this book has demonstrated, this often paralyzes work-family reconciliation policy reform processes. Apart from some modest provisions such as an increased working-time flexibility (Picot and Tassinari 2015), there have been hardly any reform efforts to tackle the reconciliation of family life and work since the end of this book's study period.

At the same time, Germany experiences a more continuous path towards the support of the dual-earner model. Apart from the care allowance (*Betreuungsgeld*)[1] coming into effect in 2013 (but being abolished in 2015), recent policy proposals further developed measures to support mothers' employment and foster fathers' involvement in care. Most recently, a "Family Working-Time Benefits Model" is debated that promotes a state-financed wage replacement for parents who both reduce their weekly working time to take care of children (Müller, Neumann, and Wrohlich 2015). Also, most parents absorbed the idea that mothers of young children work and that fathers take care of their children. Recent statistics show an increase in employment of mothers with young children. Mothers of children aged between one and three work more hours than before the reforms (Bundesministerium für Familie 2015). At the same time, an increasing share of fathers use at least two months of parental leave. While there are still many employment-restricting institutions, such as the tax splitting scheme in Germany, these developments regarding the gender division of work seem to be enduring.

Conclusion 201

This book addressed the puzzle of work-family policy change in Germany and Italy, two conservative welfare states renowned for policy blockages and characterized by the male-breadwinner model. It aimed at answering the question of why Germany deviated from the long-term, male-breadwinner model and adopted far-reaching work-family policy reforms oriented towards the dual-earner model, while Italy did not. Drawing on the rich literature on the political economy of the welfare state, I have developed and tested a theoretical framework that stresses the impact of normative beliefs, party competition and women's agency on work-family policy change in conservative welfare states. Applying a variety of methodological approaches has proven useful to capture all relevant facets of the causes and the conditions which enable work-family policy change.

In summary, the triangulation of quantitative evidence with the findings from the process tracing has revealed that, first, work-family policy reforms are more likely if the normative beliefs of the population become progressive and parties have an incentive to compete for more progressive voters. Second, the probability of policy reforms is higher if women's representation in parliament has reached a critical mass, female policy entrepreneurs espouse the reforms' advancement and are supported by the government leader. Thus the answer to the question why reforms took place in Germany lies in the combined incidence of a change of normative beliefs towards the support of the dual-earner model, an increased salience of the issue of work-family policies for party competition, high women's representation in parliament and the commitment of female policy entrepreneurs who were supported by the chancellors. The answer to the question why reforms did not take place in Italy has to be seen in the persistently traditional normative beliefs of the population, the disincentives for parties to compete on the issue of work-family reconciliation policies, the comparably low share of women representatives in government and the low support of female policy entrepreneurs by the political leadership.

The comparative conclusion at this point recalls and connects the findings of the analyses. I start with the review of the results regarding the interplay of normative beliefs and the dynamics of party competition. In a second step, the findings on women's agency are presented. Subsequently, I discuss the contributions and the limits of the study. The chapter ends with some proposals for future research avenues and political implications.

Normative beliefs, parties and the dynamics of party competition

A key argument put forward in this book is that a shift toward more progressive normative beliefs in the population regarding mothers' employment and childcare should result in dual-earner-family-model-oriented policies (*policy responsiveness*). The comparison of individual survey data between Germany and Italy in Chapter 5 demonstrated a noticeable change towards more progressive beliefs in Germany between 1990 and 2008. By contrast, traditional beliefs remained largely constant in Italy. This average change in Germany is interpreted as a general shift in normative beliefs in a society and as evidence for the argument that the population's general normative beliefs towards mothers' employment and childcare influences the probability of work-family policy reform. Chapter 5 has, moreover, shown that particular subgroups of the population favor or disfavor policies that support the dual-earner model independent of the country: women, Germans living in the eastern states, Italians living in the northwest and more highly educated people have more modern normative beliefs. By contrast, religious and less-educated persons, as well as men, western Germans and Italians from all regions except for the northwest tend to advocate for the male-breadwinner model. These relationships have become more significant over time.

How does a change of normative beliefs shape policymaking? Power resources theory and the related partisan theory, which predicts a particular commitment of left-wing governments to more progressive work-family policies and gender equality (Brady 2009, Huber and Stephens 2000, Korpi 1983) can only partly be confirmed for Germany. Center-left governments did not bring about the paradigmatic changes; however, their contribution should be acknowledged. During its second legislative period, the Social Democratic Party (SPD) prepared the ground with the parental leave proposal and the childcare reform. Furthermore, when the 2006 and 2008 reforms were adopted, the SPD was a government party. Yet it should have been easier for the ideologically coherent center-left government that was in office between 1998 and 2005 to force through path-deviant reforms. In Italy, partisanship did matter for the probability of work-family policy reforms. Both the parental leave reform and efforts to push the provision of childcare (even though both reforms were restricted in scope) occurred under the center-left governments. Despite the fact that they emphasized the importance of the family, the center-right coalitions put no value on work-family policies.

If partisanship cannot be held responsible for work-family policy change, what else accounts for the reforms in Germany? I have argued that the configuration of the party system influences which groups of voters are targeted in elections (Picot 2012, Sartori 1976). Consequently, parties propose the kinds of policies that are favored by the voters they are competing for. In both Germany and Italy, centripetal competition prevails – that is, competition for the political center. Theoretically, in a system of centripetal party competition, a shift towards dual-earner-oriented policies should be the result of a change to more progressive normative beliefs of the political center. The analysis of the evolution of normative beliefs has confirmed this assumption. The average German – i.e. the centrist voter, has become more modern. Hence the general change in normative beliefs in Germany constitutes a necessary condition for policy change. Work-family policy reform happens when normative beliefs change and political competition is centripetal. If it had not been for this average shift towards more progressive normative beliefs, the reforms likely would not have occurred. This conclusion is reinforced by the fact that in Italy, where beliefs remained traditional on average, a work-family policy change has not taken place to the same extent.

At the same time, the dynamics of party competition changed in Germany. The two largest parties faced challenges related to structural changes in their electorates and had to deal with an overall declining share of votes. Both CDU's and SPD's core constituencies – religious and low-educated voters, respectively – dropped in number and, consequently, in electoral relevance for the vote-seeking parties. The core constituencies' normative beliefs were and are traditional. Hence there is no evidence for the hypothesis that a change in the normative beliefs of the parties' core constituencies was responsible for the parties' change in policy responses. Rather, as the core constituencies' potential for winning elections decreased, both parties tried to appeal to the more libertarian groups of voters, particularly women.

Germany: a continuous process towards the adoption of work-family policies

The process tracing of the German case has revealed why, when and how SPD and CDU started to compete on the issue of work-family policies. I first showed that both parties adapted their policy positions in a continuous process starting in the late 1990s – a long time before the actual decision-making processes that lead to the reforms. For example, the definition of the family and family responsibilities, the work-family policy proposals and their use for election campaigns were subject to mutual adaptations. The SPD had endorsed the CDU's definition of the family's role as an institution that fulfils important tasks for society in 2001. The CDU's position had begun to near the SPD's position on this issue, which is that the state should play a larger role in providing childcare and help to facilitate work-family reconciliation, as early as 1999. Both did so with the intention of appealing to the centrist voter as well as the more libertarian voters. When the SPD used work-family policies for its election campaign in 2002 in the hope of electoral payoff, the CDU adapted its campaign accordingly. Yet it was not until the closely fought 2005 election that the CDU fully realized the potential of work-family policies as a vote-seeking strategy. This mutual adaptation helped to mitigate the ideological controversies about motherhood and proper care between the two parties and facilitated policymaking in the grand coalition.

Second, I showed that the first trigger for the CDU to change its stance on work-family policies was the 1998 election. The persistent loss of votes and the crushing defeat of 1998 made a realignment of the party inevitable. Thus a cautious development toward more progressive policy stances started, which also targeted issues regarding the family and gender roles. The close elections of 2002 and especially 2005 were a second trigger for a change of policy positions. The 2002 defeat paved the way for more progressive CDU politicians. When in the election of 2005, women proved to be more likely to have voted for the SPD, the CDU – in view of the declining support – was consequently under even more pressure to look beyond their traditional constituency and adapt its policy approach accordingly.

Third, I showed that these changes involved intra- and inter-party conflicts, which influenced the design of the work-family policies that were ultimately adopted. The shift towards dual-earner family support represented a stronger paradigm shift for the CDU, but the SPD also struggled with internal conflicts. Take the example of the parental leave reform proposals. The proponents of the dual-earner family support within the SPD had to prevail over those party members who criticized the income-related leave benefit as a gift to rich families and who advocated for focusing policy instruments on low-income families. The proponents of the parental leave reform in the CDU, by contrast, had to put up with traditionalists, in particular male parliamentarians who would not warm towards the idea of fathers taking care of babies. It should be noted that the structure of the leave benefit in principle suits the CDU, because the benefit reflects a previous achievement on the labor market, while exceptions to the rule, such as the basic amount for housewives, have been provided for. The example of the two reforms regarding the expansion of publicly provided childcare places were also cases in point. Proponents and opponents within the CDU intensely struggled over the issue of proper care for children younger than three years old. In the end, the fight could only be solved with the proposal of a childcare allowance for those parents who prefer to not send their child(ren) to day nurseries. Similarly, both the red-green coalition and the grand coalition had to comply with the requests of the federal states to provide additional financial means to pay for the expansion of childcare places. Thus, in both cases – parental leave and childcare reforms – the government gave additional financial means or expanded the entitlement basis in order to pacify the opponents.

Italy: relative stability in normative beliefs and political competition

In Italy, party competition did not change in a similar way. First, the left-wing and the right-wing coalitions could always rely on their core constituencies who – as in Germany – continue to have traditional beliefs, but – in contrast to Germany – also continue to have electoral relevance. Thus, while I was also able to identify groups with progressive beliefs in Italy (women, Italians living in the northwest and more highly educated people), these groups did not play a central role for the vote-seeking party blocs. By contrast, more progressive people living in the northwest even tend to vote for the center-right coalitions, while women and more highly educated people have no party-bloc preference. Hence Italian parties of either bloc did not have an incentive to compete for more libertarian groups of voters. Second, in a system of centripetal competition neither party bloc had an incentive to compete on the basis of offering progressive work-family policies because of the political center's persistently traditional normative beliefs regarding mothers' employment and childcare.

Applying process tracing in the Italian case reinforced these arguments. Even though the parties proposed improving the situations of families and the reconciliation of work and care in their party manifestos, concrete reform efforts seldom followed. In addition, those law proposals that entered the parliamentary arena were not introduced with the intention of bringing about paradigmatic changes as had happened in Germany. The law on parental leave and the ones on the support of childcare provision were, for example, not intensively debated, in part because they did not intend to crowd out the family as the core provider of childcare. This can be interpreted as an effect of centripetal competition – that is, the attempt of the coalitions to appeal to the centrist voter who has traditional normative beliefs. Thus, progressive work-family policies were apparently not seen as vital for winning elections.

Process tracing also demonstrated the impact of within-party-bloc differences. On the right wing side – which is overall only rhetorically interested in work-family policies – decentralization, for example, is an issue that arises again and again. Providing the regions with more competencies might, however, make national state efforts in the provision of childcare impossible and is likely to result in further regional discrepancies. Inter-party struggles are more problematic for the left-wing coalitions. The opposition between the more centrist parties within the center-left coalition, which advocate more flexible working-time arrangements, for example, and those further to the left, which aim to protect workers against precarious working conditions, rendered regulations promoting part-time work difficult. Further, Catholic-oriented parties within the center-left party bloc continue to see the family as the core provider of childcare and debates about what constitutes "the family" and which kind of a "family" should be entitled to benefits hamper the progress of work-family policy reforms. The example of the law proposal concerning the DiCo demonstrated that, even if the debates do not concern work-family policies, engaging in ideological debates about the family can paralyze other law-making processes, such as the one on the *Piano Nidi*, and ultimately lead to a breakdown of a government. Together with the parties' general disinterest in these issues, a "neutral" engagement with questions concerning real family life seems difficult in a climate of ideological debates. Thus centripetal competition was a major factor that prevented structural reforms of work-family policies, but, at the same time, centrifugal tendencies complicated even tentative reforms.

All things considered, the comparative account of the developments in Germany and Italy with respect to the first set of factors has shown that, first, a general change in normative beliefs is a necessary condition for work-family policy change. Second, against the backdrop of a declining electoral importance of core constituencies, and increasingly close election results, increased party competition for more libertarian voters using the issue of work-family reconciliation policies may foster reforms oriented towards the support of the dual-earner family model. Where normative beliefs on average remained traditional and parties were able to continue to rely on their core constituencies as in Italy, parties have a lower incentive to compete with the issue of progressive work-family policies and reforms are less likely.

Women's agency: the impact of women's descriptive and substantive representation

Descriptive representation: is a high share of female parliamentarians a prerequisite for policy changes?

While a change of normative beliefs and increased party competition proved to be important conditions for work-family policy changes, women's agency played a central role in pushing the topic onto the political agenda and in enforcing policy reforms that aimed at supporting the dual-earner family model. Reforms of work-family policies are more likely when more women are represented in parliament and in government. In Chapter 6, I provided evidence that even though the number and the share of women parliamentarians and ministers increased during the last 20 years in both Germany and Italy, after 1998, it was only in Germany that women reached the critical mass levels of more than 30 percent in parliament, government and cabinets. Looking more closely at the shares during the most reform-active periods after 1998, we see that these developments are driven by women representatives from left-wing parties. A share of more than 30 percent of women representatives *in government* was only found in the case of left-wing governments (1998–2002 and 2002–2005). Due to the fact that some of the most important work-family policy reforms were adopted after the collapse of the left-wing government in 2005, it thus seems as if the quantitative representation of women in government was not a sufficient condition for work-family policy reforms in Germany. While work-family policy reforms are more likely to be enacted when women representatives reach a critical mass of 30 percent, the hypothesis should be qualified insofar as it has only proven to be true for the total share of women in parliament, but not necessarily in government. To some degree, this is also the case when we take the share of women ministers. Their share exceeded the 30 percent margin to a greater extent under the left-wing governments than under the grand coalition. Yet the more decisive reforms were adopted after 2005. Arguably, policy reforms need to be preceded by a couple of legislative periods in which women have already reached a critical mass.

It may be the case that the age composition differed between the left-wing government and the grand coalition, which might explain differences in reform efforts. However, there is no evidence that dual-earner-family-oriented work-family policy reforms are more likely when the share of younger women MPs is high. In Germany, the share of women MPs younger than 40 was highest under the red-Green governments. Yet it was comparably lower during the government term between 2005 and 2009 when far-reaching reforms were enacted. At that time, less than half of all women parliamentarians were younger than 50 years old. By contrast, during the legislative period between 2002 and 2005, almost 65 percent of all women belonged to that group of younger MPs. It could be argued that younger women, who are more likely to be new in parliament, do not have the same resources as older women who have belonged to parliament for a longer time and have better networks, etc.

In Italy, the overall share of women in parliament and the share of female MPs younger under 40 years of age were low. It was even particularly low during the most reform-active period between 1996 and 2001. Similar to Germany, the size of the share of women in governing parties and in cabinets depends on the political configuration of the government. More women are represented in left-wing governments. However, the share has also increased for right-wing governments.

Thus the lack of a clear relationship between a high share of women representatives in parliaments and policy reform efforts both in Germany and in Italy means that descriptive representation is apparently a necessary, even though not a sufficient, condition for work-family policy reforms that aim to promote the dual-earner family model. To better understand how women's agency matters for work-family policy reforms, I also analyzed the substantive representation of women in Chapters 7 and 8. Put in a nutshell, female policy entrepreneurs in high-ranking positions were enormously important for work-family policy reforms aimed at a better support of working parents both in Germany and in Italy.

Substantive representation: the impact of female policy entrepreneurs

In almost all cases of policy reforms, it was women who had put the issues onto the political agenda and promoted the issue – in some cases for several decades. In most cases, they had to persuade strong critics within or outside their parties. Thus it took a while until they were supported. Furthermore, partisanship mattered, as in both Germany and Italy it had been women representatives from left-wing parties who had first pushed the topic onto the political agenda.

Yet putting the topic onto the agenda is not sufficient for enacting policy change. As mentioned before, women had been actively engaged in the promotion of work-family policies for a long time. So why were they only successful at the turn of the century? I argue that the decisive factor is the support from the chancellor or prime minister. The two legislative periods of the red-Green governments in Germany are cases in point here. During the first term of government, the then chancellor Schröder did not emphasize work-family policy reforms. This changed in 2001 when the then vice chairperson of the SPD, who had a specific portfolio focusing on family policy, persuaded him to better support working parents, particularly mothers. When Renate Schmidt became minister for family affairs after the election of 2002, she continuously pushed the topic onto the agenda and she was supported by other cabinet members, in particular by the chancellor. Arguably, this acknowledgement and support was also connected with vote-seeking strategies. At that time, family policies had risen to prominence as an issue for party competition, as the parties had used the issue during the 2002 election campaign. Another example is the SPD's parental leave proposal of 2004, which was presented at a time when the red-Green government faced protests because of labor-market reforms – in this case, it was used to elicit a positive response.

Also in Italy, female policy entrepreneurs were supported by the prime ministers during the first legislative period under a left-wing government – although this occurred to a lesser extent than in Germany. This was arguably because of a lack of party competition on the issue of work-family policies. But at that time, many welfare state reforms were in progress, and in this "reform climate", female policy entrepreneurs could enforce work-family policy reforms. This was more problematic during the second left-wing government after 2006, when this impetus to reform had vanished and the center-left coalition was also grappling with internal problems. Interestingly, even though female policy entrepreneurs basically agree on issues of work-family policies across the two countries, these entrepreneurs' perception of part-time employment apparently differs in Germany and

Italy. In the former country, part-time employment is seen as a means to enable the combination of work and care. In Italy, by contrast, women are more skeptical because they fear it would be detrimental for women's career chances.

Female parliamentarians and policy entrepreneurs from conservative parties

The two cases also differ when it comes to the representation of women under conservative governments. Even though women were involved in work-family policy reforms in the Italian center-right coalition governments, they were not supported by the prime minister. In addition, conservative women have not been as active in pushing the topic onto the agenda as women from the left-wing parties. This was different in Germany. Women, even in the CDU, were also responsible for the "revolution". The process tracing has revealed that as far back as 1999, the new party chairperson and future chancellor, Angela Merkel, was involved in changing the CDU definition of the family and placed a priority on policies that help parents to reconcile work and care. In fact, Merkel is a remarkable constant in the history of conservative women pushing for more progressive work-family policies. As early as the beginning of the 1990s, she advocated for the expansion of childcare places for children under three. When Merkel became chancellor in 2005, she was joined by the later minister for family affairs Ursula von der Leyen (CDU) who supported these demands and played a central role both in the public and within the party. The chancellor's support was particularly important for the CDU minister because she had to persuade critics within her own party, a party that had supported the male-breadwinner model for a long time. In the CDU, and particularly in the sister party CSU, men were more likely proponents of the male-breadwinner model and, in some cases, even boycotted the reforms or forced through counter proposals such as the one introducing a childcare allowance by the CSU. Even though, initially, the CSU women together with the CDU women representatives had argued against this benefit, which many people assume incentivizes families to preserve male-breadwinner oriented work-family arrangements, in the end, they had to toe the party line.

All things considered, female policy entrepreneurs in high-ranking positions played an important role for work-family policy reforms. Yet the assumption that women from left-wing parties had a greater impact than women from conservative parties only partly holds. While left-wing governments are more likely to support female policy entrepreneurship, the most decisive work-family policy reforms in Germany occurred during the government of a Christian-democratic party, or, more precisely, a grand coalition with a Christian-democratic minister for family affairs and a Christian democratic chancellor. Hence the other factors that proved decisive for Christian Democratic advocacy for work-family policy reforms – policy responsiveness and party competition – are seemingly a necessary condition for female policy entrepreneurs to successfully enforce their policy proposals. At the same time, the reforms would likely not have occurred without women putting the topic onto the agenda. Hence the three factors – change of normative beliefs, party competition and women's agency – are interdependently responsible for work-family policy change. The example of Italy shows that even though female policy entrepreneurs in Italy were able to initiate some laws, the lack of more progressive voters, who parties could have been responsive to, impeded paradigmatic policy change.

Contributions and limits of the analysis

Studies of welfare state reform and social policy change have demonstrated the importance of socio-economic, partisan and institutional factors for the development of transfer benefits provided by the unemployment, health and pension schemes. What distinguishes the field of work-family policies is that they impinge on interpersonal or inner familial relationships and relate to the question of who should care for the family's children. As a consequence, previous literature has demonstrated the importance of including cultural factors and normative beliefs in the analysis of family policy determinants. Different than most other studies is the influence of culture, which focuses on the level of party elites, the churches or women's movement. I have analyzed the development of normative beliefs on the individual level. I was able to show the population's normative beliefs and whether or not they influence policymaking in a more direct way. Societal changes, or a lack thereof, are an important factor for policymakers. Cultural change has been ahead of a change in policies. If a change in normative beliefs does not occur, policy change is less likely. This is an important finding which supports the claims made by scholars of culture and the welfare state (Brooks and Manza 2006, Pfau-Effinger 2004, 2008, van Oorschot, Opielka, and Pfau-Effinger 2008). It is also in line with more recent claims for the role of voters in the analysis of welfare state politics (Immergut and Anderson 2007, Morgan 2013). The systematic comparison of individual normative beliefs and individual voting behavior is thus an innovative and important contribution to comparative welfare state research.

The basic argument of the literature on "dynamic representation" (Stimson, Mackuen, and Erikson 1995) is that parties do not govern in an elitist way, but respond to the demands of the population and adapt policies accordingly. My analyses have confirmed this finding. This also has implications for the traditional and influential power resources hypothesis in the study of welfare state politics. Policy development not only depends on the party in government but also on (changes in) public opinion. Leftist governments are not automatically more likely to introduce or expand work-family policies. If the public does not demand these policies, parties have no incentive to reform. Furthermore, the parties' reactions depend on the competition they face. This issue has more recently assumed a greater importance in the study of the welfare state (Kitschelt 2001, Picot 2012). In a system of centripetal competition, parties take into account the centrist voter's preferences. In a system of centrifugal competition, other groups of voters are more relevant for policymakers. It should be tested in future research whether parties in a system of centrifugal competition would have more difficulties enforcing a change, even if the general trend had moved towards more progressive normative beliefs. The case of Italy has shown how centrifugal tendencies have prevented even comparably minor reform efforts. Thus the traditional power resources theory and the related partisan theory also fall short in accounting for the competition the parties face.

Furthermore, it can no longer be assumed that the parties' policy choices depend solely on their (unchanged) traditional constituencies' preferences. There are two possible reasons why a party's body of supporters may change and parties might be inclined to adapt their policies. My analyses have demonstrated that the shrinking of the core constituencies has induced the large parties in Germany to try to attract other groups within the electorate. Thus a revised partisan theory should account for changes in the composition of the electorate and the core constituencies. Another mechanism could be that policy change is brought about by altered preferences of the core constituencies. Even though I did not find changed preferences among these groups of voters, it is plausible to include this factor in the analysis of party politics (Häusermann, Picot, and Geering 2013). Certainly, work-family policies are not the only issue for party competition. It is also unlikely that women or other people described as having libertarian attitudes[2] base their voting decision only on the parties' election proposal regarding work-family policies. However, work-family policies are one part of a party's portfolio for attracting voters with more progressive normative beliefs in many respects – e.g. regarding the family, education or environment.

My findings confirm the results of other studies, which postulate an increasing impact of libertarian constituencies on social policies (Häusermann 2010). However, libertarian beliefs do not develop by default in post-industrialized countries. There is, for instance, still substantial cross-country variance in normative beliefs regarding mothers' employment (Blome and Müller 2009). In addition, in order to fully understand the impact of an increasingly heterogeneous electorate, the individuals' voting behavior should be analyzed at the same time. This is often missing in studies of the relationship of partisan and constituencies' interests and their impact on social policy. It is noteworthy that those people who have more progressive beliefs towards mothers' employment did not have clear party preferences. Rather, my findings suggest that the timing and the dynamics of party competition matter for the impact of libertarian voters' demands. Even if libertarian voters can be considered as being more relevant for leftist parties, under the condition of changing party competition, even a Christian-democratic party, such as the German CDU, might include them in their vote-seeking strategy. Or, as the Italian case has shown, they might not even play a role at all because of centrifugal tendencies within the leftist coalition.

My analyses also have implications for theories of political institutions and their use for welfare state analyses. Since political institutions did not change during the observation period of my study, they were not specifically analyzed as potential determinants of work-family policy change. However, they were accounted for as context factors. I was able to show that policy change was possible in Germany despite institutional and partisan veto players. If parties were interested in policy change because they wanted to use a modernized work-family policy approach to appeal to voters, they were able to find strategies how to circumvent institutional veto players such as the upper chamber. In addition, the veto player theory has difficulties predicting the impact of a partisan veto player that changes its mind. For example, from the analysis of the 2005 party manifestos, we would have expected the CDU and the SPD to be partisan veto players in the grand coalition because they had two distinct proposals regarding family policies. When in government, however, the CDU changed its work-family policy approach and the previously ideologically distant parties became very similar. The veto player theory does not account for such a party's change in normative beliefs and is therefore not able to account for unexpected changes or mutual adaptations to policy positions. Immergut's veto points' approach (1992a, 1990, 1992b) is more suitable for the analysis of change, because it defines the veto potential as a point of strategic uncertainty where political actors are still able to use veto points strategically. It could therefore be of great value to analyze the impact of veto points on work-family policies with a research design that assembles cases that differ with respect to political institutions.

In recent years, the study of discourses has become influential in research on the welfare state (e.g. Béland 2009, Schmidt 2000). My analyses have demonstrated that certain discourses impede or accelerate work-family policy reforms. In Italy, the work-family policy reforms of the late 1990s were enacted during a climate of reform that had been brought about by the recommendations of an expert commission on welfare issues. In contrast, the reforms of the second left-wing period were hampered by the ideological debates about the family and what constitutes a family. On the other hand, discourses may not actually explain policy change, as in spite of changes in rhetoric, concrete policies often do not follow suit. In Italy, policymakers have been aware of the increasingly pressing issue of work-family reconciliation, and they were also influenced by European-level discourses that put pressure on the national states to improve the situation of working parents. Yet concrete action seldom followed rhetorical endeavors. To fully understand discourse and its influence on policy, we need to also pay close attention to the role of actors and their interests behind the discourses. Vote-seeking strategies arguably play a central role, but the degree of societal demand, which is associated with these strategies, certainly does also.

My analyses have, moreover, contributed to the study of women's agency and policy entrepreneurship in welfare state analysis. An increase in the share of female parliamentarians is decisive for state support of the dual-earner model. When it comes to female policy entrepreneurs, studies often discriminate between women from left-wing parties and women from conservative parties. More recently, research has focused on conservative women's claims (Celis and Childs 2012). Even though progressive work-family policies apparently seem to be a goal women share across parties, the decisive difference between female policy entrepreneurs coming from a leftist party and those who are members of a conservative party is the degree of support by the prime minister or chancellor who has an important voice in the party. Arguably, the chancellor's interest depends on vote-seeking strategies. Thus future research on women's interests and policy entrepreneurs should take the role of policy entrepreneurs in their parties, their relationship with the government leader, and issues of party's vote-seeking and party competition more systematically into account.

Finally, this book contributes to the literature on conservative or Bismarckian welfare states. Within-regime studies are not widespread in comparative research, even though such similar-cases comparisons make a lot of sense from a methodological point of view. In particular, Germany and Italy are seldom subject to comparison (see, however, Erler 2005, Picot 2012). My analyses have shown that, in contrast to conventional wisdom, conservative welfare states are capable of structural reforms and path departures in family policies. Some argue that Germany does not fit into the category of conservative welfare states any longer (see Bleses and Seeleib-Kaiser 2004, Fleckenstein 2011). In recent years, Germany has managed to reform its pension scheme, the unemployment insurance, the long-term care insurance, etc. Family policy reforms were not top priority, but such reforms did eventually occur. The reforms have in common that they are centered on adult employment and activation, but also on universal social rights for those in need of care (Schiller 2016). It could thus be argued that the formerly conservative German welfare state has moved in the direction of a Scandinavian welfare state with respect to the goals – without, however, challenging some of the basic principles of a conservative welfare state – e.g. the reliance on earnings-related benefits and their financing via earnings-related contributions. Similarly, Lamping and Rüb conclude that Germany is both saying "farewell to Bismarck" and "moving forward back to Bismarck" to describe this dual tendency (Lamping and Rüb 2010).

Future research

My results suggest mainly three avenues for further research. First, since changes in normative beliefs apparently influence policymaking, an as yet unanswered question is why normative beliefs change in the first place. Some argue that the increased labor-force participation of women has altered their attitudes, yet there might be reverse causality. In Germany, unification arguably plays a role. Women in the former GDR were predominantly in employment and subsidized childcare was universally available. On the other hand, the GDR was never seen as a role model by the West German population. Instead, policymakers referred to the Scandinavian countries or to France, both of which provide support for dual-earner families. Hence the exact mechanisms of diffusion remain unclear. Further, the role of the media for the public image of women might be explored. The way women are presented in public might influence the population's perception of their role. In fact, some interviewees mentioned that Italian women on TV are often objectified, while men take over the serious jobs as journalists. Large-N quantitative analyses that control for several intervening factors might help us to understand the relationship between changes to normative beliefs and policy development. But also case studies might be of extra value. For example, the German Longitudinal Election Study (GLES) could be explored to analyze the effect of the dynamics of party competition before and after an election, the media coverage of certain subjects, the role of the chancellor candidates and so forth.

Second, given the parties' central role in policymaking, future research should try to disentangle the exact components of parties' strategies and when and why they change. This could be done with a large-N research design that explores the parties' policy positions before and after election campaigns, the role of voters and the composition of the parties' constituencies. For this, we need better data. For example, in surveys on voting behavior, people are usually not asked whether a party's policy position on issues regarding the family has affected their voting decision. Also, the available data on party manifestos do not include family policies as an issue to derive a party's position in the political space. Yet including this information would make the argument regarding an increase in importance of a certain issue for party competition more convincing. Third, and last, as mentioned earlier, future research could refine the analysis of individual's voting behavior and normative beliefs by using more elaborate variables to measure what constitutes a libertarian or a centrist or rightist individual.

In addition, while I have mainly focused on vote-seeking strategies and electoral competition, future research might also take into account office-seeking strategies. As I pointed out earlier, due to the shrinking electoral support from its core constituency, the CDU must be able to both attract new voters and also be attractive for other parties to ally with the CDU. This is also true for Italy, where the decision of a party on who to support in a coalition affects its policy position and its strategies during and after elections. Also the effect of a party's organization (and its change) on policymaking should be tested (Rüb 2011). There is exciting new research on how certain types of organizations facilitate the input of various internal party groups, including women, and shapes policymaking (Wiliarty 2010). Systematic and detailed process tracings may be useful to analyze what parties do. An additional avenue could be to analyze the composition of the parties in parliament in terms of socio-demographic characteristics and test whether there is a relationship between the individual MPs' characteristics and policy outputs.

Political implications

The shift in German work-family policies toward providing a coherent framework of dual-earner-family-model support is not yet finalized. Yet I argue that the reforms initiated mark the starting point for further changes. Without doubt, in the long run, the issue of work-family reconciliation will differ significantly from what had been considered typical of continental welfare states. So far, there has been a doubling of publicly subsidized childcare places for children younger than three between 2007 and 2015, which represents an increase of mothers' employment of about ten percentage points for women with children aged between one and three and an increased share of fathers using at least some months of parental leave (Blome 2015). At the same time, the transition to a dual-earner model is not complete. For example, fiscal incentives, a free co-insurance for unemployed married partners in the health-care scheme and benefits within the parental leave scheme such as the basic allowance for housewives continue to benefit the male-breadwinner model. At the same time, most of the work-family policy reforms targeted women. Wives and mothers are expected and encouraged to enter the labor market to a much larger degree than fathers are encouraged to enter the area of childcare.

Therefore, some scholars have been skeptical of the sustainability of the reforms (e.g. Fleckenstein 2011). Yet I argue that even though implementation is far from perfect, the transformation of the work-family reconciliation support through policies is irreversible. There are two reasons for this. First, the general shift in public opinion is sustainable. Second, and connected with this, the former proponent of the male-breadwinner model, the CDU, cannot afford opposition against the trend toward the dual-earner family model any longer. To be competitive with the center-leftist parties, the CDU arguably has no alternative than to follow the societal demand. The abolishment of the highly contested childcare allowance demonstrated that a return to the traditional regime was impossible. In the spring of 2012, a large cross-party alliance led by women parliamentarians, together with the social partners, mobilized against the childcare allowance. This resistance even had the potential to cause the government's collapse.[3] In the end, it was a benefit unpopular in the population and among all parties except for the CSU. Its abolition in 2015 was a logical step. The intense disputes are another example of how much work-family policy has increased in importance as far as the parties' vote-seeking strategies and party competition are concerned.

At the same time, the adoption of progressive work-family policies as part of an overall transformation may have long-term implications for the party system and government formation. Looking at the developments not only from the perspective of vote-seeking but also from the perspective of office-seeking, the CDU is pressurized to be open to coalition partners other than the "naturally" set liberal party FDP. In case the two parties do not reach absolute majority in an election, the CDU might then have to ally with other parties – e.g. the Greens – a party that would not accept traditional work-family policies. On the other hand, the tracing of the reform processes has demonstrated that the shift in the CDU was an acid test for the party. During the consultations regarding the childcare reform in 2007, some conservative representatives urged the CDU to "think more again of the parties' roots" (Mappus et al. 2007). By now, there are some conservative politicians that defy the official party line announced in 2010 that adopts a progressive approach to compete for center voters and voters further to the left.[4] As a matter of fact, the CDU's move has opened a gap on the right wing of the party system, and it might be that a splinter group of conservative former CDU party members will form. A split of this nature also happened to the SPD when the party adopted reforms of the labor-market policies and disappointed party members formed the WASG, which later fused to form *Die Linke* (the Left).

From a democratic perspective, it is important to know whether parties are responsive – i.e. whether they do what the voters want. Giving citizens the opportunity to influence public policy in democratic systems is the classical idea of democracy and representation. From this point of view, both the German and the Italian political systems perform the function. It could further be argued that, if decisions about policy developments depend on the dynamics of party competition, then not all citizens' interests are considered equally. Those groups of voters who are targeted by certain policy proposals have more political weight than others. In the case of work-family policies, women and other libertarian voters were at the heart of competition and were arguably the main beneficiaries of the policy change in Germany. Nonetheless, these claims were supported by a general shift in normative beliefs and demands in society. Hence the issue was seemingly seen as a benefit to society as a whole. Since the support and facilitation of qualitative caring time also benefits children, arguably these changes include citizens in politics who have no voice so far – namely, children.

In addition, the impact of a social group on policymaking can be strengthened by an increase of both its descriptive and substantive representation. This is even more important if this social group does not have a "natural" ally with a stake in social policymaking such as the social partners. As argued elsewhere, the representation of weak interests, such as issues of childcare, depends upon strong interest organizations or representational organs in society to take up their concern (von Winter and Willems 2000). The increase of the number of women in parliament and in government enhances the likelihood that women will benefit from this representation in terms of entitlements and benefits. For systems of democratic representation, this implies that parties should provide for a better social balance within their organizations.

A final relevant question is whether welfare states are able to meet new social demands in times of budget austerity. As argued earlier, the fact that many European welfare states have expanded the rights and benefits in the field of work-family policies is telling. Yet my analyses concern the period before the financial crisis hit Europe. Nonetheless, it seems as if the countries that have decided to follow the path of supporting dual-earner families are sticking to this choice. Even though it could be argued that Germany was not as badly affected by the crisis as other countries, the country does wish to lower its state deficit, but at the same time it is providing even more funds to finance the expansion of childcare places (and the childcare allowance). Thus it seems as if Germany has incorporated the view that it needs to invest in women and children to be able to remain financially viable. Italy, by contrast, was hit much harder by the financial crisis. Recent reform efforts rely on cutbacks, but not on social investment policies. In March 2012, the minister of labor announced a "program for a greater inclusion of women in the economic life". It, however, only consisted of the introduction of a right to three days paternity leave and a voucher for a babysitter to use within the first 11 months after the baby's birth as an alternative to parental leave.[5] It is difficult to imagine how such measures can really facilitate the reconciliation of work and care, since three days of paternity leave will not degender the division of work. Further, even if parents decide to make use of the voucher to enable the mother's return to the labor market, the question is what to do with the child after those 11 months when there are no childcare places available. The fact that other, more intuitive and even costless measures such as making part-time work available for parents on parental leave have not been considered shows the persistently low priority Italian policymakers accord to issues of childcare (Saraceno 2012). It underlines once more what seems to be the Italian way of dealing with work-family reconciliation and issues of family policies: Most of my interview partners told me that *chiacchiere* (babbling) instead of *affrontare* (acting) is their motto. So even now, in the middle of the 2010s, there is no end in sight to what Saraceno (1994) has labeled the Italian family paradox. While the family is highly valued as an institution, it is not at all supported in its function.

Notes

1 A care allowance of 150 Euros was paid to families who did not make use of a publicly subsidized childcare place for their children aged two to three.
2 Libertarian values emphasize, for example, personal and political freedom, equality, and concern over quality-of-life issues and environment, while authoritarian values concern security and order, as well as support for traditional religious and moral ideas (Flanagan 1987).
3 Being annoyed by the ongoing protests within the coalition partners CDU and FDP against the care allowance, CSU party leader Seehofer announced in May 2012 that she would not participate in the coalition committee until the decisions with respect to the care allowance were transformed into a law proposal (see e.g. Die Zeit 13.05.2012).
4 After the CDU's *"Berliner Erklärung"* of 2010, the *"Aktion Linkstrend stoppen"* (Stop the trend towards the left) formed, which tries to mobilize conservative party members and voters.
5 A third proposal concerns the prevention of the so-called *dimissioni in bianco*, which refer to the practice of having new employees pre-emptively sign a letter of dismissal which may be used by the employer. This practice is often used in the case of pregnancy.

References

Béland, Daniel. 2009. "Gender, Ideational Analysis, and Social Policy." *Social Politics: International Studies in Gender, State & Society* 16 (4):558–581. doi: 10.1093/sp/jxp017.

Bleses, Peter, and Martin Seeleib-Kaiser. 2004. *The Dual Transformation of the German Welfare State*. New York: Palgrave Macmillan.

Blome, Agnes. 2015. "Neuere familienpolitische Leistungen. Bilanz nach zehn Jahren." *Neue Zeitschrift für Familienrecht. Special Issue "Gesellschaftspolitische Grundentscheidungen mit Blick auf die Familie"*, edited by Jutta Allmendinger et al. 2 (23):1081–1085.

Blome, Agnes, and Kai-Uwe Müller. 2009. "Do Politics Respond to People's Attitudes? The Case of Work/care Policies." *ECPR Joint Sessions, Lisbon*, 14–19 April 2009.

Brady, David. 2009. *Rich Democracies, Poor People: How Politics Explain Poverty*. New York: Oxford University Press.

Brooks, Clem, and Jeff Manza. 2006. "Social Policy Responsiveness in Developed Democracies." *American Sociological Review* 71 (3):474–494.

Bundesministerium für Familie, Senioren, Frauen und Jugend. 2015. *Familienreport 2014*. Leistungen, Wirkungen, Trends. Berlin.

Celis, Karen, and Sarah Childs. 2012. "The Substantive Representation of Women: What to Do with Conservative Claims?" *Political Studies* 60 (1):213–225. doi: 10.1111/j.1467–9248.2011.00904.x.

Die Zeit. 13.05.2012. "Seehofer will Betreuungsgeld mit Druck auf CDU durchsetzen." http://www.zeit.de/news/2012–05/13/regierung-seehofer-will-betreuungsgeld-mit-druck-auf-cdu-durchsetzen-13122802: Access date: 29.05.2012.

Erler, Daniel. 2005. "Public work-family reconciliation policies in Germany and Italy. Exploring the relevance of problem pressures, institutions, and actors." Department of Comparative and European Politics, Università degli studi di Siena.

Flanagan, Scott. 1987. "Value Change in Industrial Societies." *American Political Science Review* 81 (4):1289–1319

Fleckenstein, Timo. 2011. "The Politics of Ideas in Welfare State Transformation: Christian Democracy and the Reform of Family Policies in Germany." *Social Politics* 18 (4):543–571.

Häusermann, Silja. 2010. *The Politics of Welfare Reform in Continental Europe. Modernization in Hard Times*. New York: Cambridge University Press.

Häusermann, Silja, Georg Picot, and Dominik Geering. 2013. "Review Article: Rethinking Party Politics and the Welfare State – Recent Advances in the Literature." *British Journal of Political Science* 43 (01):221–240. doi: 10.1017/S0007123412000336.

Huber, Evelyne, and John D. Stephens. 2000. "Partisan Governance, Women's Employment, and the Social Democratic Welfare State." *American Sociological Review* 65 (3):323–342.

Immergut, Ellen M. 1990. "Institutions, Veto Points and Policy Results: A Comparative Analysis of Health Care." *Journal of Public Policy* 10:391–416.

Immergut, Ellen M. 1992a. *Health Politics: Interests and Institutions in Western Europe*. Cambridge, New York, Melbourne: Cambridge University Press.

Immergut, Ellen M. 1992b. "The Rules of the Game: The Logic of Health Policy-Making in France, Switzerland and Sweden." In *Structuring Politics. Historical Institutionalism in Comparative Analysis*, edited by Sven Steinmo, Kathleen Thelen and Frank Longstreth, 57–89. Cambridge: Cambridge University Press.

Immergut, Ellen M., and Karen M. Anderson. 2007. "Editors Introduction: The Dynamics of Pension Politics." In *The Handbook of West European Pension Politics*, edited by Ellen M. Immergut, Karen M. Anderson and Isabelle Schulze, 1–45. Oxford: Oxford University Press.

Kitschelt, Herbert. 2001. "Partisan Competition and Welfare State Retrenchment: When Do Politicians Choose Unpopular Policies?" In *The New Politics of the Welfare State*, edited by Paul Pierson, 265–302. Oxford: Oxford University Press.

Korpi, Walter. 1983. *The Democratic Class Struggle*. London: Routledge & Kegan Paul.

Lamping, Wolfram, and Friedbert W. Rüb. 2010. "Introduction: Farewell to Bismarck or Moving Forward back to Bismarck? Transformations of the German Welfare State." *German Policy Studies* 6 (1):43–63.

Mappus, Stefan, Markus Söder, Philipp Mißfelder, and Hendrik Wüst. 2007. Moderner bürgerlicher Konservatismus. Warum die Union wieder mehr an ihre Wurzeln denken muss, http://www.stefan-mappus.de/uploads/media/Moderner_buergerlicher_Konserv atismus.pdf: Access date: 12.10.2011.

Morgan, Kimberly J. 2013. "Path Shifting of the Welfare State: Electoral Competition and the Expansion of Work-Family Policies in Western Europe." *World Politics* 65 (01):73–115. doi: doi:10.1017/S0043887112000251.

Müller, Kai-Uwe, Michael Neumann, and Katharina Wrohlich. 2015. "The 'Family Working-time Benefits Model' (Familienarbeitszeit): Giving Mothers more Time for Work, Giving Fathers more Time for Family." *DIW Economic Bulletin* (45+46):595–602.

Pfau-Effinger, Birgit. 2004. *Development of Culture, Welfare State and Women's Employment in Europe*. Aldershot: Ashgate.

Pfau-Effinger, Birgit. 2008. "Cultural Change and Path Departure: The Example of Family Policies in Conservative Welfare States." In *Culture and Welfare State. Values and Social Policy in Comparative Perspective*, edited by Wim van Oorschot, Michael Opielka and Birgit Pfau-Effinger, 185–204. Cheltenham and Northampton: Edward Elgar.

Picot, Georg. 2012. *Politics of Segmentation: Party Competition and Social Protection in Europe*. London: Routledge.

Picot, Georg, and Arianna Tassinari. 2015. "Politics in a Transformed Labor Market: Renzi's Labor Market Reform." *Italian Politics* 30:121–140.

Rüb, Friedbert W. 2011. "Michels und die neuere Parteientheorie – Die politischen Parteien und die Krise der Demokratie." In *Robert Michels' Soziologie des Parteiwesens. Oligarchien und Eliten – die Kehrseiten moderner Demokratien*, edited by Harald Bluhm and Skadi Krause, 241–263. Wiesbaden: VS Verlag für Sozialwissenschaften.

Saraceno, Chiara. 2012. "L'altra faccia della riforma." *La Repubblica*, 03.04.2012.

Sartori, Giovanni. 1976. *Parties and Party Systems: A Framework for Analysis*. Cambridge: Cambridge University Press.

Schiller, Christof. 2016. *The Politics of Welfare State Transformation in Germany. Still a Semi-Sovereign State?* London/New York: Routledge.

Schmidt, Vivien A. 2000. "Values and Discourse in the Politics of Adjustment." In *Welfare and Work in the Open Economy. Volume I. From Vulnerability to Competitiveness*, edited by Fritz W. Scharpf and Vivien A. Schmidt, 229–309. Oxford: University Press.

Stimson, James A., Michael B. Mackuen, and Robert S. Erikson. 1995. "Dynamic Representation." *The American Political Science Review* 89 (3):543–565.

van Oorschot, Wim, Michael Opielka, and Birgit Pfau-Effinger, eds. 2008. *Culture and Welfare State. Values and Social Policy in Comparative Perspective*. Cheltenham/Northampton: Edward Elgar.

von Winter, Thomas, and Ulrich Willems. 2000. "Die politische Repräsentation schwacher Interessen: Anmerkungen zum Stand und zu den Perspektiven der Forschung." In *Politische Repräsentation schwacher Interessen*, edited by Thomas von Winter and Ulrich Willems, 9–38. Opladen: Leske + Budrich.

Wiliarty, Sarah Elise. 2010. *The CDU and the Politics of Gender in Germany. Bringing Women to the Party*. Cambridge: Cambridge University Press.

Appendices

Table A.1 Variables in most-similar systems design in Germany and Italy, pre-reform period 1990–2000

Indicator	Germany	Italy
Dependent variable		
Work-family policy reforms	• Increased maximum paid leave duration • Increase of replacement rate • Increase of public childcare places, social right for one-year olds • Entitlement to part-time employment	• Addition of father months • Slight increase of public childcare
Context factors		
Welfare state institutions	• Bismarckian type • Employment-related cash benefits • Income-related contributions	• Bismarckian type • Employment-related cash benefits • Income-related contributions
Structure of work-family policies before reforms	• Universal family benefits • Male-breadwinner model • Benefits/incentives for married couples and single-earner families • Low level of public childcare for children < 3 (10% in 2000)	• No universal family benefits • Male-breadwinner model • No benefits/incentives for single earners, women's care implicitly assumed • Low level of public childcare for children < 3 (7.4% in 2000)
Economic structure and performance	• Industrial-sector share 2000: 33.1% • Service-sector share 2000: 64.2% • GDP/capita 2000: 25,100 Euros • GDP/capita growth 1990–2000: 37% • Total state debt/total GDP 2000: 59.7%	• Industrial-sector share 2000: 31.1% • Service-sector share 2000: 64.2% • GDP/capita 2000: 20,900 Euros • GDP/capita growth 1990–2000: 23% • Total state debt/total GDP 2000: 109.2%

(*Continued*)

Table A.1 (Continued)

Indicator	Germany	Italy
Economic and labor-market institutions	• Coordinated market economy • Skill formation: vocational training, dual system • High skill level of women (share of higher secondary education 2000: 44.3%, share of tertiary education 2000: 42.4%)	• Elements of a coordinated market economy • Skill formation: vocational training, company based • High skill level of women (share of higher secondary education 2000: 48.7%, share of tertiary education 2000: 55.6%)
Socio-demographic structure	• Fertility rate 2000: 1.34 • Old-age dependency ratio 2000: 23.9	• Fertility rate 2000: 1.26 • Old-age dependency ratio 2000: 26.8
Women's labor-market integration	• Women's FTE employment rate 2000: 46.1% • Women's share of total employment in service sector 2000: 54% • Women's share of total employment in industrial sector 2000: 23.7%	• Women's FTE employment rate 2000: 36,7% • Women's share of total employment in service sector 2000: 46.4% • Women's share of total employment in industrial sector 2000: 24%
Political structures and institutions	• Electoral system: mixed proportional/majoritarian • Government type: coalition • Parliamentary system: bicameral • Exclusive policy competencies of the federated states: yes • Judicial revision: strong	• Electoral system: mixed proportional/majoritarian • Government type: coalition • Parliamentary system: bicameral • Exclusive policy competencies of the regions: yes • Judicial revision: not effective
Explanatory variables		
Normative beliefs	• Shift towards more modern normative beliefs	• Relatively stable traditional belief structure
Party competition	• Centripetal competition • Increased party competition about work/care issues • Structural changes of electorate	• Centripetal competition • Work/care issues no salient issue in party competition • Hardly any change of traditional constituencies' importance
Women's agency	• Increased number of women representatives • More female policy entrepreneurs in decision-making positions	• The share of women representatives remains low

Table A.2 List of interviewees

No.	Function	Organization	Location	Date
IT1	Social policy expert	Social Study and Research Institute Censis	Roma	01/2010
IT2	Social policy expert	Università degli studi di Milano	Milano	01/2010
IT3	Professor of law	Università degli studi di Verona	Verona	12/2009
IT4	Chief of cabinet	Ministry for Equal Opportunities, centre-right government	Roma	01/2010
IT5	Professor of sociology of the family	Università degli studi di Torino	Torino	12/2009
IT6	Federation secretary	Italian Confederation of Worker's Trade Unions (CISL)	Roma	01/2010
IT7	Head of department "Measures for reconciliation" and General director of office "family policies"	Department of Family Policies, subordinated to the president of the council	Roma	01/2010
IT8	Gender consultant	Freelance professional	Milano	12/2009
IT9	Professor of sociology of the family	Social Science Research Center (WZB), Università degli studi di Torino	Berlin, Torino	12/2009
IT10	Minister	Ministry of Social Solidarity (1996–2001), Ministry of Health (2006–2008), former member of PC, now PD	Roma	01/2010
DE1	Minister	Ministry for Family Affairs, SPD	Berlin	11/2010
DE2	Management	Women's Union, CDU	Berlin	04/2010
DE3	Civil servant	Ministry for Family Affairs	Berlin	04/2009
DE4	Member of Parliament	Acting spokeswoman on Family Affairs in the German Parliament, SPD	Berlin	07/2010

Table A.3 The development of parties in Italy after 1992

Category	Abbreviation	Party name		Year founded	Ideological orientation	Founding and merger details
Post-Communist parties	PRC	Partito della Rifondazione Comunista	Communist Refoundation	1990	Neo-communist	Part of former *Partito Comunista Italiano* (PCI) plus *Democrazia Proletaria* (DP, in 1991), separated from DS
	PdCI	Partito di Comunisti Italiani	Party of Italian Communists	1998	Post-Communist	PdUP members joined (in 1991), separated from PRC
Greens	Verdi	Federazione dei Verdi	Greens	1986	Green	
Left parties, social democratic parties	PSI	Partito Socialista Italiano	Italian Socialist Party	1892	Democratic-socialist	Now: Nuovo PSI
	PDS	Partito democratico della sinistra	Left Democrats	1991	Leftist	Transformation of the former *Partito Comunista Italiano* (PCI)
	DS	Democratici di Sinistra	Left Democrats	1998	Leftist	Transformation of PDS
	SDI	Socialisti Democratici Italiani	Italian Social Democrats	1998	Social democratic	Transformation of the former Socialist party (PSI)
		I Socialisti Italiani	The Italian Socialists	2006	Social democratic	Separated from NPSI
	PS	Partito Socialista	The Socialist Party	2007	Social democratic	Merger of SDI, *I Socialisti Italiani* and *Associazione per la Rosa nel Pugno*, also some members of the NPSI joined
	NPSI	Nuovo Partito Socialista Italiano	New Italian Socialist Party	2001	Liberal, social democratic	Transformation of the former *Socialist Party* (PSI)

Category	Abbr.	Italian name	English name	Year	Ideology	Notes
Leftist Christian Democratic parties	CS	Cristiano Sociali	Social Christians	1993	Social Christian	Now a faction of the DP
	I Democratici	The Democrats	1999	Social democratic	Founded by R. Prodi. Since 2002, the party has merged into the new formation *La Margherita – Democrazia è Libertà*, as of 2007: PD
	DL	Democrazia e libertà – La Margherita		2002	Social Christian	Formed from *Democrazia e Libertà*, *Rinnovamento Italiano* and a fraction of the former *Popular Party* (PPI)
	PD	Partito Democratico	Democratic Party	2007	Center-left	Formed from DS and *Democrazia e libertà – La Margherita*, UD
Christian Democratic parties	CCD	Centro Cristiano Democratico	Christian Democratic center	1994	Christian democratic	Transformation of the former *Christian Democratic Party* (DC)
	PPI	Partito Popolare Italiano	Italian People's Party	1994	Christian democratic	Transformation of the former *Christian Democratic Party* (DC)
	RI	Rinnovamento Italiano	Italian Renewal	1996	Liberal-centrist	Part of *l'Ulivo*, in 2001/2002 joined *La Margherita*; in 2007 parts of RI joined *Liberal Democrats* who later joined PdL.
	CDU	Cristiani Democratici Uniti	Christian Democratic Party	1995	Christian democratic	Transformation of the former *Popular Party* (PPI), separated from CCD
	UDEUR	Unione Democratici per l'Europea	Christian Democratic	1999	Christian democratic	Emerged in May 1999 after the break up of UDR (founded in 1998). Merger of CDU, CDR (splinter of CCD) and PS (Patto Segni)
	UDC	Unione dei Democratici Cristiani e di Centro	Union of Christian and Center Democrats	2002	Christian democratic	Merger of CDU, CCD and DE (Democrazia Europea, a minor Christian democratic party founded in 2000)
	PP	Partito Pensionati	Pensioners' Party	1987	Centrist	

(*Continued*)

Table A.3 (Continued)

Category	Abbreviation	Party name		Year founded	Ideological orientation	Founding and merger details
Liberal parties, leftist		Lista Pannelli	Radical liberal	1989	Liberal	Also Panella-Sgarbi Lista. Resolved in 1999, merged into Radicali
	PR	Radicali	Radicals	2002	Social liberal	Transformation of the former radical party (PR)
	La Rete	Movimento per la Democrazia – La Rete	Movement for Democracy – The Net	1991	Social liberal	The party renamed in 1996: La Rete per il Partito Democratico and merged with I Democratici in 1999
		Patto Segni		1993	Liberal	Founded by Mario Segni, separated from AD on the base of the social movement *Popolari per la Riforma*,
	AD	Alleanza Democratica	Democratic Alliance	1993	Social liberal	
	DU	Unione Democratica	Democratic Union	1996	Social liberal	Evolved from the AD
		Italia dei valori – Lista di Pietro		2000		New party
Liberal parties, right-wing	FI	Forza Italia	Forward Italy	1994	Conservative liberal	
	PdL	Il Popolo della Libertà	The People of Freedom	2007	Conservative liberal	Successor of *FI*, The party was launched by Silvio Berlusconi on 18 November 2007 and officially founded in a party congress on 27–29 March 2009 when *FI* merged with National Alliance
	PL	Partito liberale	Liberal party	1994	Liberal	2004 merged into *Partito Liberale Italiano*, PLI
	PRI	Partito Repubblicano Italiano	Italian Republican Party	1895	Liberal	

Territorial parties	LN	Lega Nord	Northern League	1991	Federalist	Formed from Liga Veneta and Lega Lombarda
Right-wing parties	AN	Alleanza Nazionale	National Alliance	1995	Right wing	Transformation of the former post-fascist party (MSI), merged to *Il Popolo della Libertà* in 2009
	MSI	Movimento Sociale Italiano – Fiamma Tricolore		1995	Neo-fascist	Part of the former post-fascist party (MSI), separated from AN

Source: Ferrera and Jessoula (2007), Cotta and Verzichelli (2007), my additions

Table A.4 Definition of variables

Variable	Definition/Coding
Working mom preschool child suffers	A preschool child is likely to suffer if his or her mother works: 1-agree, rather agree; 0-disagree, rather disagree
Working mom warm relationship	A working mother can establish just as warm and secure a relationship with her children as a mother who does not work: 1-disagree, rather disagree; 0-agree, rather agree
Regions (Germany)	Eastern Germany: Mecklenburg-Western Pomerania, Brandenburg, Berlin, Saxony-Anhalt, Saxony, Thuringia Western Germany: Schleswig-Holstein, Hamburg, Bremen, Lower Saxony, North Rhine-Westphalia, Hesse, Rhineland-Palatinate, Saarland, Baden-Wuerttemberg, Bavaria (specified as set of dummies)
Regions (Italy)	Northwest: Piemonte, Lombardia, Liguria Northeast: Trentino Alto Adige, Veneto, Friuli, Emilia-Romagna Central: Toscana, Umbria, Marche, Lazio South: Abbruzzo, Molise, Puglia, Campania, Basilicata, Calabria Islands: Sardegna, Sicilia (specified as set of dummies)
Gender	Dummy: 1-Women; 0-Men
Family status	Single, Married, Widowed, Separated, Divorced (specified as set of dummies)
Employment status	Dummy: 1-Employed; 0-Not employed
Children in household	Dummy: 1-Children in household; 0-No children in household
Age	64 years or older, below 35 years, 35–44 years, 45–54 years, 55–64 years (specified as set of dummies)
Confession (Germany)	Protestant, Catholic, Other denomination, No confession (specified as set of dummies)
Confession (Italy)	Catholic, All other confessions, No confession (specified as set of dummies)
Actively religious	Dummy: 1-Actively religious (attend religious services at least once per month), 0-Not active (attend religious services less than once per month)
Union membership	Dummy: 1-Member, 0-Non-member
Education	Medium education: (upper) secondary education, post-secondary non-tertiary education Low education: pre-primary education or none education, primary education or first stage of basic education, lower secondary or second stage of basic education High education: first or second stage of tertiary education (specified as set of dummies)

Parties (Italy)

1994: Center-left: Partito della Rifondazione Comunista, Partito Socialista Italiano, Partito Democratico della Sinistra, Cristiano Sociali, Radicali, Alleanza Democratica, Lista Pannella, La Rete, Verdi. Center-right: Forza Italia, Partito Repubblicano Italiano, Lega Nord, Alleanza Nazionale, Movimento Sociale Italiano. Other parties: Centro Cristiano Democratico, Partito Popolare Italiano, others.

2001: Center-left: Ulivo, Lista Bonino, Radicali, Lista di Pietro – Italia dei Valori. Center-right: Casa delle libertà, Fiamma tricolore. Other parties: Democrazia Europea – Sergio d'Antoni, others.

2006: Center-left: Rifondazione Comunista, Verdi, Democratici di Sinistra, La Margherita, Socialisti Democratici, Radicali. Center-right: Forza Italia, Lega Nord, Alleanza Nazionale. Other parties: Udeur, UDC, Partito pensionati, others.

2008: Center-left: Sinistra Arcobaleno, Partito Socialista, Partito Democratico, Italia dei Valori. Center-right: Popolo delle Libertà, Lega Nord, La Destra. Other parties: Unione di centro, others.

Source: European Values Study 1990, 1999, 2008; Nachwahlstudie Bundestagswahl 1994; CSES 1998, 2002, 2005, 2009; ITANES 1994, 2001, 2006, 2008

Table A.5 Development of normative beliefs about mothers' employment and childcare

Year	Germany		Italy	
	Child suffers[1]	Warm relationship[2]	Child suffers[1]	Warm relationship[2]
Descriptive statistics: share of progressive beliefs in population				
1990	0.175	0.470	0.222	0.634
1999	0.450	0.755	0.186	0.641
2008	0.498	0.787	0.242	0.692
Pooled logistic regression model: time dummies with year 1990 as reference category[3]				
1999	0.242***	0.219***	−0.044***	0.003
	(0.013)	(0.011)	(0.013)	(0.015)
2008	0.319***	0.259***	0.018	0.075***
	(0.014)	(0.012)	(0.015)	(0.016)

Notes:
1 Measured as disagreement to the statement, "A preschool child is likely to suffer if his or her mother works".
2 Measured as agreement to the statement, "A working mother can establish just as warm and secure a relationship with her children as a mother who does not work".
3 Average marginal effects for probability of having progressive normative beliefs (standard errors in parentheses). Control variables in the regression (effects not shown in table): region, gender, age, employment status, marital status, children, confession, religiosity, union membership, level of education.

*** Significant at 1% level,
** significant at 5% level,
* significant at 10% level.

Source: European Values Study 1990, 1999, 2008; my calculations

Table A.6 Logistic regression, dependent variable: individual attitudes towards mothers' employment and childcare[1], Germany, 1990, 1999, and 2008, average marginal effects (AME) for probability of supporting mothers' employment (standard errors[2] in parentheses)

Variable	1990 AME	Std. Err.[2]	1999 AME	Std. Err.[2]	2008 AME	Std. Err.[2]	Pooled model AME	Std. Err.[2]
Time trend (base = 1990)								
1999							0.246***	(0.013)
2008							0.322***	(0.014)
Region Eastern Germany (base = West)	−0.004	(0.018)	0.300***	(0.027)	0.190***	(0.027)	0.143***	(0.013)
Female (base = male)	0.053***	(0.013)	0.111***	(0.022)	0.170***	(0.022)	0.092***	(0.010)
Marital status (base = single)								
Married	0.008	(0.022)	−0.017	(0.043)	−0.045	(0.037)	−0.016	(0.019)
Widowed	−0.026	(0.033)	0.031	(0.062)	−0.075	(0.052)	−0.045	(0.027)
Separated, divorced	0.082*	(0.038)	−0.011	(0.055)	−0.005	(0.044)	0.030	(0.025)
Employed (base = not employed)	−0.006	(0.018)	0.001	(0.024)	0.052*	(0.026)	−0.017	(0.013)
Children in household (base = no children)	−0.008	(0.021)	−0.012	(0.037)	−0.020	(0.031)	−0.012	(0.016)
Age (base = above 64)								
Below 35	0.093***	(0.025)	0.112*	(0.046)	0.087	(0.043)	0.096***	(0.020)
35–44	0.075**	(0.026)	0.058	(0.043)	0.067	(0.040)	0.073***	(0.020)
45–54	0.050*	(0.025)	0.076	(0.044)	0.006	(0.039)	0.049*	(0.020)
55–64	0.024	(0.023)	0.069	(0.039)	0.072	(0.038)	0.053**	(0.019)
Religious denomination (base = Protestant)								
Catholic	0.012	(0.017)	−0.026	(0.032)	−0.017	(0.032)	−0.004	(0.015)
Other denomination	0.131	(0.088)	−0.166**	(0.053)	0.054	(0.030)	0.009	(0.018)
No religious denomination	0.065***	(0.018)	0.078***	(0.030)	0.195***	(0.039)	0.087***	(0.015)
Actively religious (base = not active)	−0.089***	(0.016)	−0.043	(0.029)	−0.077*	(0.032)	−0.087***	(0.014)
Union membership (base = not a member)	0.014	(0.016)	0.032	(0.039)	0.084*	(0.043)	−0.012	(0.015)

(Continued)

Table A.6 (Continued)

Variable	1990		1999		2008		Pooled model	
	AME	Std. Err.[2]	AME	Std. Err.[2]	AME	Std. Err.[2]	AME	Std. Err.[2]
Education (base: medium)								
Low education	[3]		−0.077**	(0.027)	−0.145***	(0.031)	[3]	
High education	[3]		−0.036	(0.035)	0.091**	(0.028)	[3]	
Uncond. prob. of mothers' employment support	0.175		0.450		0.498			
Log-likelihood	−1,450		−1,098		−1,180		−3,853	
Number of observations	3,288		1,868		1,946		7,125	

Notes:
1 Measured as disagreement to the statement, "A preschool child is likely to suffer if his or her mother works".
2 Huber-White robust standard errors. 3-Variable omitted in regression if it was not asked in the respective year.

*** Significant at 1% level,
** significant at 5% level,
* significant at 10% level.

Source: European Values Study 1990, 1999, 2008; my calculations

Table A.7 Logistic regression, dependent variable: individual attitudes towards mothers' employment and childcare[1], Italy, 1990, 1999 and 2008, average marginal effects (AME) for probability of supporting mothers' employment (standard errors[2] in parentheses)

Variable	1990		1999		2008		Pooled model	
	AME	Std. Err.[2]	AME	Std. Err.[2]	AME	Std. Err.[2]	AME	Std. Err.[2]
Time trend (base = 1990)								
1999							−0.048***	(0.013)
2008							0.014	(0.014)
Region (base = Northwest)								
Northeast	−0.065*	(0.029)	0.005	(0.029)	−0.060	(0.034)	−0.043*	(0.017)
Central	−0.072*	(0.029)	−0.047	(0.026)	−0.014	(0.036)	−0.051**	(0.017)
South	−0.059*	(0.028)	−0.053*	(0.026)	−0.202***	(0.029)	−0.099***	(0.016)
Islands	−0.164***	(0.030)	−0.030	(0.032)	−0.110**	(0.039)	−0.103***	(0.020)
Female (base = male)	0.036	(0.021)	0.045*	(0.019)	0.064**	(0.023)	0.050***	(0.012)
Marital status (base = single)								
Married	−0.034	(0.039)	−0.014	(0.035)	−0.020	(0.042)	−0.027	(0.023)
Widowed	−0.064	(0.055)	−0.045	(0.051)	−0.137*	(0.054)	−0.088**	(0.030)
Separated, divorced	−0.025	(0.064)	0.023	(0.057)	0.048	(0.065)	0.027	(0.037)
Employed (base = not employed)	0.028	(0.023)	0.053*	(0.023)	−0.058*	(0.027)	0.057***	(0.012)
Children in household (base = no children)	−0.022	(0.036)	0.043	(0.030)	−0.039	(0.039)	−0.005	(0.020)
Age (base = above 64)								
Below 35	0.055	(0.039)	0.035	(0.039)	−0.001	(0.043)	0.048*	(0.021)
35–44	0.053	(0.039)	0.041	(0.038)	0.046	(0.043)	0.057**	(0.020)
45–54	−0.011	(0.037)	−0.012	(0.035)	0.070	(0.043)	0.018	(0.019)
55–64	−0.032	(0.036)	−0.017	(0.033)	0.049	(0.041)	0.004	(0.019)
Catholic (base = Non-Catholic)	−0.059*	(0.029)	−0.045	(0.027)	−0.084**	(0.031)	−0.066***	(0.017)
Actively religious (base = not active)	−0.046*	(0.021)	−0.027	(0.021)	−0.024	(0.025)	−0.029*	(0.013)
Union membership (base = no member)	0.070	(0.043)	0.028	(0.038)	−0.035	(0.044)	0.034	(0.025)

(Continued)

Table A.7 (Continued)

Variable	1990 AME	Std. Err.[2]	1999 AME	Std. Err.[2]	2008 AME	Std. Err.[2]	Pooled model AME	Std. Err.[2]
Education (base: medium)								
Low education	[3]		−0.026	(0.025)	−0.101***	(0.025)	[3]	
High education	[3]		0.075**	(0.028)	0.006	(0.030)	[3]	
Uncond. prob. of mothers' employment support	0.222		0.186		0.242			
Log-likelihood	−940		−786		−677		−2,463	
Number of observations	1,850		1,748		1,388		4,986	

Notes:
1 Measured as disagreement to the statement, "A preschool child is likely to suffer if his or her mother works".
2 Huber-White robust standard errors.
3 Variable omitted in regression if it was not asked in the respective year.

*** Significant at 1% level,
** significant at 5% level,
* significant at 10% level.

Source: European Values Study 1990, 1999, 2008; my calculations

Table A.8 Logistic regression, dependent variable: individual beliefs towards mothers' employment and childcare[1], Germany, 1990, 1999 and 2008, average marginal effects (AME) for probability of supporting mothers' employment (standard errors[2] in parentheses)

Variable	1990		1999		2008		Pooled model	
	AME	Std. Err.[2]	AME	Std. Err.[2]	AME	Std. Err.[2]	AME	Std. Err.[2]
Time trend (base = 1990)								
1999							0.221***	(0.011)
2008							0.260***	(0.012)
Region Eastern Germany (base = West)	0.080***	(0.023)	0.205***	(0.023)	0.125***	(0.022)	0.143***	(0.013)
Female (base = male)	0.114***	(0.018)	0.088***	(0.020)	0.086***	(0.019)	0.092***	(0.011)
Family status (base = single)								
Married	0.062*	(0.031)	−0.020	(0.039)	−0.014	(0.031)	0.018	(0.020)
Widowed	−0.053	(0.043)	−0.009	(0.052)	−0.029	(0.043)	−0.043	(0.028)
Separated, divorced	0.121**	(0.047)	−0.010	(0.050)	−0.017	(0.038)	0.050	(0.026)
Employed (base = not employed)	−0.015	(0.023)	0.051*	(0.022)	0.030	(0.023)	−0.023	(0.017)
Children in household (base = no children)	−0.026	(0.027)	−0.018	(0.033)	−0.026	(0.026)	−0.024	(0.017)
Age (base = above 64)								
Below 35	0.085*	(0.036)	0.042	(0.039)	0.021	(0.037)	0.065**	(0.021)
35–44	0.055	(0.037)	−0.039	(0.038)	0.062	(0.033)	0.042*	(0.021)
45–54	0.005	(0.035)	0.049	(0.037)	0.025	(0.034)	0.034	(0.021)
55–64	−0.069*	(0.033)	0.037	(0.032)	0.016	(0.032)	−0.006	(0.021)
Religious denomination (base = Protestant)								
Catholic	0.036	(0.022)	−0.087***	(0.026)	−0.029	(0.026)	−0.013	(0.014)
Other denomination	−0.047	(0.093)	−0.157**	(0.049)	0.084***	(0.025)	0.039	(0.022)
No denomination	0.096***	(0.024)	0.030	(0.025)	0.111***	(0.031)	0.069***	(0.015)
Actively religious (base = not active)	−0.128***	(0.022)	−0.057*	(0.024)	−0.056*	(0.026)	−0.103***	(0.014)
Union membership (base = no member)	0.013	(0.021)	−0.065	(0.037)	0.045	(0.033)	−0.023	(0.015)

(*Continued*)

Table A.8 (Continued)

Variable	1990		1999		2008		Pooled model	
	AME	Std. Err.[2]	AME	Std. Err.[2]	AME	Std. Err.[2]	AME	Std. Err.[2]
Education (base: medium)								
Low education	[3]		−0.044*	(0.022)	−0.061*	(0.027)	[3]	
High education	[3]		0.076*	(0.031)	0.038	(0.023)	[3]	
Uncond. prob. of mothers' employm. support	0.470	(0.500)	0.755	(0.430)	0.787	(0.409)		
Log-likelihood	−2,134		−899		−920			
Number of observations	3,268		1,900		1,983		7174	

Notes:
1 Measured as agreement to the statement, "A working mother can establish just as warm and secure a relationship with her children as a mother who does not work".
2 Huber-White robust standard errors.
3 Variable omitted in regression if it was not asked in the respective year.

*** Significant at 1% level,
** significant at 5% level,
* significant at 10% level.

Source: European Values Study 1990, 1999, 2008; my calculations

Table A.9 Logistic regression, dependent variable: individual beliefs towards mothers' employment and childcare[1], Italy, 1990, 1999 and 2008, average marginal effects for probability of supporting mothers' employment (standard errors[2] in parentheses)

	1990		1999		2008		Pooled model	
Variable	AME	Std. Err.[2]	AME	Std. Err.[2]	AME	Std. Err.[2]	AME	Std. Err.[2]
Time trend (base = 1990)								
1999							0.001	(0.015)
2008							0.063***	(0.016)
Region (base = Northwest)								
Northeast	0.038	(0.032)	−0.023	(0.033)	−0.104**	(0.035)	−0.022	(0.019)
Central	0.037	(0.031)	−0.074*	(0.032)	−0.074*	(0.035)	−0.037	(0.019)
South	−0.066*	(0.031)	−0.106**	(0.032)	−0.202***	(0.034)	−0.117***	(0.019)
Islands	−0.131**	(0.041)	0.003	(0.038)	−0.147***	(0.044)	−0.090***	(0.024)
Female (base = male)	0.074**	(0.024)	0.134***	(0.024)	0.090***	(0.025)	0.103***	(0.014)
Family status (base = single)								
Married	−0.075	(0.045)	0.014	(0.046)	0.039	(0.049)	−0.005	(0.027)
Widowed	−0.166*	(0.065)	−0.029	(0.063)	−0.023	(0.069)	−0.093*	(0.039)
Separated, divorced	−0.042	(0.077)	−0.027	(0.075)	0.088	(0.069)	0.027	(0.043)
Employed (base = not employed)	0.089**	(0.028)	0.082**	(0.028)	0.014	(0.031)	0.095***	(0.014)
Children in household (base = no children)	−0.014	(0.042)	−0.010	(0.041)	−0.023	(0.045)	−0.034	(0.025)
Age (base = above 64)								
Below 35	0.099*	(0.045)	0.034	(0.046)	0.008	(0.052)	0.074**	(0.027)
35–44	0.038	(0.045)	−0.028	(0.046)	0.034	(0.046)	0.023	(0.026)
45–54	−0.032	(0.044)	0.039	(0.043)	0.071	(0.044)	0.023	(0.026)
55–64	0.020	(0.041)	−0.027	(0.038)	0.054	(0.042)	0.011	(0.024)
Catholic (base = non-Catholic)	−0.041	(0.032)	0.006	(0.032)	0.004	(0.034)	−0.022	(0.019)
Actively religious (base = not active)	0.009	(0.024)	−0.048	(0.025)	−0.011	(0.027)	−0.012	(0.015)
Union membership (base = no member)	0.051	(0.045)	0.019	(0.045)	−0.023	(0.053)	0.029	(0.027)

(*Continued*)

Table A.9 (Continued)

Variable	1990		1999		2008		Pooled model	
	AME	Std. Err.[2]	AME	Std. Err.[2]	AME	Std. Err.[2]	AME	Std. Err.[2]
Education (base: medium)								
Low education	[3]		−0.096**	(0.031)	−0.154***	(0.030)	[3]	
High education	[3]		0.150***	(0.032)	0.039	(0.037)	[3]	
Uncond. prob. of mothers' employm. support	0.634	(0.482)	0.641	(0.480)	0.692	(0.462)		
Log-likelihood	−1,185		−1,087		−804			
Number of observations	1,889		1,760		1,393		5042	

Notes:
1 Measured as agreement to the statement, "A working mother can establish just as warm and secure a relationship with her children as a mother who does not work".
2 Huber-White robust standard errors.
3 Variable omitted in regression if it was not asked in the respective year.

*** Significant at 1% level,
** significant at 5% level,
* significant at 10% level.

Source: European Values Study 1990, 1999, 2008; my calculations

Table A.10 Logistic regression, dependent variable: individual attitudes towards mothers' employment and childcare[1], Germany, 1991, 1992, 1996, 2000, 2004, 2008, average marginal effects (AME) for probability of supporting mothers' employment (standard errors[2] in parentheses), pooled models[3]

Time trend (base = 1991)	Germany		Western Germany		Eastern Germany	
	AME	Std. Err.[2]	AME	Std. Err.[2]	AME	Std. Err.[2]
1992	0.022	(0.012)	0.015	(0.013)	0.047	(0.025)
1996	0.032**	(0.012)	0.013	(0.013)	0.084***	(0.024)
2000	0.087***	(0.012)	0.068***	(0.013)	0.145***	(0.023)
2004	0.183***	(0.012)	0.156***	(0.014)	0.255***	(0.022)
2008	0.237***	(0.012)	0.214***	(0.014)	0.295***	(0.020)
East Germany (Dummy)	0.215***	(0.010)				
Number of observations	19638		12700		6938	

Notes:
1 Measured as disagreement to the statement, "A preschool child is likely to suffer if his or her mother works".
2 Huber-White robust standard errors.
3 Controlled for sex, region, employment status, marital status, children in household, age, confession, religious practice, education.

*** Significant at 1% level,
** significant at 5% level,
* significant at 10% level.

Source: ALLBUS 1991, 1992, 1996, 2000, 2004 & 2008; my calculations

Table A.11 Multinomial logistic regression, dependent variable: voting behavior, Germany, 1994–2009, average marginal effects (AME) for probability of voting for 'FDP' (standard error¹ in parentheses)

	1994		1998		2002		2005		2009	
	AME	Std. Err.	AME	Std. Err.	AME	Std. Err.	AME	Std. Err.	AME	Std. Err.
Region Western Germany (base = East)	−0.006	(0.012)	0.026*	(0.013)	0.030*	(0.013)	−0.010	(0.018)	0.052*	(0.026)
Female (base = male)	−0.022	(0.012)	0.005	(0.012)	−0.026	(0.014)	−0.036*	(0.017)	−0.056**	(0.020)
Marital status (base = single)										
Married	0.017	(0.020)	−0.007	(0.016)	0.025	(0.020)	−0.060	(0.041)	0.047	(0.032)
Widowed	0.032	(0.026)	0.006	(0.026)	0.054	(0.032)	−0.079	(0.047)	0.011	(0.047)
Separated, divorced	−0.011	(0.034)	−0.027	(0.027)	−0.011	(0.031)	−0.069	(0.043)	0.002	(0.044)
Employed (base = not employed)	0.005	(0.013)	−0.003	(0.014)	0.006	(0.015)	0.008	(0.019)	−0.019	(0.024)
Children in household (base = no children)	−0.012	(0.016)	0.002	(0.015)	−0.023	(0.020)	−0.012	(0.025)	−0.027	(0.028)
Age (base = above 64)										
Below 35	0.019	(0.026)	−0.007	(0.024)	0.072*	(0.032)	0.040	(0.036)	0.041	(0.042)
35–44	0.021	(0.024)	−0.039	(0.027)	0.065*	(0.030)	0.023	(0.036)	0.065	(0.040)
45–54	0.014	(0.022)	−0.022	(0.026)	0.060*	(0.027)	−0.004	(0.034)	0.014	(0.039)
55–64	0.021	(0.018)	−0.029	(0.024)	0.064**	(0.024)	−0.023	(0.034)	0.008	(0.033)
Religious denomination (base = Protestant)										
Catholic	−0.013	(0.014)	−0.016	(0.015)	−0.017	(0.018)	0.028	(0.022)	0.046	(0.024)
Other denomination	−0.549	(25.095)	0.057	(1.915)	0.061	(0.035)	−1.445	(52.145)	−0.016	(0.037)
No denomination	−0.035	(0.018)	−0.000	(0.018)	0.005	(0.015)	−0.014	(0.019)	0.014	(0.034)
Religious activities (base = never in church)										
Sometimes in church	0.015	(0.015)	0.035*	(0.016)	−0.016	(0.025)	0.000	(0.029)	0.020	(0.027)
Frequently in church	0.027	(0.020)	0.044*	(0.020)	0.116	(4.646)	−1.421	(91.534)	0.016	(0.040)

Union membership (base: not a member)	−0.040*	(0.019)	−0.032	(0.020)	−0.021	(0.018)	−0.108***	(0.031)	−0.033	(0.030)
Education (base: low education)										
Low secondary education	0.028*	(0.013)	0.004	(0.017)	−0.008	(0.018)	0.040	(0.022)	0.058*	(0.025)
High secondary education	0.007	(0.022)	0.034	(0.017)	0.014	(0.020)	−0.003	(0.030)	0.123***	(0.031)
Tertiary education	−0.023	(0.025)	0.040*	(0.020)	−0.013	(0.019)	−0.001	(0.027)	0.094**	(0.031)
Unconditional probability of voting for FDP[2]	0.043		0.065		0.082		0.112		0.159	
Pseudo R-squared	0.145		0.133		0.096		0.072		0.089	
Log-likelihood	−1,641		−1,850		−2,224		−2,419		−2,010	
Number of observations	1,455		1,597		1,767		1,763		1,480	

Notes:
[1] White/Huber robust standard errors.
[2] Please note that the results do not always reproduce the official election results exactly, because the applied weights adjust for the demographic structure, not for the election result.

*** Significant at 1% level,
** significant at 5% level,
* significant at 10% level.

Sources: Nachwahlstudie Bundestagswahl 1994; CSES 1998, 2002, 2005, 2009; my calculations

Table A.12 Multinomial logistic regression, dependent variable: voting behavior, Germany, 1994–2009, average marginal effects (AME) for probability of voting for "Greens" (standard error [1] in parentheses)

	1994		1998		2002		2005		2009	
	AME	Std. Err.	AME	Std. Err.	AME	Std. Err.	AME	Std. Err.	AME	Std. Err.
Region Western Germany (base = East)	0.082***	(0.017)	0.049**	(0.015)	0.075***	(0.017)	0.038*	(0.016)	0.063**	(0.023)
Female (base = male)	0.031*	(0.015)	0.012	(0.014)	0.017	(0.016)	0.025	(0.015)	0.031	(0.017)
Marital status (base = single)										
Married	−0.050*	(0.022)	−0.018	(0.018)	−0.066**	(0.024)	−0.056	(0.040)	−0.029	(0.025)
Widowed	−0.105	(0.056)	−0.011	(0.047)	−0.025	(0.041)	−0.029	(0.044)	−0.044	(0.044)
Separated, divorced	−0.038	(0.031)	0.050*	(0.023)	−0.006	(0.031)	−0.012	(0.041)	−0.047	(0.035)
Employed (base = not employed)	−0.020	(0.016)	−0.012	(0.016)	−0.025	(0.019)	−0.018	(0.017)	0.038	(0.020)
Children in household (base = no children)	−0.012	(0.019)	0.012	(0.017)	0.048*	(0.024)	−0.033	(0.024)	0.019	(0.022)
Age (base = above 64)										
Below 35	0.078	(0.044)	0.088*	(0.040)	0.017	(0.038)	0.078*	(0.037)	0.063	(0.038)
35–44	0.095*	(0.043)	0.069	(0.040)	0.035	(0.036)	0.109**	(0.036)	0.055	(0.037)
45–54	0.081	(0.042)	0.036	(0.042)	0.052	(0.034)	0.073*	(0.036)	0.040	(0.036)
55–64	0.054	(0.043)	0.028	(0.040)	0.060	(0.031)	0.067	(0.035)	0.014	(0.035)
Religious denomination (base = Protestant)										
Catholic	0.005	(0.019)	−0.002	(0.018)	0.021	(0.021)	−0.052*	(0.022)	−0.051*	(0.021)
Other denomination	0.027	(1.869)	0.106	(4.057)	0.014	(0.059)	0.191	(5.744)	−0.033	(0.030)
No denomination	−0.003	(0.021)	−0.028	(0.019)	0.035	(0.019)	0.003	(0.017)	−0.029	(0.027)
Religious activities (base = never in church)										
Sometimes in church	−0.030	(0.019)	−0.045**	(0.017)	0.048	(0.026)	0.029	(0.028)	−0.012	(0.021)
Frequently in church	−0.029	(0.033)	−0.040	(0.024)	0.012	(7.898)	0.223	(10.083)	−0.030	(0.039)

	(1)		(2)		(3)		(4)		(5)	
Union membership (base: not a member)	−0.011	(0.017)	0.009	(0.018)	−0.000	(0.021)	−0.003	(0.022)	−0.006	(0.024)
Education (base: low education)										
Low secondary education	0.086***	(0.024)	0.056	(0.029)	−0.011	(0.028)	−0.023	(0.022)	0.039	(0.023)
High secondary education	0.131***	(0.026)	0.142***	(0.029)	0.117***	(0.027)	0.058*	(0.024)	0.048	(0.028)
Tertiary education	0.152***	(0.026)	0.153***	(0.029)	0.108***	(0.026)	0.079***	(0.022)	0.091***	(0.026)
Uncond. probability of voting for Greens [2]	0.086		0.076		0.122		0.099		0.118	
Pseudo R-squared	0.145		0.133		0.096		0.072		0.089	
Log-likelihood	−1,641		−1,850		−2,224		−2,419		−2,014	
Number of observations	1,455		1,597		1,767		1,763		1,480	

Notes:
1 White/Huber robust standard errors.
2 Please note that the results do not always reproduce the official election results exactly, because the applied weights adjust for the demographic structure, not for the election result.
*** Significant at 1% level,
** significant at 5% level,
* significant at 10% level.

Sources: Nachwahlstudie Bundestagswahl 1994; CSES 1998, 2002, 2005, 2009; my calculations

Table A.13 Multinomial logistic regression, dependent variable: voting behavior, Germany, 1994–2009, average marginal effects (AME) for probability of voting for 'Die Linke' (standard error[1] in parentheses)

	1994		1998		2002		2005		2009	
	AME	Std. Err.	AME	Std. Err.	AME	Std. Err.	AME	Std. Err.	AME	Std. Err.
Region Western Germany (base = East)	−0.110***	(0.025)	−0.214***	(0.031)	−0.157***	(0.024)	−0.108***	(0.020)	−0.082***	(0.023)
Female (base = male)	−0.009	(0.016)	−0.015	(0.015)	0.007	(0.014)	−0.017	(0.017)	−0.001	(0.019)
Marital status (base = single)										
Married	−0.011	(0.027)	−0.014	(0.021)	0.008	(0.022)	0.033	(0.053)	−0.022	(0.031)
Widowed	−0.009	(0.037)	−0.013	(0.039)	−0.009	(0.032)	0.042	(0.056)	−0.031	(0.043)
Separated, divorced	−0.020	(0.036)	0.016	(0.026)	0.004	(0.027)	0.048	(0.055)	0.041	(0.038)
Employed (base = not employed)	−0.024	(0.019)	−0.028	(0.018)	−0.034*	(0.016)	−0.024	(0.020)	−0.051*	(0.024)
Children in household (base = no children)	−0.002	(0.024)	0.009	(0.019)	0.009	(0.022)	−0.001	(0.026)	−0.014	(0.029)
Age (base = above 64)										
Below 35	−0.019	(0.037)	−0.030	(0.035)	−0.099**	(0.032)	−0.043	(0.040)	0.046	(0.041)
35–44	−0.021	(0.035)	0.012	(0.035)	−0.076**	(0.028)	−0.015	(0.038)	0.038	(0.040)
45–54	−0.040	(0.031)	−0.014	(0.034)	−0.055*	(0.024)	0.051	(0.034)	0.033	(0.035)
55–64	−0.016	(0.025)	−0.021	(0.031)	0.004	(0.020)	0.026	(0.033)	0.003	(0.032)
Religious denomination (base = Protestant)										
Catholic	−0.012	(0.047)	−0.061	(0.043)	−0.073	(0.043)	−0.041	(0.033)	−0.001	(0.030)
Other denomination	0.102	(1.573)	−0.951	(38.404)	0.009	(0.074)	0.249	(8.371)	0.084**	(0.033)
No denomination	0.138***	(0.034)	0.031	(0.020)	0.073***	(0.015)	0.088***	(0.019)	0.040	(0.031)
Religious activities (base = never in church)										
Sometimes in church	−0.006	(0.040)	−0.059**	(0.020)	0.018	(0.026)	−0.016	(0.032)	−0.096***	(0.027)
Frequently in church	−0.028	(0.063)	−0.125**	(0.047)	−0.875	(64.342)	0.292	(14.695)	−0.171**	(0.054)

Union membership (base: not a member)	0.047**	(0.017)	−0.001	(0.019)	0.042**	(0.015)	0.048*	(0.022)	0.100***	(0.024)
Education (base: low education)										
Low secondary education	0.017	(0.021)	0.022	(0.024)	0.078***	(0.023)	0.033	(0.023)	−0.030	(0.023)
High secondary education	0.069**	(0.026)	0.036	(0.026)	0.084**	(0.026)	−0.039	(0.034)	−0.052	(0.034)
Tertiary education	0.073***	(0.022)	0.079**	(0.026)	0.073**	(0.023)	−0.013	(0.029)	−0.031	(0.031)
Uncond. probability of voting for Left Party[2]	0.099		0.047		0.038		0.085		0.121	
Pseudo R-squared	0.145		0.133		0.096		0.072		0.089	
Log-likelihood	−1,641		−1,850		−2,224		−2,419		−2,014	
Number of observations	1,455		1,597		1,767		1,763		1,480	

Notes:

1 White/Huber robust standard errors.

2 Please note that the results do not always reproduce the official election results exactly, because the applied weights adjust for the demographic structure, not for the election result.

*** Significant at 1% level,
** significant at 5% level,
* significant at 10% level.

Sources: Nachwahlstudie Bundestagswahl 1994; CSES 1998, 2002, 2005, 2009; my calculations

Table A.14 Multinomial logistic regression, average marginal effects (AME) for probability of preferring the SPD/left-wing coalition and the CDU/right-wing coalition[1] of people having progressive normative beliefs[2] in Germany and Italy, 1990, 1999 and 2008 (standard errors[3] in parentheses)

Party/Coalition[4]	1990		1999		2008	
	AME	Std. Err.	AME	Std. Err.	AME	Std. Err.
Germany: SPD	0.015	(0.024)	0.095**	(0.029)	−0.014	(0.027)
Germany: CDU/CSU	−0.070**	(0.025)	−0.041	(0.032)	−0.055*	(0.028)
Italy: Left-wing coalition	0.031	(0.033)	0.108**	(0.041)	0.074	(0.043)
Italy: Right-wing coalition	−0.001	(0.017)	−0.095*	(0.043)	−0.054	(0.035)

Notes:
1 Respondents' answer to the question, "If there was a general election tomorrow, which party would you vote for?"
2 Measured as agreement to the statement, "A preschool child is likely to suffer if his or her mother works".
3 Huber-White robust standard errors.
4 Control variables in the regression (effects not shown in table): region, gender, age, employment status, marital status, children, confession, religiosity, union membership, level of education.

*** Significant at 1% level,
** significant at 5% level,
* significant at 10% level.

Source: European Values Survey 1990, 1999, 2008; my calculations

Index

abortion 88, 90, 152
actor-centered theory 22, 33–4
advocacy groups 23, 208
ALLBUS 138n9
allowances for children *see* children's allowances
assistantes maternelles 59, 74n21
Austria: childcare provision 60, 61*t*, 62*t*, 64*t*, 65, 66–7, 66*t*; flexible work time arrangements 54, 57, 58; taxation system 68*t*, 69; work-family policies 72

baby bonus 196n39
Belgium: childcare provision 60, 61*t*, 62*t*, 63, 64*t*, 66*t*, 67; flexible work time arrangements 54, 57, 58; taxation system 68*t*; work-family policies 71
Benelux states 54; *see also* Belgium; Luxembourg; Netherlands
Bergmann, Christine 154
Berlusconi, Silvio 116
Biagi reform 189
Bindi, Rosy 192
Böhmer, Maria 160
budget austerity 36n2, 186, 215

cabinets, women in 146–8, 146*t*; *see also* government, women in
care culture 23
care ideal 4, 23, 114
career-break schemes 58
Catholic Church 15, 23; and private kindergarten 88; influence on politics 118, 128, 132, 134, 192, 197n51
Catholic political parties 190
CCD *see* Christian Democratic Center
CDU *see* Christian Democratic Party (*Christlich Demokratische Union Deutschlands, CDU*, in Germany); Christian Democratic Party (Partito dei Cristiano Democratici, CDU, in Italy)

CDU Women's Union (*Frauen Union*) 162, 164, 167–9
Child and Youth Aid Act (KHJG) 161
Child Support Law (*Kinderförderungsgesetz*, Kifög) 97
childcare allowance (*Betreuungsgeld*) 167, 169, 204, 214
childcare provisions 22, 51–2, 165–7; affordability 63–5; availability 59–63, 61*t*, 62*t*; for children younger than three 160–2; crèches 88, 103, 188, 196nn46–7; daycare centers 8, 151; day nurseries 59, 74n19; debate in Italy 88, 179–80; in East Germany 93; family day care 59–60, 74n21; in Germany 60, 61*t*, 62*t*, 63, 64*t*, 66*t*, 66–7, 75n27, 96–7, 97*t*, 152; in Italy 100–4, 101*t*, 184–5, 188–9; private 35, 47, 49, 60, 63–4, 74n22, 100–2, 108n43, 109n56, 161; public 1–3, 9–10, 26, 29, 35, 47–8, 51–2, 63–7, 74n22, 87, 88, 90, 94, 97*t*, 100, 101*t*, 102–4, 106n17, 109n56, 114, 152–3, 157, 160, 165, 167, 169, 184, 185, 191, 194n12, 204, 213; quality, 65–7; regional variations in 97*t*, 101*t*
childcare workers 35, 59, 74n21, 87, 97, 150–1
children: legal rights of 92; legal status of 87; legislation supporting 191; *see also* childcare provisions; children's allowances
children's allowances 52–3, 67–8, 70; in Germany 105n5, 154, 157; in Italy 85; in West Germany 83, 86, 87; *see also* childcare allowance; family allowances
Christian Democratic Center (*Centro Cristiano Democratico*, CCD) 117
Christian-democratic parties 25–8, 31, 90–2, 115, 117; and policy reform 31; and the role of women 25, 28;

246 Index

supporting the work-family approach 2–3, 26–8; and the values cleavage 25–6
Christian Democratic Party (*Christlich Demokratische Union Deutschlands, CDU*, in Germany) 3, 4, 12, 15, 17n1, 26, 28, 90–2, 115–16, 129–31, 134, 137n3, 160, 165, 168, 208, 210; coalition with FDP 149; constituencies of 136, 153; on family policies 157–8, 162–70; on parental leave 150–1; shrinking share of votes 129–30, 131*f*; Women's Union (*Frauen Union*) 162, 164, 167–9
Christian Democratic Party (*Partito dei Cristiano Democratici Uniti, CDU*, in Italy) 117, 179
Christian Democrats (*Democrazia Cristiana, DC*, in Italy) 116–17, 118, 179
Christlich Demokratische Union Deutschlands see Christian Democratic Party (CDU, in Germany)
Christlich Soziale Union (CSU) 121, 135, 157–8, 164–9, 208, 214
church-state cleavage 25, 36n3
citizenship theory 47
civil union 192, 200
CME (Coordinated Market Economics) 35
cohabiting couples 191, 200
Communist party: in Germany 12, 137n3; in Italy 116–17, 179, 181
Communist Refoundation Party (*Partito della Rifondazione Comunista, PRC*) 116
Comparative Study of Electoral Systems (CSES) 120–1
Confederazione Italiana Sindacati Lavoratori (CISL) 184
conservative parties 26–7; constituencies of 24–7, 31, 122–3, 131; in Germany 150–1, 155–7, 161–2, 164, 168; in Italy 116, 180, 193; support for work-family policies, 31–2, 201; women voting for 122, 150, 161, 193, 208–9, 211; and the welfare state 9, 24, 212, 214; *see also* right-wing parties
Convention of Herrenchiemsee 82
Coordinated Market Economies (CME) 35
crèches 88, 103, 188, 196nn46–7
CSES (Comparative Study of Electoral Systems) 120–1
CSU *see Christlich Soziale Union (CSU)*

data sources 14
day-care centers 8, 151; *see also* childcare provisions

Day-Care Expansion Act (*Tagesbetreuungsausbaugesetz*, TAG) 96–7, 160
daycare provisions *see* childcare provisions
day nurseries 59, 74n19; *see also* childcare provisions
DC *see* Christian Democrats
decentralization 9, 185, 205
decommodification 22
defamilization 47–8
Deligöz, Ekin 165
Democracy and Liberty – the Marguerite (*Democrazia e libertà – La Margherita, DL*) 117
Democratic Party of the Left (*Democratici di Sinistra, DS*) 116, 118, 190
Denmark: childcare provision 61, 61*t*, 62*t*, 64*t*, 65, 66–7, 66*t*, 74nn25–6; flexible work time arrangements 54, 57; taxation system 68*t*; work-family policies 71
Die Linke (the Left) 115, 121, 214
discourses, study of 211
divorce 88, 106n20
DL *see* Democracy and Liberty – the Marguerite
DS *see* Democratic Party of the Left
dual-earner model 47, 70*f*, 73n5, 164, 169, 182; in Germany 3, 94, 103, 200–1, 213; lack of support for 149, 152; state support for 24; steps toward 155; support for 122–3, 136
dynamic representation 23, 209

East Germany: childcare provisions 93; socialist education 92–3; women in the labor force 92–3; *see also* Germany
Eimer, Norbert 151
Elterngeld 164–5
empirical analyses 15; age 122–3, 127–8, 130–1, 134; education 123, 129, 132, 134, 136, 137n2; employment 122, 127; explanatory variables 121; marital status and children in household 122, 127; multinomial logistic regression 135*f*; normative beliefs about mother's employment 119–20, 124–9; region of residence 121; religious denomination and religious activity 123, 128, 131–2, 133*t*, 134, 136; sex 122, 126–8, 130, 134, 136–7; union membership 123–4, 132, 134; voting behavior 120–1
employment, precarious 182; *see also* part-time employment
employment rates of women, Germany vs. Italy 6, 7*f*

Index 247

European Union 10, 23, 58, 99, 103, 184
European Value Survey (EVS) 119, 125, 132

family, support for 118, 154–5; *see also* marriage, and family
family allowances 48, 84–5, 91–2, 157, 162; *see also* children's allowances
family day care 59–60, 74n21
family law reform: in Italy 87–8; in West Germany 86–7
family planning clinics 88
family policies: changes in 154–5; and political party competition 156; in the 2002 election campaign 157–8; after the 2002 election 158–60; in the 2005 elections 162–3; after 2005 163–9; sustainable 158–60, 172n31, 214; day care for children younger than three 160–2; *see also* work-family policies
fascism 15, 34
FDP *see* Free Democratic Party
Federal Republic of Germany (FRG) *see* West Germany
federalism 8, 116, 165, 186–7
feminism, "abstract" 179
feminist issues 29
feminist scholarship 47
feminist theories of representation 29
fertility rates of women, Germany vs. Italy 6, 7*f*
Fiamma Tricolore 116
Finland: childcare provision 61, 61*t*, 62*t*, 64*t*, 65, 66*t*, 67, 74n23; flexible work time arrangements 54, 57, 58; taxation system 68*t*, 69; work-family policies 72
Fiorino, Giuseppe 185
Forza Italia (FI) 116, 117, 118, 179
France 28; childcare provision in 60, 61*t*, 62*t*, 63, 64*t*, 65, 66*t*, 67; flexible work time arrangements in 54, 57; taxation system 68*t*, 69; work-family policies in 72
Frauen Union (CDU Women's Union) 162, 164, 167–9
Free Democratic Party (FDP) 115, 143
FRG (Federal Republic of Germany) *see* West Germany
functionalist theories 4, 22, 33–4

gay couples 192, 200
GDP per capita 10*f*
gender consciousness 30
gender equality 34, 83, 88, 91, 93, 150, 152, 162, 170n8

gender quotas 142–3, 148n1
gender relations 22
gender roles 4, 27
German Civil Code 82–3
German Democratic Republic (GDR) *see* East Germany
German legislation: Alliance for the Family 158; childcare allowance 167–8, 174n51; Day Care Expansion Act 160; *Elterngeld* 164–5; on the financing of childcare 165–6; legal right to childcare 164, 167, 169; parental leave reform 159–60, 164–5; reform of federalism 165–6; reform of the German Child and Youth Aid Act (KHJG) 161
German Longitudinal Election Study (GLES) 212–13
German work-family policy reform 2, 5, 71, 136, 149–50, 169–70, 202–3, 212–14; male-breadwinner model (1990–1998) 150–3; shift in work-family policy (1998–2002) 153–5; party competition and initial reforms (2002–2005) 156–63; under the grand coalition (after 2005) 163–9
Germany: analysis of voting behavior 129–32; as coordinated market economy 11; as frozen landscape 8; childcare provision 60, 61*t*, 62*t*, 63, 64*t*, 66*t*, 66–7, 75n27, 96–7, 152; children's allowances (*Kinderzuschlag*) 67–8, 105n5; compared to Italy 3, 6, 7*f*, 103–4, 104*t*, 114, 201, 205; division of competencies 8–9; dual-earner model 94, 103; flexible work time arrangements 54, 57, 59, 95–6; GDP per capita 10*f*; male-breadwinner model 103–4; normative role of mother 1–2, 5, 114, 119–26, 129–30, 134–7, 153, 155, 158, 163, 168, 202–3; parental leave 94–6; parliamentary election results 115*t*; part-time legislation 58; party system 114–16; policy developments 15; regional variations in childcare 97*t*; reunification of 94, 132, 152; taxation system 68*t*, 68–9, 154; welfare regime 9–10; women as MPs 143, 144*f*, 145*f*; women in cabinets 146, 146*t*; *see also* East Germany; German legislation; German work-family policy reform; West Germany
globalization 33
government, women in 22–3, 143–6, 154; *see also* cabinets, women in; parliament, women in

grand coalition 4, 12, 16, 24, 115, 134, 143, 163, 169, 203, 204, 206, 208
Greece: childcare provision 60, 61*t*, 62*t*, 64*t*, 65, 66, 66*t*; children's allowances 67–8; flexible work time arrangements 54, 57, 58; taxation system 68, 68*t*, 69; work-family policies 2
Greens 115; coalition with SPD 153, 156, 159–60

housing subsidies 83

income inequality 33
income splitting 68–9, 75n31, 83, 86
institutional theories 4, 6, 22, 35
Ireland: childcare provision 61*t*, 62*t*, 63, 64*t*, 65, 66, 66*t*; flexible work time arrangements 54, 57; taxation system 68*t*; work-family policies 71
Italian legislation: on childcare provision 184–5, 188–91, 204; law 53/2000 194n14; on part-time workers and reduced working hours 183–4, 189, 194n14; Provision for the Support of Mother- and Fatherhood, for the Right to Care and Education and for the Coordination of City Times 181–3, 194n6; Provisions of the Promotion of Rights of Childhood and Adolescence 184–5; supporting family and childcare 185–6, 192, 194n12, 204
Italian National Election Studies (ITANES) 121
Italian People's Party (*Partito Popolare Italiano, PPI*) 117
Italian work-family policy reform 16, 72, 85–6, 178–9, 192–3; neglect of the issue (1994–1996) 179–80; movement toward reconciliation policies (1996–2001) 180–7; curtailing the progress of reforms (2001–2006) 187–90; new reform initiatives (2006–2008) 190–2
Italy: analysis of voting behavior 132–5; center-left party bloc voting 132*f*, 136; center-right party bloc voting 133*f*, 134, 136; childcare provision 60, 61*t*, 62*t*, 63–4, 64*t*, 66, 66*t*, 88–9, 100–4; children's allowances 67, 85; compared to Germany 3, 6, 7*f*, 94, 103–4, 104*t*, 114, 201, 205; compared to West Germany 86, 89–90; as frozen landscape 8; debt ratio 11; development of the Italian executive 118*t*; division of competencies 8–9; family law reform 87–8; flexible work time arrangements 54, 57, 58–9, 99–100;
GDP per capita 10*f*; labor rights 103; male-breadwinner model 84–6, 91–2, 94, 103; new reform initiatives 190; normative role of mother 1–2, 5, 90, 178, 180, 181, 187, 193, 201–5; parental leave 3, 73n14, 98–9, 103–4; parliamentary elections 117*t*; party system 116–19, 179; reasons for slower work-family policy reform 136–7; regional variations in childcare 101*t*; social services in 185–6; taxation system 68*t*, 69, 89; welfare regime 9–10; women as MPs 143, 144*f*, 145*f*; women in cabinets 146–7, 147*t*; working time flexibility 99–100; *see also* Italian legislation; Italian work-family policy reform

kindergartens 8, 87–8, 90, 96, 150
Kohl, Helmut 116

l'Unione (center-left coalition) 190–91, 196n44
La Margherita 116, 117, 118, 190
labor rights, in Italy 3, 103
leave regulations 50–1, 53–7; *see also* parental leave
leftist parties, 2, 24–6, 31–3, 36n2, 122, 130, 159, 165, 179–80, 185, 188, 209–11; *see also* left-wing parties
left-wing parties: competing with Christian-democratic 28; in Germany 28, 115, 159, 165, 202; in Italy 100, 116, 118, 121, 136, 143, 146–7, 179–81, 183, 187, 196n44, 200, 204–5, 207–8, 211; and the libertarian vote 26; and social equality 123; and union membership 134; and the working class 25; and women's votes 122, 145–6, 206–8; *see also* left-wing parties
Lega Nord 116, 118, 121, 179
Liberal Market Economies (LME) 35, 37n14
liberal parties 27, 116, 122, 214
libertarian parties 25–6, 122–3, 156, 158, 163, 168, 203, 204, 205, 210, 213, 215, 216n2
Linkspartei.PDS 115, 165
Lisbon Strategy 23
Luxembourg: childcare provision in 60, 61*t*, 62*t*, 63, 64*t*, 66*t*; flexible work time arrangements in 54, 57; taxation system 68*t*; work-family policies in 71

male-breadwinner model 2–3, 15, 34, 47–8, 70*f*, 73n5, 169; in Germany 103–4, 152; Germany's move away

from 201; in Italy 84–6, 94, 103, 186–8; in West Germany 81–4; support for 122–3, 149
marriage and family: in Italy 192; in West Germany 82–3
Mastella, Clemence 192
maternity leave 29, 53–4, 55f, 89, 105n10, 173n43; in Italy 85, 98; replacement rates 56f
Merkel, Angela 150, 152–3, 155, 158, 161, 162–3, 165, 168
Merz, Friedrich 157, 158
Mixa, Walter 166
modernization 36n7
Mother's Cross 82
mothers' employment, normative beliefs about 125f; in Italy 1–2, 5, 90, 178, 180, 181, 187, 193, 202–5; in Germany 1–2, 5, 114, 119–26, 129–30, 134–7, 153, 155, 158, 163, 168, 202–3
Movimento Sociale Italiano (MSI) 116
multivariate regression analysis 15–16

National Alliance (*Alleanza Nazionale, AN*) 116, 118
National Fund for the Construction and Operation of Crèches and Child Minders within the Working Place (Italy) 196n36
Netherlands: childcare provision in 60, 61t, 62t, 63, 64t, 66t; flexible work time arrangements in 54, 57–9; taxation system 68t, 69; work-family policies in 71
Nordic countries 28; childcare provision 60, 63; taxation system 69; *see also* Denmark; Finland; Sweden
normative beliefs 22–4, 30–2; analysis of 209–10; changes in 168, 201; a comparison between Germany and Italy 124–6; effect on work-family policies 136–7; in Germany 1–2, 5, 114, 119–26, 129–30, 134–7, 153, 155, 158, 163, 168, 202–3; in Italy 1–2, 5, 90, 178, 180, 181, 187, 193, 201–5; on mothers' employment and childcare 119–20, 125f, 124–9, 127f, 128f, 134, 152–3; and party competition 201–3; and party preference 135–6; share of progressive beliefs in Germany and Italy 124f; across subgroups of population 126–7; and voting behavior 120–1
Northern League (*Lega Nord*, LN) 116, 118, 121, 179
Nuremberg racial laws 82

Olive Tree coalition 180
Onofri Commission 180
output perspective 49–50

parental leave 3, 22, 50, 53–4, 55f, 57, 90, 151, 153, 157, 159, 173n43, 182, 194n8; debate in Italy 180; in Germany 2, 94–6; income-related 164; in Italy 3, 98–9, 73n14, 103–4, 192–3, 200; reform 2, 150, 163–5; replacement rates 56f; in West Germany 87; *see also* maternity leave; paternity leave
parliament, women in 142–4, 169, 180, 205–7; *see also* government, women in
parties *see* political parties
partisan theory 4, 202
Partito Democaratico (PD) 185
Partito Democratico della Sinistra (PDS) 116, 117, 180
Partito Popolare Italian (PPI) 117, 179
part-time employment 1–3, 57–8, 73n15, 74n17, 183–4, 189; in Italy 91–2, 99–100
Party of Democratic Socialism 115
Party of Italian Communists (*Partito di Comunisti Italiani, PCI*) 92, 116, 179, 181–3
party systems: centripetal competition in 4, 5, 12, 15, 28, 31, 31f, 32f, 114, 116–19, 136, 168, 180, 193, 201–2, 204, 205, 209; in Germany 114–16; in Italy 116–19; *see also* political parties
paternity leave 73n11, 215; *see also* parental leave
PCI *see* Party of Italian Communists (*Partito di Comunisti Italiani, PCI*)
PDS *see Partito Democratico della Sinistra (PDS)*
Piano nidi 191, 193, 196n47, 205
PISA (Programme for International Student Assessment) 23
Pisanelli's civil code 84
play groups 59, 74n20
polarization, ideological 28
policy entrepreneurs 5–6, 14–16, 30, 150, 154, 156, 168, 164, 178–9, 193, 201, 207–9, 211–12
policy responsiveness theory 5, 22, 23
political institutions, theories of 34–5
political parties: competition among 22, 27–8, 30–2, 36n4, 156–63; constituencies of 31; Greens 115, 153, 156, 159–60; in Italy 179; normative beliefs of constituencies 26–7; policy choices of 27–8; religiously-based

28, 118; responsiveness to electorate 214–15; role of 24–5; strategies of 213; and the values cleavage 25–6; *see also* Christian-democratic parties; Christian Democratic Party (CDU); Christian Democratic Party (*Partito del Cristiano Democratici Uniti*); Communist party; conservative parties; leftist parties; left-wing parties; libertarian parties; party systems; right-wing parties; social-democratic parties
political-institutionalist approach 35
Pollastrini, Barbara 192
Portugal: childcare provision it0, 61t, 62t, 63, 64t, 66–7, 66t; children's allowances 67; flexible work time arrangements in 54, 58; taxation system 68, 68t, 75n31; work-family policies in 71
power resources theory 4, 24, 27, 31, 34, 36n1, 202
PPI see *Partito Popolare Italian (PPI)*
PRC see Communist Refoundation Party
Prestigiacomo, Stefania 182
Procaccini, Maria Burani 188
process tracking 13–14
Prodi, Romano 180, 192
Programme for International Student Assessment (PISA) 23
Projekt 21 155
public opinion 23–4, 155, 209, 214

qualitative research 13, 215
quantitative research 13, 30, 34, 40, 137, 142, 149, 169, 201, 212

Radicali Italiani 190
Ramsauer, Peter 165
Reiche, Katharina 157
reproductive rights 29
right-wing parties: and feminist issues 29; in Germany 134, 136, 214; in Italy 116, 118, 121, 130, 131, 146, 185, 204–6; *see also* conservative parties
Rönsch, Hannelore 150

Scandinavian countries 33; *see also* Denmark; Finland; Nordic countries; Sweden
Schmidt, Renate 155, 156, 158, 159, 161, 164, 166, 169–70
Schröder, Gerhard 154, 156, 157, 160
SDP see Social Democratic Party (SDP)
sibling's bonus 96
Singhammer, Johannes 164
skill formation, systems of 35

social Christian party 117
social democracy thesis 26
social-democratic parties 25–6, 28; constituencies of 26–7, 123–4; in Italy 190; support for working mothers by 33; and the values cleavage 25–6; and the welfare state 4, 24, 37n10
Social Democratic Party (SDP) 4, 16, 115–16; coalition with Greens 153, 156, 159–60; constituencies of 129, 132–4, 136, 153; encouraging employment for women 152; in Germany 166, 202; in Italy 117; on parental leave 151; shrinking share of votes 129–30, 130f; support for women and families, 83, 115; and the women's vote 28; and work-family policy reform 150, 153–4, 156–68
social policy: gridlock in 34; institutional characteristics of programs 49; theoretical explanations for change 4–6
social rights 3, 50
socialism, in East Germany 92–3
Socialist Unity Party 115
Sozialdemokratische Partei Deutschlands (SPD) see Social Democratic Party
Spain: childcare provision 60, 61t, 62t, 63, 64t, 66–7, 66t; children's allowances 67; flexible work time arrangements 57; taxation system 68t; work-family policies 71
SPD see Social Democratic Party (SDP)
Steinmeier, Frank-Walter 159, 160
Stoiber, Edmund 157, 167–8
students' movements 86
Sweden: childcare provision 61, 61t, 62t, 63, 64t, 65, 66t, 67, 74n24; flexible work time arrangements in 54, 57, 58; taxation system 68t, 69; work-family policies in 71–2

TAG (Day-Care Expansion Act), 96–7, 160
Tagesmütter 59, 74n21, 87, 97, 150–1
Tagesväter 97, 160
taxation issues 52–3, 68–71; in Germany 68t, 68–9, 154; in Italy 68t, 69, 89
theories of political institutions 34–5
three-phase model 150, 151
triangulation 13, 201
Turco, Livia 180, 182

UDEUR 190, 192
unemployment 1, 11, 17n6, 33, 68, 161, 163, 165, 172n32, 189, 209
unemployment insurance 28, 49, 172n32, 212

union membership 87, 89, 92, 99, 120, 123–4, 129, 132, 134, 158, 181, 183–4, 189–90
United Kingdom: childcare provision 60, 61*t*, 62*t*, 63, 64*t*, 65, 66–7, 66*t*; flexible work time arrangements 54, 57, 58; taxation system 68*t*; work-family policies 71

values: authoritarian 25; concerning gender relations and child rearing 14, 22; cultural 23; libertarian 25–6, 216n2; normative 33; and norms 4, 5; religious vs. secular 25; traditional 134; *see also* European Values Study (EVS); normative beliefs
veto player theory 211
veto players 34–5, 37n13, 87, 160, 210–11
veto points 4, 34–5, 211
von der Leyen, Ursula 162, 164, 166–7, 169–70
voters: centrist 116, 155, 183, 202; role of 4–6, 24; *see also* voting behavior
voting behavior: and normative beliefs 120–1; normative beliefs and party preference 135–6; regional differences in 121, 129–30; of social groups 129–35; *see also* voters

Wahlalternative Soziale Gerechtigkeit (WASG) 115, 214
Weimar Constitution 81–2
welfare states: beneficiaries of 22; conservative 37n10; development theories 33–6; generosity of 33, 50; in Germany 9–12; in Italy 9–10; liberal 37n10; policies of 24; retrenchment of 24, 27, 49, 179; social-democratic 37n10; studies of 22, 47
West Germany: childcare provisions 90–1; children's allowances 83, 86, 87; compared to Italy 86, 89–90, 93–4; family law reform 86–7; growth in family policies 90–1; male-breadwinner model 81–4; regression in family policies 90; "three-phase model" 91; *see also* Germany
women: agency of 29, 142, 205–9, 211–12; in cabinets 146–8, 146*t*; in conservative parties 208–9, 211; as critical actors 30, 142, 153; and the decision-making process 16; educational attainment of 11*f*, 73n8; in the electorate 28; employment rates of 6, 7*f*; fertility rates of 6, 7*f*; in government 22–3, 143–6, 154; impact on work-family policies 28–30, 32; influence of in German legislation 152; influence on lawmaking,152, 158; in the labor market 47; as MPs 169, 189–90; in parliament 142–4, 180, 181, 205–9, 211–12; as policy entrepreneurs 207–8, 211–12; political representation of 16; in politics 5, 6; reluctant to intervene in Italy 189–90; on television 212; as voters 156, 180; the workforce 6, 7*f*, 84–5
women's movement 86
women's organizations 23
work-family policies: children's allowances and taxation 14–15, 22, 30–2, 46–8, 52–3, 67–71; changing approaches to 154–5; dimensions of 53*t*; effect of changing normative beliefs and voting behavior 136–7; how to measure change in 48–50; leave regulations and working-time flexibility 50–1, 53–9; state support for 46–8; *see also* childcare provision; family policies; German work-family policy reform; Italian work-family policy reform; parental leave; working-time flexibility
working-time flexibility 50–1, 53; in Germany 54, 57, 59, 95–6; in Italy 54, 57–9, 99–100